Palgrave Studies on Leadership and Learning in Teacher Education

Series Editors
Maria Assunção Flores
Institute of Education
University of Minho
Braga, Portugal

Thuwayba Al Barwani
College of Education
Sultan Qaboos University
Al Khod, Muscat, Oman

The series focuses on original and research informed writing related to teachers and leaders' work as it addresses teacher education in the 21st century. The editors of this series adopt a more comprehensive definition of Teacher Education to include pre-service, induction and continuing professional development of the teacher. The contributions will deal with the challenges and opportunities of learning and leading in teacher education in a globalized era. It includes the dimensions of practice, policy, research and university school partnership. The distinctiveness of this book series lies in the comprehensive and interconnected ways in which learning and leading in teacher education are understood. In the face of global challenges and local contexts it is important to address leadership and learning in teacher education as it relates to different levels of education as well as opportunities for teacher candidates, teacher educators education leaders and other stakeholders to learn and develop. The book series draws upon a wide range of methodological approaches and epistemological stances and covers topics including teacher education, professionalism, leadership and teacher identity.

More information about this series at
http://www.palgrave.com/gp/series/16190

Tony Townsend
Editor

Instructional Leadership and Leadership for Learning in Schools

Understanding Theories of Leading

Editor
Tony Townsend
Griffith Institute for Educational Research
Griffith University
Mt Gravatt, QLD, Australia

ISSN 2524-7069   ISSN 2524-7077 (electronic)
Palgrave Studies on Leadership and Learning in Teacher Education
ISBN 978-3-030-23735-6   ISBN 978-3-030-23736-3 (eBook)
https://doi.org/10.1007/978-3-030-23736-3

© The Editor(s) (if applicable) and The Author(s), under exclusive licence to Springer Nature Switzerland AG 2019
This work is subject to copyright. All rights are solely and exclusively licensed by the Publisher, whether the whole or part of the material is concerned, specifically the rights of translation, reprinting, reuse of illustrations, recitation, broadcasting, reproduction on microfilms or in any other physical way, and transmission or information storage and retrieval, electronic adaptation, computer software, or by similar or dissimilar methodology now known or hereafter developed.
The use of general descriptive names, registered names, trademarks, service marks, etc. in this publication does not imply, even in the absence of a specific statement, that such names are exempt from the relevant protective laws and regulations and therefore free for general use.
The publisher, the authors and the editors are safe to assume that the advice and information in this book are believed to be true and accurate at the date of publication. Neither the publisher nor the authors or the editors give a warranty, express or implied, with respect to the material contained herein or for any errors or omissions that may have been made. The publisher remains neutral with regard to jurisdictional claims in published maps and institutional affiliations.

This Palgrave Macmillan imprint is published by the registered company Springer Nature Switzerland AG.
The registered company address is: Gewerbestrasse 11, 6330 Cham, Switzerland

This book is dedicated to my grandson Jasper Townsend and to the teachers and school leaders who will lead his learning as he moves towards adulthood.

Preface

The International Council on Education for Teaching (ICET) has been a consistent presence for more than six decades, contributing to the ongoing development of international partnerships aimed at improving the quality of teacher education, and thus the quality of teachers, from a time way before internationalisation and globalisation became buzzwords made easy by technology. It has contributed to teacher education in virtually every aspect of its study and development for more than half a century, a claim that can rarely be argued by other international organisations.

The mission of ICET is to "improve the educational experiences and outcomes of learners in all parts of the world by providing opportunities for those involved in their education to share knowledge, practice, resources, and expertise and establish active partnerships that are designed to enhance the quality of teaching and learning and improve life opportunities for young people".

The first ICET conference was held in Oxford in 1953, and since that time, the conference has been held in many countries. I first attended ICET in Sydney in 1988, where the theme was "Progress and Promise in Teacher Education". If we reflect on that theme more than 30 years later, there is evidence of much progress in that time, but to paraphrase Robert Frost's *Stopping by Woods on a Snowy Evening*, "we still have promises to keep, and miles to go before we sleep".

I came back to ICET in Windhoek, Namibia, in 2000, and have been involved ever since. I have been President and have organised conferences (Melbourne, 2003 and Glasgow, 2011) and continue to serve as an Emeritus Board Member. During this time, I have been able to reflect on teacher education and on what are some of the promises that we still need to keep.

Internationally, there are probably still around 20 million young people (mostly girls) who do not get to go to school, so the first issue is access. It is also the case that for many students who are lucky enough to be in school in the first place, they will have a teacher who may be not qualified, who may be underqualified or who, for one reason or another, has not kept fully up to date with the changes in strategies that ensure high levels of learning for all students, so the second issue is teacher quality.

The International Task Force on Teachers for Education 2030: Strategic Plan 2018–2021 (available from https://unesdoc.unesco.org/ark:/48223/pf0000261708) identifies these two issues as critical and addresses them in three ways, through advocacy, through knowledge creation and sharing and through country support and engagement. The issue of access is something that the current book cannot address, but we firmly believe that we have something to say about the quality of teaching and learning and how it might be improved and supported in school communities around the world.

This book, as part of the Palgrave Studies in Leading and Learning in Teacher Education, aims to support all three of these strategies, by advocating for the importance of leadership, not only by school leaders, but by everyone in the school; by sharing the knowledge related to this that has been generated by both researchers and practitioners, from universities, from education systems, from agencies and from the community; and by promoting country support through chapters by authors from seven different countries. In doing so, we gain an understanding of how different parts of the world address the same underlying issue, that of supporting high levels of learning for all students, in very different ways.

The book looks at two theoretical positions, instructional leadership and leadership for learning, and then considers how these have been perceived in various parts of the world and how they have been used as a basis for leadership development. It then considers how school leadership has supported the development of teacher leadership and the leadership of others in the school community. It discusses professional learning across school networks and through using the resources of other agencies in the community.

We hope that in doing so we provide the reader with a better understanding of how progress is being made in teacher education through school leadership, some of it focusing on instruction and some focusing on learning, and how everyone in the community can play a part in this process we call schooling. One of the world's most ancient group of human cultures, those on the continent of Africa, is identified as the source of the statement "It takes a Village to Raise a Child", but it is interesting to look at some of the literal translations used to generate that statement. In Western Uganda, there is a proverb that says "Omwana takulila nju emoi" whose literal translation is "A child does not grow up only in a single home". For the Bahaya people in Tanzania, "Omwana taba womoi" translates as "A child belongs not to one parent or home". For the Jita in Tanzania, "Omwana ni wa bhone" means that regardless of a child's biological parents, its upbringing belongs to the community, and in Swahili, a language that covers a number of African countries, "Asiye funzwa na mamae hufunzwa na ulimwengu" means "Whomsoever is not taught by the mother will be taught with the world". As the chapters of the book progress, it becomes clear that school leaders cannot be the only people responsible for the successful education of children. If providing every single child, from every country in the world, with a quality education, one that will see them make a smooth transition into adulthood, is the promise that education systems make, then to be successful in this quest, school leaders will need to engage teachers, parents and students themselves, and will need to work with other schools and with community agencies. This is the first promise that schooling needs to keep.

There is now an additional level of urgency as the world becomes a more divided and oppositional place. As I write this, New Zealand has just experienced the most horrific shooting in mosques in Christchurch, by an Australian self-professed extremist white supremacist. As an Australian educator, I ask myself, where did we go wrong? But a second question has to be, how do we change the current climate of division and hate? To answer this, perhaps we can turn to a man of peace. "If we are to reach real peace in this world … we shall have to begin with children" (Gandhi, October 28, 1931).

If we are to begin with the children, the question then becomes, how do we help children to learn to live peaceful lives? The first step in this quest would be to provide the teacher quality and teacher numbers that both ICET and the International Task Force see as major goals, sufficient in numbers and quality to ensure that every child has access to school with teachers who are able to help them learn. We then need to think about what children need to learn. We should remember Everett Reimer's statement from his 1971 book *School Is Dead*:

> No child … fails to learn from school. Those who never get in, learn that the good things of life are not for them. Those who drop out early, learn that they do not deserve the good things of life. The later dropouts learn that the system can be beaten, but not by them.

This has messages for the way in which education needs to be delivered. Education should no longer be seen as a competition, where some are successful and others are not, but as a birthright for everyone. And this would be the second promise that schooling needs to keep.

So, although we still might have promises to keep, we are at least much more aware of what they are, and how we might address them, than we were when ICET was first formed all those years ago. Hopefully, this book will provide some new insights into how we might keep our promises.

Mt Gravatt, QLD, Australia   Tony Townsend
                                                                    July 2019

Acknowledgements

I wish to acknowledge each of the people involved in the creation of this book. It will come as no surprise to the reader that the world of education, like many other fields of endeavour, is facing increasing intensiveness as we learn more about learning and how to support the development of young people. Change—in technology, in the environment in which we live, and even in the values that we hold—has led to an intensification of expectations. There are now increased expectations on the range of things that schools are seen to be responsible for and for the level of performance that students will achieve. With a rapidly rising level of general education in the population, there has been increased scrutiny as well as increased expectation. This has brought about changes in the range and rate of data collected, as we address higher levels of accountability for learning outcomes across a range of areas, to an extent never seen before.

The authors of this book are all living within this intensification and have themselves increasingly busy lives as professors, as students, as members of education systems or as directors of community agencies. All of them have had to quarantine some time to enable the works that you find in this book to be produced. In many cases, finding this time has not been easy, and I wish to acknowledge the work done by the authors.

Much of the work that you read about in this book discusses the findings of the research or other activity in schools, across schools and in communities. This activity is being led by school leaders, not only principals but others in the school or community as well, those who have dedicated their lives to improving the lives of children. I wish to acknowledge the work of teachers, of school leaders, of parents and of others in the community who support them, for their never-ending efforts to improve the quality of teaching and learning in their schools and in their communities. Without their work, there would be nothing worth reporting.

Praise for *Instructional Leadership and Leadership for Learning in Schools*

"This is a groundbreaking work of scholarship that brings together pre-eminent voices from around the world to think together and about two of the most critical concepts in the field of education, leadership and learning. In the process, longstanding ideas are uprooted such as the singular, heroic leader in a hierarchical system that can single-mindedly drive a school to perform according to set targets. This book, by contrast, demands a more democratic leadership built around the collective strengths of followers, in which not only children learn, and which pursues education outcomes far beyond a narrow preoccupation with test scores. This remarkable book should be required for every education leadership student anywhere in the world."

—Jonathan Jansen, Distinguished Professor, *Stellenbosch University, South Africa*

"Great teachers are first great listeners. The authors in this collection have had the opportunity to listen and to learn from schooling sites around the world. They've brought that privilege and that experience to this book. Paraphrasing part of the liturgy of one religion – If you are interested in being less of what you used to be and more of what you ought to be – then this is guidance in the shift from managing schools to leading learning. A welcome summary that deserves attention – and action. All premised on the analysis of these experts."

—Dale Mann, Professor Emeritus, *Teachers College, Columbia University, USA*

"With school and system leadership now acutely recognized as critical factors in explaining high performing Learning Systems, this impressive international volume on Leading Learning in schools could not be more timely. Tony Townsend brings together a collection of compelling, international authors who reveal the importance of leadership competencies for complexity, new approaches to leadership learning, the conditions which enable the collective leadership of learning and the leadership impact on learning."

—Anthony Mackay, President and CEO, *National Center for Education and the Economy, USA*

Contents

1 Changing Understandings of School Leadership   1
Tony Townsend

Part I   Theoretical Approaches to Leading Schools   13

2 Instructional Leadership   15
David Ng Foo Seong

3 Leadership for Learning   49
John MacBeath

Part II   International Responses to the Theory   75

4 Australian Considerations in Relation to Instructional Leadership and Leadership for Learning   77
David Gurr

Contents

5   **Leadership for Learning in the US**   105
David Imig, South Holden, and Dale Placek

6   **Leading Learning in Schools in Challenging Times: Findings from Research in Portugal**   133
Maria Assunção Flores and Fernando Ilídio Ferreira

Part III   Responding to the Theory   163

7   **Future-Ready Leadership Development**   165
David Ng Foo Seong

8   **Professional Autonomy and the Future of Leadership for Learning in Australia**   193
Brian J. Caldwell

9   **Leaders of Learning: Recovering the Pedagogical Role of School Leaders and Promoting Leadership at All Levels in Scotland**   219
Margery A. McMahon

10   **Instructional Leadership Development for Principals: A South African Context**   237
Parvathy Naidoo and Raj Mestry

Part IV   Practising School Leadership: Putting the Theories into Practice   267

11   **Principals as Literacy Leaders (PALL): Leading Learning by Improving Instructional Practices in Australia**   269
Anne Bayetto and Tony Townsend

12	Promoting Teacher Collaborative Learning in Lesson Study: Exploring and Interpreting Leadership to Create Professional Learning Community *Toshiya Chichibu, Tetsuro Uchizaki, and Yumiko Ono*	299
13	Creating and Leading Powerful Learning Relationships Through a Whole School Community Approach *George Otero*	317
14	The Power of Collective Leadership for Learning *Suzanne Cridge*	347
15	Leading Place-Based Interventions to Improve Outcomes in Low Socio-economic Settings *Christopher Chapman, Alison Drever, Maureen McBride, Craig Orr, and Sarah Weakley*	379

Part V	Summary and Conclusions: What Do We Now Know About School Leadership?	401
16	Leadership for Learning: Embracing Purpose, People, Pedagogy and Place *Neil Dempster*	403

Index 423

Notes on Contributors

Anne Bayetto is lecturer in special education at Flinders University in South Australia where she teaches both undergraduate and postgraduate topics focused on school students with literacy and/or numeracy difficulties. She has previously been a mainstream and special class teacher, adaptive education teacher and a district-wide disability support coordinator. Since 1989, she has worked closely with the Specific Learning Difficulties Association of South Australia where she has taught courses and been an academic mentor to the directors. She has published books about reading and spelling for Oxford University Press and was their lead researcher for Stages 2 and 3 of the Oxford Wordlist Project as well as being one of their academic consultants. She regularly provides professional learning sessions and consultancy for teachers, leaders, and managers in education sectors across Australia.

Brian J. Caldwell is Principal Consultant at Educational Transformations and professor emeritus at the University of Melbourne where he is a former Dean of Education. Previous academic appointments include Dean of Education at University of Tasmania. He has held teaching and leadership appointments in schools in Victoria, Australia, and Alberta, Canada. He holds a Doctor of Philosophy (1977) from University of Alberta and was awarded the degree of Doctor of Education *honoris causa* by the Education University of Hong Kong in 2012. International work includes more than 600 presentations, projects and other professional assignments in or for 42 countries or jurisdictions on six continents. He has authored, co-authored or co-edited 19 books, including *The Autonomy Premium* (2016) and *The Alignment Premium* (2018). He has served as the President of the Australian Council for Educational Leaders and as Deputy Chair of the boards of the Australian Council for Educational Research and the Australian Curriculum, Assessment and Reporting Authority.

Christopher Chapman is Chair of Educational Policy at University of Glasgow where he is Director of Policy Scotland, the University's Research and Knowledge Exchange Unit for Public Policy and Co-Director of the Robert Owen Centre for Educational Change. Chapman is the key architect and Principal Investigator for Children's Neighbourhoods Scotland and the Network for Social and Educational Equity. His research focuses on school and system reform, public service leadership and networking and collaboration for improvement. He has over 150 publications in these related areas. Chris has advised governments and universities across the world and is Senior Academic Advisor to Scottish Government and a member of the First Minister's International Council of Education Advisors.

Toshiya Chichibu is a Senior Researcher at the National Institute for Educational Policy Research of Japan. His research interest is lesson study, which is becoming popular in the world. While sustained Lesson Study can develop their teaching skills and strengthen pedagogical content knowledge, Lesson Study contributes to establishing professional learning communities in the school. Chichibu visits schools at least 20 times a year as an external advisor of Lesson Study. He visits schools not only in Japan but also in Kazakhstan and China. He served as a Lesson Study advisor for presidential schools in Kazakhstan in 2013.

Suzanne Cridge joined Social Ventures Australia (SVA) in 2013 and is responsible for designing and leading the SVA Bright Spots Schools Connection. The Connection provides an innovative response to the issues of educational disadvantage in Australia's most challenged communities. In 2015, Cridge was acknowledged with an award from the Australian Council Educational Leaders and was a nominee for Pro Bono Australia Impact 25 recognition in 2019. She has been acknowledged as an Outstanding Education Leader by the state of Victoria in 2003 and was awarded a Sir Winston Churchill Fellowship in Education in the same year while working in disadvantaged schools across the government education system. She also served as a volunteer teacher of English in a refugee camp for the United Nations. Suzanne's international experience extends to 5 years spent as the Executive Director of Citizen Schools New Mexico, USA, establishing a model of expanded learning opportunities for underserved public schools as part of a national US education reform initiative. Upon returning to Australia, she led the Innovation Programme at the Australian Institute for Teaching and School Leadership.

Neil Dempster is emeritus professor in Educational Leadership at Griffith University and former Dean of its Faculty of Education. His research interests are leadership for learning, school governance, school improvement and the role that professional development plays in leadership work, policy implementation and institutional change. Dempster is a Fellow of the Australian Council for Educational Leaders and a Fellow of the Australian College of Educators where he held the post of National President in 2006–2007. He has published widely on the learning and development needs of school leaders.

Alison Drever is National Director of Children's Neighbourhoods Scotland. She was previously a Senior Education Officer with the national inspection and improvement agency, Education Scotland where she held a number of different leadership roles, including lead officer and Attainment Advisor for the Scottish Attainment Challenge. Prior to that she led professional learning and provided support for improvement for local authorities, headteachers and teachers across Scotland for different areas of strategic curriculum development and design. Before joining Education Scotland, Alison held a variety of teaching and leadership roles in the education system in the primary and secondary sectors and at local authority level, including headteacher and improvement officer.

Fernando Ilídio Ferreira is associate professor at University of Minho, Portugal, where he received his PhD in Child Studies. He teaches Sociology of Education, Education Policies, Intercultural Education, Qualitative Research, Educational Practicum in Preschool and Primary School Institutions, among other subjects. He taught at the National University of East Timor in 2014–2015 and was a visiting scholar at the Federal University of Bahia, Brazil, in 2017–2018. His research interests include teacher education, leadership, continuing education, community development, early childhood and primary education, childhood studies and children's rights. He supervises master's and PhD theses and dissertations in the broad areas of Education and Child Studies and has published a number of books, chapters and articles on these topics both nationally and internationally.

Maria Assunção Flores is associate professor at University of Minho, Portugal. She holds a PhD from the University of Nottingham, UK. She was a visiting scholar at University of Cambridge, UK, in 2008–2009, and at University of Glasgow, UK, in 2016–2017. Her research interests include teacher professionalism and identity, teacher education and professional development, teacher appraisal, leadership and higher education. She has published extensively on these topics both nationally and internationally. She is Chair of the International Study Association on Teachers and Teaching and is former Chair of the Board of Directors of the International Council on Education for Teaching (ICET). She is executive editor of the journal *Teachers and Teaching: Theory and Practice* and co-editor of the *European Journal of Teacher Education*.

David Gurr is associate professor in educational leadership within the Graduate School of Education at the University of Melbourne and has a 40-year background in secondary teaching, educational psychology, school supervision and research in educational leadership. He has more than 170 publications and has presented more than 175 times at international and local conferences, and has led or been involved in research classified grants worth more than $26,000,000. David is editor of *International Studies in Educational Administration* and senior associate editor of the *Journal of Educational Administration*. He is a founding member of the International Successful School Principalship Project and the International School Leadership Development Network. An active member of the Australian Council for Educational Leaders, Gurr received the association's highest honour, the Gold Medal, in 2014.

South Holden is a doctoral student at University of Maryland, College Park in the College of Education's Department of Teaching, Learning, Policy, and Leadership. Before beginning his doctoral studies, Holden received his Masters' of Teaching in Elementary Education from University of Virginia and taught at The Intergenerational School in Cleveland, Ohio. South's research interests include teacher education and teacher educator development. He is focusing his efforts on studying how doctoral students develop their practices, identities and self-efficacy as teacher educators.

David Imig teaches in the Teaching and Learning, Policy and Leadership programme at University of Maryland, College Park. He studies and writes in the area of school leader preparation and teacher education research, policy and practice. He is former chair of the National Policy Board for Educational Administration. He is leading an effort to transform the Doctor of Education (EdD) degree in the USA and has worked in the area of policy and politics as President of the American Association of Colleges for Teacher Education. He serves as a senior fellow for the Carnegie Foundation for the Advancement of Teaching and as co-leader of a Foundation initiative called Improvement Leadership Education for the Advancement of Teaching. He holds three academic degrees from University of Illinois, Urbana-Champaign, and an honorary doctorate from Bridgewater State University in Massachusetts.

John MacBeath is professor emeritus at University of Cambridge where he held the Chair of Educational Leadership from 2000 to 2012. From 1997 to 2001, he was a member of the Tony Blair Government Task Force on Standards, and from 1997 to 1999, he was a member of the Scottish Government Action Group on Standards. He served as President of the International Congress on School Effectiveness and Improvement from 2007 to 2009 and served on the ICSEI board for 10 years. He was awarded the Order of British Empire (OBE) for services to education in 1997 and an honorary doctorate from University of Edinburgh in 2009. He has authored and co-authored 20 books on leadership, self-evaluation and school improvement.

Maureen McBride is research associate on the Children's Neighbourhoods Scotland project, based at University of Glasgow. She is a sociologist whose research interests include poverty, class inequalities, racialisation and racism, religion and nationalism. She completed her Economic and Social Research Council (ESRC)-funded PhD, entitled "Rethinking Sectarianism in Scotland", in 2018. Much of her research focuses on public policy responses to social inequalities, and she has previously worked on research projects through What Works Scotland and the Scottish Centre for Crime and Justice Research. She has co-edited and contributed to *No Problem Here: Understanding Racism in Scotland*, a book published in January 2018.

Margery A. McMahon is Professor of Educational Leadership and Head of the School of Education, University of Glasgow. In 2013–2014, she was seconded to the National Implementation Board for *Teaching Scotland's Future* where she led the scoping and initial set up of the Scottish College for Educational Leadership. She is the author and co-author of a range of books and articles focusing on professional learning and leadership including Mowat, J., G., & McMahon, M. (2018), "Interrogating the Concept of 'Leadership at All Levels': A Scottish Perspective", *Professional Development in Education* (Early Online Publication). McMahon serves as an adviser and consultant to national and international agencies on leadership development and institutional capability building. She is the UK Representative for the International Study Association for Teachers and Teaching and co-convenor of the Leadership in Scottish Education Network.

Raj Mestry is emeritus professor in the Department of Education Leadership and Management, and previously served as Head of Department at University of Johannesburg. His field of expertise includes education leadership and management with a special emphasis on social justice and equity. His forte is in human resources management and school financial management in education. He has been rated as a researcher by the National Research Foundation and serves on the executive of the Education Association of South Africa. He also served on the executive of the South African Education Law Association. He has published extensively nationally and internationally in accredited journals and has co-authored and edited multiple books and chapters. He was awarded the Research Medal in 2012 and Medal of Honour in 2017 by the Education Association of South Africa.

Parvathy Naidoo is lecturer in the Department of Leadership and Management at University of Johannesburg, South Africa. She has held various positions: teacher, head of department, deputy principal and principal under the auspices of the Department of Education, Gauteng, South Africa, before transitioning to tertiary education when awarded a Next Generation Scholarship to pursue a PhD in school leadership development. On a national and international level, she is involved in various research projects in her field of expertise. She also serves as critical examiner, moderator and reviewer for several tertiary institutions, national and international journals and book publishers. Her publications in accredited journals include instructional leadership, leadership for learning, professional leadership development, school financial management and propagation of leadership equity.

David Ng Foo Seong is Head of Academic Quality and associate professor in the Policy and Leadership Department at the National Institute of Education (NIE), Nanyang Technological University, Singapore. He provides overall leadership, management and improvement in academic, student and programmes quality. He also leads the planning, review and effective implementation of the Strategic Planning Academic Quality's initiatives, research and evaluation studies that guide future strategic directions of the institute. He was also the Associate Dean for Leadership Programmes at NIE from 2004 to 2010. He was responsible for designing and implementing innovative leadership programmes for system superintendents, school principals, Heads of Departments and middle-level leaders.

Yumiko Ono is research associate at the Institute of Teacher Education, Waseda University, Tokyo. She has been interested in effective schools for less advantaged groups and researched to find factors to improve students' learning. Since 1999, she has been committed to education development through Japan International Cooperation Agency. The countries where she has worked include South Africa, Afghanistan, Kenya, Rwanda and Myanmar. Based on these experiences, she is carrying out a research project focused on international education policy transfer. Her publications include Maeda, M. and Ono, Y. (2019), "Diffusion of Lesson Study as an Educational Innovation", *International Comparative Education and Development,* 21(1), 46–60, and Ono, Y. & Chikamori, K. (2018), "Challenging Tasks for South African Teachers: Realization of Democratic Education", in Okitsu, T. and Kawaguchi, J. (Eds.), *Teacher Education Policy and International Cooperation,* Akashi-Shoten, pp. 127–150 (n Japanese).

Craig Orr is Lecturer in Childhood Practice at University of Glasgow, following over a decade of working in both policy and practice within the Early Learning and Childcare sector in Scotland. Also studying towards a PhD, Orr is exploring the ways in which leadership and multiagency collaborations may support children's educational outcomes. Through social network analysis, Orr aims to investigate the ways in which professional capital can be developed and distributed throughout professional networks, such as the Children's Neighbourhoods Scotland initiative.

George Otero is an educational consultant and has worked as a teacher, educator, international consultant and social entrepreneur and is also an author. He and his wife, Susan, operate the Center for RelationaLearning, based in Santa Fe, New Mexico. He has worked for many years in Australia and the UK as well as the USA. His work with schools and community leaders in transforming schools is an outgrowth of his 20 years of work creating and directing a multicultural community learning centre in Taos, New Mexico, attended by over 50,000 people. His work focuses on new ways for schools and communities to secure equity, inclusion and social justice leading to transformations in relationships by clarifying the issues and problems within the context of their communities. He has authored more than ten books designed to support teachers to develop global thinking with their students.

Dale Placek is a doctoral student at University of Maryland (UMD), College Park, in the College of Education's Department of Teaching, Learning, Policy, and Leadership. Before beginning his doctoral studies, Placek received his Master's in Teacher Leadership from UMD, College Park, and served as the Chair of Performing Arts, and later the IB Programme Coordinator, at The Academy of the Holy Cross in Kensington, Maryland. His research interests include teaching, teacher education and professional development, and he is focusing his efforts on studying unforeseen moments in classroom teaching and educational applications of theatrical improvisation.

Tony Townsend (Editor) has worked all over the world. He has worked at Monash University as associate professor, and as professor at Griffith University and University of Tasmania in Australia, Florida Atlantic University in the USA and University of Glasgow in the UK. He has been a visiting professor in Michigan in the USA; Johannesburg and Durban in South Africa; Saskatoon in Canada; Macau; Kuala Lumpur in Malaysia; Brno in the Czech Republic; and Dublin in the Republic of Ireland. He has been a consultant for the United Nations Educational, Scientific and Cultural Organization (UNESCO), the Commonwealth Trust, the National Education Council of Chile and the Balochistan Education Department in Pakistan. He has worked with school leaders in many countries including Mongolia, the Maldives, the UK, Germany, the Czech Republic and Slovenia. He has published 12 books and numerous articles, chapters and papers, in the areas of leadership, school effectiveness, school improvement, teacher education and community education and development, in Australia, Europe and North America. He has been President and is a life member of both the International Congress for School Effectiveness and Improvement (ICSEI) and the International Council on Education for Teaching (ICET).

Tetsuro Uchizaki is adjunct professor at Himeji University, School of Education. After graduating university with a teaching licence, he first got a job in business instead of teaching. However, his aspiration for the teaching profession did not diminish. After 1-year, he quit the job and started his career as a teacher. He worked at large schools where he experienced the importance of addressing diversity and individual needs of children. Uchizaki enjoyed administrative positions in a board of education, but he believes he can feel first-hand the change and growth both in children and teachers in schools. After retiring as a principal, he worked as an advisor and facilitator at Prefectural Education Center to provide support to newly appointed school administrators. He has contributed to many teachers' magazines and journals.

Sarah Weakley is a Research and Impact Acceleration Officer in Policy Scotland at University of Glasgow. In this role, she is an affiliated researcher with Children's Neighbourhoods Scotland. She is a quantitative social researcher by training and her work is focused on poverty, the welfare state and young people's transitions to independence. She holds a PhD in Social Policy (University of Edinburgh, UK), a Master of Research in Urban Research (University of Glasgow, UK), a Master of Public Administration (George Washington University, USA) and a Bachelor of Arts in English (Washington State University, USA).

List of Figures

Fig. 2.1	A framework of instructional leadership. (Hallinger & Murphy, 1985, 1986)	16
Fig. 2.2	Far West Lab instructional management model. (Bossert et al., 1982, p. 40)	17
Fig. 2.3	Adaptation of the Far West Lab instructional management model. (Bossert et al., 1982, p. 40)	18
Fig. 4.1	Australian model of successful principal leadership. (Gurr et al. 2006, 2007)	91
Fig. 7.1	Employment in services (% of total employment) country comparison 1991–2018	167
Fig. 7.2	Multi-dimensional framework for school success	168
Fig. 7.3	Singapore's economy 1960–2017	171
Fig. 7.4	Singapore's employment by economic sectors 2016. (Source: mom.gov.sg)	172
Fig. 7.5	Three learning environments in schools	174
Fig. 7.6	Evolution of educational leadership development	176
Fig. 7.7	Knowledge creation (complexity learning) through an innovation project	186
Fig. 11.1	The leadership for learning blueprint	271
Fig. 12.1	Unit curriculum plan form	305
Fig. 12.2	Lesson study reform based on unit curriculum	308
Fig. 13.1	The variables influencing a child's life chances and wellbeing. (West-Burnham et al., 2007)	328

Fig. 13.2	A framework for leading learning relationally	335
Fig. 14.1	Collaborative action cuts through complexity	354
Fig. 14.2	Programme Logic Frame Bright Spots Schools Connection, Social Ventures Australia	361
Fig. 14.3	Leveraging the cycle of collaboration for action	362
Fig. 14.4	Core features of CLDN	362
Fig. 14.5	Connection Hub school target outcomes for evaluation of progress in 2017	371
Fig. 15.1	Harnessing models of collaboration for collective impact. (Henig et al., 2015)	385
Fig. 15.2	Creating a common agenda: questionnaire sent to partners in the planning phase of CNS	388

List of Tables

Table 2.1	Instructional leadership—quantitative method	30
Table 2.2	Instructional leadership—qualitative methods	31
Table 2.3	Social network	37
Table 2.4	Complexity science research methods	38
Table 5.1	The principles associated with instructional leadership and leadership for learning	112
Table 7.1	Learning assumptions of twentieth and twenty-first centuries	173
Table 8.1	Principals' engagement in leadership activities in lower secondary education in Australia (percentage of principals reporting 'very often' or 'often' as reported in TALIS 2013)	199
Table 8.2	Distribution of actions of leaders in lower secondary schools in Australia (percentage of principals as reported in TALIS 2013)	200
Table 9.1	Advice for schools from HMIe related to the leadership of learning	226
Table 9.2	Professional standards and career stages in Scottish education	229
Table 10.1	Definitions of instructional leadership by various scholars	245
Table 14.1	Summary of SVA connection activities	363
Table 14.2	Summary of pilot Hub school participation 2015–2016, after 1 year of participation	369

Table 14.3	Outcomes analysis after 1 year of a 3-year planned engagement	373
Table 15.1	Neighbourhood profile for Parkhead and Dalmarnock	392
Table 16.1	Domains and dimensions of a Unified Leadership Framework	411
Table 16.2	*Carpe Vitam* Leadership for Learning principles and practices	412

1

Changing Understandings of School Leadership

Tony Townsend

Over the past 30 or so years, I have been incredibly lucky to have been able to see educational systems in many parts of the world. Not only have I held tenured positions in Australia, the United States and Scotland, but I have also had shorter periods of being a visiting professor in other countries, such as Canada, Ireland, Macau, Malaysia, Oman and South Africa, as well as presenting, either at conferences or in professional workshops, in more than 50 countries. One of the things that I have found in these travels is that education is very different, whilst having the same underlying aims. How different parts of the world see things differently can be shown in many ways, but one simple way is to describe how I was identified when being introduced. In Australia, I was usually introduced as Tony Townsend, but in the Middle East and Asia I was Prof Tony, in the United Kingdom I was Professor Townsend, in the United States I was Dr Townsend and in some European countries I was Professor Dr Townsend.

T. Townsend (✉)
Griffith Institute for Educational Research, Griffith University,
Mt Gravatt, QLD, Australia
e-mail: t.townsend@griffith.edu.au

In each case, I was being treated with respect, but each of these introductions signified a slight difference in local perceptions of the importance of various qualifications or positions. In the United States, most people who work in universities are professors, whether assistant, associate or full, so having a doctorate was a higher symbol of recognition, to the point where I had great difficulty in even getting my colleagues to call me Tony. In the United Kingdom, most people who work in universities have doctorates, but only about 5% of those in universities become full professors (with maybe 20% associate professors), so professor becomes the term of respect. In Europe (especially Germany), both the doctorate and the professorship are considered as a mark of excellence, so both are used, and in the Middle East and Asia, there is an endearing respectful friendliness of the shortened 'Prof' and the use of one's first name. But in Australia, I was just me. None of these is more or less respectful than the others, they just happen to have their own histories attached.

We need to be just as respectful when it comes to looking at education systems and what they are trying to do. Underlying every education system is the ultimate aim of providing for students within their care the best possible start to their adult life. But when it comes to seeing how they do this, once again difference becomes the norm. We have some systems of education that span more than 800 years and others that are less than 50 years. The three universities that I worked for over an extended period of time demonstrate this. The University of Glasgow was formed in 1451, but both Monash University in Australia and Florida Atlantic University in the United States had their first students more than 500 years later, in 1961. Some countries in the Middle East and Asia did not have any university until the 1990s.

Many school systems, especially the religious ones, date back to the middle ages, many government school systems came about in the mid- to late-1800s and some countries did not really have a system of education (just a few schools here and there) until the 1970s. We have some countries that are well resourced, where every child gets to go to school, and we have others that struggle to ensure an education for every child. By 2030, there may be up to 50 million children (with, unfortunately, girls being in a strong majority) that will never step foot inside a school. In the past 30 years, we have talked about school, classroom and system effectiveness and what that might mean, but can a system ever be effective if some of its students never go to school and a substantial proportion leave school without the knowledge, skills and attitudes they need to become a successful adult, as a worker, parent or citizen?

The school effectiveness and improvement research that really started to take shape in the 1980s has been very influential and many countries have drawn on the research from these two areas of study to shape the education systems of today. One of the things that can be confirmed is the important role that school leadership plays in the process of improving individual schools and, ultimately, educational systems. However, the concept of school leadership is a comparatively recent one. Until the 1980s, the term commonly used was 'school management and administration'. Schools in the 1800s had a headmaster or a principal, but the oversight of the management and administration of the school emerged on both sides of the Atlantic in 1837 when in the United Kingdom, two inspectors were appointed by the British Government to oversee grants made to religious schools, and in the United States, the Buffalo Common Council appointed the first superintendent of schools as the Chief School Administrator. These systems of inspection in the United Kingdom and superintendency in the United States remain intact even today, although the roles have changed substantially.

However, after the Second World War, history tells us that school education moved into the modern age. A substantial and rapid growth in the size of educational systems in many parts of the world in the early 1960s was brought about by a post-war baby boom, coupled with an increasing demand for more schooling by societies around the world, during a time of economic strength. Subsequent to this period of rapid growth, a downturn in birth rates in many parts of the Western world enabled some countries to turn their attention from expanding education towards assessing the quality of what was being offered.

In the United Kingdom, works such as *The Home and the School* (Douglas, 1964), *Children and Their Primary Schools* (the Plowden Report, 1967) and *Parents and Teachers: Partners or Rivals* (Green, 1968) had considered the relationship between family background and success at school. When these were followed up by such documents as *The Crisis in Education* (Boyson, 1975) and *The Black Papers* (Cox & Boyson,

1977), the standard of students' academic performance in the United Kingdom became a critical issue. The British Government's response to these concerns was the establishment of the Assessment of Performance Unit within the Department of Education and Science in 1974.

In the United States, formal reports such as *A Nation at Risk* (National Commission on Excellence in Education, 1983), *Education and Economic Progress* (Carnegie Corporation, 1983), *Investing in Our Children* (Committee on Economic Development, 1985) and *Who Will Teach Our Children?* (Commons, 1985) indicated a similar level of government and public concern about the outcomes of the schooling system and this created a climate in which the relationship between education and competitiveness on the international market became inextricably linked, leading to a situation where schools were charged with turning out, in the most cost-effective way, the maximum number of graduates with the 'right' skills and knowledge as possible.

Concerns for the effectiveness of schools in the United Kingdom (Rutter, Maughan, Mortimore, & Ouston, 1979) and the United States (Edmonds, 1979) were exacerbated in the 1980s by these countries having a seemingly diminished status as the economic superpowers of the world, when other countries such as Japan and Germany attracted increased economic and political status in world affairs.

Concerns for the efficiency of education, related to the cost of education, became associated, as in business, with outputs. Given that a large proportion of government spending was directed towards education, governments were asked to account for their spending in terms similar to those used in business. The issue of the effectiveness of schools became related to the number of students who completed school successfully and the qualities those graduates had, ones that would enable graduates of schooling systems either to become employed or to enter higher education. Thus, the twin concerns of quality and quantity merged and the concept of market-driven education was born.

The notion of the market upturned the previous concept of school systems, where individual educational systems oversaw the operations of the schools within them, to one where each school was charged with doing what was required to ensure that the students within the school achieved the levels reflected by all students in the system. More pressure was applied on individual head teachers and principals to ensure that 'their' school was one that could be considered effective.

This movement of responsibility from the system level to school level in many school systems around the world changed the way in which the administration of schools was undertaken. Concepts such as school-based decision-making or self-managing schools (Caldwell & Spinks, 1988) emerged in government systems in England and Wales, Canada, New Zealand and Australia, all in the 1980s, and with them came the understanding that school leaders would require a range of new skills and knowledge to be able to undertake the tasks as required. However, in each case the relationship between governments, education systems and individual schools was slightly different. In England and Wales, from 1988, some schools were able to opt out of the Local Education Authority (LEA) system to become Grant-Maintained schools, and received funding directly from the government, while others stayed within the LEA. Edmonton, Canada, pioneered site-based decision-making in 1976 and expanded it to all its schools in 1980 while Victoria, Australia introduced Schools of the Future, where schools became self-managing, in the early 1990s. In New Zealand, from 1988, the government funded the schools directly and there was no education system in between. On the other hand, the United States maintained the relationship between the school district and individual schools until the first charter schools, semi-autonomous public schools that received public funding, were established in Minnesota in 1991. With the support of the Bush Government, which promoted them as a viable alternative to the public school system, more than 5000 (and growing) charter schools now operate across the country, many of them being for profit, which makes them very different from other forms of self-management.

Government funding of schools also varies substantially in different parts of the world: some countries such as the United States only fund public education (but with increasing under-the-table funding for non-government education, through voucher systems); some countries such as Australia have mixed funding, with states mostly funding government schools and partially funding non-government schools, while the Commonwealth government provides the majority of funding to non-government schools with some funding for government schools; some governments pay for teachers' salaries if the local community is able to finance the building of the school; and yet other countries in Asia and Europe fund both government and non-government schools in equal measures, to make all schools 'public' schools.

What this brief overview provides is a short analysis of just some of the ways that education, although it may have the same underlying purpose globally, has very different approaches locally to actually fulfilling that purpose. One area that has changed over the three decades that have passed since many of the changes described briefly above were introduced is the nature and responsibility of school leadership.

If we think back to the 1970s, leadership (or management) of schools was systematic and hierarchical. Ministers of Education made decisions that were implemented by Education Departments. The fidelity of the implementations was ensured by inspectors (or superintendents) who oversaw the work of school principals. School principals' responsibilities were to implement (faithfully) the decisions made by others and to ensure that teachers followed the requirements related to their employment. The 1980s and 1990s saw that hierarchical approach start to change as more and more responsibilities were shifted from the system level to the school level. These first steps have continued over the past 20 years to the point where we now see school leadership in a different light. Three major shifts have occurred.

The first shift is that we used to see leadership as being the sole responsibility of a single person—the school principal—and everyone else in the organisation was subservient to this person. Now, we see leadership as being a collective activity, with the more people involved and taking part, the more likely that all the issues arising in the increasingly complex environment that schools face these days will be addressed.

The second major shift is related to the first, in that leadership previously was seen as positional: principals were the leaders because they were principal, not because of anything they might do. Principals had been appointed (mostly) because they had been around longer than anyone else, rather than because they were seen to be good at leading a school. Now we see leadership as being an activity; we still have principals, but how they get to become principals now involves them demonstrating that they understand how to lead other people. We also now recognise that people other than the principal can also be leaders in their schools. In fact, we could argue that for a school to be really successful, everyone needs to be a leader; administrators might lead the school, but teachers need to lead learning in their classrooms and students are most successful when they are leaders of their own learning. So, in many primary schools, we have moved from the principal managing classroom teachers (or in secondary schools, from the principal and department heads overseeing classroom teachers) to leadership teams and professional learning communities where teachers take responsibility for the issues directly affecting them and their students.

The third major shift is that we used to think that leadership was generic. If you could lead in one place, you could lead anywhere. However, numerous examples abound of principals who had led some schools to high levels of success but were not as effective in other places. We recognised that leadership is context specific and that leading a school that is successful is not the same as leading a school that is not. A leader of a school that goes from being less to more successful requires that the leader changes style as the success builds. We also recognise that leadership is purpose specific: we must know why we are leading and be sure to build a common, moral purpose within the school community, if we are to be successful.

These changing understandings of leadership were brought about, in part, during the 1980s when a number of leadership terminologies entered educational conversations. These included transformational leadership (Leithwood & Jantzi, 2000), shared leadership (Lambert, 2002) or distributed leadership (Cox, Pearce, & Perry, 2003; Gronn, 2002; Spillane, Halverson, & Diamond, 2001, 2004). Many other terms have emerged as well: moral leadership, teacher leadership, servant leadership and so on. To try and consider all of these in some depth would be an almost impossible task.

However, instructional leadership, which emerged in the United States in the mid-1980s and leadership for learning, which emerged in the United Kingdom in the second half of the 2000s, are leadership theories worthy of being considered in some detail, for two main reasons. First, these might be considered as successful models of school leadership across many countries. Second, on the surface, they might be seen as opposing theories, with a strong focus on student outcomes promoted by instructional leadership, on the one hand, and an equally strong focus on developing the processes associated with learning (for everyone in the school) promoted by leadership for learning, on the other. One seems to promote a hierarchical approach to leadership, where the leader tells others what needs to be done, then ensures that it happens, and the other seems to be promoting a much broader involvement of others in the school in the process of leading the school forward and then establishing processes that enable this to occur.

Instructional leadership emerged in the early 1980s and was researched and conceptualised by Hallinger and Murphy (1985). The authors proposed three main dimensions—defining the school mission, managing the educational programme and promoting a positive school-learning climate—with a number of specific tasks that are undertaken within each of those dimensions. Leadership for learning was developed by the University of Cambridge through its Carpe Diem project (Swaffield & MacBeath, 2006), and identifies five different principles: a focus on learning (for everyone in the school), the conditions for learning, dialogue, shared leadership and shared accountability.

The focus of this book is to consider whether instructional leadership and leadership for learning can be seen as two sides of the same coin, underpinned by the question, 'How do we provide the best possible educational experience for young people as they move through schools?', or whether they are two very different approaches to leading school improvement. It is clear that, as school leaders, we need to focus on student outcomes and achievement on the one hand, but on the other, we also need to think about the processes that we use to increase learning across the school. It could be argued, however, that the choice made by a practising principal, to be either an instructional leader or a leader of learning, will influence the strategies and actions taken by that principal to lead the school towards improvement.

In order to consider this issue in some detail, we will first focus our attention on the theory behind these two approaches to school leadership, followed by chapters that consider how these theories have impacted on school leadership developments in different parts of the world and then others that provide a better understanding of how school leaders are developed and then use what they have learned to implement approaches to school improvement.

The Chapters to Come

The chapters of this book are collected into a number of parts. The first part of the book contains chapters by David Ng Foo Seong and John MacBeath that provide us with the theoretical underpinnings of the two leadership theories that are the focus of the book, instructional leadership and leadership for learning. Here, we get a better understanding of the history and theoretical bases of the two approaches to school leadership.

The second part of the book looks at how these theories of school leadership are seen and used in various parts of the world, with chapters from David Gurr looking at research into school leadership and how it influences student learning in Australia, then from David Imig, South Holden and Dale Placek, who consider whether or not the United States has moved away from instructional leadership and towards a leadership for learning approach, and Maria Assunção Flores and Fernando Ferreira providing a European perspective from Portugal that considers both school and teacher leadership in times of economic downturn.

The third part of the book considers how the two leadership approaches may have been incorporated into the preparation of school leaders, with David Ng Foo Seong from Singapore providing an Asian perspective on what it means for school leaders to be prepared for an uncertain future and whether leadership for learning approaches might support this challenge. Then Brian Caldwell considers leadership development in Australia, making the case for professional autonomy, rather than structural autonomy, as a way of empowering school leaders to enable school systems to become more adaptable in the future. Margery McMahon provides information on leadership at all levels from the Scottish context, where the focus on leadership for learning has intensified after a recent report in teaching and school leadership, and then Parvany Naidoo and Raj Mestry consider the development of school principals in South Africa, where making principals effective instructional leaders takes priority when the massive changes required after Apartheid continue to create challenges.

The fourth part of the book considers putting the theoretical and professional learning elements of the two theories into practice, in different ways, in different parts of the world. Anne Bayetto and Tony Townsend, using case studies, consider the impact of a programme designed to improve school leader support for changes in literacy in Australian schools using a leadership for learning approach, and Toshiya Chichibu, Tetsuro Uchizaki and Yumiko Ono consider a case of instructional leadership as it applies to lesson study in Japan. We then move beyond the school in three very different ways, with George Otero looking at school leaders working with the whole school community in the United States, with a recognition that relationships within the school community must be developed if we are to be successful, not only in academic terms but in other ways as well. Suzanne Cridge discusses an example of a not-for-profit agency working with schools to enable them to network with other schools in ways that support and promote student learning success in disadvantaged schools in Australia and Chris Chapman, Alison Drever, Maureen McBride, Craig Orr and Sarah Wheatley look at schools networking with other agencies within their communities, in a project called Children's Neighbourhoods, Scotland, to provide a comprehensive approach to student learning and wellbeing in the United Kingdom.

Finally, Neil Dempster uses the information provided in the chapters, together with further research findings, to draw some conclusions about school leadership and focuses particularly on the two main approaches we have discussed, instructional leadership and leadership for learning. In doing so, he identifies four main characteristics that must be considered when any form of school leadership exists: purpose (why we are doing what we are doing), pedagogy (how we will do it), people (who we are doing it for, and with) and relationships (which bring the other three issues together into a single focus). In doing so, he covers what Townsend and Bogotch (2008) called the 'what' and the 'how' of school leadership. His conclusion is that leadership for learning and instructional leadership are two very different approaches to leading schools and that leadership for learning has the best chance of fulfilling the moral purpose of education: to liberate all students through learning.

References

Boyson, R. (1975). *The crisis in education*. London: Woburn.
Caldwell, B., & Spinks, J. (1988). *The self managing school*. Lewes, UK: Falmer Press.
Carnegie Corporation. (1983). *Education and economic progress: Towards a national economic policy*. New York: Carnegie Corporation.
Committee on Economic Development. (1985). *Investing in our children: Business and the public schools*. New York: Committee on Economic Development.
Commons, D. L. (Chair). (1985). *Who will teach our children? A strategy for improving California's schools*. Sacramento, CA: California Commission on the Teaching Profession.
Cox, C. B., & Boyson, R. (Eds.). (1977). *Black paper 1977*. London: Temple Smith.
Cox, J., Pearce, C., & Perry, M. (2003). Toward a model of shared leadership and distributed influence in the innovation process: How shared leadership can enhance new product development team dynamics and effectiveness. In C. L. Pearce & J. A. Conger (Eds.), *Shared leadership: Reframing the hows and whys* (pp. 48–76). Thousand Oaks, CA: Sage.
Douglas, J. W. B. (1964). *The home and the school*. London: Panther Books.
Edmonds, R. (1979). Effective schools for the urban poor. *Educational Leadership, 37*(1), 15–27.
Green, L. J. (1968). *Parents and teachers: Partners or rivals*. London: Allen and Unwin.
Gronn, P. (2002). Distributed leadership as a unit of analysis. *Leadership Quarterly, 13*, 423–451.
Hallinger, P., & Murphy, J. (1985). Assessing the instructional management behaviour of principals. *The Elementary School Journal, 86*(2), 217–248.
Lambert, L. (2002). A framework for shared leadership. *Educational Leadership, 59*(8), 37–40.
Leithwood, K., & Jantzi, D. (2000). The effects of transformational leadership of organisational conditions and student engagement with school. *Journal of Educational Administration, 38*(2), 112–129.
National Commission on Excellence in Education. (1983). *A nation at risk: The imperative for educational reform*. Washington, DC: U.S. Government Printing Office.
Plowden Report. (1967). *Children and their primary schools*. London: HMSO.

Rutter, M., Maughan, B., Mortimore, P., & Ouston, J. (1979). *Fifteen thousand hours: Secondary schools and effects on children.* Boston: Harvard University Press.

Spillane, J. P., Halverson, R., & Diamond, J. B. (2001). Investigating school leadership practice: A distributed perspective. *Educational Researcher, 30*, 23–28.

Spillane, J. P., Halverson, R., & Diamond, J. B. (2004). Towards a theory of leadership practice: A distributed perspective. *Journal of Curriculum Studies, 36*, 3–34.

Swaffield, S., & MacBeath, J. (2006). Embedding learning how to learn in school policy: The challenge for leadership. *Research Papers in Education, 21*(2), 201–215.

Townsend, T., & Bogotch, I. (Eds.). (2008). *The elusive what and the problematic how: The essential leadership questions for school leaders and educational researcher.* Rotterdam, The Netherlands: Sense Publishers.

Part I

Theoretical Approaches to Leading Schools

2

Instructional Leadership

David Ng Foo Seong

An Overview of Instructional Leadership

In the 1970s, four studies investigated factors contributing to high-achieving schools in the United States: Weber (1971), State of New York—Office of Education Performance Review (1974), Madden, Lawson, and Sweet (1976) and Brookover and Lezotte (1977). Synthesising these studies, Edmonds (1979) suggested six hallmarks of effective schools: strong administrative leadership; high expectations for all students; orderly environment conducive to teaching and learning; academic emphasis; flexible resource mobilisation to better teaching and learning activities; and frequent monitoring of student progress. These claims highlight the importance of a good balance between effective management and instructional leadership of school leaders. However, there was no substantial attempt in conceptualising the construct of instructional leadership at that time.

D. Ng Foo Seong (✉)
Nanyang Technological University, Singapore, Singapore
e-mail: david.ng@nie.edu.sg

© The Author(s) 2019
T. Townsend (ed.), *Instructional Leadership and Leadership for Learning in Schools*, Palgrave Studies on Leadership and Learning in Teacher Education, https://doi.org/10.1007/978-3-030-23736-3_2

It was not until the 1980s that competing and alternative conceptualisations of instructional leadership burgeoned in scholarly works (e.g., Andrews & Soder, 1987; Bossert, Dwyer, Rowan, & Lee, 1982; Glickman, 1985; Hallinger & Murphy, 1985; Leithwood & Montgomery, 1982). Of these early conceptualisations, Hallinger and Murphy's (1985) model, shown in Fig. 2.1, has been the most fully tested and widely adopted in the research on instructional leadership (Southworth, 2002). This model proposes three dimensions for the instructional leadership construct: defining the school's mission, managing the instructional programme, and promoting a positive school learning climate.

Two functions in defining the school's mission are framing the school's goals and communicating the school's goals. They concern the principal's role in working with staff to ensure that the school has clear and measurable goals that are focused on the academic progress of its students. It is the principal's responsibility to ensure that these goals are widely known, supported, and communicated throughout the school community.

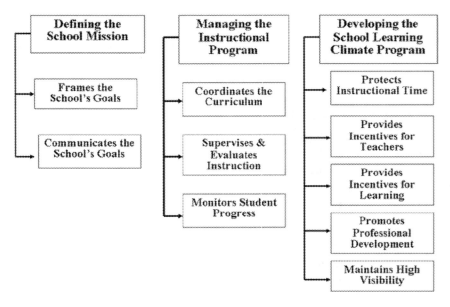

Fig. 2.1 A framework of instructional leadership. (Hallinger & Murphy, 1985, 1986)

The second dimension, managing the instructional programme, incorporates three leadership functions: supervising and evaluating instruction, coordinating the curriculum, and monitoring student progress. These functions require the leader to be deeply engaged in the school's instructional development. In larger schools, it is clear that the principal cannot be the only person involved in leading the school's instructional programme. Yet, this framework assumes that the development of the academic core of the school is a key leadership responsibility of the principal (Hallinger & Murphy, 1985).

The third dimension, promoting a positive school learning climate, includes several functions as shown in Fig. 2.1. This dimension is broader in scope and intent than the other two. It conforms to the notion that effective schools create an 'academic press' through developing high standards and expectations and a culture of continuous improvement.

This early conception of instructional leadership did not account for the school context or the characteristics of school leaders in instructional leadership. An influential framework that sought to conceptualise principal instructional leadership beyond the three dimensions in Hallinger and Murphy's model was proposed by Bossert et al. (1982), as shown in Fig. 2.2. This Far West Lab instructional management model proposed that instructional leadership is exercised in a complex organisational context and impacts student outcomes through indirect linkages. The model

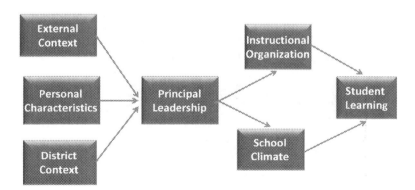

Fig. 2.2 Far West Lab instructional management model. (Bossert et al., 1982, p. 40)

guided subsequent qualitative studies that sought to describe how principals enacted the instructional leadership roles in the context of different school settings (e.g., Dwyer, Lee, Rowan, & Bossert, 1983; Hallinger & Murphy, 1986). Together, these reviews and early qualitative research provided a foundation for the subsequent development of survey instruments (e.g., Hallinger & Murphy, 1985; Heck, Larson, & Marcoulides, 1990) for use in large-scale quantitative research. Over the ensuing three decades a maturing literature was built upon this foundation through large-scale empirical research conducted in North America (e.g., Hallinger & Heck, 1996; Heck et al., 1990; Leithwood, Patten, & Jantzi, 2010; Marks & Printy, 2003), Europe (Day et al., 2010; Witziers, Bosker, & Kruger, 2003), and Australia (Mulford & Silins, 2009).

Bossert and his colleagues (1982) advanced theoretical discourse in educational leadership by explicitly highlighting the impact of the school's context on principals. The acknowledgement that the school's context is important resulted in an adaptation of the Far West Lab model for the instructional leadership model during the mid-1990s. Subsequently, the Far West model includes the dimension of socio-cultural and national/institutional contexts, as shown in Fig. 2.3 (Bajunid, 1996; Cheng, 1995; Hallinger, 1995; Hallinger & Leithwood, 1998).

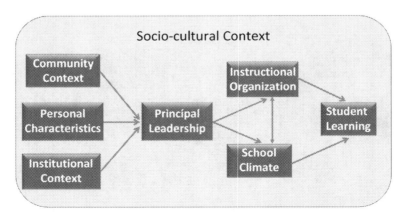

Fig. 2.3 Adaptation of the Far West Lab instructional management model. (Bossert et al., 1982, p. 40)

A number of other models of instructional leadership were also proposed. These include Andrews and Soder (1987); the more recent Robinson, Lloyd, and Rowe's (2008) five-dimension model; and OECD's (2009) three-dimension model. These models qualify instructional leadership as a multidimensional construct.

Although these instructional leadership (IL) dimensions are somewhat competing with one another, they share commonalities. Generally, principals, with the assistance of vice-principals, are expected to fulfil roles pertaining to the following aspects: vision development and alignment, management of instruction, curriculum coordination, promoting a positive school climate, and supporting teacher professional development.

Reviewing studies conducted in the 1980s, Hallinger (2003, 2005) highlighted five notable descriptions of principals as effective instructional leaders: (1) principals as 'strong, directive leaders'; (2) principals as managers of instructional and curricular activities; (3) principals as 'culture builders'; (4) principals as 'goal-oriented leaders'; and (5) principals leading from 'a combination of expertise and charisma'. The first two characteristics have invited criticism for instructional leadership owing to its being heavily directive, hierarchical, and centralised. Traditional instructional leadership models seem to consider the principal as a sole source of influence and expertise and downplay the influence of other leaders such as middle managers or teacher leaders.

Due to these concerns and school restructuring initiatives in the USA in the 1990s, scholars shifted attention to other models such as transformational leadership, distributed leadership, shared leadership, and teacher leadership (Gronn, 2000; Hallinger, 2003; Harris, 2008; Leithwood, 1992, 1994; Leithwood & Jantzi, 2005). The 2005 review by Hallinger indicated an intermediate drop in the number of studies on instructional leadership between 1991 and 2000.

Instructional leadership regained its prominence in the leadership discourse in the early 2000s. A review was conducted of articles relevant to instructional leadership published in eight core journals on educational leadership from 2000 to 2016 (Ng, Nguyen, Wong, & Choy, 2015). The review surfaced a substantial number of studies (at least 340 articles). There are several reasons for this remarkable resurgence of instructional leadership research.

First, international educational reforms in the early 2000s emphasised school accountability measures that are linked directly to improving student learning (Hallinger, 2003, 2005; Pan, Nyeu, & Chen, 2015; Walker, Hu, & Qian, 2012). The principal as an 'instructional leader', or more often under the new label 'leadership for learning', took central focus in accountability educational reforms.

Second, the conceptual models of instructional leadership in the 1980s appear to be still effective and convenient instruments for positivist/post-positivist researchers, particularly novice researchers. For example, Hallinger (2011) identified that at least 130 doctoral dissertations used the Principal Instructional Management Rating Scale (PIMRS) over the course of nearly three decades.

Finally, instructional leadership has documented positive effects over other leadership models. Robinson and her colleagues conducted a meta-analysis review on the impact of school leadership on student learning. This 2008 review concluded, 'the average effect of instructional leadership on student outcomes was three to four times that of transformational leadership' (p. 635). Robinson et al. (2008) further added to the conceptualisations of instructional leadership by proposing five dimensions: (1) establishing goals and expectations; (2) strategic resourcing; (3) planning, coordinating, and evaluating teaching and the curriculum; (4) promoting and participating in teacher learning and development; and (5) ensuring an orderly and supportive environment (p. 656).

Evolving Assumptions of Instructional Leadership: Principal Leadership to Distributed Instructional Leadership

Principal Instructional Leadership

The centrality of the principal as the educational leader has been expansively written about in school improvement literature from the 1970s. The principal as *the* instructional leader emerged from the 1980s era of 'instructionally effective elementary schools' (Edmonds, 1979; Hallinger, 2005). Earlier reviews consistently reported a preference among scholars for studying school administrators at the elementary school level (Bossert et al., 1982; Bridges, 1982; Erickson, 1967; Hallinger, Bickman, & Davis, 1996). This ushered in the conception of the influential principal instructional leader who exercised strong and directive instructional leadership in turning schools around (Bamburg & Andrews, 1991; Bossert et al., 1982; Hallinger, 2005). The instructional leadership roles of the principal are encapsulated in Hallinger and Murphy's (1985) model. This widely adopted model described *the* instructional leader *(principal)* defining the school's mission, managing the instructional programme, and promoting the school learning climate.

Principals were described as providing the vision and direction for the school. Hence, principals as instructional leaders exercised leadership and management of schools to achieve the goals derived from the school vision (Bamburg & Andrews, 1991; Glasman, 1984; Goldring & Pasternak, 1994; Hallinger & Murphy, 1986; Heck et al., 1990; Leithwood, Begley, & Cousins, 1990; Leitner, 1994; O'Day, 1983). The effective principal instructional leader was described as able to align the strategies and activities of the school with the school's academic mission.

The centrality of the principal as the instructional leader could be significantly attributed to the use of the PIMRS. The instrument, developed by Hallinger during the early 1980s, was the most frequently used instrument to study instructional leadership (Hallinger & Murphy, 1985). It assumes that coordination and control of the academic programme of the school are key leadership responsibilities of the principal. Over 45% of the 130 doctoral studies reviewed (Hallinger, 2011; Hallinger & Chen, 2015) showed a continuing preference for studying principals at the elementary school level.

The Western literature has stressed the importance of the principal's role in fulfilling accountability of standards through classroom evaluation of teaching and learning (Darling-Hammond, Meyerson, LaPointe, & Orr, 2009; Hallinger, 2005; Leithwood, Louis, Anderson, & Wahlstrom, 2004; Mendels, 2012). Not only do effective principals focus attention on monitoring curriculum and teaching, the literature widely touts that principals must also have strong knowledge related to teaching and learning (Mazzeo, 2003). More specifically, some studies regarded regular classroom visits and feedback as principals' effective channel to influence the teaching and learning process (Blase & Blase, 1999; Ovando, 2005) and as a valuable tool in professional development (Joyce & Showers, 2002).

An emerging question is whether school principals need to exert more instructional leadership on instructional evaluation and supervision and whether this is feasible in the context of large schools. According to Horng and Loeb's (2010) review of empirical studies, the traditional model mentioned above is ideal, but it is 'actually poorly suited to the reality of many of today's schools' (p. 66). They add that the principal's involvement in the classroom has only a marginal impact on the quality of teaching and learning. Even principals who are very determined to be more heavily involved in classrooms meet numerous and varied challenges (Hallinger, 2000). Instead, principals can improve instruction by strategically managing activities such as recruiting and retaining highly qualified staff and allocating budgets and resources.

Distributed/Shared Instructional Leadership

The reality, through reviews of studies on instructional leadership, contradicts the ideal notion that instructional leadership is the main responsibility of the principal (Cuban, 1984; Hallinger & Murphy, 1987). In fact, the 2005 review by Hallinger found few studies indicating principals' hands-on involvement in classroom instruction at either the primary or secondary school level.

The role of giving feedback and evaluating teachers is performed by Heads of Department or middle-level leaders in Singapore (Ng et al., 2015). This finding provided empirical evidence of the devolvement of classroom observation of teaching and learning to the other leaders instead of the school principal.

By the turn of the century, educational leadership scholars began to focus on a diffused centrality of influence beyond the individual principal. There were a number of conceptions such as 'shared instructional leadership' (Harris, 2003; Jackson, 2000; Lambert, 2002; Marks & Printy, 2003), 'teacher leadership' (Harris, 2005; York-Barr & Duke, 2004), and 'distributed leadership' (Bennett, Wise, Woods, & Harvey, 2003; Gronn, 2002; Spillane, 2006; Woods, 2004). This shift towards diffused centrality of influence was further elaborated in Printy's (2010) review of the influence of leadership on the quality of instruction in U.S. schools. Printy pointed out that there is strong evidence that teachers' leadership efforts are more important than the principal's involvement in making instructional choices. These leadership efforts among teachers are through appointed leadership roles such as instructional coaches.

The conclusion drawn from educational leadership scholars in the last decade is that the phenomenon of leadership is shared or distributed and does not solely rest on the individual principal. Naturally, the processes of influence and implementation will be more complex as they involve multiple interactions and interrelationships between and among stakeholders. Instructional leadership requires the principal to have the capacity to create organisational conditions necessary to build pedagogical capacity, expand opportunities for innovation, supply and allocate resources, give instructional direction and support to teachers, and enable teachers to assume individual and collective responsibility for instructional improvement (e.g., Darling-Hammond et al., 2009; Hallinger & Bryant, 2013; Matthews, Moorman, & Nusche, 2007).

Therefore, the concept of the principal as the instructional leader should focus on the principal's role in the development and distribution of the understandings, skills, and attributes across the school organisational spectrum. As Gronn (1986, 1999, 2003) has argued, the term 'school leadership' does not refer to the leadership of the principal alone. Although the principal remains a key player in organisational change, schools cannot rely on the 'power of one'. Rather, concepts such as leader–teacher relationship, collegiality, collaborative culture, learning organisation, and teacher leadership suggest that the power to make decisions to improve teaching and learning in the classroom must be distributed throughout the organisation.

Gronn (2002) introduced one of the early distributed leadership conceptualisations in education. He identified three types of distributed leadership: (1) spontaneous collaboration, (2) intuitive working relations, and (3) institutionalised practices. Gronn also suggested that distributed leadership is more about 'concertive action', rather than only 'numerical action' that refers to multiple individuals contributing to the exercise of leadership (p. 429). Spillane (2006) proposed three types of distributed leadership patterns, namely, collaborated distribution, collective distribution, and coordinated distribution. Both Gronn and Spillane agreed that leadership is not the sole responsibility and action of the typical hierarchical leader.

A synthesis of several notable empirical studies addressing shared/distributed instructional leadership is discussed by Marks and Printy (2003), who suggested a model of 'shared instructional leadership' to supplant a hierarchical and procedural perspective with a more heterarchical orientation. This model suggests the active collaboration between a principal and teachers on curricular, instructional, and assessment matters. Marks and Printy claimed at least two benefits of shared instructional leadership: first, this model promotes synergy amongst individuals in the school, and second, it pragmatically allows principals to share their increasing workload.

Hallinger and Lee (2012) investigated how instructional leadership was distributed in International Baccalaureate (IB) schools. Specifically, the researchers identified four distributed instructional leadership practices in IB schools: (1) 'the development of subject vertical and horizontal articulation documents', (2) 'teachers teaching in more than one programme', (3) collaboration between programme coordinators, and (4) 'collaboration between teachers of each programme'.

Several other studies utilised frameworks of distributed leadership to investigate how instructional leadership is distributed in U.S. high schools (e.g., Bredeson & Kelley, 2013; Halverson & Clifford, 2013; Klar, 2012). Noticeably, Klar (2012) provided examples about how principals fostered distributed instructional leadership. Klar illuminated these principals' practices in developing their department chairs' instructional leadership capacities such as: 'creating opportunities to learn', 'modelling distributed leadership', 'modelling collaborative learning', and 'setting department chairs up for success' (p. 373).

In summary, we suggest that research on instructional leadership can further move forward to take distributed perspectives into consideration, instead of solely focusing on studying principal instructional leadership practices. To enable this, in the following sections, the three dimensions considered to be central to instructional leadership in the Western literature (Vision, Managing Teaching and Learning and Establishing a Conducive Learning Environment) are considered from an Asian context.

Evolving Substantive Theories of Instructional Leadership: Anglo-Saxon to Indigenous Knowledge

For nearly 70 years, the research on educational administration and leadership has built a comparatively rich corpus; however, the contributions to the field are still heavily reliant on Anglo-American contexts such as Australia, Canada, the UK, and the USA (Dimmock, 2011; Hallinger, Wang, Chen, & Liare, 2015; Walker & Hallinger, 2015). Research into educational management and leadership from non-Anglo-American perspectives (e.g., Asia, Africa, and South America) is still at a relative infancy. Scholars have long affirmed the significant influences of particular contexts on successful school leadership (Bossert et al., 1982; Hallinger & Ko, 2015; Lee, Hallinger, & Walker, 2012).

In order to assess the state of the research on educational management and leadership in Asia, Hallinger and Bryant (2013) conducted a review of studies published between 2000 and 2011 in eight 'core' journals in the field. The two authors reported a very limited number of empirical studies undertaken in Asian societies (Hallinger & Bryant, 2013). This finding is strongly consistent with other claims on the dearth of empirical educational leadership research in Asia (e.g., Bajunid, 1996; Dimmock, 2011; Walker & Qian, 2015).

The following section, however, provides an emerging indigenous knowledge on instructional leadership based on the original Hallinger and Murphy model of instructional leadership (1985, 1986). In general, Asian education systems are more centralised than those in the West. Therefore, the emerging indigenous knowledge in highly centralised education systems helps to create substantive knowledge of the practice of instructional leadership in such systems.

Vision

Singapore's education system provides an interesting context to study instructional leadership. The education system has been described as a 'centralised decentralisation governance' approach (Ng, 2008). The

Ministry of Education maintains centralised control of strategic directions of the education system through initiatives, policies, a common examination system, and a common syllabus. Leung (2004) noted that decentralisation happens at the decision-making level at the school and, in particular, through efforts in school-based innovations to accommodate diversity and pedagogical reforms. Several studies support the definitive role of the school principal in leading curriculum change in Singaporean schools (Dimmock & Goh, 2011; Koh, Ponnusamy, Tan, Lee, & Ramos, 2014; Ng & Ho, 2012). The school principal always refers to the school vision and mission in terms of strategic directions and student learning outcomes. At the key personnel and teacher level, there appears to be a practice of distributed leadership where a significant degree of autonomy is given to translate the vision into curriculum implementation and curriculum change (Ho, Victor Chen, & Ng, 2016; Lim-Ratnam, Atencio, & Lee, 2016).

Elmore (2004) emphasises that educators must learn to do new things in 'the setting in which they work'. This is evident in how Singaporean principals articulate their own vision of the school within the constraint of the framework imposed by the Ministry. The implication is that school vision follows system vision instead of the school having an independent vision. Principals have consistently adapted their own school vision in collaboration with the stakeholders in the school according to the school's setting and context, with the system vision provided by the Ministry of Education (Nguyen, Ng, & Yap, 2017). While it appears that school principals in Singapore's highly centralised system do not have the liberty to create their own vision for the school, the reality is that they do exercise bounded flexibility. Principals could refine, review, and change goals through a systematic process involving stakeholders, in particular, the middle-level leaders.

As an alternative approach to vision, Vietnam's Ministry of Education (e.g., see Hallinger & Huber, 2012) conceives of its school principals first and foremost as 'government officers' responsible for implementing the Ministry of Education's policies. Their roles include maintaining the socio-political norms of the society as well as ensuring that its schools have the capacity to change. The state's management of education is organised on multiple levels including Elected Governmental Bodies,

Ministry of Education and Training, Regional and District Departments of Education Services and Local Education Bureaus. The government assumes authority for education management, makes concrete educational policies, and directs national resources towards educational development (Hallinger & Truong, 2014). Vietnamese school leaders tend to develop and build an image as powerful authority figures who exercise control over subordinates (Nguyen, 2007; Truong, 2012). The implication is that the school's direction and goal are 'determined' and that decision-making is a 'top-down' approach. Patterns of one-way communication where leaders communicate the school direction/vision and goals to teachers (Lan, 2002; Pham, 2007) occur. Teachers and staff are expected to obey the leaders' decision and implement their directives and instructions.

Managing Teaching and Learning

Singapore's principals, however, do not seem to be directly involved in the domain of instructional evaluation and supervision. Instead, they tend to delegate this direct responsibility to middle managers. Principals can improve instruction by strategically managing organisational activities such as recruiting and retaining highly qualified staff, and allocating budgets and resources.

To a certain extent, Taiwan's school leaders are similar to Singaporean school leaders where they assume the role of indirect leadership more so than the role of direct leadership in managing teaching and learning (Pan et al., 2015). Studies in principal instructional leadership in Taiwan found that 'developing a supporting work environment' was the most observed behaviour, while 'ensuring teaching quality' was the least observed. Other behaviours ranked in between were 'promoting student learning climate', followed by 'developing teaching mission and goals', 'ensuring curriculum quality', and 'promoting teacher professional development' (Pan et al., 2015). The lack of legal authority to supervise teaching through walk-through observations as well as a lack of training on pedagogy and curriculum development might illustrate why Taiwanese principals executed a high level of indirect leadership such as the most frequently observed behaviour, supporting work environment.

Conducive Learning Environment

Principals in Singapore recognised the significant effects of the school physical environment on instructional activities. They typically consulted key personnel and considered functionality, structure, size, and flexibility of space in their decision. The efforts undertaken by these principals on the physical environment of the school were typical and essential for accommodating instructional activities in the twenty-first century (Ng et al., 2015).

Principals generally made efforts to promote collegiality and harmony in the school. They proactively established supporting structures such as mentoring collaborative teams, creating conditions to support staff collaboration, and promoting innovation and receptiveness of feedback in the school.

Principals generally emphasised staff well-being and scheduled celebratory and relaxation activities throughout the year to enable staff bonding. To promote harmony in the school, most principals saw the need to be open to feedback from stakeholders.

Most principals regarded establishing good relationships with teachers and students as the key to building a successful school. Almost all principals claimed to adopt an open-door policy in order to be accessible to teachers and students. This practice extends to virtual communication platforms such as email, SMS, or WhatsApp.

Many principals utilised 'walkabouts' as an opportunity to maintain high visibility and to interact with teachers and students. Some principals would occasionally visit classrooms to motivate students during the pre-examination periods or when students were delivering presentations. Principals prioritised quality instructional activities and took strong measures to protect instructional time.

Evolving Research in Instructional Leadership

Instructional leadership research in the early 1980s generally adopted a direct-effects model of bivariate leadership effects (Hallinger & Heck, 1996; Van de Grift & Houtveen, 1999), which did not account or control for the effects of mediating, antecedent and moderator variables. A review of instructional leadership research from 1980 to 1995 does not support the claim that instructional leadership is directly tied to student achievement. Instead, most research in instructional leadership points to indirect effects on student achievement (Cotton, 2003; Hallinger & Heck, 1996; Hallinger et al., 1996; Leithwood et al., 2004, 2010; Louis et al., 2010; Supovitz, Sirinides, & May, 2010).

As concepts of collaborative leadership (Heck & Hallinger, 2010), shared instructional leadership, teacher leadership, and distributed leadership emerged, the bivariate direct-effects study quickly lost its relevancy. Researchers adopted multi-variate, indirect effects using the mediated and reciprocal effects models (Hallinger & Heck, 1996; Heck & Hallinger, 2010; Leithwood et al., 2010). The following section reviews the research paradigm adopted in instructional leadership.

Educational leadership research adopts a spectrum of disciplined inquiry methods. Cronbach and Suppes (1969) defined disciplined inquiry as 'conducted and reported in such a way that the argument can be painstakingly examined' (p. 15). This section looks at the disciplined inquiry methods adopted and implemented in the past 30 years to identify the quantitative and qualitative methods that have contributed to the current body of knowledge on instructional leadership.

The author's review adopted a search for instructional leadership in schools using the following search parameters:

* Keywords in database search: AB 'instructional leadership'
* Limiters: Full Text; Scholarly (Peer-reviewed) Journals; Published Date: 1980–2016
* Narrow by Methodology: quantitative study
* Narrow by Methodology: qualitative study
* Search modes: Find all search terms
* Interface: EBSCOhost Research Databases
* Database: Academic Search Premier; British Education Index; Education Source; ERIC

The search found over 350 empirical studies that employed the constructs of instructional leadership. The author carefully read the relevant sections of the 350 studies pertaining to methodologies and extracted this information in the following tables (Tables 2.1 and 2.2).

Table 2.1 Instructional leadership—quantitative method

Data source: Questionnaire survey	
Types	Specific analytical methods
Basic statistics	Frequency distribution; mean; median; standard deviation; t-test
Analysis of variance	Analysis of covariance; analysis of variance; one-way ANOVA; Two-way ANOVA
Association and correlation	Correlation; regression
Causal Modelling	Dependent variable; independent variable; path analysis; structural equation modeling
Factor analysis	Exploratory factor analysis; factor analysis; confirmatory factor analysis; oblique rotation; rotated factor
Linear and multilevel analysis	Generalised linear model, hierarchical generalised linear model; hierarchical linear modeling
Multilevel regression	Multicollinearity; multiple regression analysis; interaction effect

The range of research quantitative and qualitative methodologies and analytical tools found in the review could be classified as follows:

Quantitative Analyses

- Univariate analysis
- Bivariate analysis
- Inferential statistics

Qualitative Analyses

- Content analysis
- Hermeneutic analysis
- Grounded theory analysis

The dominant analytical tools adopted in instructional leadership research involved relational and associational analyses of the effects of leadership actions and interventions in the school. The focus is on identifying variables, factors, and their associations in providing explanations of successful practices. The central concept of relations is based on linear causality.

Table 2.2 Instructional leadership—qualitative methods

Data source	Specific analytical methods
One-on-one interview	Thematic analysis ("coding and then segregating the data by codes into data clumps for furtheranalysis and description)
	Discrepancy theme
Focus group interview	Characteristics
Document search (e.g. writing samples, email correspondence, and district literature)	Descriptive
Field notes	Factors
Classroom observations	Roles
Semi-structured interviews	Nature
Artefacts	Content analysis
Shadowing	Causal sequence
Interview protocols (for multiple case studies)	Interactions but also in social, cultural, and institutional discourses
Interpretive description	Structured coding scheme derived from the conceptual framework
Topic-oriented	Exploratory analysis
The voices from the field	Phenomenology and constant comparative methods
Cross-cultural comparative studies	Comparative analysis: finding common themes, and contrasts
Portfolios	Detailed analytical memo
Micropolitical analysis	Vertical analysis: analysing participants' voices separately; and patterns and elucidating the differences among participants' voices.

However, this assumption predisposed researchers to accept that systems are in equilibrium. One implication is that the number of possible outcomes in a system is limited (because of the limited number of variables within a closed system). A second implication is the centrality influence of the school leader. The influence from the school leader that results in instability is short-term compared with the equilibrium time of the outcome. Hence, we measure effects or establish relationships and accept their data value as a true indicator of the cause of intervention. For this to be true, the many variables in the school (as a closed system) must be assumed as independent data points; otherwise we could have interdependence, possible mutual causality, and the occurrence of possible external influences (like political change) in the larger system.

The evolution from principal instructional leadership to distributed/shared instructional leadership as discussed in the earlier section poses issues in current research methodologies. Naturally, the processes of influence and implementation will be more complex as they involve multiple interactions and interrelationships between and among stakeholders.

Distributed/shared instructional leadership suggests active collaboration between a principal and teachers on curricular, instructional, and assessment matters. The nature of leadership is a social influence process (Conger, 1998; Yukl & Mahsud, 2010). Research on leadership has been long well entrenched; nonetheless, Parry (1998) asserts that 'mainstream leadership research methodologies have been partially unsuccessful in theorizing about the nature of these processes' (p. 85).

In studying this complexity in the system, instructional leadership research methods must be able to collect data that are associated with the dynamism and diffused centrality of leadership influence. The limitations of current, commonly used analytical tools contribute to the difficulty in distinguishing between the contributions of independent variables to that of the dependent variable as they may compete to explain much of the similar variance. Heck and Hallinger (2010, p. 248) concluded that 'Research needs to examine how leadership responds to changing environmental forces as well as to changes in organisational processes and performance outcomes over time. Given current theoretical constructs and statistical methods, conducting further reciprocal-effects studies with longitudinal data is eminently possible and highly recommended'.

Future Directions in Instructional Leadership: Research Methodologies That Parallel Evolving Assumptions of Instructional Leadership

Complexity of Schools: Systems and Structures

Murphy (2015) examined the evolution of education from the industrial era in the USA (1890–1920) to the post-industrial era from the 1980s. He concluded that post-industrial school organisations have fundamentally shifted in roles, relationships, and responsibilities. The shift is seen in the blurring of the distinctions between administrators and teachers, with general roles instead of specialisation and the need for greater flexibility and adaptability. In terms of structures, the traditional hierarchical organisation structures are giving way to structures that are flatter.

This shift contributed to the increasing complexity of schools. The involvement among a growing circle of stakeholders within the school and between government, employers, and communities clearly supports the view that schooling is no longer seen as a closed system. It is both a closed and open system (Darling-Hammond, 2010; Hargreaves & Shirley, 2009; Leithwood & Day, 2007). Open systems are 'a system in exchange of a matter with its environment' (Von Bertalanffy, 1968, p. 141). Schools as an open system are seen as part of a much larger network rather than an independent, self-standing entity.

To understand the processes extant within the school, it is critical to study interrelationships between those entities and their connections to a whole system. The interrelationships among stakeholders are nonlinear and discontinuous, so even small changes in variables can have significant impacts on the whole system. A common theme found in the education reform documents from diverse countries is the phrase 'world-class education'. This phrase has become widely associated with comparative results on international tests such as Trends in International Mathematics and Science Study, which purport to measure certain aspects of educational quality. This seemingly small aspect of change (comparing of achievement in Mathematics and Science) has impacted developing and developed nations in reforming their education system and being able to call their ongoing education reform as moving towards a 'world-class education system'.

Thus, interrelationships in an open system require sophisticated analyses of their systemic nature. A reductionist and linear sequential relationship investigation would not be sufficient to inform us to bring about further change.

Contexts: High Accountability Systems

Investigation into the shape, place, and effect of principal instructional leadership has followed numerous pathways. Among these is the role and impact of school leadership in a policy environment that demands increased school accountability for student outcomes (Cooley & Shen, 2003; Heck & Hallinger, 2009; Vanderhaar, Muñoz, & Rodosky, 2006).

A consequence of this policy trend has been to return 'instructional leadership' to a central position within reform discourse (Hallinger, 2005; Wiseman, 2004). While scholarly interest in instructional leadership has endured since the early 1980s (e.g., Bossert et al., 1982), it has returned to the limelight because of an increasing global emphasis on school accountability measures linked directly to improving student learning (Hallinger, 2005). This is accompanied by substantial empirical evidence of the positive impact of instructional leadership on teacher practices and student outcomes (Blase & Blase, 1999; Hallinger et al., 1996; Leithwood et al., 2004; Louis et al., 2010; Marks & Printy, 2003; O'Donnell & White, 2005; Robinson et al., 2008).

Scope for Indigenous Substantive Theory Building in Instructional Leadership

Similarly to the other topics in educational leadership, the research on instructional leadership still lacks empirical evidence, specifically in Asian societies and other non-Anglo-American contexts, despite its longevity. Bush (2014) argues that instructional leadership knowledge has been underpinned by research and practice in (partly) decentralised contexts, while little is known about how instructional leadership is practised in (more) centralised systems in Asia, Africa, and Eastern Europe. A number of scholars have recently confirmed the need for empirical studies on practices and effects of principal instructional leadership in Asia (e.g., Hallinger & Lee, 2011; Hallinger et al., 2015; Lee et al., 2012; Walker & Ko, 2011). One of the developmental tendencies for the research on instructional leadership is to surface indigenous understandings on instructional leadership.

What Are the Alternatives to Current Social Science Methodologies for Instructional Leadership?

As mentioned, it is important to ensure that any alternative research methodologies proposed must adhere to the characteristic of disciplined inquiry. Cronbach and Suppes (1969) stated that 'Disciplined inquiry does not necessarily follow well established, formal procedures. Some of the most excellent inquiry is free-ranging and speculative ... trying what might seem to be a bizarre combination of ideas and procedures' (p. 16).

Drawing from this, there are two other important points about disciplined inquiry that must be addressed. First, disciplined inquiry is not solely focused on establishing facts. The methods of observation and inquiry are critical if we were to state the facts. Establishment of facts can be done through a selection of observations and/or data collection methods. From a pragmatic perspective and to adhere to the characteristic of disciplined inquiry, we are proposing that one should be open to different types of observations and data collection methodologies as long as the definition of disciplined inquiry is adhered to. The field of educational leadership is not a discipline by itself. One should not be limited to a single discipline to dictate and direct the study. Instead, procedures and perspectives of different disciplines such as biology, anthropology, economics, and others can be brought to bear on the research questions that we investigate.

In the last decade, the field of complexity science has emerged as a serious paradigm for research on complex systems. Complex systems consist of many distributed interacting components. Example of systems that have adopted complexity science research methodologies include health, socio-technological, natural sciences, governance and public policies, and so on (Klimek & Thurner, 2013; Sloot, Ivanov, Boukhanovsky, van de Vijver, & Boucher, 2008).

Complexity science is not a single theory—it encompasses many theoretical frameworks and is highly inter-disciplinary. It is also the study of systems—the patterns of relationships within them, how they are sustained, how they self-organise, and how outcomes emerge (Zimmerman, Lindberg, & Plsek, 1998). Emergence is a property classically exhibited by many agent-based models, and it occurs when an attribute that can be described at a system level is not specifically encoded at the individual level. Complex systems are characterised by emergent phenomena—patterns that appear to be quite complex can often be generated by simple rules.

Social science research that has been the hallmark of educational leadership research has always been about reducing the complexity of the world to predictable regularities (Phelan, 2001). Complexity science focuses on studying the evolution of complex organisations—entities with multiple, diverse, and interconnected elements. The emergence of new patterns in an organisation is a result of iterative feedback effects, nonlinearity interactions, and self-organisation practices (Zimmerman et al., 1998).

Therefore, complexity science provides a useful alternative to the linear causality assumption of social science. The studies adopt a rigorous approach to study some of the key dimensions of organisational life. How does organisational change happen? What are the conditions for innovations in organisations? (Zimmerman et al., 1998).

The following section will highlight one of the methods used in complexity science research that provide an alternative to the limitations identified in current research methodologies in educational leadership research.

Social Network Analysis

Social network analysis (SNA) (Scott, 2000; Wasserman & Faust, 1994) focuses on relational structures that characterise a network of people. It has been used to investigate educational issues such as teacher professional networks (Baker-Doyle & Yoon, 2011; Penuel, Riel, Krause, & Frank, 2009), the spread of educational innovations (Frank, Zhao, & Borman, 2004), and peer influences on youth behaviour (Bennett, Schneider, Tang, Arnold, & Wilson, 2006). It has also been used to shed light on the variety of ways in which teachers interact and relate. The relationships between teachers can be divided into expressive and instrumental relationships, with an underlying differentiation between how independent or interdependent each relationship structure makes teachers (Moolenaar, Sleegers, Karsten, & Daly, 2012).

The following table provides examples of the types of data collected, analytical methods, and analytical tools used in social network (Table 2.3):

There are multiple methods and ways to study complexity phenomena. It is not possible to delve into these methodologies in a meaningful manner in one chapter. The following are examples of established methods used in studying complex systems (Table 2.4):

Table 2.3 Social network

Data	Types and methods
What types of data are collected for social network?	Social bonds Organisational links Media connection Identify boundaries Clarify and design questions 'Actually existing social relations' 'Perceived relations' Dynamism: 'Episodic' relations or 'typical'/'long term' ties
Methods used to collect such data	Surveys Interviews Facebook, LinkedIn Data mining (internet, emails) Archival data Observations
Analytical tools	Netlogo Netdraw UCINET NodeXL Gephi PAJEK SPAN STATNET

Conclusion

In this chapter, I have reviewed instructional leadership from its inception to current adaptations in different contexts. In particular, the discussion on the evolution from heroic individual and simple cause and effect to one of team/distributed leadership and complexity has highlighted two key points. First, instructional leadership is still relevant in improving schools and student learning, albeit with the need for adaptation and modification of the original models. Second, there are constraints in the use of current universally adopted social science methodologies and analytical tools for researching instructional leadership in context, in different cultures and within the dynamic complexity of schools.

This chapter proposes to add diversity to instructional leadership research, thus ensuring that its scholarly evolution continues. Complexity research methodologies proposed are not merely alternative or novel ways

Table 2.4 Complexity science research methods

Methods	Definition
Agent-based modelling	An agent-based model (ABM) is one of a class of computational models for simulating the actions and interactions of autonomous agents (both individual and collective entities such as organisations or groups) with a view to assessing their effects on the system as a whole. It combines elements of game theory, complex systems emergence, computational sociology, multi-agent systems, and evolutionary programming. Source: https://en.wikipedia.org/wiki/Agent-based_model
Network (social) analysis	Social network analysis (SNA) is the process of investigating social structures through the use of network and graph theories. It characterises networked structures in terms of nodes (individual actors, people, or things within the network) and the ties or edges (relationships or interactions) that connect them. Source: https://en.wikipedia.org/wiki/Social_network_analysis
Dynamical systems theory	Dynamical systems theory is an area of mathematics used to describe the behaviour of complex dynamical systems, usually by employing differential equations or difference equations. Much of modern research is focused on the study of chaotic systems. Source: https://en.wikipedia.org/wiki/Dynamical_systems_theory
Multi-agent modelling	A multi-agent system (M.A.S.) is a computerised system composed of multiple interacting intelligent agents within an environment. Multi-agent systems can be used to solve problems that are difficult or impossible for an individual agent or a monolithic system to solve. Source: https://en.wikipedia.org/wiki/Agent-based_social_simulation

of examining the problems or issues encountered. They bring with them their contrasting disciplinary roots where the types of research questions that can be raised are now made possible by adopting similar concepts from different disciplines.

Our interest in the effects of instructional leadership on school improvement can now be investigated by asking different research questions. We could indeed go deeper and ask, 'What do we wish to know about school improvement that we do not yet know enough?' Being open to diverse methodologies through a disciplined approach has nothing to lose but everything to gain in our scholastic pursuit of knowledge in the field of educational leadership. We must avoid being educational leadership researchers who see our world from the perspectives that we have lived in and must not accept without question these perspectives as the only ones.

The choice of research method or combination of methods affects the type of research questions asked. Ideally, we should not be constrained by the methods before asking our research questions. Research questions are the primary drivers for our quest for knowledge. It should be from this basis that we find the most relevant methodologies that can answer our research questions and provide us with the findings that can contribute to theory formation, knowledge building, and translation to practice.

References

Andrews, R. L., & Soder, R. (1987). Principal leadership and student achievement. *Educational Leadership, 44*(6), 9–11.

Bajunid, I. A. (1996). Preliminary explorations of indigenous perspectives of educational management. *Journal of Educational Administration, 34*(5), 50–73.

Baker-Doyle, K. J., & Yoon, S. A. (2011). In search of practitioner-based social capital: A social network analysis tool for understanding and facilitating teacher collaboration in a US-based STEM professional development program. *Professional Development in Education, 37*(1), 75–93.

Bamburg, J. D., & Andrews, R. L. (1991). School goals, principals, and achievement. *School Effectiveness & School Improvement, 2*(3), 175–191.

Bennett, D. A., Schneider, J. A., Tang, Y., Arnold, S. E., & Wilson, R. S. (2006). The effect of social networks on the relation between Alzheimer's disease pathology and level of cognitive function in old people: A longitudinal cohort study. *The Lancet Neurology, 5*(5), 406–412.

Bennett, N., Wise, C., Woods, P., & Harvey, J. (2003). *Distributed leadership: Full report*. Nottingham, UK: National College for School Leadership.

Blase, J., & Blase, J. (1999). Implementation of shared governance for instructional improvement: Principals' perspectives. *Journal of Educational Administration, 37*(5), 476–500.

Bossert, S., Dwyer, D., Rowan, B., & Lee, G. (1982). The instructional management role of the principal. *Educational Administration Quarterly, 18*(3), 34–64.

Bredeson, P., & Kelley, C. (2013). Introduction to the special issue: Distributed instructional leadership as a reform strategy: Activating teacher leadership to improve student learning in urban high schools. *Journal of School Leadership, 23*(2), 214–219.

Bridges, E. M. (1982). Research on the school administrator: The state of the art, 1967–19801. *Educational Administration Quarterly, 18*(3), 12–33.

Brookover, W. B., & Lezotte, L. W. (1977). *Changes in school characteristics coincident with changes in student achievement*. East Lansing, MI: The Institute for Research on Teaching, Michigan State University.

Bush, T. (2014). Instructional leadership in centralized contexts: Rhetoric or reality? *Educational Management Administration & Leadership, 42*(1), 3–5.

Cheng, K. M. (1995). The neglected dimension: Cultural comparison in educational administration. In K. C. Wong & K. M. Cheng (Eds.), *Educational leadership and change* (pp. 87–102). Hong Kong, China: Hong Kong University Press.

Conger, J. A. (1998). Qualitative research as the cornerstone methodology for understanding leadership. *The Leadership Quarterly, 9*, 107–121.

Cooley, V. E., & Shen, J. (2003). School accountability and professional job responsibilities: A perspective from secondary principals. *NASSP Bulletin, 87*(634), 10–25.

Cotton, K. (2003). *Principals and student achievement: What the research says*. Washington, DC: ASCD.

Cronbach, L. J., & Suppes, P. (1969). *Research for tomorrow's schools: Disciplined inquiry for education*. New York: Macmillan.

Cuban, L. (1984). Transforming the frog into a prince: Effective schools research, policy, and practice at the district level. *Harvard Educational Review, 54*(2), 129–151.

Darling-Hammond, L. (2010). *Evaluating teacher effectiveness: How teacher performance assessments can measure and improve teaching*. Washington, DC: Center for American Progress.

Darling-Hammond, L., Meyerson, D., LaPointe, M., & Orr, M. T. (2009). *Preparing principals for a changing world: Lessons from effective school leadership programs*. New York: John Wiley & Sons.

Day, C., Sammons, P., Leithwood, K., Hopkins, D., Harris, A., Gu, Q., et al. (2010). *Ten strong claims about successful school leadership*. Nottingham, UK: NCSL.

Dimmock, C. (2011). Formulating a research agenda in school leadership and organisational change for school improvement in Singapore. *School Leadership & Management, 31*(4), 321–338.

Dimmock, C., & Goh, J. W. P. (2011). Transformative pedagogy, leadership and school organisation for the twenty-first-century knowledge-based economy: The case of Singapore. *School Leadership and Management, 31*(3), 215–234.

Dwyer, D. C., Lee, G. V., Rowan, B., & Bossert, S. T. (1983). *Five principals in action: Perspectives on instructional management.* San Francisco: Far West Laboratory for Educational Research and Development.

Edmonds, R. (1979). Effective schools for the urban poor. *Educational Leadership, 37*(1), 15–24.

Elmore, R. F. (2004). *School reform from the inside out: Policy, practice and performance.* Cambridge, MA: Harvard Education Press.

Erickson, D. A. (1967). Chapter IV: The school administrator. *Review of Educational Research, 37*(4), 417–432.

Frank, K. A., Zhao, Y., & Borman, K. (2004). Social capital and the diffusion of innovations within organizations: The case of computer technology in schools. *Sociology of Education, 77*(2), 148–171.

Glasman, N. S. (1984). Student achievement and the school principal. *Educational Evaluation and Policy Analysis, 6*(3), 283–296.

Glickman, C. D. (1985). *Supervision of instruction: A developmental approach.* Boston: Allyn and Bacon.

Goldring, E., & Pasternak, R. (1994). Principals' coordinating strategies and school effectiveness. *School Effectiveness and School Improvement, 5*(3), 239–253.

Gronn, P. (1986). Politics, power and management of schools. In E. Hoyle (Ed.), *The World yearbook of education—The management of schools* (pp. 44–54). London: Kogan Page.

Gronn, P. (1999). Substituting for leadership: The neglected role of the leadership couple. *The Leadership Quarterly, 10*(1), 41–62.

Gronn, P. (2000). Distributed properties: A new architecture for leadership. *Educational Management Administration & Leadership, 28*(3), 317–338.

Gronn, P. (2002). Distributed leadership as a unit of analysis. *Leadership Quarterly, 13*(4), 423–451.

Gronn, P. (2003). Leadership: Who needs it? *School Leadership & Management, 23*(3), 267–291.

Hallinger, P. (1995). Culture and leadership: Developing an international perspective in educational administration. *UCEA Review, 36*(1), 3–7.

Hallinger, P. (2000, April). *A review of two decades of research on the principalship using the principal instructional management rating scale.* Paper presented at American Educational Research Association, Seattle, WA.

Hallinger, P. (2003). Two decades of ferment in school leadership development in retrospect: 1980–2000. In P. Hallinger (Ed.), *Reshaping the landscape of schoolleadership development: A global perspective.* Lisse, The Netherlands: Swets & Zeitlinger.

Hallinger, P. (2005). Instructional leadership and the school principal: A passing fancy that refuses to fade away. *Leadership and Policy in Schools, 4*, 221–240.

Hallinger, P. (2011). A review of three decades of doctoral studies using the principal instructional management rating scale: A lens on methodological progress in educational leadership. *Educational Administration Quarterly, 47*(2), 271–306.

Hallinger, P., Bickman, L., & Davis, K. (1996). School context, principal leadership, and student reading achievement. *The Elementary School Journal, 96*(5), 527–549.

Hallinger, P., & Bryant, D. A. (2013). Mapping the terrain of research on educational leadership and management in East Asia. *Journal of Educational Administration, 51*(5), 618–637.

Hallinger, P., & Chen, J. (2015). Review of research on educational leadership and management in Asia: A comparative analysis of research topics and methods, 1995–2012. *Educational Management Administration & Leadership, 43*(1), 5–27.

Hallinger, P., & Heck, R. H. (1996). Reassessing the principal's role in school effectiveness: A review of empirical research, 1980–1995. *Educational Administration Quarterly, 32*(1), 5–44.

Hallinger, P., & Huber, S. (2012). School leadership that makes a difference: International perspectives. *School Effectiveness and School Improvement, 23*(4), 1–9.

Hallinger, P., & Ko, J. (2015). Education accountability and principal leadership effects in Hong Kong primary schools. *Nordic Journal of Studies in Educational Policy, 1*(3), 18–29.

Hallinger, P., & Lee, M. (2011). A decade of education reform in Thailand: Broken promise or impossible dream? *Cambridge Journal of Education, 41*(2), 139–158.

Hallinger, P., & Lee, M. S. (2012). A global study of the practice and impact of distributed instructional leadership in International Baccalaureate (IB) schools. *Leadership & Policy in Schools, 11*(4), 477–495.

Hallinger, P., & Leithwood, K. (1998). Unseen forces: The impact of social culture on leadership. *Peabody Journal of Education, 73*(2), 126–151.

Hallinger, P., & Murphy, J. (1987). Instructional leadership in the school context. *Instructional leadership: Concepts, issues, and controversies*, 179–203.

Hallinger, P., & Murphy, J. F. (1985). Assessing the instructional management behavior of principals. *The Elementary School Journal, 86*(2), 217–247.

Hallinger, P., & Murphy, J. F. (1986). The social context of effective schools. *American Journal of Education, 94*(3), 328–355.

Hallinger, P., & Truong, D. T. (2014). Exploring the contours of context and leadership effectiveness in Vietnam. *Leading and Managing, 20*(2), 43.

Hallinger, P., Wang, W. C., Chen, C. W., & Liare, D. (2015). *Assessing instructional leadership with the principal instructional management rating scale.* Dordrecht, The Netherlands: Springer.

Halverson, R., & Clifford, M. (2013). Distributed instructional leadership in high schools. *Journal of School Leadership, 23*(2), 389–419.

Hargreaves, A., & Shirley, D. (2009). *The fourth way: The inspiring future for educational change.* Thousand Oaks, CA: Corwin.

Harris, A. (2003). Distributed leadership in schools: Leading or misleading? *Management in Education, 16*(5), 10–13.

Harris, A. (2005). Teacher leadership: More than just a feel-good factor? *Leadership and Policy in Schools, 4*(3), 201–219.

Harris, A. (2008). Distributed leadership: According to the evidence. *Journal of Educational Administration, 46*, 172–188.

Heck, R., Larson, T., & Marcoulides, G. (1990). Principal instructional leadership and school achievement: Validation of a causal model. *Educational Administration Quarterly, 26*, 94–125.

Heck, R. H., & Hallinger, P. (2009). Assessing the contribution of distributed leadership to school improvement and growth in math achievement. *American Educational Research Journal, 46*(3), 659–689.

Heck, R. H., & Hallinger, P. (2010). Collaborative leadership effects on school improvement: Integrating unidirectional- and reciprocal-effects models. *The Elementary School Journal, 111*(2), 226–252.

Ho, J. P. Y., Victor Chen, D. T., & Ng, D. (2016). Distributed leadership through the lens of activity theory. *Educational Management Administration & Leadership, 44*(5), 814–836.

Horng, E., & Loeb, S. (2010). New thinking about instructional leadership. *Phi Delta Kappan, 92*(3), 66–69.

Jackson, D. (2000). The school improvement journey: Perspectives on leadership. *School Leadership & Management, 20*(1), 61–78.

Joyce, B., & Showers, B. (2002). *Student achievement through staff development.* White Plains, NY: Longman.

Klar, H. W. (2012). Fostering distributed instructional leadership: A sociocultural perspective of leadership development in urban high schools. *Leadership and Policy in Schools, 11*(4), 365–390.

Klimek, P., & Thurner, S. (2013). Triadic closure dynamics drives scaling laws in social multiplex networks. *New Journal of Physics, 15*(6), 063008.

Koh, E., Ponnusamy, L. D., Tan, L. S., Lee, S. S., & Ramos, M. E. (2014). A Singapore case study of curriculum innovation in the twenty-first century: Demands, tensions and deliberations. *The Asia-Pacific Education Researcher, 23*(4), 851–860.

Lambert, L. (2002). A framework for shared leadership. *Educational Leadership, 59*(8), 37–40.

Lan, P. T. P. (2002). *Mapping values in educational management and leadership in Vietnam: The impact of culture.* Unpublished master thesis, Dunedin College of Education, Dunedin, New Zealand.

Lee, M., Hallinger, P., & Walker, A. (2012). A distributed perspective on instructional leadership in International Baccalaureate (IB) schools. *Educational Administration Quarterly, 48*(4), 664–698.

Leithwood, K. (1992). The move toward transformational leadership. *Educational Leadership, 49*(5), 8–13.

Leithwood, K. (1994). Leadership for school restructuring. *Educational Administration Quarterly, 30*(4), 498–518.

Leithwood, K., Begley, P., & Cousins, B. (1990). The nature, causes and consequences of principals' practices: An agenda for future research. *Journal of Educational Administration, 28*(4), 5–31.

Leithwood, K., & Day, C. (2007). *Successful school leadership in times of change.* Toronto, ON: Springer.

Leithwood, K., & Jantzi, D. (2005). A review of transformational school leadership research 1996–2005. *Leadership and Policy in Schools, 4,* 177–199.

Leithwood, K., Louis, K. S., Anderson, S., & Wahlstrom, K. (2004). *How leadership influences student learning.* Toronto, ON: Center for Applied Research and Educational Improvement and Ontario Institute for Studies in Education.

Leithwood, K., & Montgomery, D. (1982). The role of the elementary school principal in program improvement. *Review of Educational Research, 52*(3), 309–339.

Leithwood, K., Patten, S., & Jantzi, D. (2010). *Testing a conception of how school leadership influences learning.* Unpublished paper, University of Toronto/OISE, Toronto, Canada.

Leitner, D. (1994). Do principals affect student outcomes? An organisational perspective. *School Effectiveness and School Improvement, 5*(3), 219–239.

Leung, F. K.S. (2004). Educational centralization and decentralization in East Asia. Paper presented at the APEC Educational Reform Summit, January 2004. Beijing. Retrieved from URL http://www.apecneted.org/resources/downloads/LeungSystemicreform.pdf

Lim-Ratnam, C., Atencio, M., & Lee, C. K. E. (2016). Managing the paradox of control: The case of ground-up implementation of active learning in Singapore's primary schools. *Educational Research for Policy and Practice, 15*(3), 231–246.

Louis, K. S., Leithwood, K., Wahlstrom, K. L., Anderson, S. E., Michlin, M., & Mascall, B. (2010). Learning from leadership: Investigating the links to improved student learning. *Center for Applied Research and Educational Improvement/University of Minnesota and Ontario Institute for Studies in Education/University of Toronto, 42*, 50.

Madden, J. V., Lawson, D., & Sweet, D. (1976). *School effectiveness study*. Paper presented at the annual meeting of the American Educational Research Association, San Francisco.

Marks, H., & Printy, S. (2003). Principal leadership and school performance. *Educational Administration Quarterly, 39*(3), 370–397.

Matthews, P., Moorman, H., & Nusche, D. (2007). *School leadership development strategies: Building leadership capacity in Victoria, Australia*. A case study report for the OECD activity improving school Leadership.

Mazzeo, C. (2003). *Improving teaching and learning by improving school leadership*. Washington, DC: National Governors Association Center for Best Practices.

Mendels, P. (2012). The effective principal. *Journal of Staff Development, 33*(1), 54–58.

Moolenaar, N. M., Sleegers, P. J. C., Karsten, S., & Daly, A. J. (2012). The social fabric of elementary schools: A network typology of social interaction among teachers. *Educational Studies, 38*(4), 355–371.

Mulford, B., & Silins, H. (2009). Revised models and conceptualisation of successful school principalship in Tasmania. In B. Mulford & B. Edmunds (Eds.), *Successful school principalship in Tasmania*. Launceston, TAS: University of Tasmania.

Murphy, J. (2015). Forces shaping schooling and school leadership. *Journal of School Leadership, 25*(6), 1064–1087.

Ng, F. S. D., & Ho, J. M. (2012). How leadership for an ICT reform is distributed within a school. *International Journal of Educational Management, 26*(6), 529–549.

Ng, F. S. D., Nguyen, T. D., Wong, K. S. B., & Choy, K. W. W. (2015). Instructional leadership practices in Singapore. *School Leadership & Management, 35*(4), 388–407.

Ng, P. T. (2008). The phases and paradoxes of educational quality assurance: The case of the Singapore education system. *Quality Assurance in Education, 16*(2), 112–125.

Nguyen, D. (2007). The role of high school principal nowadays (Vai trò của Hiệu trưởng trường THPT hiện nay). *Journal of Education Science, 18,* 29–31. (in Vietnamese).

Nguyen, D. T., Ng, D., & Yap, P. S. (2017). Instructional leadership structure in Singapore: A co-existence of hierarchy and heterarchy. *Journal of Educational Administration, 55*(2), 147–167.

O'Day, K. (1983). *The relationship between principal and teacher perceptions of principal instructional management behavior and student achievement.* Doctoral dissertation, Northern Illinois University, Normal, IL.

O'Donnell, R. J., & White, G. P. (2005). Within the accountability era: Principals' instructional leadership behaviors and student achievement. *NASSP Bulletin, 89*(645), 56–71.

Organization for Economic Co-operation and Development (OECD). (2009). *Creating effective teaching and learning environments: First results from TALIS.* Paris: OECD.

Ovando, M. N. (2005). Building instructional leaders' capacity to deliver constructive feedback to teachers. *Journal of Personnel Evaluation in Education, 18*(3), 171–183.

Pan, H. L. W., Nyeu, F. Y., & Chen, J. S. (2015). Principal instructional leadership in Taiwan: Lessons from two decades of research. *Journal of Educational Administration, 53*(4), 492–511.

Parry, K. W. (1998). Grounded theory and social process: A new direction for leadership research. *The Leadership Quarterly, 9*(1), 85–105.

Penuel, W. R., Riel, M., Krause, A., & Frank, K. A. (2009). Analyzing teachers' professional interactions in a school as social capital: A social network approach. *Teachers College Record, 111*(1), 124–163.

Pham, H. (2007). Teaching management at high school using the approach of total quality management (TQM). *Journal of Education Science, 25,* 12–17. (in Vietnamese).

Phelan, S. (2001). What is complexity science, really? *Emergence, 3,* 120–136.

Printy, S. (2010). Principals' influence on instructional quality: Insights from US schools. *School Leadership and Management, 30*(2), 111–126.

Robinson, V. M. J., Lloyd, C. A., & Rowe, K. J. (2008). The impact of leadership on student outcomes: An analysis of the differential effects of leadership types. *Educational Administration Quarterly, 44*(5), 635–674. https://doi.org/10.1177/0013161X08321509

Scott, J. (2000). *Social network analysis: A handbook* (2nd ed.). London: SAGE Publications.

Sloot, P. M., Ivanov, S. V., Boukhanovsky, A. V., van de Vijver, D. A., & Boucher, C. A. (2008). Stochastic simulation of HIV population dynamics through complex network modelling. *International Journal of Computer Mathematics, 85*(8), 1175–1187.

Southworth, G. (2002). Instructional leadership in schools: Reflections and empirical evidence. *School Leadership & Management, 22*(1), 73–91.

Spillane, J. P. (2006). *Distributed leadership*. San Francisco: Jossey-Bass.

State of New York, Office of Education Performance Review, A. (1974). *School factors and influencing reading achievement: A case study of two inner city schools*. Available at: ERIC, EBSCO*host*. Accessed 5 Apr 2016.

Supovitz, J., Sirinides, P., & May, H. (2010). How principals and peers influence teaching and learning. *Educational Administration Quarterly, 46*(1), 31–56.

Truong, D. T. (2012). *Confucian values and school leadership in Vietnam*. Unpublished Ph.D. dissertation, Victoria University of Wellington, New Zealand.

Van de Grift, W., & Houtveen, A. A. M. (1999). Educational leadership and pupil achievement in primary education. *School Effectiveness and School Improvement, 10*(4), 373–389.

Vanderhaar, J. E., Muñoz, M. A., & Rodosky, R. J. (2006). Leadership as accountability for learning: The effects of school poverty, teacher experience, previous achievement, and principal preparation programs on student achievement. *Journal of Personnel Evaluation in Education, 19*(1–2), 17–33.

Von Bertalanffy, L. (1968). General system theory. *New York, 41973*(1968), 40.

Walker, A., & Hallinger, P. (2015). A synthesis of reviews of research on principal leadership in East Asia. *Journal of Educational Administration, 53*(4), 554–570.

Walker, A., Hu, R., & Qian, H. (2012). Principal leadership in China: An initial review. *School Effectiveness and School Improvement, 23*(4), 369–399.

Walker, A., & Ko, J. (2011). Principal leadership in an era of accountability: A perspective from the Hong Kong context. *School Leadership & Management, 31*(4), 369–392.

Walker, A., & Qian, H. (2015). Review of research on school principal leadership in mainland China, 1998-2013: Continuity and change. *Journal of Educational Administration, 53*(4), 467–491.

Wasserman, S., & Faust, K. (1994). *Social network analysis: Methods and applications*. Cambridge, UK: Cambridge University Press.

Weber, G. (1971). *Inner-city children can be taught to read: Four successful schools* (CBE Occasional Papers, 18). Washington, DC: Council for Basic Education.

Wiseman, A. W. (2004). *Principals Under Pressure: The Growing Crisis*. Lanham, MD: Scarecrow Press.

Witziers, B., Bosker, R., & Kruger, M. (2003). Educational leadership and student achievement: The elusive search for an association. *Educational Administration Quarterly, 34*(3), 398–425.

Woods, P. A. (2004). Democratic leadership: Drawing distinctions with distributed leadership. *International Journal of Leadership in Education, 7*(1), 3–26.

York-Barr, J., & Duke, K. (2004). What do we know about teacher leadership? Findings from two decades of scholarship. *Review of Educational Research, 74*(3), 255–316.

Yukl, G., & Mahsud, R. (2010). Why flexible and adaptive leadership is essential. *Consulting Psychology Journal: Practice and Research, 62*(2), 81.

Zimmerman, B., Lindberg, C., & Plsek, P. (1998). A complexity science primer: What is complexity science and why should I learn about it. Adapted From: *Edgeware: Lessons from Complexity Science for Health Care Leaders*. Dallas, TX: VHA Inc.

3

Leadership for Learning

John MacBeath

Instructional leadership (IL) and leadership for learning (LfL), it had been argued, are synonymous, a simple matter of terminology. But words have a latent power.

How we think is so saturated with language that it makes it virtually impossible to recast the concepts which shape our thoughts and often frustrate our attempts to communicate ideas.

When A.N. Whitehead (1929) referred to 'inert ideas', he reminded us that thinking critically requires a new cognitive vocabulary, new ways of seeing the all-too familiar. So, does it matter that 'instruction' has been progressively redefined to mean something quite different from its historical roots? Does it matter that it resides in a form of authority and mode of 'delivery', famously captured in England's Chief Inspector pronouncement, 'Teachers teach and children learn. It's as simple as that' (2002). Or, as he might have added, leaders lead and followers follow.

J. MacBeath (✉)
University of Cambridge, Cambridge, UK
e-mail: jecm2@cam.ac.uk

Why is it important to recast terminology so that we privilege leadership for learning over other definitions? Why indeed should we take the trouble if other definitions serve us equally well? Perhaps because the history and connotations of 'instruction' place the teacher, parent or authority figure at centre stage while 'learning', by contrast, refers to the individual or the collective process of transformational change.

This is not to argue, however, that leadership for learning is free of ambiguity or misconception. After all, it contains not only two big ideas but also a highly contentious connecting proposition. What is it 'for'? Its very ambiguity opens the door to a deeper exploration of the contested connections between two forms of activity which, after a few thousand lifetimes, we still struggle to fully comprehend.

If we are to suggest new ways of leading and new ways of leading learning, we have to recognise the power of language and an embedded discourse of leading. We have to revisit our long-held assumptions of positional authority and the reflex nature of followership. We easily fall into the familiar language in which policies are couched, referring almost reflexively to school *leaders* as the principal actors. The term *principal* is widely used in North America, Australasia, Singapore and Hong Kong, for example. In countries where English in not the first language—in Europe for example—the French *proviseur* is the provider; *preside,* in Italian, is the one who presides.

Richard Elmore (2008) refers to this as the 'default culture' because it is rarely challenged, and even when it is challenged, there are powerful forces which push back to the status quo. The democratic, free and alternative schools of the 1970s enjoyed a relatively brief life, perhaps because we are so culturally wedded to hierarchy, or more persuasively perhaps, because they were overtaken by accountability, performance management and 'league tables'.

In this world of 'detailed deliverology', write Hargreaves and Shirley (2009), there is no spare energy for teachers to contest the conditions and oppressive aspects of their work. In addition to (or as a concomitant of) pressure from above, writes Ann Lieberman (1992), strong teacher norms of egalitarianism can also be powerful inhibitors, dissuading anyone from presumptuous initiatives, from sticking their neck out too far, engendering a reluctance to exercise leadership without formal invitation or approval.

So powerful and so seductive are the accolades which fall to successful schools, and by association to successful leaders, that the essential purposes of what it means to lead are easily forgotten. Fullan (2011) attributes these inimical policy effects to what he calls the 'wrong policy drivers', a too-ready compliance with convention and external authority.

There is a 'deeply entrenched tendency to underestimate the contribution of more than a few key figures … [stemming] from thousands of years of cultural conditioning' and, as such, [it] remains incredibly difficult to change, even if the evidence points elsewhere (Bolden, 2011, p. 254).

What could be more obvious or self-evident than 'leadership'? We elect our national and party leaders, and virtually all secular and religious organisations that we belong to are 'led' by elected, self-appointed or anointed individuals. The lessons of history are that however misguided, incompetent or destructive they may be, we are often powerless to either influence their decisions or remove them from office.

What happens, however, when decisions made by elected leaders have far-reaching and potentially destructive consequences? How many party-political appointees have actually been competent to make critical decisions on school curricula and assessment? Recent history in England provides evidence of leaders making decisions based on their own school experience, perceived 'public opinion' or nostalgia for a mythical golden age.

Leadership Coming of Age

The creation of a chair in Educational Leadership in 2000 in Cambridge was, in part, a recognition of a gap in provision, a growing emphasis on leadership, politically and academically, and a need for rethinking what we understand by the language and embedded assumptions of 'leading' and 'learning'.

One of the first initiatives of the newly created leadership team was to build on international connections and previous collaboration with colleagues in other countries. The intention was to explore how leadership was understood and how it was instrumental in creating an environment in which a 'learning' discourse was embedded in routine practice.

The six countries which eventually signed up to a 4-year comparative project (*Carpe Vitam* in honour of its Swedish funding body) could hardly have been more different, culturally and politically. Denmark and Norway had a longstanding tradition of democratic leadership, absence of hierarchy or explicit accountability. In Greece, leadership was synonymous with the principal, and in Austria, there was caution in its approach to the language of leaders (Fuhrer) and leadership (Fuhrung), as the country was embarking on radical reappraisal of longstanding conventions. In the US (from Seattle in the west to Princeton in the east), together with Australia in the deep south, accountability, and its handmaiden 'performativity', were already deeply embedded in policy and practice.

What was becoming increasingly common over the 4-year period of the study was the emphasis on leadership as positional and on senior leaders as accountable for the performance of their schools. In 1983, Geert Hofstede compared 'power distance' between the highest and lowest levels of the educational hierarchy among countries, a measure of democracy in schools. Denmark, along with its Nordic neighbours, was one of the countries with the smallest power distance. However, as Lejf Moos in Denmark and Jorunn Møller in Norway wrote in 2003, both countries were experiencing an inexorable shift from a strong traditional belief in shared leadership, equality, comprehensive schools and democratic participation into the brave new world of comparative performativity.

> The focus is shifting to detailed national performance standards and competitive advantage. The democratic approach which left many curriculum decisions to professional leaders and teachers, in collaboration with students and parents, has been superseded by mandated standards, decentralisation, consumer choice, competition, outcomes, effectiveness, efficiency, inter-school and inter-country comparisons. (Moos & Møller, 2003, p. 35)

Five Key Principles

In 2001, teachers and senior leaders, participants in the *Carpe Vitam* project, met to agree on an agenda and a common purpose for research and development. Three and a half years later five key principles had been agreed. The fifth principle (accountability) was a late addition from the U.S. partners, who had expressed surprise that such a salient issue had originally been overlooked. The five principles have not only survived over the ensuing decade and a half but have been widely adopted in other countries as culturally diverse as Egypt, Macedonia, Turkey, Hong Kong and Ghana. The principles are as follows:

* Sharing leadership
* Maintaining a focus on learning
* Sustaining a learning dialogue
* Creating an environment for learning
* Reframing accountability

Sharing Leadership

This first principle may be seen as underpinning and sustaining the other four. By challenging conventional images and revisiting what it means to lead, we are brought closer to rethinking the nature and place of learning, the importance of dialogue, the environment in which it occurs and how we account to one another for the practice which flows from that. We are so inured to the notion of leadership as an individual quality, or activity, that it is challenging to think of how a genuine sharing of leadership might be enacted in the day-by-day business of schools.

In a high-stakes accountability environment principals/head teachers have become acutely aware that the 'buck' stops with them and that while they may delegate, any risk they may take with their colleagues carries with it a personal, rather than an institutional, accountability.

At the same time, within increasingly demanding and complex circumstances, it was becoming daily clearer that no single leader could have all of the skills to effectively perform the range of leadership tasks now required. As Richard Elmore would write in 2008, senior leaders have little option but to trust colleagues and create an environment in which that trust is reciprocated.

> When teachers exercise their agency beyond the classroom, with colleagues, with parents and other agencies or with policy, they exercise leadership. When they do so as part of a collective endeavour, leadership becomes a shared activity. Despite a body of writing on teacher leadership, much of it fails to grasp or explore the connections between individual agency and the collective. Teacher leadership is construed as a role or as status within the institutional hierarchy rather than captured in the flow of activities. The roles and activities of leadership flow from the expertise required for learning and improvement, not from the formal dictates of the institution. (Elmore, in OECD, 2008, p. 38)

Where leadership lies and the form it assumes can prove difficult to disentangle, requiring careful study as to where the initiative occurs, how decisions are made and by whom. It demands a sophisticated grasp of how differences are resolved and how resources are identified and used. Intelligence and creativity, it has been found, do not necessarily lie within individuals but between them. As Spillane writes (2012), equating leadership with the actions of those in leadership positions is inadequate for three reasons: First, because leadership practice typically involves multiple leaders, some with, and some without, formal leadership positions. Second, because leadership practice is not something done to followers. Approaching this from a distributed perspective, 'followers' may be seen as simply one of the multiple essential aspects of all leadership practice. Third, it is not the actions of individuals, but the interactions among them, that are critical in leadership practice. It has to be understood, argues Gronn, as a group, rather than simply an individual, activity.

> Distributed leadership is not something 'done' by an individual 'to' others, or a set of individual actions through which people contribute to a group or organization…. [it] is a group activity that works through and within relationships, rather than individual action, offering the promise of a new 'unit of analysis' through which leadership could be understood in a holistic

sense rather than simply as the aggregation of individual contributions. (Gronn, 2002, p. 425)

Maintaining a Focus on Learning

It is through the second principle that a distribution, or sharing, of leadership may be realised, in situations where learning is genuinely the focus of the schools' endeavours. It is a demanding precept.

As with leadership, we tend to approach 'learning' as institutionally located, involving being taught or directed by others. So, in an educational context, the questions 'Who are the learners?' and 'Who are the leaders?' receive a default answer in the implicit structures and conventions of schools. Both leadership and learning are made apparent in the everyday conduct of school life, in the arrangements of classrooms, and in the hierarchies of access and privilege. It needs no conversation for the new pupil, or the new graduate student, the novice teacher or the visiting parent to know who learns, who leads and who follows.

Problematising learning is unlikely to take place without a common commitment to inquiry and challenge, an openness to critique and an ability to offer it in a way that can be heard. The larger challenge is to share this exploratory endeavour with the parent body, many of whom may, unsurprisingly, hold a more performance-orientated perspective. With reference to learning-friendly leaders, MacBeath and Townsend (2011, p. 87) write:

> [T]hey find ways to release the creative energy of teachers and students, for this is the force that fosters experimentation and that breathes life, excitement, and enthusiasm into the learning environment for students and for teachers. This implies, of course, that leaders are comfortable with ambiguity, that they are more interested in learning than in outcomes, and that they trust teachers and students to work their magic in the classrooms.

In Hong Kong, a principal talked about using his first year in post 'to listen and learn, to feel and experience the culture', to engage in dialogue with a range of stakeholders, each day inviting a different group of students or teachers to conversations over lunch in his office. Only when he felt he had gained their trust, did he begin to encourage teachers 'to venture forth' and to learn from their colleagues and from their students. Professional development grew from a recognition of the force field of 'satisfiers' and 'dissatisfiers' and a recognition of the nesting of teachers' experience, within their own classrooms, their departments, their schools, their local neighbourhoods, local policy and national politics, and the international standards agendas which touch, however invisibly or insidiously, on teachers' daily work.

The idea of leadership as *emerging in the flow of practice* invests a collective power to those who put pedagogical practice under scrutiny so as to understand it better and, in turn, to influence, shaping future practice. In so doing, it adds meaning to their own professional practice, their own sense of agency and, at the same time, revisits the concept of leadership itself.

Sustaining a Learning Dialogue

The word 'dialogue' has been used by teachers to refer to a process which is, by definition, about voice but refers to something more than speaking and listening. It is about a shared search for meaning and mutual understanding. It is not a one-off event but a continuous process. It is not reserved for special places or special occasions but is an essential aspect of the school's ethos. It has been captured in Robin Alexander's notion of the dialogic classroom and the dialogic school, in Senge's 'learning school' and in McGilchrist and colleagues' 'intelligent school'. It is readily acknowledged, however, that this is an ideal state which is not simply or easily achieved and that the journey towards it is by starting small, by modelling being a living example, and, over time, making the implicit explicit and a matter of planned intervention.

Javed (2013) refers to 'disciplined dialogue' as a process which is teacher-led, in which there is co-construction of professional knowledge, evidence-based and sustained through a culture which is unafraid of challenge to conventional wisdom and authority. In Javed's own research in Pakistan into the practical applications of LfL in schools, he describes the reach of dialogue to encompass all stakeholders (principals, teachers, students and parents) in order to establish a shared vision for effective learning. Dialogue emerged very strongly as 'the missing link' in embedding change, bringing together different people, levels and aspects of a school community, curriculum, assessment and accountability. Adapting the LfL model and the wording of the principles, he describes a particular challenge, but one which also serves to clarify and sharpen the concept.

> When working with people in the more remote areas of Pakistan for whom English is their fourth or fifth language, I have to modify the terminology and I am more focused on the meaning that I want to convey. (in Swaffield Dempster, Frost, & MacBeath, 2014, p. 5)

While it may seem patently obvious that learning should be meaningful, the hard work of making meaning is most commonly left to the student, often attended by sanctions and ultimately reflected in poor grades. 'How many students were rendered callous to ideas? How many lost the impetus to learn because of the way in which learning was experienced by them?', wrote John Dewey in 1937.

Creating an Environment for Learning

School and classroom life is a prolonged process of making meaning within the place one finds oneself, its constraints, demands and opportunities. In Amsterdam, a teacher uses the first day with a new class to problematise the classroom as an environment for learning. He or she asks pupils to use the first period in the day to explore the room, to rearrange furniture, to open drawers and cupboards, to examine teaching materials. They then discuss the arguments for and against different configurations and deployment of resources so as to maximise opportunities for learning.

In her book *Assessing Children's Learning*, Mary Jane Drummond (1993) writes about how often children struggle to make sense of what is going on around them, seeing what the teacher may fail to see in her relentless quest for the right and wrong answers. She cites a pupil conscientiously answering 36 questions on a test and getting a raw score of two correct answers. She writes:

> We have little evidence from this test of his learning in the cognitive domain but we can see how much he has learned about the social conventions of school – how to keep his pencil sharp, how to stay in his seat, how to take a test, how to be a pupil. In the affective domain we can see Jason has learned not to express dissatisfaction or disquiet when meaningless demands are made on him. And yet we can also see signs – small but perhaps significant– that in limited ways left open to him, Jason is still struggling to make sense of what goes on around him in the puzzling world of school. (Drummond, 1993, p. 5)

Reframing Accountability

Accountability is not a particularly friendly word. It tends to have negative connotations and associations with control and hierarchy. It seems to imply that one cannot be trusted without some form of oversight and justification for behavioural choices. There is nothing as corrosive within an organisation as mistrust, and nothing as destructive within a school than a lack of trust between those who lead and those who follow, teachers and students, teachers and their colleagues, teachers and parents, teachers and senior leaders. None of these negative constructs are desirable or necessary. How we account to one another takes us back to an environment which nurtures dialogue and shares agency. In his book *The Speed of Trust* Stephen Covey argues that in organisations in which there are high levels of trust, business is affected faster, more effectively and more productively. Where there is high trust there is much less need for tedious bureaucracy, supervision, accounting and accountability. With high levels of trust there is an implicit sense of mutual accountability— what we owe to others in return for the trust invested in us. This does imply, as Day and Sammons (2008, p. 18) write:

> [A] shift away from the conventional, hierarchical patterns of bureaucratic control toward what has been referred to as a network pattern of control, that is, a pattern of control in which line employees are actively involved in

[making] organisational decision[s] [and] staff cooperation and collegiality supplant the hierarchy as a means of coordinating work flows and resolving technical difficulties.

Whether 'supplanting' hierarchical structures and cultures will ever become a reality, as both Gronn and Spillane contend, we need to approach this issue with a more sophisticated understanding of the policy-practice relationship and the nature of the 'force field' which may promote, but may also inhibit, a more radical agenda.

A major quantitative study (Wahlstrom & Louis, 2008) identified four essential and inter-related characteristics of successful schools, which researchers described as effective dialogue, collective responsibility, deprivatised practice and shared norms. In relation to the first of these four criteria—effective dialogue—the most discriminating questionnaire item was: *'How often in this school year have you had conversations with colleagues about what helps students learn best?'* This was found to be closely related to the second criterion, 'collective responsibility' which was tested by the question *'How many teachers in this school feel responsible to help each other improve their instruction?'* This was, again, coincident with 'deprivatized practice' and the questionnaire item *'How often in this school year have you had colleagues observe your classroom?'* The fourth criterion 'shared norms' was found to be particularly significant in relation to the statement *'Most teachers in our school share a similar set of values, beliefs, and attitudes related to teaching and learning'*.

Taken together, these findings coincide with the conclusions of other major studies, that when the focus of the teachers' conversations centres on the quality of student learning and on collaborative work, teachers are more likely to adopt practices that enhance that learning. By these measures, improvement rests most significantly with a culture and ethos in which teachers not only talk together about their practice but listen to, and learn from, their colleagues.

As the authors conclude:

> When teachers share ideas about practice, discuss them, or demonstrate them regularly, they may have decreased dependence on their principal as a direct source of expert knowledge. This lessened dependence may help to

account for the diminished impact of trust in leadership when we take the level of professional community into account. In other words, perhaps only where professional community is weak do teachers look to the principal for direct instructional support. (Wahlstrom & Louis, 2008, p. 468)

The Challenge of Convention and Hierarchy

Changing a culture is 'hard work for everyone', concludes Seashore Louis, the complexity of the challenge exemplified in a 3-year initiative in Florida. Its purpose was to encourage collaborative teacher leadership—'a new brand of teacher leadership, where the state's most effective classroom practitioners would spread the teaching expertise'. It was recognised as a bold promise given a daunting body of international evidence as to embedded traditions and systemic obstacles to both 'sharing' and 'spreading'. The programme was founded on a lateral process of diffusion which relied on either a receptive school climate or the space and ability to create one. This, it was promised, would be achieved through a Teacher Leader Fellowship designed to:

> empower teachers professionally so that they improve their own practice and that of their colleagues in ways that ultimately support the creation of more rich and meaningful learning experiences for students and result in greater college and career success. (Wahlstrom & Louis, 2008, p. 3)

Among the positive accolades and enthusiastic testimonies from participants, highlighted in the Cambridge-led evaluation, there were some participating Fellows who described being disempowered by authority, characterised by one participant as 'deferential vulnerability'. This was in sharp contrast with the personal and professional authority that these teachers had experienced within the collegial meeting ground of the programme workshops. Acute disappointment was expressed in relation to gatekeepers—senior staff—who could deny access to the levers of change, frustrating the potential to make a wider impact. As one teacher leader put it, senior staff had not learned 'to view it as an asset rather than a threat'. This underlined the importance of holding workshops for senior leaders. One of the University team made this telling observation:

> Part of what this programme has surfaced for me is that you cannot work on teacher leadership without simultaneously working on principal leadership. Because the fact is that what our teachers have got [to do] is seldom experienced by the people they report to. It's a lonely uncollaborated fear-driven experience.

Speaking at the *International Conference on School Effectiveness and Improvement* in Stavanger in 2019, Amanda Datnow emphasised an essential quality of senior leaders as recognising the emotional nature of teachers' collaborative work. They understand how leadership is shared and how teachers become a resource for their colleagues. This presumes an ability among those senior leaders to understand teachers' emotional investment in their work, to appreciate the nature of stress and the resilience required not only to lead the learning of one's students but also of one's colleagues. It also presumes an ability to recognise the vulnerability and frustration which teachers experience when such support is absent: in short, both a lack of effective leadership and a lack of effective learning.

This stands in stark contrast with a London school where the head teacher, Sir Alan Steer, presided over a school in which he would walk the corridors to ensure that all classroom doors were closed, that children were facing the front and that the only voice to be heard was that of the teacher.

Rather than creating space for teachers to lead, this powerful model of leadership effectively closed off opportunities to exceed the tight boundaries of their designated role. With reference to policy and pedagogy, Sir Alan is quoted as saying, 'This policy has got a lot of me in it. It's largely me', and 'that wasn't from the staff. That was from myself... It was quite brutal. It was tough. It was me' (in James et al., 2007). At the same time, the reference to teacher autonomy was, by his own admission, disingenuous. 'I think teachers have got to feel that they're making decisions but what I suppose I'm forcing them to do is make those decisions'.

His vocabulary, scattered with terms such as 'tough', 'brutal', and 'forcing', appeared to be widely accepted as 'strong leadership', raising the stakes, creating followership, willing or otherwise. A telling measure of this autocratic regime was for young people in their first year of university to return to the school to complain of the inhibiting legacy of unquestioning compliance with authority which had robbed them of initiative and the ability to think for themselves.

The language of leadership gives us insights into its origins and effects. Tough and brutal may be extreme but more commonly we meet terms such as 'strong', 'powerful', 'directive' and 'charismatic'. This 'hard' language contrasts with a softer, even horticultural, language of nurturing, growth and qualities such as empathy and even vulnerability. In Datnow's reference to the successful teacher-empowering schools, she talks about the emotional nature of leading, learning and the resilience that comes from collegial sharing.

Unlike many newly appointed principals whose first step it to stamp their authority on the school, in Hong Kong a newly appointed principal devoted his first year to learning, to understanding the unique culture of the school of which he had been privileged to become a part. He was alert to potential resentment as well as possible enthusiasm for change and a mix of differing expectations and latent assumptions about 'authority'. He knew of leaders who had moved too quickly to assert their presence and power, who 'owned' their school.

Who Owns the School?

In 2016, a group of teachers in the Netherlands invented a board game 'We Own the School' in which the players explore where authority, principles, conventions and the wellsprings of learning lie. The playing board contains six segments each with a different type of school, the object being to debate the qualities that are most desirable, what it might mean to realise them in practice and, as pupils, to 'own' one's learning. The six are described as follows:

(1) *The Traditional School,* in which formal roles take centre stage, in which delegation of responsibilities is executed through top-down structures, in which knowing and performing designated roles is

practised as a norm. Who leads, who learns and who follows is transparent and unambiguous.
(2) *The Strategic School* is one in which leadership is less role-bound, less reliant on hierarchy than on clearly defined remits, tasks allocated and engaged in according to talent, individual aptitude and specialisation. It might be described as a meritocracy.
(3) In the *Pragmatic School*, personal relationships are at a premium and although roles and responsibilities are assigned by senior leaders, they tend to be ad hoc and fluid, responsive and supportive, encouraging of staff's sense of ownership of the school.
(4) *The Incremental School* is described as both pragmatic and strategic, bottom-up and top-down, more people- than task-orientated, and progressively building student leadership as essential to creating a flatter organisation in which leadership is seen and nurtured as a common endeavour.
(5) *The Competent School* thrives on the ownership and ambition of its members, on their collective ambition and 'competence' and on a resilient belief in the skills of all its members, encouraging 'leading' as both individual and collegial.
(6) In the *Cultural School*, student ownership is the core driving value, defining the nature and ethos of an organisation in which roles are secondary to values so that decisions as to who leads and who follows are fluid and dependent on situation and task.

The purpose of the game is to open up discussion and appeal to evidence regarding the latitude for dissent and the locus of areas (or potential areas) where pupil or teacher leadership may lie. The degree to which pupils or teachers may claim to 'own' the school depends on the scope that exists for initiative, agency and a climate open enough to accept risk and to be constantly self-renewing.

If posed the question of ownership, the most common reply would be to cite the principal or head teacher. For their part, teachers might claim to 'own' the classroom, the locus of ownership clearly signalled in the language of 'my school' and 'my classroom'. In their own homes, many children and young people lay claim to their bedroom as their own private space, explicitly signalled by the seven-year-old whose bedroom door boasts a 'No Entry' traffic symbol, an instruction to knock before entering, and in large letters, *Emmanuelle's Room*.

A challenge to conventions of ownership is the example cited above of the teacher who, on the first school day, invites children to problematise the classroom as a learning environment, always coming back to the question 'is this a good place in which to learn, to share ideas, to think again?'

A much-used reference is to Roger Hart's ladder of student participation, from manipulation to shared decision-making. A variation on this comes from Fielding and McGregor (2005) who write about 'new spaces for dialogue' and the nature of 'participation', in which students in a 'lived democracy' are 'knowledge creators'. On the bottom rung of the ladder, students are characterised as a data source, their achievements used to measure and report on progress. Moving up the ladder, students are seen as 'active respondents', invited into the learning dialogue. 'Students as co-inquirers' extends their role further into a more collaborative partnership with their teachers. A further step on the ladder is to for students to be in the lead role with their teachers in a facilitated and supportive role—'students as knowledge creators'. 'Students as joint authors' moves further into action planning which, in turn, leads to the top, most ambitious, step of 'intergenerational learning in a lived democracy' in which there is a shared commitment to, and responsibility for, the common good.

Children's World of Learning

In his award-winning book *Children, their World, their Education*, Robin Alexander finds little evidence in policyspeak of children as knowledge creators or 'joint authors'. He draws attention to the layered complexity of school, learning and leadership and their historical legacy and identifies nine inter-related aspects of practice which define how learning may be understood and may be led.

1. Children: their characteristics, development and upbringing.
2. Teaching: its planning, execution and evaluation.

3. Learning: how it can best be motivated, achieved, identified, assessed and built upon.
4. Curriculum: the various ways of knowing, understanding, doing, creating, investigating and making sense of what is most important for children to encounter, and how these are most appropriately translated and structured for teaching.
5. School, as a formal institution, a microculture and a conveyor of pedagogical messages over and above those of the classroom.
6. Policy, national and local, which prescribes or proscribes, enables or inhibits, what is taught and how.
7. Culture: the web of values, ideas, institutions and processes which inform, shape and explain a society's views of education, teaching and learning and which throw up a complex burden of choices and dilemmas for those whose job it is to translate these into a practical pedagogy.
8. Self: what it is to be a person, an individual relating to others and to the wider society, and how through education and other early experiences selfhood is acquired.
9. History: the indispensable tool for making sense of both education's present state and its future possibilities and potential. (Alexander, 2010a)

His plaint 'Still no pedagogy' refers, in part, to the inhibitions of language used to refer to learning and leadership. Reframing active understanding implies coming to recognise this less as a matter of what leaders or teachers do but what learners do, or how learning is made manifest. His nine dimensions offer a 'counter discourse' to 'the technical science-driven conceptions of teaching that dominate the language of educational policy'.

Writing in *The Guardian*, Alexander (2010b) pointed out the extent to which the compliance culture in England had impacted on schools and on teachers' professional lives. He questioned the way governments, since the 1990s, had chosen to tackle the task of raising primary school standards by using high-stakes tests, league tables, prescriptive national teaching strategies, procedures for inspection, initial teacher training, continuous professional development and 'school improvement', all requiring strict compliance with official accounts of what primary education is about and how it should be undertaken. At the same time, teachers professed to be 'fed up with interference, mindless paper work, lurches in policy, and daily announcements of gimmicky initiatives' (cited in MacBeath, 2010, p. 37).

If school leaders, teachers and young people have a genuine belief that 'we own the school' it ought to be made visible in commitment and resistance to mindlessness, not simply an embrace of a counter discourse but a demonstration of what a learning community can look and feel like. As Hesselbein, Goldsmith, Beckard, and Drucker (1996, p. 78) have argued in relation to school leaders, their distinguishing strength is the ability to push themselves out of their comfort zone into risky territory. The same may be said of leading-edge teachers. 'They are open to people and ideas even at a time in life when they might reasonably think—because of their success—that they know everything'.

'Nothing fails like success', wrote Peter Senge in his discourse on organisational learning disabilities. Familiarity breeds complacency, write Mayer, Pecheone, and Merino (2012, p. 115), arguing for a more refined critique of routine practice.

> Challenging curriculum expectations and more diverse learners mean that teachers have to be more sophisticated in their understanding of the effects of context and learner variability on teaching and learning. Instead of implementing set routines, teachers need to become ever more skillful in their ability to evaluate teaching situations and develop teaching responses that can be effective under different circumstances.

'Under different circumstances' is a telling phrase because it challenges the contained setting of the classroom. It challenges the comfort zone of those who know telling those who don't know. It opens to scrutiny the nature of behaviour settings and 'construction sites'. The former refers to the powerful shaping of the conditioned response of human beings to the dictats of the physical environment in which they find themselves. The latter refers to ways in which intelligence is 'constructed' by the places and people with whom we congregate, who either constrain or enhance desire and determination.

'There is a well-established gap between what teachers would like to do and what they do, between their aspiration and achievement', wrote UNESDOC in their *Competency Framework for Teachers* (2011). 'It will take time for teachers to understand these new approaches to teaching but it clearly goes beyond understanding'.

How Teachers Lose, and Gain, Their Voice

There are resonances here with Yendol-Silva and Dana (2004) journal article in which they describe the challenges in encouraging classroom teachers to assume a more challenging leadership role. They suggest four key responsibilities: teacher as a decision-maker, teacher as a teacher-educator, teacher as a researcher and teacher as a political advocate. Each of these demand leadership of some kind, individual or collegial, but requiring liberation, sometimes painful, from the tight boundaries of classroom instruction. This does not come easily, argue Yendol-Silva and Dana, given the weight of history and convention, reminding their readers of teachers' struggles to use the space and find their voice.

There is a compelling relationship between space and voice. Within the classroom, it is teachers' voice that rules and is rarely questioned. Outside the classroom, that voice appears to lose its authority, except perhaps in relation to parents. The weight of convention is a powerful deterrent, especially to neophyte teachers for whom the classroom is their predetermined place. Their pre-service education may not have included examination of the politics and micropolitics of organisations. Drawing on Foucault's work, Yendol-Silva and Dana (2004) describe teachers' struggles with roles, relationships and power. Having a prescribed role as a classroom teacher, they write, commonly brings with it, perceptions of limited power and a necessary subordination to convention and expectation. Being 'just a teacher' carries within it a self-limiting convention and an implicit virtue of knowing one's place. They write that teachers 'did not find their power until they began acting, interacting, and understanding the new micropolitics of the new spaces and their new voice'. However, they further argue, 'simply creating spaces for teachers to assume responsibility for decision-making, and educating teachers as to their potential agency, is not enough. All members of the community need to work hard to construct, navigate, and protect these new spaces in productive and meaningful ways. They need to continually analyse ways in which these spaces are being occupied, who is benefiting from the spaces being created, whose voices are being heard, and who is left out' (p. 130).

The opportunity to find new spaces for learning and leadership and the relationship between them is exemplified in Hong Kong where students are released from the dictats of curriculum and assessment and the authority of teachers through 'other' forms of individual and collegial learning.

Other Learning Experiences

In Hong Kong, 15% of the curriculum has, over the last decade, been devoted to what are known as Other Learning Experiences, or OLE. Teachers there have attested to a profound impact on their knowledge and professional expertise when they work with young people in unfamiliar, or less tightly structured and prescriptive, contexts than the classroom. This includes community projects, work experience, trips to Macau or Singapore or to mainland China. It is a liberating experience not to be cast in the teacher/teller role but to be free not to know, not to be the expert or the ultimate authority. As one member of staff described it:

> I suddenly felt I wasn't the teacher any more. Here we were traveling and learning together, sharing our thinking and constantly surprising each other with what we knew and didn't know. It was embarrassing at first not to know the answers, and for children to explain to me when I didn't understand, but I soon became comfortable with it because I got so much from how much it empowered them to know more than their teacher. (unpublished evaluation of Other Learning Experiences)

As teachers explore the potential of OLE, they discover different forms of leading and following, more exciting forms of pedagogy and more imaginative ways of making learning active, interactive and student-led. While school principals were rarely involved directly in OLE it was critical for them to understand its potential for raising achievement by re-invigorating a sense of agency for young people as well as for participating teachers.

The 2007 Cambridge external evaluation of OLE provided evidence of the success of the programme in not only extending and enriching learning but in offering opportunities for leadership. Students described how they had learned to accept others' ideas, becoming open to differing perspectives, team working and dealing with people, time management, self-discovery and self-reliance, an ability to deal with challenging situations, perseverance, dealing with setbacks and self-presentation in interview. Asked to identify their least and most enjoyable and useful learning experiences on a 4-point scale, those which were given a one (the lowest grade) referred to lessons:

- which did not allow student-student interaction;
- were dominated by teacher talk; and
- were predominantly focused on writing, copying or note taking.

Those given a 4 as enjoyable and memorable learning experiences were described as:

- taking place in sites out of school;
- requiring active participation or problem solving;
- engaging students' interest and abilities;
- related to career or life beyond school; and
- offering opportunities for leadership.

These students profited from the experience to become, in Fielding and McGregor's (2005) taxonomy, knowledge creators and joint authors.

Have Terminology Will Travel

These experiences in learning and leading within and beyond the classroom not only extend our understanding of learning but also remind us of how limited is the notion of 'instruction' and 'instructional leadership'. Leading without instruction, leading collegially all challenge the vocabulary and essential limitations of what has become a pervasive and limiting vocabulary. It requires a rigorous and time-consuming research to find a paper or a reference which challenges the terminology that is now so deeply embedded that it has become the descriptor of choice and has travelled world-wide. A Google search reveals that its origins in the United States in the 1980s emerged from the school effectiveness movement.

> Instructional leadership is generally defined as the management of curriculum and instruction by a school principal. This term appeared as a result of research associated with the effective school movement of the 1980s, which revealed that the key to running successful schools lies in the principal's role.
>
> Instructional leadership is a critical aspect of school leadership. The work of instructional leaders is to ensure that every student receives the highest quality instruction each day.

The following is to be found in a 2009 OECD publication:

> Principals in every country have adopted the instructional leadership styles which are central to today's paradigm of effective school leadership. (*Leading to Learn: School Leadership and management Style*)

In the chapter preceding this, the term 'instructional leadership' is used 106 times. How many references are there, by contrast, to emotions, vulnerability, risk and self-doubt?

Leadership with Feeling

In a Cambridge University seminar in 2011, Jonathan Jansen, South Africa's first black Dean, spoke about the 'deeply emotional' nature of leadership and the challenges of being a learner, open to change and dealing with your own vulnerability and emotions.

What have been the most formidable obstacles you have faced in trying to achieve your vision?

Dealing with myself. I do not lead outside of my own emotions, hurts, experiences and troubles. Leading is a deeply personal and indeed emotional experience. Knowing yourself, being open to change and adjustment even as you lead, and yet knowing what is worth pursuing, are critical elements in credible and effective leadership. (Inform, no. 11, June)

Here is the meeting ground of leading and learning, recognising both as fraught with emotion—with risk, challenge, failure, achievement, celebrating the success and leadership of others. The emotional aspect of leadership has been subject to much less research than the 'strong' directive qualities, but it is the human aspect of leadership, the empathy and genuine concern for others that defines, in many respects, what it means to lead.

Ackerman and Maslin-Ostrowski (2002) counsel 'wounded leaders' who are hurt by their disappointments, by the deaths of students or colleagues, or by the bullying and betrayals of superiors, to accept and express rather than deny their vulnerability. In this way, they argue, leaders become more human, more open to being cared for as well as caring, more connected to, and therefore even more capable of, leading others around them.

We return to where we first started with a challenge to inert ideas, with new ways of seeing the all-too-familiar and with a challenge to the language of 'instruction'. We come to understand learning and leadership not as roles but as activities. While acknowledging the hierarchies, constraints and accountabilities of the institutions we have created, we are reminded that their primary purpose is for learning. A few hundred years B.C., the heretic Qin Yueren was murdered for his views on leadership for learning which he captured in four words—to look, to listen, to ask and to feel the pulse.

References

Ackerman, R. H., & Maslin-Ostrowski, P. (2002). *The wounded leaders; how real leadership emerges in times of crisis*. San Francisco: Jossey-Bass.

Alexander, R. J. (Ed.). (2010a). *Children, their world, their education: Final report of the Cambridge primary review*. London: Routledge.

Alexander, R. (2010b, April 27). Post-election priorities from the Cambridge review. *The Guardian*. Retrieved from https://www.theguardian.com/education/2010/apr/27/primary-education-cambridge-review-election

Bolden, R. (2011). Distributed leadership in organizations: A review of theory and research. *International Journal of Management Reviews, 13*, 251–269.

Day, C., & Sammons, P. (2008). *Successful school leadership*. London: Education Development Trust.

Dewey, J. (1937). Democracy and educational administration. *School and Society, 45*(April 3), 457–467.

Drummond, M. J. (1993). *Assessing children's learning*. London: David Fulton Publishers.

Elmore, R. (2008). Leadership as the practice of improvement. In B. Pont, D. Nusche, & D. Hopkins (Eds.), *Improving school leadership, volume 2: Case studies on system leadership* (pp. 37–67). Paris: OECD.

Fielding, M., & McGregor, J. (2005, April 11–15). *Deconstructing student voice: New spaces for dialogue or new opportunities for surveillance*. Paper presented at the American Educational Research Association Annual Conference (AERA), Montreal, Canada.

Fullan, M. (2011). *Choosing the wrong drivers for whole system reform*. Melbourne, Australia: Centre for Strategic Education.

Gronn, P. (2002). Distributed leadership as a unit of analysis. *Leadership Quarterly, 13*, 423–451.

Hargreaves, A., & Shirley, D. (2009). *The fourth way*. Thousand Oaks, CA: Corwin.

Hesselbein, F., Goldsmith, M., Beckard, R., & Drucker, P. (1996). *The leader of the future*. San Francisco: Jossey-Bass.

Hofstede, G. (1983). Culture's consequences: International differences in work-related values. *Administrative Science Quarterly (Johnson Graduate School of Management*, Cornell University), *28*(4), 625–629.

James, M., McCormick, R., Black, P., Carmichael, P., Drummond, M. J., Fox, A., et al. (2007). *Improving learning how to learn: Classrooms, schools and networks. TLRP Improving Learning Series*. London, UK: Routledge.

Javed, U. (2013). *Leadership for learning: A case study in six public and private schools of Pakistan*. Unpublished PhD thesis, University of Birmingham, Birmingham, UK.

Lieberman, A. (1992). Teacher leadership: What are we learning? In C. Livingston (Ed.), *Teachers as leaders: Evolving roles*. Washington, DC: National Education Association.

MacBeath, J. (2010). *Education and schooling: Myth, heresy and misconception*. London: Routledge.

MacBeath, J., & Townsend, T. (2011). *Leadership and learning: Paradox, paradigms and principles* (International handbook of leadership for learning). Rotterdam, The Netherlands: Springer.

Mayer, D., Pecheone, R., & Merino, N. (2012). Rethinking teacher education in Australia: The teacher quality reforms. In L. Darling-Hammond & A. Lieberman (Eds.), *Teacher education around the world: Changing policies and practices* (pp. 110–129). Abingdon, UK: Routledge.

Moos, L., & Møller, J. (2003). Schools and leadership in transition: The case of Scandinavia. *Cambridge Journal of Education, 33*(3), 353–371.

Spillane, J. (2012). *Distributed leadership*. San Francisco: Jossey Bass.

Swaffield, S., Dempster, N., Frost, D., & MacBeath, J. (Eds.). (2014). *Leadership for learning travels*. Inform No. 17. Cambridge, UK: Faculty of Education, University of Cambridge.

UNESDOC. (2011). *Competency framework for teachers*. Retrieved from https://unesdoc.unesco.org/ark:/48223/pf0000213475

Wahlstrom, K., & Louis, K. S. (2008). How teachers perceive principal leadership. *Educational Administration Quarterly, 44*(4), 458–495.

Whitehead, A. N. (1929). *The aims of education and other essays*. New York: The Free Press.

Yendol-Silva, D., & Dana, N. F. (2004). Encountering new spaces: Teachers developing voice within a professional development school. *Journal of Teacher Education, 55*(2), 128–140.

Part II

International Responses to the Theory

4

Australian Considerations in Relation to Instructional Leadership and Leadership for Learning

David Gurr

Introduction

This chapter considers Australian research about leadership and learning. It begins with a review of instructional leadership and leadership for learning (LfL) from research outside of Australia. The next section provides a range of sources of information about the study of school leadership in Australia and includes a review of successful school leadership and descriptions of three major ongoing research projects and two review papers. In terms of the concepts of instructional leadership or leadership for learning, there is not much specific support for either concept in the Australian literature. However, there is a concern to explore how leadership influences student learning, and there are many examples of small and large projects that are doing this and which contribute to the global study of this important topic.

D. Gurr (✉)
University of Melbourne, Melbourne, VIC, Australia
e-mail: d.gurr@unimelb.edu.au

© The Author(s) 2019
T. Townsend (ed.), *Instructional Leadership and Leadership for Learning in Schools*, Palgrave Studies on Leadership and Learning in Teacher Education, https://doi.org/10.1007/978-3-030-23736-3_4

A Brief Review of Instructional Leadership and Leadership for Learning

The Coleman report (Coleman et al., 1966) and Jencks' reanalysis of this and other material (Jencks et al., 1972; and see Coleman, Pettigrew, Sewell, and Pullum (1973), for a critique of this reanalysis) focussed discussion about the impact of schools on student achievement. The Coleman report has, halfway through a complex document of 737 pages, an oft-used quote: 'schools bring little to bear on a child's achievement that is independent of his background and general social context' (Coleman et al., 1966, p. 325). Jencks et al. (1972) argued, amongst other matters, that equalising the quality of schools and increasing resources was likely to have minimal impact on student learning. Whilst one interpretation of these findings was that schools had only a small impact on student learning, there was ambiguity and complexity with, for example, Coleman et al. (1966) noting that schools in challenging contexts had a far greater influence on student learning. One result of these reports was the birth of the effective schools' movement, which sought to explain why some schools seem to be contributing more to student learning outcomes than others. Based on his own and the research of others on effective schools, and his work with schools to improve teaching, Edmonds wrote a short article in Association for Supervision and Curriculum Development (ASCD's) journal, *Educational Leadership*, which led to the development of an enormously influential view of effective schools (Edmonds, 1979). There were six claims made about the characteristics of effective schools.

> I want to end this discussion by noting as unequivocally as I can what seem to me the most tangible and indispensable characteristics of effective schools: (a) They have strong administrative leadership without which the disparate elements of good schooling can neither be brought together nor kept together; (b) Schools that are instructionally effective for poor children have a climate of expectation in which no children are permitted to fall below minimum but efficacious levels of achievement; (c) The school's atmosphere is orderly without being oppressive, and generally conducive to the instructional business at hand; (d) Effective schools get that way partly

by making it clear that pupil acquisition of basic skills takes precedence over all other school activities; (e) When necessary, school energy and resources can be diverted from other business in furtherance of the fundamental objectives; and (f) There must be some means by which pupil progress can be frequently monitored. (Edmonds, 1979, p. 22)

This, and other research on effective schools (e.g., Rutter, Maughan, Mortimore, Ouston, & Smith, 1979), led to the development during the 1980s of a view of leadership that seemed to typify what was observed in these schools—instructional leadership. This view was often linked to the school effectiveness literature, with, for example, evidence that the extent of instructional leadership is one differentiating aspect between high- and low-achieving schools (Bamburg & Andrews, 1991; Heck, Marcoulides, & Lang, 1991). Two central figures in the development of this view were Murphy and Hallinger, who were colleagues at Peabody College at Vanderbilt University and who developed one of the first comprehensive views of instructional leadership (Hallinger & Murphy, 1985). This involved three dimensions—defining the school mission, managing the instructional programme, and creating a positive school climate—and ten instructional leadership functions: framing and communicating clear school goals; supervising and evaluating instruction, coordinating curriculum, and monitoring student progress; protecting instructional time, promoting professional development, maintaining high visibility, providing incentives for teachers, and providing incentives for learning. With a dedicated survey tool, this view has become the most used in empirical research (Hallinger, 2009). Building on this, and through a major review of the instructional leadership literature that included studies of administrative work activities, analyses of administrative training programmes, and investigations of administrative coordination and control, Murphy (1990) proposed a more elaborate framework for viewing instructional leadership which included four major dimensions:

- **Developing mission and goals** which included framing and communicating school goals. Effective principals were described as having a vision and the ability to develop shared purpose through the way they communicated their vision for their school.

- **Managing the educational production function** which included promoting quality instruction, informally supervising instruction, evaluating instruction, allocating and protecting instructional time, active involvement in coordinating the curriculum, extending content coverage by developing and enforcing homework policies that require regular homework, and actively monitoring student progress.
- **Promoting an academic learning climate** which included establishing positive expectations and standards, maintaining high visibility in the classroom and around the school, providing incentives for teachers (e.g., increased responsibility, personal support, public and private praise, and encouragement) and students (e.g., school-wide recognition systems, special emphasis on academic excellence), and promoting and encouraging professional development of teachers.
- **Developing a supportive work environment** which included creating a safe and orderly learning environment through emphasising effective discipline programs, providing opportunities for meaningful student involvement (e.g., system-wide activity programs, formal recognition for successful student participation, use of school symbols to bond students to school), developing staff collaboration and cohesion through having clear goals and opportunities for teachers to be involved in professional interchanges and decision making, securing outside resources in support of school goals, and forging links between the home and the school.

Whilst instructional leadership was linked to school effectiveness, it was troubling that research suggested that principals devoted relatively little time to it, and that teachers didn't see instructional leadership as a primary principal responsibility, nor did they want them doing this (Murphy, 1990). Principals were caught in a bind as decentralisation and an emphasis on school-based management was emphasising instructional leadership, yet increased administrative tasks were limiting what principals could do (Murphy & Hallinger, 1992); this was not a new dilemma, however, as Bridges had also described this in 1967 (see Hallinger, 2011, for a discussion of this).

Despite a renewed emphasis on instructional leadership in the 2000s with the emergence of meta-analytic research highlighting its greater impact on student learning compared to competing leadership models like transformational leadership (e.g., Robinson, Lloyd, & Rowe, 2008), criticisms were mounting, with many arriving at the view that instructional leadership as conceived in the 1990s was by itself not sufficient (e.g., Day, Gu, & Sammons, 2016; Townsend, Acker-Hocevar, Ballenger, & Place, 2013). There have been moves over the last two decades to develop leadership for learning views which have a central concern to improve teaching and learning, but which incorporate a wider range of ideas about how to do this. Two views are described next.

Over the last decade, Hallinger has developed a more complex leadership model that built upon his earlier instructional leadership model and which he has labelled as leadership for learning (Hallinger, 2011, 2018). In this model, principals and others could be the sources of leadership action, and they could have multiple foci in their work. The core elements of the model are vision and goals, academic structures and processes, and people capacity. Leadership influences these elements and it is these that influence student outcomes. The leader brings to their work their own values and beliefs and knowledge and experience. Importantly, this work is contained within a complex environment that includes societal culture, an institutional system, staff and community characteristics and school organisation.

Paralleling the renewed emphasis on instructional leadership in the 2000s was the emergence of the leadership for learning (LfL) project (www.educ.cam.ac.uk/networks/lfl/). This was formed in 2001 with an agenda to challenge educational policy and current views of educational leadership (MacBeath, Frost, Swaffield, & Waterhouse, 2003). Stimulated by the establishment of a professorial chair at Cambridge in 2000, Leadership for Learning: The Cambridge Network was established, and with philanthropic support from the *Carpe Vitam* Foundation, the *Carpe Vitam* Leadership for Learning (LfL) project began. Across 2002–2006, a series of meetings was held to establish what a leadership for learning focus would contribute to knowledge about school leadership. Seven countries (Australia, Austria, Denmark, England, Greece, Norway, and the United States of America) and eight research groups (two were in the USA) were involved in a longitudinal study that comprised researchers and critical friends working with three schools from each country (see below for more details about the methodology). The central research questions were:

- What is understood by learning in different contexts?
- What is understood by leadership?
- What are the links between leadership and learning?

Four annual meetings (Cambridge, Innsbruck, Copenhagen, and Athens) helped unpack what was meant by leadership, learning, and the conjunction 'for'. The resulting LfL model had four common framing values: leadership for learning, democratic values, critical friendship, and moral purpose. At the base of the model, leadership and learning are bookended by activity and agency to emphasise that 'leading and learning are necessary forms of activity, enacted by those with a strong sense of their own human agency' (MacBeath, Dempster, Frost, Johnson, & Swaffield, 2018, p. 42). There are four tiers to represent leadership from students, teachers, senior managers, and communities of learners. The LfL model views leadership as an activity that can be exercised by anyone, and learning applies to all. The leadership actions are guided by five principles at the top of the model: focusing on learning, sharing leadership, engaging in dialogue, sharing accountability, and creating favourable learning conditions.

In this truncated and highly selective view of complex and substantial research over many years, it appears that whilst instructional leadership (largely as conceived in the 1980s and 1990s) remains a focus for many, it is being replaced by leadership for learning views. Two such views are Hallinger's own expansion of his earlier view of instructional leadership, with the other being a view developed from a grounded empirical project that connected leadership and learning.

School Leadership Research in Australia

Research about school leadership has a relatively short history in Australia. For example, in reviews of successful school leadership in Australia (Gurr, 2008, 2009, 2012), I have described how substantial research in the area has a 60-year history and a predominant focus on principals. The 1960s saw research and teaching on educational administration emerge, particularly fuelled by the work of Walker and colleagues at the University of New England, and Bassett and colleagues at the University of Queensland. This work relied on overseas research and a somewhat unsophisticated view of school leadership, with the overwhelming view that this resided in the male head of a school, in an individualistic and positional pursuit to influence others to improve: '[a] good school has good staff … Given a reasonable basis on which to work, the headmaster can *create* a good staff' (Bassett, Crane, & Walker, 1967, p. 3); '[e]ven if he [the Headmaster] (sic) already has a good school, he can look forward to leading an infinitely better one' (Bassett et al., 1967, p. 32).

In the 1970s, research and writing remained largely focused on principal leadership, and there continued to be a lack of major Australian research. This changed with 'The Australian School Principal: A National Study' (Duignan et al., 1985), a study that heralded the beginning of interest in exploring Australian school leadership that impacts on student learning. Using interviews with principals, parents, teachers, and students from government and non-government schools in all Australian states and territories, a survey administered to 1600 principals, and 14 case studies of highly effective schools from across Australia, it was the first major study in Australia to explore principal leadership and effectiveness. A model relating principal role to goal achievement was presented. This model described principals in terms of personal (confidence, willingness to accept criticism, sensitivity, tolerance, honesty, integrity, consistency, approachability, intellectual acuity, good judgement, tough-mindedness, resilience, a sense of perspective, and a sense of humour) and professional qualities (leadership, effective communication, effective relationships, knowledge of learning processes and instructional design, initiating change, and innovation), and the nature of their work in terms of the role complexity and ambiguity evident. Through focusing on task, process and function strategies, principal work was shared between school (e.g., stimulating and motivating staff), classroom (e.g., monitoring programmes and instructional processes) and out-of-school (e.g., facilitating parent and community involvement) factors to influence directly the improvement of teaching and, ultimately and indirectly, the improvement of student learning.

In the ensuing years, there have been many more contributions that have explored leadership and its impacts on student and school success. Some of these are described briefly below (in many cases, a more detailed discussion of these can be found in Gurr, 2009).

There are many books on how principals and others lead school improvement and success (e.g., Beare, Caldwell, & Millikan, 1989; Caldwell & Spinks, 1992; Dinham, 2008, 2016; Simpkins, Thomas, & Thomas, 1987; Thompson, E.B., 1994, 1995; Thompson, A.R., 2000), research focused on describing successful Australian practice within a world focus (e.g., Caldwell & Harris, 2008), and principals writing about what they do (Anderson & Cawsey, 2008; Degenhardt & Duignan, 2010; Fleming & Kleinhenz, 2007). A substantial contribution to describing principal practice was the publication and distribution to all Australian schools of a book of 17 stories about the exhilaration of being a principal, *Leading Australia's Schools* (Duignan & Gurr, 2007a). Analysing the 17 chapters, Duignan and Gurr (2007b, pp. 158–164) found that the principals seemed to have: a clearly articulated philosophy and deep moral purpose; an unwavering focus on all students and their learning needs; a passionate belief in the significance of what they do; a commitment to making a difference; a focus on, and valuing of, people; strong support for learning, growth, and development of themselves and others; an expectation for high professional standards; an ability to develop a collaborative, collegial, and inclusive school culture; a view in which leadership was seen as service; an attitude that hard work was accepted; a 'can do' attitude to all that they did; and a high-level enjoyment and satisfaction from what they do.

There have been many small-scale case studies of successful principal leadership. Three that were mentioned by Gurr (2009) were: Dimmock and O'Donoghue (1997) who used life history portraits to explore the successful leadership of six innovative secondary school principals; Drysdale (2001, 2002) who explored, through multiple perspective case studies of seven schools, how a market-centred orientation by principals led to school success; and the leadership of a successful Christian school through a complex immersion case study (Twelves, 2005). All showed elements of how principals influenced teaching and learning, but all showed that there was considerable complexity beyond this to have a successful school. Even notions of success were challenged, with, in the case of the Christian school, the main indicator of success being the extent to which students maintained their faith (Twelves, 2005). Another example of a small-scale study is that from a group of Australian researchers from Griffith University involved in the LfL project (Dempster, 2006; Dempster & Johnson, 2006). Two schools were involved in a complex three-year project as described by Dempster (2006, p. 56):

> The LfL Project was conducted over three years, in a number of phases. The first of these was the 'mapping' of perceptions and practices regarding leadership, learning and possible connections between the two. The mapping process was comprised of a baseline survey of teachers and students aimed at ascertaining key insights about leadership, learning, and the school context. In addition, a school profile was compiled consisting of information that school leaders and teaching staff viewed as important in presenting an authentic portrayal of the institution, its purposes and achievements. A students' portrait of the school was also generated, focusing especially on the meaning that the school had for them. The mapping process included qualitative inquiry entailing semi-structured interviews and focus group discussions with school leaders, teachers, and students—the students being followed over three years as they progressed through years 8, 9, and 10. The purpose of the mapping exercise, the baseline survey and interviews was to identify leadership and/or learning matters on which each school should concentrate during the three years of the study. These matters constituted the second phase of the project, namely, the development of 'interventions' or initiatives designed by the participants (with help from a 'Critical Friend' if necessary) to address selected issues uncovered in the baseline survey, interviews, and portraits. Phase three involved taking the necessary action to implement one or more initiatives within the school over the following two years. Finally, in the fourth phase, teachers' and students' views about learning were revisited at the end of the three years with a view to identifying and describing possible links between leadership and learning.

Leadership and learning were shown to be linked, and the development of student leadership was considered important in the secondary context (Dempster, 2006). Dempster and Johnson (2006) concluded that for learning success there must be a focus on learning (e.g., learning for students and staff, appropriate pastoral structures to support student learning), conditions favourable to learning must be created (e.g., learning culture, reflection on learning, staff professional learning), leadership must be shared (e.g., supportive structures like leadership teams, staff collegiality and collaboration, targeted professional learning), and the connection between leadership and learning must be explicit (e.g., agency of staff in relation to supporting student learning, leadership structures, learning culture).

Small-scale studies like these struggle to contribute in a cumulative way to knowledge-building (Leithwood, 2005) and so there is a need for more expansive research, such as those that use high response surveys, case study research with large case numbers, and mixed-method research. Some examples of these are now considered.

A major school effectiveness study was the *Australian Effective Schools Project*. The Australian Council for Educational Research (ACER) conducted a national survey of parents, students, teachers, principals, schools, and community members on their views on effective schools (McGaw, Piper, Banks, & Evans, 1993a, 1993b). It remains as one of the most ambitious educational research projects conducted in Australia and pioneered the large-scale use of qualitative analysis software. From a distribution of more than 300,000 survey booklets, there were over 7000 responses from nearly one-third of Australian schools to questions on areas identified as contributing to school effectiveness, including the important components of an effective-school curriculum, and the extent of parent and teacher roles and goals for student learning. Among the findings was that effective schools had: a central focus on learning and a conducive school climate; a concern for the learning and welfare of all students; a committed and professional staff; an organisational culture characterised by collaborative decision-making and effective educational leadership; a curriculum that is relevant, coherent, and inclusive; and a focus on ongoing professional development and parent involvement. This study adopted a wide view of school outcomes, with student academic achievement being only one of several outcomes identified as being important for effective schools. While this research was not specifically focused on school leadership, it was one of the elements identified as being important.

Leadership for Organisational Learning and Student Outcomes (LOLSO) was a large survey-based study exploring leadership, organisational learning, and student outcomes (Mulford & Silins, 2003; Mulford, Silins, & Leithwood, 2004). LOLSO involved surveys of 3500 students and 2500 teachers in 96 government secondary schools in two Australian states, South Australia and Tasmania (including all of the eight secondary schools in Tasmania at the time). The research demonstrated that leadership makes a difference in schools in an indirect manner: 'leadership contributes to organisational learning, which in turn influences what happens in the core business of school—the teaching and learning' (Mulford & Silins, 2003, p. 183). In a model describing the findings, 15 variables were included with principal transformational leadership, impacting on teacher leadership and administrative team leadership to influence organisational learning, which in turn influences teacher work, and through this student participation and engagement and ultimately academic achievement. School size, home educational environment, and socioeconomic status variously influenced the outcomes of this process. For example, larger school size negatively influenced principal transformational leadership, teacher leadership, and student participation, but positively influenced academic self-concept. Mulford (2007) noted that this model placed much less emphasis on organisational, managerial and strategic elements, and more on dispersed leadership and organisational learning cultures.

The study, An Exceptional Schooling Outcomes Project (ÆSOP) (Dinham, 2005, 2007), explored middle-level leadership through multiple perspective case studies of 50 Australian secondary school subject departments and cross-school programmes (e.g., student welfare) across 38 secondary schools. All were able to demonstrate outstanding educational outcomes over at least a four-year period. The middle leaders were found to promote success through: a focus on students and their learning; high-level interpersonal skills, and generally being well-liked and trusted; high-level professional capacity and strategic resource allocation; promotion and advocacy of their departments and maintaining good external relations with the school; influencing department planning and organisation; developing common purpose, collaboration and sense of team within their department; fostering teacher learning and developing a culture of shared responsibility and trust; and having clear vision, high expectations of themselves and others, and developing a culture of success. While the focus of the research was on the outstanding faculties and teams, it found that principal leadership was a key to success. Principals promoted success through: external awareness and engagement with the wider environment; a bias towards innovation and action; high-level interpersonal skills and generally being well-liked and trusted; having a clear vision, high expectations and fostering a culture of success; encouraging teacher learning and responsibility and showing trust; promoting student support, developing common purpose and encouraging teacher collaboration; and having a core focus on students, learning, and teaching. This research highlighted the importance of the principal in 'providing the conditions where teachers can operate effectively and students can learn' (Dinham, 2005, p. 355).

Further examples of complex and large-scale research are three major ongoing projects relevant to the leadership for learning focus of this chapter, and these are now described.

Innovative Designs for Enhancing Achievements in Schools (IDEAS) is an extensive and ongoing school improvement project that has developed a framework for establishing professional learning communities to improve school outcomes (e.g., Crowther, Ferguson, & Hann, 2009; Lewis & Andrews, 2007). In an overlapping time frame with the LOLSO and ÆSOP projects, a team from the University of Southern Queensland were refining school improvement ideas from a project that began in 1997 and which was designed to explore how school-based management could be constructed to ensure it had a positive effect on classrooms (Andrews et al., 2004; Crowther, Andrews, Morgan, & O'Neill, 2012; Crowther et al., 2009; Crowther, Kaagan, Ferguson, & Hann, 2002; Lewis & Andrews, 2007). In particular, the research was concerned with establishing professional learning communities to improve school outcomes. IDEAS involved three components: a research-based framework for enhancing school outcomes that includes development of strategic foundations, cohesive community, appropriate infrastructure, school-wide pedagogy, and professional learning; a five-phase school-based implementation strategy—initiating, discovering, envisioning, actioning, and sustaining (this is a process version of the IDEAS acronym; Crowther et al., 2012); and parallel leadership in which the principal and teachers engage in mutualism (mutual trust and respect), a sense of shared purpose and an allowance of individual expression. IDEAS promoted teacher leadership (these are generally middle leaders like in the ÆSOP project) and defined the core roles of the principal to include: facilitating the development of a shared vision, creating cultural meaning through identity generation, supporting organisational alignment, distributing power and leadership, and developing networks and external alliances. IDEAS has been shown to lead to improved school outcomes, often concerned with changes associated with teachers and teaching practice such as increased teacher confidence, self-reflection and review, and the development of a professional learning community (Lewis & Andrews, 2007). Whilst there was less focus on reporting student outcomes in the early stages of the programme and less surety about the impact of IDEAS on students (e.g., Andrews et al., 2004; Lewis, 2006), in more recent years there has been clear evidence for improved student learning and behavioural outcomes (Crowther et al., 2012). More substantial evidence of the success of the programme, with a focus on the sustainability of success, and more research from those outside the project would be useful to confirm the importance of IDEAS (see Wildy & Faulkner, 2008, and Gurr & Drysdale, 2016a, for discussion of these points). However, student outcomes have not been a focus for IDEAS because it is a process that helps schools embark on a major school-wide change to teaching and learning, and acts to establish those conditions that will lead to improved student outcomes, rather than directly impacting on the outcomes. It works through the parallel leadership of teachers (focus on pedagogical development) and principals (focus on strategic development) combining to activate and integrate culture-building, organisation-wide professional learning, and development of school-wide pedagogy, which lead to school alignment and an enhanced school community capacity to improve school outcomes. In terms of understanding successful school leadership, its main contribution is to highlight the importance of principals in direction setting (as meta-strategists), in supporting change and the work of teachers, and in promoting a distributed view of leadership through the concept of teacher and parallel leadership to support principal efforts in driving school improvement (Crowther et al., 2009; Lewis & Andrews, 2007).

The Australian arm of the International Successful School Principalship Project (ISSPP) and the International School Leadership Development Network (ISLDN) are examples of Australian research involvement in major international research projects. The ISSPP began in 2001 and Australia has had representation through research groups in Tasmania and Victoria. The ISLDN began in 2009 and the initial Australian representation was through research groups in Western Australia and Victoria. There is considerable overlap in the research agenda of the two projects. For the ISSPP, 14 multiple perspective case studies involving individual and group interviews with senior leadership, teachers, parents, students, and school council members were conducted in the states of Victoria and Tasmania between 2003 and 2005 and covering primary, secondary, and special schools. The five case studies in Tasmania were conducted under the leadership of Mulford and nine cases from Victoria were conducted under the supervision of Gurr and Drysdale. Three of the schools in Victoria have been subsequently revisited to explore the sustainability of success, this time including observation of the life of the school as well as multiple perspectives through interviews (Goode, 2017). More recently, three multiple perspectives and observational studies of Victorian secondary schools that had been underperforming were conducted (Gurr, Drysdale, Longmuir, & McCrohan, 2018; Longmuir, 2017). These case studies of underperforming schools overlap with the ISLDN methodology (Gurr et al., 2018) and form part of an Australian contribution to the ISLDN, with the other case being an interview with the principal of a remote school in Western Australia (Gurr, Drysdale, Clarke, & Wildy, 2014). The ISSPP studies have led to the production of leadership models with the one based on Australian only research (Gurr, Drysdale, & Mulford, 2006, 2007) shown in Fig. 4.1 (this is a slightly modified version that eliminates some errors in the original).

In this model, principals exert an influence on student outcomes (broadly conceived) through a focus on teaching and learning (curriculum, pedagogy, assessment, and reporting) which is driven by their own values and vision, establishing an agreed school vision, using elements of

4 Australian Considerations in Relation to Instructional...

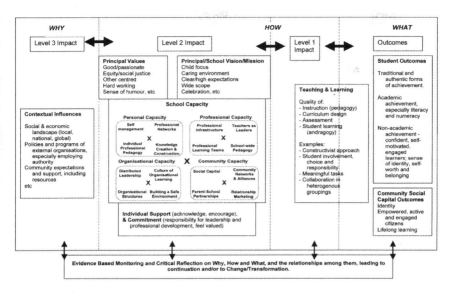

Fig. 4.1 Australian model of successful principal leadership. (Gurr et al. 2006, 2007)

transformational leadership (individual support), and increasing school capacity across four dimensions (personal, professional, organisational, and community), taking into account and working within the school context, and using evidence-based monitoring and critical reflection that leads to change and transformation in the school. Level 1 interventions have the most impact on student outcomes. Level 2 interventions are focused on school direction and culture (supportive, high expectation), and capacity building (through the areas of individual, professional, organisational, and community capacity building, with each area specified with four parts—see Fig. 4.1). Level 2 interventions have a more indirect impact on student outcomes. In Level 3, principals were found to be responsive to external and other influences, and also to shape some of these by, for example, contributing to the district- and system-level policy development, and being involved in networks and professional associations. This model provides several conceptual frameworks to allow principals to locate their work. It indicates that they can impact both directly and indirectly on student learning, but that mostly the impact is indirect. An interesting aspect of this model is that it can be applied to those school personnel holding other leadership positions, especially those in coordinating roles (see Gurr & Drysdale, 2013, for a discussion of this). For example, the 16 elements of the 4 × 4 capacity-building section are relevant for anyone who has a supervisory role – an important aspect of educational leadership is helping to develop the capacities of staff. Drysdale and Gurr (2011) have developed a version of this model that focused on leader qualities, school context, and capacity building, and Gurr (2015) described a further refinement of the model that included findings from several other models developed in ISSPP research from other countries. Gurr, Drysdale, and Mulford (2007, 2009) noted that the ISSPP research supports leadership impact on student learning, but at the principal and senior leadership levels this is mostly indirect, with direct influence more typically found in the work of middle leaders like department/faculty/area leaders. They argued that there is not much evidence in the Australian context for instructional leadership of the type championed by Hallinger and Murphy (1985), with only one of the 14 principals showing these qualities.

The Principals as Literacy Leaders (PALL) project formed as a response by a principal association, the Australian Primary Principals Association (APPA), to a federal government call for projects to address educational disadvantage. The APPA saw an opportunity to develop primary principals as literacy leaders, and so, in 2009, a collaboration was born that involved associations with a federal and state education department, three universities (Griffith, Edith Cowan, and the Australian Catholic University), and the government, Catholic and independent school jurisdictions from the Northern Territory, Queensland, South Australia and Western Australia. PALL was a professional learning opportunity, a school improvement programme and a leadership for learning research project. Dempster et al. (2017) described how the project has expanded to three further research projects and programmes in all six states and two territories—it is a vibrant, impactful learning, and research programme designed to 'provide principals with both the literacy knowledge and leadership support they need to assist their teachers to improve reading performance in their schools' (Dempster et al., 2017, p. 150). The PALL project has strong connections with the LfL project, which is not surprising as researchers like Dempster and Johnson were involved in both. It is a project that clearly links leadership with learning and does so in the important area of reading development.

An initial review of relevant literature established a programme framework, the leadership for literacy learning blueprint, that had five components (shared leadership, professional development participation, enhancing the physical, social and emotional conditions for learning, planning and coordinating the curriculum and teaching across the school, and connecting with parent and community support) surrounding a core that had developing shared moral purpose around improving student learning and performance, disciplined dialogue and a strong evidence base to inform practice (Dempster et al., 2012). Schools participated in a two-year programme that included completion of five modules (leadership for learning, learning to read, gathering and using reading achievement data, designing and implementing literacy interventions, and intervention evaluation) and the construction of a literacy improvement plan in the first year, and implementation of the plan in the second year. It was a programme that focussed on what is called the BIG 6: oral language, vocabulary, phonological awareness, letter-sound knowledge, comprehension, and fluency. Principals were supported by a literacy achievement advisor (usually a system-based peer mentor), and this role was considered to be very important (the importance of having critical friends to support school improvement is well known: Butler et al., 2011; Huerta Villalobos, 2013; Swaffield, 2004; Swaffield & MacBeath, 2005). The programme was clearly focussed on principals and provided considerable support and opportunities for principals to be literacy leaders, and there was evidence that with support they could become better at doing this. Importantly, from the beginning, the project adopted an inclusive view of leadership, and the development of teachers in leadership roles, such as literacy leaders, or class teachers who become more widely influential, were features of many of the case study schools (Dempster et al., 2017). Teacher leadership (positional and non-positional) was seen to be 'central to school-wide action' (Dempster et al., 2017, p. 94). Dempster et al. (2017, p. 150) reported on findings from six PALL studies and concluded that in terms of impact on student achievement, and despite some methodological difficulties in the studies (such as the relatively short nature of the programme and problems in getting principals to complete programme evaluations), 'there is certainly considerable evidence of increases in student achievement in reading—at the individual, class, and school level'. However, as with IDEAS, the core focus of the programme was not student outcomes per se, but rather changes in what happened in schools. In the case of PALL, changes in how principals led their schools were demonstrated, with flow-on effects to how other staff worked across curriculum, pedagogy, assessment, and reporting. In many cases, this led to improved student learning outcomes in a short time, with the project leaders hopeful that as time progresses more substantial and sustainable evidence of learning gain will be shown. In some cases, there was evidence of impact on families, although the family engagement was an area identified as needing more development and one that was being explored in further studies.

The final section of this exploration of Australian school leadership research considers two related review papers. In 2007 Mulford published, through the Australian Council for Educational Leaders, an overview of Australian educational leadership research from 2001 to 2005 through an examination of articles published during this period in the four leading Australian-based education journals (*Australian Journal of Education, Australian Educational Researcher, Leading and Managing*, and the *Journal of Educational Administration*). The justification for the years selected was that this period reflected 'a period of major ferment in the area, and of major change in views about schooling and school leadership' (Mulford, 2007, p. 4). Through a detailed exploration of the papers, Mulford provided what he described as reliable, evidence-based conclusions in the areas of leadership (indirect impact on student outcomes of positional and distributed leadership), transformational leadership (direct impact on organisational effectiveness and learning), distributed leadership (importance for school success, but successful leadership is contingent on the context elements), school organisation and student outcomes (school organisational arrangements impact on student cognitive and emotional outcomes; teacher perceptions of schools as learning organisations is positively related to student perceptions about teachers and student outcomes), job satisfaction/stress and leader supply/demand (difficulties with principal recruitment, satisfaction, work intensification, leading small/rural/isolated schools, and ICT implementation), system and community issues (need for professional autonomy and ownership; development over performance management; limited impact of school councils on classrooms; community support for national goals but ambivalence about how to achieve them), and survey instruments (availability of valid and reliable survey instruments). Of relevance to the current chapter, there were no papers focussed on instructional leadership and only a few that made a contribution to how leadership influences learning, with these main papers reporting on the LOLSO, IDEAS, ÆSOP, and ISSPP projects as described above. Gurr and Drysdale (2016b) built upon Mulford's, 2007 review by considering articles published between 2006 and 2013 in the same journals that Mulford reviewed. They found only five papers that described Australian research that had some connection with principal leadership for learning. Surveying West Australian teachers about their perception of principal leadership, Cavanagh (2007) found, through structural equation modelling, that in an 11-element principal leadership model, giving attention to individuals (attention to individual teachers, provision of professional development, coaching of teachers, and recognition of teacher and student effort) and promoting renewal of schooling (advocating need for morally positioned changes to education) were higher order leadership functions that impacted directly on seven of the nine remaining elements. In particular, principal leadership of pedagogy was dependent on both of these elements. Pepper and Wildy (2008, 2009) explored the implementation of a sustainability initiative, noting principal understanding of the concept, sharing of leadership responsibilities, and enthusiasm for the initiative, were important elements of successful implementation. Reviewing research on the influence of school leadership on student outcomes, Marsh (2012) identified the challenges faced by contemporary leaders (accountability, educational reform, ambiguity of leadership) and suggested that leadership needs to go beyond the current notion of position-based concepts of leadership through a leadership for learning view that was community focused and involving anyone who had the potential to influence student outcomes. Cranston, Mulford, Keating, and Reid (2010) reported on a national survey of government primary school principals that explored their perception of the purpose of education. Principals reported a disconnection between what they considered should be the purposes of education, the strategies for achieving them and the realities of what was actually occurring. They concluded that principals believed schools are not orientated towards public purposes to the extent that they thought they should be, nor were they enacting practices that supported public purposes.

Reflection

Instructional leadership and leadership for learning, like most concepts, have ambiguity and lack of clarity through the production of competing views. In the early part of the paper, two versions of the most researched view of instructional leadership, and two different views of leadership for learning were described. As others have noted (e.g., Boyce & Bowers, 2018) there is now considerable overlap between the views. In the Australian research considered in this chapter, neither view appears to be widely used, yet there is clearly a substantial body of research that is describing how school leadership influences student learning. In many ways in the Australian context, it seems to be assumed that this is true and the need to label it is not important. For example, the Australian Institute for Teaching and School Leadership (AITSL) has developed a leadership standard that is being adopted by many systems/jurisdictions in Australia, and which describes a leadership model that has leading teaching and learning as one of five professional practices for principals:

> Principals create a positive culture of challenge and support, enabling effective teaching that promotes enthusiastic, independent learners, committed to life-long learning. Principals have a key responsibility for developing a culture of effective teaching, for leading, designing and managing the quality of teaching and learning and for students' achievement in all aspects of their development. They set high expectations for the whole school through careful collaborative planning, monitoring and reviewing the effectiveness of learning. Principals set high standards of behaviour and attendance, encouraging active engagement and a strong student voice. (AITSL, 2011, p. 9)

This practice is not labelled, other than to say it is about leading teaching and learning. With the other four leadership practices (developing self and others; leading improvement, innovation and change; leading the management of the school; engaging and working with the community) and four leadership requirements (vision and values, knowledge and understanding, personal qualities, social, and interpersonal skills), AITSL provide a complex contemporary view of school leadership that has elements of instructional leadership and leadership for learning views, but which is not encased in either. There are few Australian studies that use either instructional leadership or leadership for learning, and even when they do, often it is because of a relationship with overseas literature or projects. For example, I have been involved with several papers that used instructional leadership in the title (Gurr et al., 2007, 2010; Gurr, Drysdale, Ylimaki, & Moos, 2011). These reported on a reanalysis of cases from the ISSPP by focussing on the concept of instructional leadership, with the need for this analysis driven by ISSPP colleagues from the USA. Whilst we used instructional leadership in the title, we argued that instructional leadership was not a term commonly used in Australian educational leadership research, and as a concept to explain the work of our successful principals, it was not sufficient to capture the complexity of their work. We found instructional leadership to be a dated term reflective of a past era from the USA, and not well suited to leading in contemporary Australian schools. In the Australian context, some academics, such as Dinham, hold on to the instructional leadership label, but even then there is confusion, because whilst Dinham set up the Master of Instructional Leadership at The University of Melbourne, when he came to write a book related to this, it was entitled, *Leading Teaching and Learning* (Dinham, 2016).

Of course, Australian research does proffer examples of significant projects that provide insight into the connections between leadership and learning. LOLSO, ÆSOP, IDEAS, ISSPP/ISLDN, and PALL are examples that have richness and complexity that this chapter cannot hope to describe adequately. There are also many research and professional books, case study, survey and mixed-method research, and so forth, that provide additional knowledge, with several examples of each described in this chapter. It is troubling, however, when major publication sources for

Australian school leadership research are reviewed, that the quantity of publications focussed on leadership and learning is not large, and the quality is somewhat uneven, with a reliance on small-scale studies and with limited collaboration between researchers from different universities (Gurr & Drysdale, 2016b; Mulford, 2007). Projects like PALL are notable exceptions to this observation and show the way in terms of collaboration, quality, and potential impact; it is time for Australian school leadership researchers to engage in more collaborative and complex endeavours to advance understanding of educational leadership broadly.

In terms of the concepts of instructional leadership or leadership for learning, there is not much specific support for either concept in the Australian literature. However, there is a concern to explore how leadership influences student learning, and there are many examples of small and large projects that are doing this. There is research about leadership and learning that is worth attending to and which contributes to the world knowledge about this.

References

Anderson, M., & Cawsey, C. (2008). *Learning for leadership*. Melbourne, Australia: ACER.

Andrews, D., Conway, J., Dawson, M., Lewis, M., McMaster, J., Morgan, A., et al. (2004). *School revitalisation the IDEAS way, Monograph, 34*. Melbourne, Australia: Australian Council for Educational Leaders.

Australian Institute for Teaching and School Leadership (AITSL). (2011). *National professional standard for principals*. Canberra, Australia: Australian Institute for Teaching and School Leadership.

Bamburg, J. D., & Andrews, R. L. (1991). School goals, principals and achievement. *School Effectiveness and School Improvement, 2*(3), 175–191.

Bassett, G. W., Crane, A. R., & Walker, W. G. (1967). *Headmasters for better schools* (2nd ed.). St Lucia, Australia: University of Queensland Press.

Beare, H., Caldwell, B. J., & Millikan, R. H. (1989). *Creating an excellent school*. London: Routledge.

Boyce, J., & Bowers, A. J. (2018). Toward an evolving conceptualization of instructional leadership as leadership for learning: Meta-narrative review of

109 quantitative studies across 25 years. *Journal of Educational Administration, 56*(2), 161–182.

Butler, H., Krelle, A., Seal, I., Trafford, L., Drew, S., Hargreaves, J., et al. (2011). *The critical friend: Facilitating positive change in school communities*. Camberwell, Australia: ACER Press.

Caldwell, B. J., & Harris, J. (2008). *Why not the best schools? What we have learned from outstanding schools around the world*. Melbourne, Australia: ACER Press.

Caldwell, B. J., & Spinks, J. M. (1992). *Leading the self-managing school*. London: The Falmer Press.

Cavanagh, R. (2007). The driving school leadership forces: Attention to individuals and promoting renewal of schooling. *Leading and Managing, 13*(2), 99–112.

Coleman, J. S., Campbell, E. Q., Hobson, C. J., McPartland, J., Mood, A. M., Weinfield, F. D., et al. (1966). *Equality of educational opportunity*. Washington, DC: National Center for Educational Statistics, U.S. government Printing Office.

Coleman, J. S., Pettigrew, T. F., Sewell, W. H., & Pullum, T. W. (1973). Inequality: A reassessment of the effect of family and schooling in America. *American Journal of Sociology, 78*(6), 1523–1544.

Cranston, N., Mulford, B., Keating, J., & Reid, A. (2010). Primary school principals and the purposes of education in Australia: Results of a national survey. *Journal of Educational Administration, 48*(4), 517–539.

Crowther, F., Andrews, D., Morgan, A., & O'Neill, S. (2012). Hitting the Bullseye of school improvement: The IDEAS project at work in a successful system. *Leading and Managing, 18*(2), 1–33.

Crowther, F., Ferguson, M., & Hann, L. (2009). *Developing teacher leaders* (2nd ed.). Thousand Oaks, CA: Corwin Press.

Crowther, F., Kaagan, S., Ferguson, M., & Hann, L. (2002). *Developing teacher leaders*. Thousand Oaks, CA: Corwin Press.

Day, C., Gu, Q., & Sammons, P. (2016). The impact of leadership on student outcomes: How successful school leaders use transformational and instructional strategies to make a difference. *Educational Administration Quarterly, 52*(2), 221–258.

Degenhardt, L., & Duignan, P. (2010). *Dancing on a Shifting Carpet: Reinventing Traditional Schooling for the 21st Century*. Camberwell, Australia: ACER Press.

Dempster, N. (2006). Leadership and learning: Possible links at the gap state high school. *Leading and Managing, 12*(2), 54–63.

Dempster, N., & Johnson, G. (2006). Inter-relationships between leadership and learning: Some findings from Southside high. *Leading and Managing, 12*(2), 29–39.

Dempster, N., Konza, D., Robson, G., Gaffney, M., Lock, G., & McKennariey, K. (2012). *Principals as literacy leaders: Confident, credible and connected.* Kingston, Australia: Australian Primary Principals' Association.

Dempster, N., Townsend, T., Johnson, G., Bayetto, A., Lovett, S., & Stevens, E. (2017). *Leadership and literacy: Principals, partnerships and pathways to improvement.* Cham, Switzerland: Springer International Publishing.

Dimmock, C., & O'Donoghue, T. (1997). *Innovative school principals and restructuring. Life history portraits of successful managers of change.* London: Routledge.

Dinham, S. (2005). Principal leadership for outstanding educational outcomes. *Journal of Educational Administration, 43*(4), 338–356.

Dinham, S. (2007). The secondary head of department and the achievement of exceptional student outcomes. *Journal of Educational Administration, 45*(1), 62–79.

Dinham, S. (2008). *How to get your school moving and improving.* Melbourne, Australia: ACER Press.

Dinham, S. (2016). *Leading learning and teaching.* Melbourne, Australia: ACER Press.

Drysdale, L. (2001). Towards a model of market Centred leadership. *Leading and Managing, 7*(1), 76–89.

Drysdale, L. (2002). *A study of marketing and market orientation in selected Victorian Schools of the future.* PhD thesis, University of Melbourne, Australia.

Drysdale, L., & Gurr, D. (2011). The theory and practice of successful school leadership in Australia. *School Leadership and Management, 31*(4), 355–368.

Duignan, P., & Gurr, D. (Eds.). (2007a). *Leading Australia's schools.* Sydney, Australia: ACEL and DEST.

Duignan, P., & Gurr, D. (2007b). Hope for a better future. In P. Duignan & D. Gurr (Eds.), *Leading Australia's Schools* (pp. 157–164). Sydney, Australia: ACEL and DEST.

Duignan, P., Marshall, A. R., Harrold, R. I., Phillipps, D. M., Thomas, E. B., & Lane, T. J. (1985). *The Australian school principal: A summary report.* Canberra, Australia: Commonwealth Schools Commission.

Edmonds, R. (1979, October). Effective schools for the urban poor. *Educational Leadership, 37*(1), 15–24.

Fleming, J., & Kleinhenz, E. (2007). *Towards a moving school: Developing a professional learning and performance culture.* Melbourne, Australia: ACER Press.

Goode, H. (2017). *A study of successful principal leadership: Moving from success to sustainability.* Doctor of Philosophy thesis, The University of Melbourne, Australia.

Gurr, D. (2008). *Principal leadership: What does it do, what does it look like, and how might it evolve? Monograph* (Vol. 42). Melbourne, Australia: Australian Council for Educational Leaders.

Gurr, D. (2009). Successful school leadership in Australia. In N. Cranston & L. Erlich (Eds.), *Australian educational leadership today: Issues and trends* (pp. 369–394). Brisbane, Australia: Australian Academic Press.

Gurr, D. (2012). Successful schools, successful leaders: The Australian case. In C. Day (Ed.), *The Routledge international handbook on teacher and school development* (pp. 458–467). London: Routledge.

Gurr, D. (2015). A model of successful school leadership from the international successful school principalship project. *Societies, 5*(1), 136–150.

Gurr, D., & Drysdale, L. (2013). Middle-level school leaders: Potential, constraints and implications for leadership preparation. *Journal of Educational Administration, 51*(1), 55–71.

Gurr, D., & Drysdale, L. (2016a). Successful and effective school leadership: Insights from Australasia. In P. Pashiardis & O. Johansson (Eds.), *Successful school leadership: International perspectives* (pp. 139–154). London: Bloomsbury.

Gurr, D., & Drysdale, L. (2016b). Australia: The principal as leader – A review of Australian principal research, 2006–2013. In H. Ärlestig, C. Day, & O. Johansson (Eds.), *A decade of research on school principals: Cases from 24 countries* (pp. 187–209). Dordrecht, The Netherlands: Springer.

Gurr, D., Drysdale, L., Clarke, S., & Wildy, H. (2014). High needs schools in Australia. *Management in Education, 28*(3), 86–90.

Gurr, D., Drysdale, L., Longmuir, F., & McCrohan, K. (2018). Leading the improvement of schools in challenging circumstances. *International Studies in Educational Administration, 46*(1), 22–44.

Gurr, D., Drysdale, L., & Mulford, B. (2006). Models of successful principal leadership. *School Leadership and Management, 26*(4), 371–395.

Gurr, D., Drysdale, L., & Mulford, B. (2007). Instructional leadership in three Australian schools. *International Studies in Educational Administration, 35*(3), 20–29.

Gurr, D., Drysdale, L., & Mulford, B. (2010). Australian principal instructional leadership: Direct and indirect influences. *Magis, 2*(4), 299–314.

Gurr, D., Drysdale, L., Ylimaki, R., & Moos, l. (2011). Preparing instructional leaders. In R. Ylimaki & S. Jacobson (Eds.), *US and cross-national policies, practices and preparation: Implications for successful instructional leadership, organizational learning, and culturally responsive practices* (pp. 125–152). Dordrecht, The Netherlands: Springer-Kluwer.

Hallinger, P. (2009). *Leadership for 21st century schools: From instructional leadership to leadership for learning.* Hong Kong, China: The Hong Kong Institute of Education.

Hallinger, P. (2011). Leadership for learning: Lessons from 40 years of empirical research. *Journal of Educational Administration, 49*(2), 125–142.

Hallinger, P. (2018). Bringing context out of the shadow. *Educational Management Administration & Leadership, 46*(1), 5–24.

Hallinger, P., & Murphy, J. (1985). Assessing the instructional leadership behavior of principals. *Elementary School Journal, 86*(2), 217–248.

Heck, R. H., Marcoulides, G. A., & Lang, P. (1991). Principal instructional leadership and school achievement: The application of discriminant techniques. *School Effectiveness and School Improvement, 2*(2), 115–135.

Huerta Villalobos, M. (2013). *The role of the critical friend in leadership and school improvement.* Master of Education thesis, The University of Melbourne, Australia.

Jencks, C., Smith, M., Acland, H., Bane, M. J., Cohen, D., Gintis, H., et al. (1972). *Inequality: A reassessment of the effect of family and schooling in America.* New York: Basic Books.

Leithwood, K. (2005). Understanding successful principal leadership: Progress on a broken front. *Journal of Educational Administration, 43*(6), 619–629.

Lewis, M. (2006). It's a different place now: Teacher leadership and pedagogical change at Newlyn Public School. *Leading and Managing, 12*(1), 107–121.

Lewis, M., & Andrews, D. (2007). The dance of influence: Professional relationships evolve as teachers and administrators engage in whole school renewal. *Leading and Managing, 13*(1), 91–107.

Longmuir, F. (2017). *Principal leadership in high-advantage, improving Victorian secondary schools.* Doctor of Philosophy thesis, The University of Melbourne, Australia.

MacBeath, J., Dempster, N., Frost, D., Johnson, G., & Swaffield, S. (Eds.). (2018). *Strengthening the connections between leadership and learning.* London: Routledge.

MacBeath, J., Frost, D., Swaffield, S., & Waterhouse, J. (2003). *Making the connections: The story of a seven-country odyssey in search of a practical theory*. Cambridge, UK: University of Cambridge, Faculty of Education.

Marsh, S. (2012). Improving student learning in schools: Exploring leadership for learning as a community activity. *Leading and Managing, 18*(1), 107–121.

McGaw, B., Piper, K., Banks, D., & Evans, B. (1993a). *Improving Australia's schools: Executive summary of making schools more effective*. Melbourne, Australia: ACER.

McGaw, B., Piper, K., Banks, D., & Evans, B. (1993b). *Making schools more effective: Report of the Australian effective schools' project*. Melbourne, Australia: ACER.

Mulford, B. (2007). *Overview of research on Australian educational leadership, 2001–2005, Monograph, 40*. Melbourne, Australia: Australian Council for Educational Leaders.

Mulford, B., & Silins, H. (2003). Leadership for organisational learning and improved student outcomes. *Cambridge Journal of Education, 33*(2), 175–195.

Mulford, W., Silins, H., & Leithwood, K. (2004). *Educational leadership for organisational learning and improved student outcomes*. Dordrecht, The Netherlands: Kluwer Academic Publishers.

Murphy, J. (1990). Principal instructional leadership. In P. W. Thurston, N. A. Prestine, L. S. Lotto, & P. P. Zodhiates (Eds.), *Advances in educational administration: Changing perspectives on the school, 1 (part B)* (pp. 163–200). Greenwich, CT: JAI Press.

Murphy, J., & Hallinger, P. (1992). The principalship in an era of transformation. *Journal of Educational Administration, 30*(3), 77–88.

Pepper, C., & Wildy, H. (2008). Leading for sustainability: Is surface understanding enough? *Journal of Educational Administration, 46*(5), 613–629.

Pepper, C., & Wildy, H. (2009). Leading and education for sustainability in Western Australian secondary schools. *Leading and Managing, 15*(1), 42–52.

Robinson, V., Lloyd, C., & Rowe, K. (2008). The impact of leadership on student outcomes: An analysis of the differential effects of leadership types. *Educational Administration Quarterly, 44*(5), 635–674.

Rutter, M., Maughan, B., Mortimore, P., & Ouston, J. with Smith, A. (1979). *Fifteen thousand hours: Secondary schools and their effects on children*. London/Boston: Open Books/Harvard University Press.

Simpkins, W. S., Thomas, A. R., & Thomas, E. B. (Eds.). (1987). *Principal and change: The Australian experience*. Armidale, Australia: University of New England.

Swaffield, S. (2004). Critical friends: Supporting leadership, improving learning. *Improving Schools, 7*(3), 267–278.

Swaffield, S., & MacBeath, J. (2005). School self-evaluation and the role of a critical friend. *Cambridge Journal of Education, 35*(2), 239–252.

Thomas, A. R. (Ed.). (2000). *Challenges of the principalship*. Point Lonsdale, Australia: Professional Reading Guide for School Administrators.

Thomas, E. B. (Ed.). (1994). *What every principal needs to know about leadership skills. Point Lonsdale*. Point Lonsdale, Australia: Professional Reading Guide for School Administrators.

Thomas, E. B. (Ed.). (1995). *What every principal needs to know about good schools*. Point Lonsdale, Australia: Professional Reading Guide for School Administrators..

Townsend, T., Acker-Hocevar, M., Ballenger, J., & Place, A. W. (2013). Voices from the field: What have we learned about instructional leadership? *Leadership and Policy in Schools, 12*(1), 60–88.

Twelves, J. B. (2005). *Putting them in the hands of god: A successful Christian school in Australia*. Unpublished doctoral dissertation, The University of Melbourne, Australia.

Wildy, H., & Faulkner, J. (2008). Whole school improvement Australian-style: What do IDEAS and RAISe offer? *Leading and Managing, 14*(2), 83–96.

5

Leadership for Learning in the US

David Imig, South Holden, and Dale Placek

> *The leadership issue of our time is how human communities productively confront complex systemic issues where hierarchical authority is inadequate.*
> Peter Senge, Carnegie Foundation Summit on Improvement Science, 2017

The most recent reauthorization of the *Elementary and Secondary Education Act of 1965* (ESEA) offered policymakers the opportunity to better define the role of the elementary and secondary school principal in the US. The outcome of the nearly seven-year effort was the *Every Student Succeeds Act of 2015* (ESSA), which defined a school leader as "a principal or assistant principal who is responsible for the daily instructional leadership and managerial operations in the elementary or secondary school building" (ESEA, 2015). The law authorized substantial monies for "principal improvement activities" that have the potential to shape

D. Imig (✉) • S. Holden • D. Placek
University of Maryland, College Park, MD, USA
e-mail: dplacek@umd.edu

principal actions "associated with improved student outcomes" (Herman, Gates, Chavez-Herrereasm, & Hares, 2017). The law also called upon states to prepare expansive plans for the implementation of the law and to submit these to the US Department of Education for approval. In these state plans, despite the legislative definition of a school leader, there is evidence of much ambiguity relative to the roles and responsibilities of the school principal.

Earlier federal policymaking in the US pertaining to principal roles and responsibilities was consistent with research evidence that confirmed that principal leadership was second only to teacher effectiveness in promoting student learning (Seashore-Louis, Leithwood, Wahlstrom, & Anderson, 2010). The 2015 law was enacted at a time when there was positive movement by students on measures of student achievement and an insistence that school improvement needed to be maintained. While the US Department of Education was viewed by a majority of policymakers and practitioners as having "overreached" during the Obama administration, there was also a determination to maintain things that had worked from the previous decade in the new legislation. High on that list was an emphasis on strong leadership for schools. While ESSA promoted greater state and local authority for schooling, Washington insisted that school leadership had to be a prominent component of state and district planning for school improvement. ESSA called for the Education Department to formulate policies but leave to states significant discretion in ways of implementing those policies for the 13,500 school districts and 100,000 schools in the US.

This chapter will argue that despite efforts by practitioner organizations and academic scholars to promote a new construct for school leadership that explicitly promotes "leadership for learning" (LfL) or "leading learning", recent education policy formation in the US has sought to maintain a traditional form of instructional leadership. This view of the instructional leader is one of the "strong, directive principal", who is "the master teacher" with exceptional teaching skills, able to mentor beginning teachers and model outstanding instruction for experienced teachers across the broad range of academic courses offered by the school (Honig & Rainey, 2014). While professional standards setting for principal licensure and preparation that preceded passage of ESSA presented a more nuanced view of the principal as instructional leader, focusing on the principal's role in professional capacity building and the promotion of professional learning communities (NPBEA, 2015), the dominant narrative that remains after passage of ESSA is that strong leaders are necessary to "drive" school improvement. The principal as a heroic, visionary, charismatic, and effective instructional leader, who manages both the operation and the conduct of the school, embodies that narrative.

The concept of the principal as an instructional leader is well established in policy formation and practice in the US. Defined by Hallinger and Murphy (1985) as the management of curriculum and instruction, it remains the dominant paradigm in school leadership in the US. Major school administrator and curricular organizations promoted this concept over the past 40 years as school heads or principals struggled to find ways to handle "the managerial imperative" (Cuban, 1988) while realizing the promise of being an instructional leader. Emerging in contrast to the traditional instructional leader construct is a different concept of leadership that has strong roots in Europe (MacBeath, Dempster, Frost, Johnson, & Swaffield, 2018), that has crossed the Atlantic to the US and is found in many contemporary efforts to transform schools. While some argue that this is merely a refinement of the traditional instructional leadership paradigm to put more emphasis on learning as the central focus of schools, others see the emphasis on the capacity building of teachers and staff, greater reliance on multiple forms of teacher leadership and teacher collaboration, and more attention to the school as a learning organization (Knapp, Copland, Honig, Pleki, & Portin, 2010; Murphy, Elliott, Goldring, & Porter, 2006, 2007; Schlechty, 2009) as a significant advancement.

This chapter contends that ESSA promised investment in "new ways" that states and districts could leverage principals to become more effective in their roles as school leaders, but then allowed states to retain an emphasis on the school leader's managerial responsibilities. The retention of much of the accountability framework from the earlier *No Child Left Behind Act of 2001* (NCLB) seems to be causing schools and systems to expect that principals will maintain a prominent role in the shaping of classroom instruction. The strong or heroic or singular school leader remains the dominant model for policymakers and is reflected in the ESSA authorization and in many of the state plans submitted to detail implementation priorities. As we will show, an expansive review of the state plans for the implementation of ESSA indicates that the promise of leading learning seems to have escaped those who either wrote relevant provisions of the law or created rubrics for states to use in developing their plans for the implementation of the law.

Background for Instructional Leadership as a Dominant Narrative

Instructional leadership as a construct for school leadership emerged at least as early as the 1960s but was reinforced by the effective schools' movement of the 1970s and 1980s (Bridges, 1967; Bossert, Dwyer, Rowan, & Lee, 1982; Edmunds, 1979). The principal as an instructional leader challenged the then conventional managerial role of the principal. Slow to "take off" because it was perceived as requiring "deep knowledge of subject matter" and "expansive pedagogical expertise" that was beyond the capacity of many principals, the concept also ran counter to the traditional promotion practices of school districts that focused on a principal's managerial responsibilities. It, nevertheless, was viewed by policymakers and stakeholders as essential in a standards-based education climate. It fit the prevailing narrative that strong leadership would produce effective schools that, in turn, would promote student learning. The idea of the instructional leader as essential for schools to succeed, gave added importance to the idea of the principal as a hierarchical and unidirectional leader in a well-organized school, who exerted maximum influence on all school practices. Many of those who wrote about this form of instructional leadership argued that the principal's authority was derived from their position as a principal in a system where they were charged with implementing district policies and managing well the resources they were provided. As the concept evolved, instructional leadership was viewed as requiring strong individuals making "top-down" decisions regarding the instructional programme of the school, monitoring student progress, and evaluating teacher performance to ensure compliance with district policies and practices.

The Obama administration (2009–2017) greatly expanded the concept of strong school leadership with added accountability expectations and greater reliance on student scores as the measure of principal effectiveness. Also occurring at this time was the impact of the 2008 economic recession that resulted in the loss of administrative staff (assistant principals and curriculum specialists and subject chairs) that forced principals to assume more and more instructional responsibilities. Noteworthy was the fact that fewer administrators necessitated other staff to assume new responsibilities and reinforced the perception that teachers could and should play a much greater role in instructional leadership. The combination of increased accountability and diminished staffing contributed to an expectation that the 2015 reauthorization of ESEA would produce clarity on principal role definition and more resources for principal development. As this chapter will show, what ESSA produced was a call for continued principal leadership by strong leaders in unidirectional roles who both manage the operation of schools and lead the learning of teachers and students.

Chapter Organization

In each of the following sections of this chapter, we examine more closely policies at the federal, state, and district levels. At the federal level, we outline the major changes impacting school leaders from the No Child Left Behind Act of 2001 (NCLB) to ESSA (2016)—the most recent reauthorization of the 1965 Elementary and Secondary Education Act (ESEA). At the state level, we conduct an "Instructional Leadership" (IL) and "Leadership for Learning" (LfL) review of the 50 ESSA State Plans—which outline state-specific strategies to meet the federal ESSA requirements. At the district level, we investigate how current methods of principal evaluation (mostly prior to ESSA implementation) demonstrate evidence of the "Instructional Leadership" and "Leadership for Learning" philosophy at the local level. Throughout these sections, we consider whether these policies demonstrate a "shift" *from* IL and *towards* LfL ideas in the US. In a concluding section, however, we acknowledge that while we have not found evidence of that shift, the relationship might in fact be more complicated than a simple *before* and *after* picture. We follow with a summary of challenges to a more full adoption of "Leadership for Learning" in the US and conclude with a statement regarding the limitations to our review.

ESEA, and the Shift from NCLB to ESSA

In December 2015, President Obama signed Congress's reauthorization of the 1965 Elementary and Secondary Education Act (ESEA). This reauthorization, known as the Every Student Succeeds Act (ESSA), replaced the previous 2002 Bush Administration reauthorization known as No Child Left Behind (NCLB).

Although many parts of ESSA address the roles and responsibilities of principals either directly or indirectly, the primary area where shifts from NCLB to ESSA may have been the greatest was in Title II—"Preparing, Training, and Recruiting High-Quality Teachers, Principals, or Other School Leaders". These Title II provisions, according to the National Association of Elementary School Principals (NAESP), can potentially help the US establish a "robust principal pipeline" that not only ensures a highly qualified principal in every school but also meets the increasing demand for more principals that the US will experience in the coming years (NAESP, 2016).

Part A of Title II of ESSA authorizes a number of programmes intended to (a) increase student achievement consistent with challenging State academic standards; (b) improve the quality and effectiveness of teachers, principals, and other school leaders; (c) increase the number of teachers, principals, and other school leaders who are effective in improving student academic achievement in schools; and (d) provide low-income and minority students greater access to effective teachers, principals, and other school leaders. States can now use up to 3% of Title IIA funds for the development and support of principals (a new provision). The law also requires states to consult with principals on how to best put those principal development funds to use (ESSA, 2015). In addition to these Title IIA funding provisions, ESSA also allows states to create teacher, principal, and school leadership academies, expand "job-embedded" professional development activities, and require that professional development should be collaborative with the ability for teachers to apply what they learn with immediacy. In addition, Title II retitles the "Teacher Incentive Fund" programme as the "Teacher and School Leader Incentive Grants" programme which provides monies to states and districts for performance-based preparation programmes or for other ways to develop human capital. The law also allows states to develop new forms of teacher and principal evaluations but stipulates that if states/districts use Title II funds to create or improve teacher evaluation, that those evaluations must be based "in part" on student achievement and rely on other multiple measures such as observations or student surveys.

State ESSA Plans

ESSA required that each state submit a "State ESSA Plan" to outline how they intended to meet the requirements of the law, as well as how they generally envisioned using the authorized funds available to them. Templates for these state plans were developed and transmitted to each Chief State School Officer (and later modified by the incoming Trump administration). The authors of this chapter have used these state plans to analyse whether states have put a premium on new forms of instructional leadership or chosen to embark in new directions for leading learning. By next examining the state plan responses to the ESSA law, the authors sought to gain an understanding of whether this federal legislation enables or encourages states to adopt leadership for learning or retains an emphasis on both traditional and evolving forms of instructional leadership.

The ESSA state plans provide a fairly detailed and precise description of their accountability system as required or mandated under Title 1. The details for their accountability plans are often lost in the Title IIA section where the majority of state plans devote only a few pages to their planning for teacher and principal development. These pages are often dominated by descriptions of professional learning systems and teacher preparation pipelines, with only a few sentences describing the role of leadership in schools. For example, North Dakota devotes over 60 pages to describing accountability measures for schools, principals, teachers, and students and three pages to describing their plan to support principal and educator development. The result is that many ESSA plans provide a surface-level description of the anticipated role that leadership will play in schools, failing to provide details about the actions and roles school leaders will take in their states. Despite the ambiguity of the plans, certain themes about principals, leadership, and professional learning emerge.

When reviewing the ESSA plans, we found an absence of the term "leadership for learning" (LfL), showing that the terminology has not made its way into the vocabulary of most state actors. As LfL was not clearly stated, we looked for evidence of the principles of IL as described by Hallinger and Murphy (1985) and the principles of LfL described by MacBeath and Cheng (2008) (see Table 5.1 below).

We found that states' responses to ESSA's focus on leadership were a miscellany of approaches for principals to support effective educators in schools. The dominant approach to leadership in schools appears to be managerial (Hallinger & Murphy, 1985). States that adopted this approach often focused on the principal as a strong leader, the need to focus on data and evaluation, and the prescribed nature of professional learning. Teacher leadership and collaborative learning approaches were popular concepts among states, showing signs of moving towards a focus on shared leadership and learning (MacBeath & Cheng, 2008). However, the meaning and application of these terms seems to diverge, showing little consensus for what it means to learn collaboratively and draw on teacher leadership. Finally, there are some states that recognize the Learning Forward standards, inspired by LfL. However, these states do

Table 5.1 The principles associated with instructional leadership and leadership for learning

Instructional Leadership (Hallinger & Murphy, 1985)	Leadership for Learning (MacBeath & Cheng, 2008)
1. Defines the School Mission 2. Manages the Instructional Programme 3. Promotes a Positive School-Learning Climate	1. Maintains a Focus on Learning as an Activity 2. Creates Conditions Favourable to Learning as an Activity 3. Creates a Dialogue About LfL 4. Shares Leadership 5. Shares Accountability

not appear to have planned for how to create a leadership system that shares accountability for student growth (MacBeath & Cheng, 2008). The themes that emerge from the ESSA plans show a wide variety of approaches to school leadership.

Heroism, Evaluation, and Data

Hallinger and Murphy (1985) described the ideal principal as an instructional leader having strong-mindedness, directness, top-down management skills, and charisma. They contended that the principal is *the* leader of the school, defining the school mission, managing the instructional programme, and promoting a positive school-learning climate. The majority of states appear to have maintained this instructional leadership role for the principal in their ESSA plans.

Heroism

The principal as a charismatic and strong leader, ready to drive school improvement, appears in multiple ESSA plans. Massachusetts and Tennessee provide examples of how state plans explicitly stated the importance of the principal. Massachusetts focused on the principal as the key factor in transforming high-need schools, using "turnaround schools" strategies for effective intervention and sustainable improvement. Similarly, Tennessee has created an Academy for School Leaders that focuses on the preparation of transformational principals who drive growth to achieve improved student outcomes. Tennessee's "equation to success" appears to be a strong principal with many skills (such as instructional leader and staff manager) using evidence-based interventions that result in student success. The Governor of Tennessee, in 2013, captured the heroic principal notion in a statement that the Tennessee ESSA plan quotes:

> Principals are responsible for hiring and retaining great teachers, being the instructional leaders of their schools, creating positive learning environments and managing complex operations within their buildings. Successful

organizations have great leaders at the top, and one of the most important things we can do to transform our schools is to have each one led by a great principal. Tennessee has many great principals already, and we want even more. (Tennessee ESSA Plan)

This heroic view of the principal is consistent with the concept of instructional leadership (Hallinger & Murphy, 1985), but states did not always explicitly use this term in their plans. Many states represented the managerial aspect of the principal's role explicitly or implicitly through descriptions of the principal relying on an array of data and the use of teacher evaluation protocols. Evaluation and the reliance on data are seen as key to learning in schools.

Evaluation and the Use of Data

For the majority of ESSA plans, evaluation of student learning and teacher instruction (student assessment and observation data) receives more attention than the process of learning for teachers (professional learning). This focus means that the role of principals is more heavily weighted towards evaluating teachers and using data from the evaluations to assign professional learning rather than understanding and creating a process for teachers to learn. Iowa, Mississippi, and South Carolina's plans are examples of slightly different ways that student assessment and teacher observation data are expected to be used by principals. All of these plans require the principal to adopt the role of manager for professional learning, gathering as much data as possible to construct professional development interventions (Hallinger & Murphy, 1985). Iowa's plan suggests that school leaders should "provide learning opportunities" for others through a cycle of data collection, goal setting, content providing, and measuring outcomes (Iowa ESSA Plan, p. 100). Mississippi and South Carolina both utilize state-run educator evaluation systems to determine professional learning needs. Principals are charged with aligning teacher needs to professional learning activities based on data gathered from these evaluations systems.

For some states, the principal's role in professional learning appears to be more manager than prescriber. Colorado and Arizona are examples of plans that have the state as a major determiner of professional learning. Colorado uses gathered data to identify what should be learned by teachers and then provides targeted technical assistance to schools and a list of evidence-based interventions and strategies (Colorado ESSA Plan, p. 95). Arizona also offers free and low-cost training aimed at strengthening teachers' content knowledge and instruction (Arizona ESSA Plan, p. 53). The principal's role in these state-driven professional learning systems is sometimes unclear. One can assume that the principal is charged with monitoring the state-mandated professional learning intervention.

The focus on outcomes and instruction when states and principals decide on professional learning means that there is a lack of focus on how teachers learn and improve. There appears to be an assumption, in many state plans, that delivering content to teachers, through face-to-face, blended, or online learning formats, will be enough to help them improve in the classroom. This prescriptive form of teacher learning fails to meet the principle of learning for all that is championed by LfL (MacBeath & Cheng, 2008). There are some states that do recognize the need for a focus on teacher learning by advocating the use of professional learning communities (PLCs). However, as we discuss later, the process of learning within a PLC is not "fleshed out" in detail in most state plans.

Teacher Leadership and Collaborative Learning: Patchwork Approach to Changing School Leadership in an Evaluation Environment

The terms "teacher leadership" and "collaborative learning" are used in many of the ESSA plans. Teacher leadership carries with it different definitions and is recognized as something different from district to district and state to state. Maryland's state plan calls for the state agency to find a common definition and promote its use throughout the state. The terms "teacher leadership" and "collaborative learning" appear to align with the concepts of shared leadership and a focus on learning (MacBeath & Cheng, 2008). However, there does not appear to be a clear and consistent definition of the term and the role of the principal and, therefore, it is difficult to say that states have adopted key principles of LfL.

Teacher Leadership

The concept of shared leadership, where multiple members of the school community are responsible for learning, is an important part of LfL (MacBeath & Cheng, 2008). Teacher leadership, as a form of shared leadership, is a popular concept of many of the ESSA plans. However, what teacher leadership is, what a teacher leader does, and how you learn to become a teacher leader are not well defined. Indiana's ESSA plan describes the development of a "Teach to Lead" initiative; however, the roles and responsibilities of the teacher leader are missing from the plan. Other state plans, such as Illinois', recognize the importance of shared leadership, but call for more efforts to increase understanding of the role and work of teacher leaders (Illinois ESSA Plan, p. 98). Without a clear understanding of the role and work of teacher leaders, it is difficult to know what role the principal is expected to take in teacher leadership.

There are some states that have defined teacher leadership more clearly, but they appear to apply it to the top-down approach of instructional leadership. For example, Idaho describes a teacher leader as someone who delivers professional learning experiences to other teachers. Louisiana provides a more detailed description of a teacher leader and what they do. In Louisiana, 5000 teacher leaders (about three per school), receive training and a monthly newsletter from the state. They are then charged to share what they learn with other members of the school. Even though the state has adopted the term "teacher leader", they are not using it as a form of shared leadership, but rather as a form of top-down leadership.

Collaborative Learning and Professional Learning Communities

Collaborative learning is also a component of shared leadership in LfL (MacBeath & Cheng, 2008). Many states have championed the idea of developing a more collaborative professional learning environment. Texas focuses on the role of the principal in that collaborative environment. The principal is expected to meet with teachers to analyse student work and formative assessment data, to observe and coach teacher leaders who work with their peers, and to promote collaborative analysis of data and promote teacher use of root cause analysis as a form of self-reflection.

PLCs are a popular approach to teacher learning. For example, Tennessee plans to promote personalized learning through PLCs and more frequent coaching and feedback (Tennessee ESSA Plan, p. 247). However, the form and function of a PLC is not fully developed. Given Tennessee's support of the need for a principal as "great leader" (discussed earlier), there are contradictory concepts being championed in one state plan. Arkansas hints at what happens in a PLC, stating that they must be facilitated by expert, experienced teachers. However, it is unclear whether the PLC is structured for the expert teacher to teach the other teachers or for the expert teacher to facilitate shared leadership. The inner workings of PLCs and the role of principals in facilitating them is not well enough defined in the ESSA plans to say whether states have adopted the principles of LfL. Despite the ambiguity around PLCs, there are some ESSA plans that do hint at the possibility of moving towards principles of LfL.

A Real Change?

The leadership for learning concept of *the school as a learning organization* emerged in a few states. Things that matter in this vision, in addition to student performance, are professional learning communities, the building of trusting relationships between teachers, students, administrators, and parents, networks focused on student and adult learning, reliance on a shared vision, and promoting collective practices and shared learning. Here, the principal is a facilitator or enabler of learning, cultivating leadership in others, who recognizes the potential of teacher learning as the way to strengthen instructional practices.

Learning Forward Adopters

State plans from New Hampshire, Maryland, North Carolina, Oklahoma, Illinois, and Delaware indicate that these states are adopters of the Learning Forward standards. These standards are a departure from earlier standards for professional development. They borrow heavily from LfL concepts and acknowledge efforts by academics in Australia, New Zealand and Canada to frame and use the standards (Hirsh, 2018). They call for new forms of educator learning in which educators are enrolled "as active partners in determining the content of their learning, how their learning occurs, and how they evaluate its effectiveness". The standards put a premium on learning communities, call for a commitment to continuous improvement, promote collective responsibility, create opportunities for alignment and accountability, and rely on data to determine student and teacher learning needs. While other states champion many of the principles of LfL and embrace Learning Forward's Standards for Professional Learning, these concepts are not pervasive in ESSA state planning.

Delaware adopted the Learning Forward standards in 2012 and focuses its efforts on creating a "meaningful and differentiated form of professional learning" (Delaware ESSA Plan, p. 79) that goes beyond evaluation and incorporates individualized coaching. Principals are viewed in the Delaware plan as the driving force behind collaborative and individual teacher learning. New Hampshire promotes personalized learning options for teachers and is working to develop collective responsibility for improved student performance. In both of these plans, principals are the drivers for professional learning for teachers.

An Expanding Definition of the School Leader

Nebraska and Oklahoma both adopted the Learning Forward standards, but still maintain systems that focus heavily on the school principal as the traditional instructional leader. Oklahoma is not as descriptive in their discussion of the role of the principal, despite adopting the Learning Forward standards, but appeals for a strong instructional leader in every school (Oklahoma ESSA Plan, p. 149). Nebraska's plan is more detailed, and calls for mobilizing schools, districts, and education service units (ESUs) to embrace systems of evaluation and support continual and focused growth, produce evidence to inform professional growth activities, and build capacity of building administrators to serve as instructional leaders (Nebraska ESSA Plan, p. 161). Nebraska seems to rely heavily on the Learning Forward concepts but seeks to expand the role and definition of the modern-day principal to be someone who must be an instructional leader, a visionary community organizer, a data analyst, a change agent, a team builder, and a cultivator of leadership in others. The Nebraska state plan contends that the modern-day principal must be prepared to engage in the processes of hiring and dismissing of teachers, serving as a coach for teachers' continual improvement, cultivating a safe and secure learning environment, and nurturing a collaborative culture of shared accountability. Seemingly, the modern principal can do everything.

Against the Hero Narrative

Michigan's ESSA plan seems to be the most adoptive of the LfL principles. They use language to emphasize that the goal is ***not*** a single superhero principal whose individual "herculean" effort is responsible for school improvement that is not sustainable. Instead, they see the principal as part of a collective staff that aims to provide students with access to an "effective learning environment" (Michigan ESSA Plan, p. 74). This distributive leadership model puts learning at its centre. However, they still see the value of using locally adopted formative and summative evaluation systems for teachers and leaders to receive individualized professional learning. What that individualized learning looks like is not fully explored. Coaching and mentoring seem to be the primary learning approach for teachers and leaders and teacher leader voices are seen as important to regional and state-level policy. It is unclear whether states are going to move towards Michigan's focus on learning or remain fixated on prescriptive forms of professional learning. We explore principal evaluation at the district level to see if concepts of IL and LfL seen in the ESSA plans have made their way to local practices.

IL and LfL in Action: Principal Evaluation at the District Level

Principal evaluation grew from the push for standards and accountability that began in the 1980s with *A Nation at Risk* (1983) and continued with the school leadership "paradigm wars" of the 1990s (Murphy, Seashore-Louis, & Smylie, 2017). By looking at how a sample of large US school districts are currently evaluating their principals (either before, after, or in addition to ESSA implementation), we sought to gain further understanding of whether (or how) ideas associated with IL and LfL are influencing leadership policy and practice in schools in the US. First, however, we briefly recount efforts by national education organizations (since the 1990s) to establish a shared set of educational leadership standards and principal evaluation methods. Others (e.g., Canole & Young, 2013) have traced these histories in much greater depth, but the summary that follows aims to provide sufficient context for understanding current evaluation protocols in major school districts in the US.

In 1996, the National Policy Board for Educational Administration (NPBEA), in partnership with the Council of Chief State School Officers (CCSSO), created what they hoped would be the first set of national standards for educational leadership in the US. A coalition of NPBEA and CCSSO members formed the Interstate School Leaders Licensure Consortium (ISLLC) and created the instructional leadership-focused ISLLC Standards for School Leaders. In the next decade, 46 states either adopted these standards outright or used them as a template to develop their own state- or district-level standards (Canole & Young, 2013). In 2008, in part due to increased demands on principals as a result of the accountability measures of No Child Left Behind, the consortium revised the standards to produce the 2008 ISLLC Standards for Educational Leadership. These standards included the following domains of effective principal leadership (Shipman & Murphy, 1996; Van Meter & Murphy, 1997):

1. Vision, mission, and goals;
2. Teaching and learning;
3. Managing organizational systems and safety;
4. Collaborating with families and stakeholders;
5. Ethics and integrity; and
6. The educational system.

In 2015, the consortium once again revised the ISLLC 2008 standards (newly named the Professional Standards for Educational Leaders, or PSELs) in an effort to respond to an increasingly technology-driven, diversity-focused, and globally interconnected world. The new and modified standards addressed the CCSSO and NPBEA insistence that the 2015 PSELs have (a) a stronger, clearer emphasis on success (academic and general well-being) for "each" and "all" students; (b) a more systemic view of leadership work with evidence that links leadership practices to learning; and (c) components of equity and cultural responsiveness, including promoting meaningful engagement of families and communities (NPBEA, 2015). The standards use neither instructional leadership nor leading learning, but a new Standard 7 puts emphasis on "[empowering] and [entrusting] teachers and staff with collective responsibility" (p. 22), and Standard 6 encourages school leaders to "foster continuous improvement of individual and collective instructional capacity" (p. 20). The PSELs were quickly embraced by states and districts seeking ways of both defining the principal's role and responsibilities, and fashioning evaluation protocols to be used to assess principal performance.

Parallel to the development of the PSELs, NPBEA sought to create a reliable evaluation system to measure the capacities and capabilities of practising principals as part of its portfolio. Eventually, they turned to the National Board for Professional Teaching Standards (NBPTS) to use its resources to develop a valid and reliable assessment protocol. Despite their best efforts to develop such a protocol that was based on another set of standards, NBPTS shuttered this initiative in 2014, after a five-year and $3.5 million effort proved to be financially untenable (Maxwell, 2014), but left the community with the Accomplished Principal Standards, which emphasize nine priorities (NBPTS, 2010):

1. Leadership for Results
2. Vision and Mission
3. Teaching and Learning
4. Knowledge of students and adults
5. Culture
6. Strategic Management
7. Advocacy
8. Ethics
9. Reflection and Growth

Although these standards, as well as the PSELs, show evidence of principles and practices associated with LfL (especially standards pertaining to the principal's responsibility for building the professional capacity of school personnel), they stop short of a full embrace of the principles associated with leading learning. This shortcoming might ultimately be because the very notion of principal evaluation is, in itself, rooted in the ideas of "instructional leadership". That we might go into a school to observe the practice of the one school leader and come away with an understanding of how successful that person is or is not at leading the school to success is an important assumption that underlies much of the leadership standards work of the last 20–30 years, and that we therefore see throughout evaluation systems as they still exist today. While countless evaluation protocols used to assess the effectiveness of school leaders have emerged, few of them embody the concepts and principles inherent in leading learning.

Principal Evaluation in Large US School Districts: IL, LfL, or Both?

The 25 most populous school districts in the US account for 50.3 million students—11.7% of all students attending public schools in the US (NCES, 2016), and represent varying levels of academic performance and yearly per-pupil school funding (see US Department of Commerce, 2015). Examination of these districts' practices for evaluating principals (sometimes known as school-based administrators, or SBAs) affirms that, while we may be moving towards LfL in small or fragmented ways, ideas associated with IL still weigh most heavily on how we think about the job of a principal in schools in the US.

The districts in our sample of 25 currently evaluate their principals in strikingly similar ways to one another. In light of the history of the development and early 2000s adoption of the original ISLLC standards, this commonality is not surprising. As mentioned above, New York State uses the PSELs outright, while the Los Angeles Unified School District (LAUSD) has created their own school leadership framework that specifically cites the corresponding PSEL and California Professional Standards for Educational Leadership (CPSEL) standards. One of the CPSEL standards comes close to embodying LfL principles. That standard (CPSEL Standard 5) reads as follows: "I. Leadership and Professional Growth—School: Leaders have a responsibility to be the 'chief learner' at a school site, modelling reflective practice, ethical decision-making, professional growth, and other learning-centred leadership behaviours" (Los Angeles Unified School District, 2016).

In contrast to LAUSD's language above, other principal evaluation systems from our sample of districts seem to lean heavily on the tenets of Hallinger and Murphy's (1985) framework for IL. Several of the districts even use the exact term "Instructional Leadership" as a broad section header, standard, or criterion (e.g., LAUSD; Fairfax County Public Schools, VA; Clark County Public Schools, Las Vegas NV; Houston Independent School District, Texas). Additionally, nearly all of the above systems list the following tasks as essential priorities for principal practice: (a) defining and communicating the school's mission or leadership vision; (b) supervising and evaluating teachers and administering or coordinating professional development; (c) fostering positive and professional relationships with, between, and among students, teachers, parents, and staff; and (d) collecting, evaluating, and using data to set the school improvement agenda. Also vital to principal evaluation systems in these districts is the combination of "professional practice" (or some similar principal behaviour-focused heading) with some kind of "student performance" metric. That is, the tasks above may account for only half of a principal's evaluation data, while student attendance, retention, and performance on standardized district and state assessments account for the other 50%. School systems from our sample that make use of this approach are the New York City Public Schools, Clark County Schools (Las Vegas NV), Prince George's County Public Schools (MD), and all Florida School Leadership Evaluation System schools, which include Miami-Dade, Broward County (Ft. Lauderdale), Hillsborough County (Tampa), Orange County (Orlando), Duval (Jacksonville), and Palm Beach County Schools. This practice in principal evaluation is still in line with requirements from No Child Left Behind, and we are yet to see changes emanating from ESSA, which leaves much more discretion to districts and states in the formulation of new evaluation protocols. Additionally, all of the approved ESSA state plans require districts to put into place a school-ranking system for all schools that makes similar demands on districts.

Similar to our findings from examining state ESSA plans, principal evaluation protocols in the 25 largest US school districts demonstrate little systematic commitment to the ideas of LfL. LAUSD's and NYC Public Schools' protocols make *some* headway, referencing "shared leadership", "professional collaboration", and the building of leadership capacity in teachers, students, families, and other members of the greater school community (LAUSD School Leadership Framework, NYC Principal Performance Review, PPO Scoring Tool). In most other cases, however, the word "shared" references the principal's role in ensuring that the mission and goals of the school are *shared* ones. While this task of developing and communicating a shared vision or mission *could* be highly collaborative, the language, in practice, seems to refer more to a hierarchical process of achieving community adherence to a principal-defined mission and school goals (i.e., it is the principal's job to ensure that school stakeholders *share* the *principal's vision* for the school).

While the criteria in IL-centric principal evaluation systems may be important for school success, proponents of LfL might argue that in examining school leadership practice through only the hierarchical lens of the principal, we are missing the bigger picture of what it means for a school to be a place where *everyone* takes on roles of teacher and learner—where *everyone* is responsible for leading their *own* learning, as well as contributing to the learning of others. The Comprehensive Assessment of Leadership for Learning (CALL) is an example of a leadership evaluation system that subverts that hierarchical approach in favour of a *school-wide* assessment (Kelley & Halverson, 2014). The CALL (developed over the last decade by Carolyn Kelley, Richard Halverson, and James Shaw at the University of Wisconsin-Madison) is a 40-minute-long online survey for all teachers, administrators, and student support staff that is specifically *not* a method of evaluating a school's principal, but rather a way of characterizing both formal and informal leadership *practices* in areas such as professional development, teacher collaboration, parent/teacher conferences, faculty meetings, discipline policies, and serving students from special populations. While the CALL is not yet widely used in the US, it does provide a vision for where school leadership evaluation could be headed in the years to come.

Chapter Limitations and LfL Challenges in the US

In this chapter, we have alluded to limitations of our investigation, as well as to challenges that widespread adoption of LfL faces in the US. We conclude with a brief summary of both, followed by some thoughts on the relationship between the two leadership paradigms.

Limitations

Although President Obama signed ESSA in 2015, we are, 4 years later, still very much in a time of transition between NCLB and ESSA. Ironically, legislation that was intended to constrain the Obama administration's oversight and direction for school reform now limits the Trump administration from exercising sweeping changes in the form and function of public schools in the US. Expansive federal authorizations like ESSA generally "phase in" over an extended period and a change of presidential administrations (including the appointment of a new Secretary of Education) has led to different interpretations of (and guidance on) aspects of the law. Thus far, Congress has been unwilling to embrace school policy proposals generated by the Trump administration and states and districts seem slow to enact changes mandated by ESSA. During this time of transition, states have filed for and received various extensions on state plan submission or enactments of aspects of the law. At the time of the writing of this chapter, all 50 states plans have been approved by the Department of Education with an expectation that implementation will begin with the beginning of the school year 2018–19.

It is also still too early for us to determine how states will put into action the conceptions of, and priorities for, leadership expressed in ESSA state plans. Most ESSA plans involve outlines of programmes and priorities with the expectation that state governance will do additional planning and budgeting before actually implementing their plans. Furthermore, although ESSA gives states the ability to allocate up to 3% of Title IIA funding for principal development, this additional funding for principals is not a requirement. Since states are also now allowed to spend up to 100% of Title IIA funds on Title I activities, we may find in the future that ESSA implementation contributes to *less* funding for the recruitment and training of high-quality teachers and school leaders.

Leadership for Learning in the US: Challenges and Considerations

Throughout this chapter, we have found repeatedly that the conception and practice of school leadership in the US is weighted heavily towards ideas associated with IL. Although our investigation revealed federal, state, and district consideration of some ideas associated with LfL (e.g., PLCs, cultivating leadership in others, creating a climate for learning, teacher leadership), implementation of these ideas is often hierarchical or inconsistent across states or levels of government. While networks of schools and school leaders in several states now embrace concepts from LfL, we found no systematic attempt by national, state, or local education authorities to adopt LfL or its associated ideas as a consistent school leadership philosophy.

The authors identified several challenges to widespread adoption of LfL (or its associated ideas) in the US. A first challenge is the organization of the American educational system. Because education is a state responsibility, nationwide educational movements are extraordinarily complex and lead to a fierce debate about governmental overreach, big vs. small government, and states' rights. Although states *could* come together to redefine not only leadership standards (as with the PSELs) but the way we think about leadership for schools in the US, there are few incentives to do so at this time.

Another challenge is our deeply ingrained systems of accountability, evaluation, and data collection/analysis. US accountability and evaluation systems prioritize individual responsibility and duties over collective responsibility, and our data collection emphasizes primarily quantitative data measuring "student results" without much deep analysis of situated causes or processes to explain "root causes" for learning (or lack thereof). These systems seem to lend themselves to conversations about blame and guilt, and therefore shorter tenures for principals and superintendents.

Conclusion

Townsend, in Chap. 1, asked whether instructional leadership and leading learning were two sides of the same coin. The review of the literature and of the state plans prepared in response to ESSA and selected principal evaluation protocols suggest that they are distinctly different. Embedded in the instructional leadership construct is the heroic leader dominating every aspect of the school environment. While there are a few references to the other side of the coin, with the principal as the *lead learner* for a school, these are infrequent references and found in very few state plans and evaluation protocols. The PSEL standards promote a new form of leadership without explicit reference to LfL that captures many of the features of leading learning. We did not find much evidence that these standards are being implemented. This may be a variation on the theme of instructional leadership but it also may presage a fundamental shift in the way that teachers and students and leaders learn together. In this model, hierarchical leadership gives way to leadership that promotes a professional community of learners engaged in a common purpose of ensuring all students learn.

The chapter review also suggests that while instructional leadership remains the dominant paradigm for school leadership, there is an emerging consensus that schools need to be very different from those that dominate the American landscape. This time, however, the change will come from within schools and come from the bottom up. Driving such change will not be massive federal mandates but, rather, much experimentation by states and districts with new assessments and curriculum, teacher assignments and school structures. It may be exhaustion from a decade of efforts by Washington to reform schools, but what is emerging is a landscape of local efforts to make schools more student-centric with students having a greater voice in their own learning. Individualization or personalization is much talked about, with philanthropic foundations supporting experimentation with these ideas, but at the heart of these new designs resides an ambition that students will cross traditional disciplinary and age-based boundaries and engage with other students with similar interest and proficiency. The American aversion to tracking—based on the sordid history of racial segregation and assignment—seems to be giving way to new ways of grouping by interest and opportunity. The disciplinary curriculum is giving way to more problem-based study with flexible assignments and the end of traditional age groupings in favour of individual learning. The challenges of transforming thousands of schools in hundreds of school districts in the US are enormous but ESSA has created a space and an opportunity for this to occur.

References

Bossert, S. T., Dwyer, D. C., Rowan, B., & Lee, G. V. (1982). The instructional management role of the principal. *Educational Administration Quarterly, 18*(3), 34–64.
Bridges, E. (1967). Instructional leadership: A concept re-examined. *Journal of Educational Administration, 5*(2), 136–147.
Canole, M., & Young, M. (2013). *Standards for school leaders: An analysis.* Washington, DC: Council of Chief State School Officers. Retrieved from http://www.ccsso.org/Documents/Analysis%20of%20Leadership%20Standards-Final-070913-RGB.pdf
Cuban, L. (1988). *The managerial imperative and the practice of leadership.* Albany, NY: SUNY Press.
Edmunds, R. R. (1979). Effective schools for the urban poor. *Educational Leadership., 37*(1), 15–24.
ESSA. (2015). Every Student Succeeds Act of 2015, Pub. L. No. 114-95 114 Stat. 1177 (2015–2016).
ESSA Implementation Begins. (2016, March). Retrieved July 31, 2016 from http://www.nea.org/essabegins
Hallinger, P., & Murphy, J. (1985). Assessing the instructional leadership behavior of principals. *Elementary School Journal, 86*(2), 217–248.
Herman, R., Gates, S., Chavez-Herrereasm, E. R., & Hares, M. (2017). *School leadership interventions under the ESSA: Evidence review.* Washington, DC: RAND.
Hirsh, S. (2018). Personal Communication, May 17.
Honig, M. I., & Rainey, L. R. (2014). Central office leadership in principal professional learning communities: The practice beneath the policy. *Teachers College Record, 116*(4), 48.
Kelley, C., & Halverson, R. (2014). *CALL one page.* Retrieved from Comprehensive Assessment for Leadership for Learning: https://drive.google.com/file/d/0B23hYAPyfdPdLWVtVmMwUWJjX0E/view
Knapp, M. S., Copland, M. A., Honig, M., Pleki, M. L., & Portin, B. S. (2010). *Learning-focused leadership and leadership support: Meaning and practice in urban systems.* Seattle, WA: University of Washington, Center for the Study of Teaching and Policy.
Los Angeles Unified School District. (2016, May 20). Retrieved May 2018, from LAUSD School Leadership Framework v4: https://achieve.lausd.net/

cms/lib/CA01000043/Centricity/Domain/434/LAUSD%20School%20 Leadership%20Framework.pdf

MacBeath, J., & Cheng, Y. C. (2008). *Leadership for learning: International perspectives*. Rotterdam, The Netherlands: Sense Publishers.

MacBeath, J., Dempster, N., Frost, D., Johnson, G., & Swaffield, S. (2018). *Strengthening the connections between leadership and learning: Challenges to policy, school and classroom practice*. London: Routledge.

Maxwell, L. A. (2014, April 12). *National board votes to end principal-certification program*. Retrieved June 2018, from *Education Week*: http://blogs.edweek.org/edweek/District_Dossier/2014/04/national_board_votes_to_end_pr.html

Murphy, J., Elliott, S., Goldring, E., & Porter, A. (2006). *Learning centered leadership: A conceptual foundation*. Nashville, TN: Learning Science Institute, Vanderbilt University.

Murphy, J., Elliott, S. N., Goldring, E., & Porter, A. C. (2007). Leadership for learning: A research-based model and taxonomy of behaviors. *School Leadership and Management, 27*(2), 179–201.

Murphy, J., Seashore-Louis, K., & Smylie, M. (2017). Positive school leadership: How professional standards for education leaders can be brought to life. *Phi Delta Kappan, 99*(1), 21–24.

National Board for Professional Teaching Standards. (2010). *National board certification for educational leaders: Accomplished principal standards*. Retrieved June 2018, from http://npbea.org/wp-content/uploads/2017/05/NBPTS-Certification-Standards.pdf

National Center for Education Statistics. (2016). *Table 215.30: Enrollment, poverty, and federal funds for the 120 largest school districts, by enrollment size in 2014: Selected years, 2013–14 through 2016*. Retrieved from National Center for Education Statistics: https://nces.ed.gov/programs/digest/d16/tables/dt16_215.30.asp?current=yes

National Commission on Excellence in Education. (1983). A nation at risk: The imperative for educational reform. *The Elementary School Journal, 84*(2), 113–130.

National Policy Board for Educational Administration. (2015). *Professional standards for educational leaders 2015*. Reston, VA: Author.

NCLB. (2001). No Child Left Behind Act of 2001, Pub. L. No. 107-110, 20 U.S.C. 6319 (2002).

Schlechty, P. P. (2009). *Leading for learning: How to transform schools into learning organizations*. San Francisco: Wiley.

Seashore-Louis, K., Leithwood, K., Wahlstrom, K. L., & Anderson, S. E. (2010). *Learning from leadership: Investigating the links to improved student learning*. St. Paul, MN: University of Minnesota, Center for Applied Research and Educational Improvement.

Shipman, N., & Murphy, J. (1996). *Interstate school leaders' licensure consortium: Standards for school leaders*. Washington, DC: Council of Chief State School Officers.

US Department of Commerce. (2015, June). *Public education finances: 2013*. Retrieved from United States Census Bureau: https://www2.census.gov/govs/school/13f33pub.pdf

Van Meter, E., & Murphy, J. (1997). *Using ISLLC standards to strengthen preparation programs in school administration*. Washington, DC: Council of Chief State School Officers.

6

Leading Learning in Schools in Challenging Times: Findings from Research in Portugal

Maria Assunção Flores and Fernando Ilídio Ferreira

Introduction

Leadership has been the subject of discussion, reflection and investigation over the last decades, particularly in the English-speaking world (for a synthesis, see, for instance, English, 2005 and Townsend & MacBeath, 2011). As Townsend and MacBeath (2011) state, concepts related to running organisations such as schools have evolved. Management, for instance, seems to be seen as a constraining term, associated with ensuring conformity, uniformity and stasis whereas leadership emerged as an alternative concept, linked to change, development and movement. However, they underline that 'the best managers have all the qualities of a leader, because even conformity and uniformity these days involve change and development, and the best leaders all have to manage well' (pp. vii–viii).

M. A. Flores (✉) • F. I. Ferreira
University of Minho, Braga, Portugal
e-mail: aflores@ie.uminho.pt; filidio@ie.uminho.pt

Instructional leadership and leadership for learning have been discussed in the literature from a variety of perspectives. Hallinger (1992, p. 37), for instance, states that 'the instructional leader was viewed as the primary source of knowledge for the development of the school's educational program'. In turn, Bush (2015, p. 487) stresses the limitations of the instructional model, arguing for the distributed approach and the need to revisit the balance with its central focus on learning rather than on instruction. Dimmock and Tan (2016) also highlight the need for a more critical perspective of instructional leadership associated with the expansion of principals' responsibilities. They refer, amongst other features, to instructional leadership as a multi-dimensional concept with different dimensional efficacies, to the need to challenge the so-called established truths about effective practices, to instructional leadership as a cross-cultural and comparative concept and to the reconfiguration of the school's patterns of leadership.

Teacher leadership has been expanding as a key element to improve education within a view of more distributed leadership and of schools as being the communities of learning. Yet, the existing literature points to the existence of different perspectives and understandings (Alexandrou & Swaffield, 2012; Davis & Leon, 2009), including both a formal and an informal dimension. Frost (2012) argues for a non-positional approach in which teachers are able to engage in strategic action for change and to transform their educational practice (Frost, 2017). This perspective 'does not assume leadership is automatically linked with positions in the organizational hierarchy of the school. Instead it recognizes the potential of all teachers to exercise leadership as part of their role as a teacher' (Frost, 2012, p. 210). In a similar vein, Huang (2016) distinguishes traditional views of leadership and informal leadership, the former focussing on an authorised individual (usually the principal or head teacher in the school), and the latter pointing to those who do not have a formal position in an organisation.

Literature has identified several constraints and obstacles for teachers to exercise leadership, such as isolation and individualism, role ambiguity, inadequate time for collaboration, lack of incentives (York-Barr & Duke, 2004); external accountability, teachers' capacity to undertake "extra work" and the role of senior managers (Muijs & Harris, 2006); and lack of administrative support, lack of time, dealing with teachers who are resistant to change, have too many duties and lack of professional development opportunities (Gordon, Jacobs, & Solis, 2013). Also, there is a vast literature on leadership focussing on the challenges of instructional leadership by using student achievement information for instructional improvement (Timperley, 2005), on how school leaders enact policies in context managing tensions and balancing conflicting goals (Flores & Derrington, 2017), on the interplay of the relationships between school context, principal leadership and mediating variables in leadership for learning (Paletta, Alivernini, & Manganelli, 2017), and on school leadership focusing on values embedded in the biographies of principals of successful schools and how they influence their response to systemic policy reforms (Day & Gu, 2018).

For Stevenson (2012, p. 345), much of the existing literature on teacher leadership 'is rooted within mainstream discourses of education leadership and management and fails to address more fundamental questions about the nature of leadership in an educational context'. The author identifies two main problems linked to this literature: (a) teacher leadership continues to be seen within a managerialist perspective located within managerialist tradition and hierarchies, linked to roles and structures and remaining essentially conservative and orthodox; and (b) the literature stresses the contribution of teacher leaders to educational change but seldom questions the 'fundamental nature of these changes' (p. 345). For instance, the idea widely disseminated is that teachers' resistance to change has to do, to a great extent, with the belief that change is naturally good and not as simply a decision-making process that may also inhibit or even negatively impact pupil learning. Therefore, discussing the nature of change, including its purpose, values and meaning, as well as the interests behind them, is crucial for critically leading innovation in schools. Moos (2008), for instance, emphasising critical reflection in detriment to fundamentalist beliefs, discusses contemporary demands from the perspective of notions of democratic education. He asks if leaders can contribute to building democratic communities in schools, where professionals and students participate in the interactions on the basis of inclusion in the community (participation) and on critical reflection and analysis (deliberation). In this sense, three main perspectives converge for leadership for learning: democratic learning, learning democracy and democratic leadership.

These theoretical and conceptual perspectives offer a basis for understanding the ways in which leadership for leading learning in schools and classrooms has been developing in Portugal in the light of both the national and the global political agendas but also the social, cultural and political features that characterise the Portuguese context. This chapter draws upon data arising from a wider piece of research aimed at analysing school and teacher leadership in times of economic downturn and intensive reforms. It provides a pluralistic view of leadership which includes both formal and non-formal approaches, and diverse actors within the school setting, including principals, teachers and pupils. We look at the emerging trends arising from data from the research project, the details of which will be described after a brief contextualisation to which we now turn.

The Portuguese Context

A Bureaucratic, Centralised and Compliant Tradition

For almost half of the last century, Portugal was ruled under a dictatorship. This has marked both the structures and the mindset of people in various sectors of the state and the society. In his book *Portugal hoje—o medo de existir* (Portugal, today—the fear of existing), José Gil (2005), a Portuguese philosopher, considers that some characteristics of people nowadays correspond to the heritage of the dictatorship: people are envious, resentful, always complaining and essentially, they fear: they fear risk-taking, they fear not being up to what was required.[1] During the dictatorship, known as Estado Novo (New State), the development of the country, and particularly the education sector, was stagnant. Research shows a number of repressive strategies aimed at securing a tight social control and a detailed normalisation of the schooling system (Fernandes, 1992). Educating for passivity and compliance in order to keep a civil society depoliticised was the main goal of the New State regime

(Formosinho, 1987). Schools were the last link of a long hierarchical chain commanded by the central administration and, to a great extent, this perspective is still very much present and culturally rooted in the existing school organisations.

From the Democratic Management to School Autonomy and Accountability

The Red Carnation Revolution, in 1974, marked the end of the dictatorship. Democratic school management became the mainstream notion. Yet, it became clear there was a progressive abandonment of the qualifier "democratic" in subsequent legislation. The terms used before the revolution such as rector and school director/principal were replaced by the word "president" (president of a collegial body named as directive or executive council). The president was a teacher elected amongst his/her peers.

The notion of school autonomy started to be used in the legislative texts during the transition period of the 1980s to the 1990s, and it has been associated with successive models of school administration and management. In 1998, in the Decree-Law no 115-A/98, of the 4th May, the three notions were used together for the first time: autonomy, administration and management of schools and "clusters of schools".[2] School contracts ("contracts of autonomy") between the Ministry of Education and the schools were also mentioned in this legal framework but it was only in 2006 that this process began to be fully articulated with the mechanisms of internal and external evaluation of schools. These reforms were undergirded by the premise that greater school autonomy will encourage innovation and quality teaching and drive forward school performance (Lupton, 2011; Wößmann, 2007).

In Portugal, the discourse of autonomy has influenced a rather rhetorical role but at the same time, a strategic function of recentralisation of education through renewed mechanisms typical of the "Managerial State" (Newman and Clarke, 1997). Whether concentrated or deconcentrated, the decentralisation of education is in sharp contrast to the possibilities of democratic management of the schools, as they are run and controlled by the central administration. As Lima (2014, p. 1078) states, autonomy is seen as a rhetorical condition in the face of the maintenance of centralisation, or even the recentralisation, of the powers in education: 'elections, collegiality, and participation in the decision-making process are now widely undervalued as basic dimensions of the democratic management of schools'.

The above referred to Decree-Law no 115-A/98 was in place for ten years before being replaced in 2008. The government approved a new legal framework (Decree-Law no 75/08, on 22nd April), which is still in place. Its label is the same as the previous decree law, but it introduced for the first time the concept of leadership. This has generated great controversy and debate involving policymakers, teachers' unions, academics and teachers. The principal is no longer elected but appointed by the General Council, according to a recruitment process. He/she should have adequate qualifications for the role, including either training or experience in school administration and management. According to this new legislation, the principal is given more power in order to reinforce school leadership and to enhance effectiveness, but it also represents more responsibility. He/she simultaneously assumes the presidency of the Pedagogical Council and designates the coordinators of the curriculum departments which are the main pedagogical coordinating and supervising structures at school (in the previous legislation, the coordinators of the curriculum department were elected amongst teachers who integrated each department).

The Emergence of the Concept of Leadership: Mixed and Contradictory Messages

Over the last ten years, the concept of leadership has emerged. The management and leadership discourses go hand in hand, although both discourses reveal the landmarks of a centralised and bureaucratic culture. Today, mixed notions co-exist, such as "top management" and "top leadership" as well as "intermediate management" and "intermediate leadership".

The legislation stated that the principal is "the face" and the "first responsible" for the school. It also stipulates new school governance (principal), the aim of which is to "reinforce leadership at school". The legal text uses notions such as "strong leadership" and "effective leadership" as well as the innocuous term of "good leadership". It is possible to identify in this legislation a conception of leadership as mere implementation, defining the "authority of the principal" as a way to "locally execute policy initiatives issued by the central government".

To the lexicon typical of a centralised and bureaucratic administration was added the emerging managerialistic lexicon such as efficacy, efficiency, goals and objectives, measurable and quantifiable results, standards to assess quality, competitiveness, performance, excellence, and so on. It should not be forgotten that managerialism has been growing in the educational discourse and, for much of the time, it is related to the seduction of its lexicon, which is nowadays greatly valued and used in schools, particularly by the principals. An example may be seen in the existence of "merit places", which have been institutionalised in many Portuguese schools influenced by the seductive discourse of excellence.

Economic Downturn and Austerity Measures

The research project on which this chapter draws was developed during a critical period in Portugal as the country was going through a severe financial and economic crisis (2011–2014) with implications for the education sector and particularly for teaching (see Flores, 2014; Flores & Ferreira, 2016). Schools and teachers were greatly influenced not only by the need to educate children, but also by the alarming expansion of poverty bringing with it greater social intervention demands. A number of policy initiatives were introduced to deal with the complex demands of school life as a result of the financial, economic and social crises. Since 2012, several emergency and compensatory policies, programmes and initiatives have been put in place by the Ministry of Education, including the school programme for "Food Reinforcement" (PERA Portugal, Ministério da Educação e Ciência, 2012), which aimed at providing pupils in need with a meal in the morning (around 14,000 and 12,000 pupils benefited from this programme in 2012/2013 and 2013/2014, respectively).

A number of changes in the education sector occurred after 2011 (Benavente et al., 2014), including: an increase in the number of pupils per class; increased workload for teachers; promotion of school rankings based on national exams; reinforcement of so-called key subjects, such as Portuguese and Mathematics; and reduced attention given to subjects such as physical education, artistic education, civic education and health education. Considering the effects of the austerity measures, Flores, Ferreira, and Parente (2014) identify issues such as salary cuts, high rates of unemployment, high taxation and worsening opportunities for career progression, as a few examples of the ways in which the teaching profession has been affected during this period.

Existing research pointed to the deterioration of working conditions at school for teachers not only as a result of the economic and social crisis, but also the greater challenges and pressures placed on them. Teachers had to deal with social issues such as child poverty and scarcity of resources, but also were faced with the intensification of their work, an increase in bureaucracy and low morale (Flores, 2014). Enhancing learning through leadership has, thus, become a more demanding endeavour on the part of both principals and teachers.

Methods

This chapter draws on data from a wider three-year project (January 2011–June 2014) funded by *Fundação para a Ciência e a Tecnologia* (National Foundation for Science and Technology) (PTDC/CPE-CED/112164/2009). Drawing upon the major research project, this chapter addresses the following research questions:

1. How do principals, teachers and pupils understand leadership?
2. In which ways is leadership linked to pupil learning from the point of view of principals, teachers and pupils?

Data Collection and Participants

Data were collected through in-depth interviews with 11 principals and also focus on the groups of pupils ($n = 108$) and teachers ($n = 99$) in 11 schools. Data analysis was undertaken in two phases. First, there was an analysis of data gathered in each school from the voices of teachers, pupils and the head teacher. A second phase was then carried out according to a comparative or horizontal analysis (cross-case analysis) (Miles & Huberman, 1994). In this phase, it was possible to look for common patterns as well as differences. A semantic criterion was used to look for key themes arising from the qualitative data by the research team.

Findings

The findings from the research are presented below according to the following themes: (a) common challenges faced by the schools and the exercise of leadership in demanding circumstances; (b) a plural understanding of leadership versus an emphasis on the formal roles; (c) accountability, school autonomy and the increase of the bureaucratic work and control in schools; (d) leading innovation by doing policy: a more ecological and inclusive view of leadership; and (e) leadership for learning and learning for leading: two sides of the same coin. Quotations used to illustrate the main themes are drawn from the focus groups with teachers and pupils and from the interviews with the principals.

Common Challenges Faced by the Schools and the Exercise of Leadership in Demanding Circumstances

The school principals pointed to the constraints and difficulties in exercising leadership as well as the strategies used to deal with them. Issues such as self-motivation and ability to motivate and encourage others were at the forefront of their accounts during a period marked by the feelings of frustration and disappointment, on the one hand, and resilience and professionalism, on the other. Teachers' negative image, especially on the part of politicians and the media, policy initiatives related to teacher evaluation, and an obsession with outcomes were examples identified in the principals' interviews:

> *Since 2008 motivation has decreased, first as a result of the implementation of teacher evaluation, which as a crazy process and has led to huge demonstrations, and then the curriculum goals to increase students' outcomes.* (Principal)

> *Motivation is very low at the moment due to the economic situation, salary cuts, high taxes. These and other aspects have led to the deterioration of the image of teachers.* (Principal)

> *A social image has been created that is not good for teachers; it is a narrative in which teachers have lots of privileges, including long holidays, great salaries that do not correspond to what they do, etc.* (Principal)

The increase of teachers' workload, the increase of the number of students per class, the increase of meetings, roles and administrative tasks, the high level of unemployment, the precarious jobs, the lack of career advancement and salary cuts, the deterioration of the teachers' image and lack of social recognition are among the key aspects that have led to the impoverishment of the teacher workforce, along with issues of insecurity, fear and lack of job satisfaction:

> *The lack of a secure job is more and more felt by the teachers. The school is not a healthy environment anymore ... there is fear.* (Principal)

> *Teachers are tired! They have gone through too many reforms, legislation, etc. Somebody needs to stop that! It is hard for teachers to find a calm situation and share their practice, it is hard to do collaborative work in such circumstances.* (Principal)

When asked to talk about themselves, the school principals revealed common feelings in regard to the ways in which they understand leadership, especially when they have to lead in demanding circumstances. In general, they feel good about their job despite the increased challenges and difficulties they need to deal with on a daily basis:

> *I am very happy doing my job. I enjoy what I do, I commit to what I do, I am perfectionist and I think people need to do well their job.* (Principal)

Principals' views of "good leadership" and "good leaders" point to personal qualities: being able to listen, to motivate, to cooperate, to influence others, to create a positive environment, to demonstrate ways to work in a team, being altruistic, being strong, to bond with other people:

Teacher leaders are able to listen, motivate and mobilise others in their groups or departments …. They are capable of provoking discussion and make others do something. (Principal)

You alone cannot do much. But if there is sharing, help and a positive climate for people to cooperate and work together … it is great. I think this is crucial in any organisation. In a school, if everybody works in an individualistic manner, it doesn't work. (Principal)

Being able to listen is key to exercise leadership. Also important are sharing and teamwork. (Principal)

A number of conceptions of leadership emerged from the participants' accounts. Issues such as "open door leadership", "democratic leadership", "shared leadership", "emotional leadership" and "motivational leadership" were but a few recurring examples in the principals' accounts.

If I am able to keep a more directive and hierarchical attitude, it tends to reinforce the bureaucratic path and organisations, and even more schools, which have to be the least bureaucratic possible in order to motivate people. (Principal)

My concern is my leadership to be as democratic as possible … sometimes you need to be more directive, other times you need to tolerate and understand the context in which things happen. (Principal)

I guess my leadership is motivational in the sense that I am motivated and I am concerned with motivating people. I also feel the effect of other people's motivation. (Principal)

I think it is about emotional leadership. We have had external evaluation in our school and one of the key features identified was leadership and teachers' engagement. When I speak about emotional leadership, I mean respecting people and give them autonomy… (Principal)

Although Principal's complain about the time and energy that they have to spend on bureaucratic tasks that prevent them from focussing on the issues of teaching and learning, they emphasise that the pedagogical dimension is the most important one for them. As Sergiovanni (1998) asserts, if one intends to improve the school, pedagogical leadership is the more effective alternative to bureaucratic leadership. To quote one principal: 'It is at the Pedagogical Council that I feel better and fulfilled, as it is the heart of the school in which you make big decisions, evaluate and devise and develop improvement strategies'.

A Plural Understanding of Leadership Versus an Emphasis on the Formal Roles

Concepts such as "leadership density" (Sergiovanni, 1992) and "leaderful practice" (Raelin, 2003) emphasise the principle that all members of a school have something to contribute. MacBeath and Townsend (2011, p. 9) assert that 'leadership may, like learning, be understood not simply as the province of those in formally defined roles but as opportunistic, emergent and collective' and they go on to say that 'opportunistic leadership occurs within cultures which encourage leadership to be taken rather than simply given, an expression of agency' (p. 10).

Both the principals and the teachers held a plural view of leadership, but the concept that emerged in their discourses was much more associated with the principal and his/her staff and with teachers who perform formal roles in the school structure such as head of departments and subject leaders.

> *Leadership is about the principal and the intermediate structures at school such as the head of departments, class tutors and the coordinator of the tutors.* (Teacher)

This emphasis on the formal dimension of leadership linked to the hierarchical structures of the school and the exercise of roles and functions is not surprising, taking into account the Portuguese context and culture and the generalised understanding of the concept (see context section above). For instance, some teachers stated that 'the principal is in charge, but coordinators are also doing their job' and 'leadership comes from the principal, but you can also identify other levels of leadership in the school'.

Despite this, some principals also spoke of informal teacher leadership in a diversity of contexts and situations, including the classroom. According to Danielson (2007), informal leaders emerge in a spontaneous and organic way among teachers; they are not selected and do not possess a formal authority. They rather take the initiative in solving problems or in the implementation of a project and their influence stems from experience, practice and respect in regard to peers.

> *Leadership in school is exercised through the roles and functions at the intermediate level of the school structures but also by the teachers themselves when they lead projects.* (Principal)

> *I think everybody can exercise leadership, for instance, the teacher in the classroom … even the pupils.* (Principal)

At the beginning of the focus group, teachers spoke of leadership in its formal dimension, but as the focus group went on, they started to talk more spontaneously and reflected on the issues under discussion. They explained the concept by highlighting teacher leadership at the interpersonal and professional level and at the level of projects and activities at school: '*you can exercise different forms of leadership in the ways in which you interact with people at school*' (Teacher); '*teachers are not only in the classroom; their practices represent the true power of the school*' (Teacher); '*The school dynamic has to do with all people at the school*' (Teacher).

In a similar vein, one principal stated that '*school is the face of teachers*' and '*a good teacher makes a good school*' through his/her daily practices and persistence.

As for the pupils, there is a clear distinction between the role of teachers and of the principal. During the focus group, when asked about who is the most influential person(s) in decision-making at school, the majority of the pupils identified the school principal: '*I think the principal is the boss*' (Pupil); '*I have never seen anyone with more power at school than the principal*' (Pupil).

However, during the focus group, pupils reflected on other forms of leadership from the part of other actors in the school: *'teachers are also leaders… this is our vision but I am not sure if they are the ones who are more influential at school'* (Pupil); *'if you talk at a personal level, teachers are leaders, if you talk at a bureaucratic level the principal is the leader and bureaucracy is ruining the school'* (Pupil).

Accountability, School Autonomy and the Increase of Bureaucratic Work and Control in Schools

In the name of autonomy, principals and teachers deal simultaneously with bureaucratic intensification and control of their work and increasing demands of accountability and performativity. These demands have become characteristic of some policy initiatives in Portugal, especially those related to schools' internal and external evaluations, teacher evaluation and pupil assessment, with a particular emphasis on national exams for new entrants into the teaching profession, and for pupils in Year 4, Year 6 and Year 9 in Portuguese and Mathematics. More pressure has been placed on schools and teachers to increase student attainment as a result of concerns with national and international assessment programmes, such as Programme for International Student Assessment (PISA).

Nevertheless, in the interviews with the principals, autonomy was one of the most critical aspects: *'there is no autonomy whatsoever!'*; *'autonomy is zero! You are kidding!'*; *'Autonomy is rhetoric there is no such thing as autonomy!'* Others said:

> *The legislative texts mention autonomy, but it is about autonomy in regard to what the Ministry of Education has regulated!* (Principal)

> *I have autonomy but to do and make others do whatever the central administration imposes on us!* (Principal)

> *The principal is asked to respond to centralised or deconcentrated services of school administration. And this is on the top of the daily work that as a principal you need to do.* (Principal)

The abundant, hurried and unstable legislation, through more and more micro-legislative texts, hyper-regulate school life. For principals and teachers, bureaucracy (usually seen as filling in documents, doing reports, etc.) implies less time and energy for reflection, discussion and other learning-oriented practices. One principal stated: '*I really would like to have autonomy at the pedagogical dimension, I would like to develop a curriculum that takes into account the socio-economical characteristics of the environment of the school*'. A teacher also claimed that '*it is all about paperwork and more paperwork … what I enjoy is being with the children.*' Other principals stated:

> *You feel suffocated by bureaucracy that does not leave space for other tasks which require reflection, proximity and discussion.* (Principal)

> *It is frustrating because people do reports and other administrative tasks, and this means less energy for other practical stuff.* (Principal)

> *Sometimes I reflect on what I do and I find myself feeling like giving up. In 5 days, 2 or 3 days are devoted to pupils and the rest to the other tasks. You feel frustrated because you do not do what you enjoy.* (Principal)

As Torres Santomé (2006, p. 131) states, 'teachers who are committed to their work, to the daily life of the school, but do not see their work recognized, became disappointed, lack motivation, generating a "culture of pessimism"'.

> *Teachers are tired of being seen in a negative way, of being mistrusted. There have been too many reforms, too much legislation and so on. There are people that are exhausted and they say "I am going to retire. I can't stand it anymore".* (Principal)

Some principals and teachers also highlight the new forms of bureaucratic control that is exercised through online platforms from the part of the services of the Ministry of Education.

> *I think we are more and more controlled at all levels, including through informatics … and online platforms.* (Principal)

We know that there is a need to register data for future analysis. But doing the same in a systematic way ... you are asked to provide the same data and you need to register the same, it is too much! (Teacher)

Principals and teachers spend much time inserting data without seeing its utility and purpose. However, this does not correspond only to administrative tasks but to new forms of "E-Government" (Henman, 2010) which are nowadays very much prevalent in schools. A recent research project carried out in Portugal has shown that "electronic bureaucracy" (Meira, 2017) is one of the most exacerbated forms of control of the schools, of principals and of teachers.

The bureaucratic paraphernalia implies less time and energy for principals and teachers for exercising leadership for learning. In addition, it creates the illusion of teachers as agents of change when they, in fact, only implement top-down programmes and initiatives. Thus, teachers stressed the change at the rhetorical level but with them having no effects in reality. They highlight the endless changes in education seen as a make-up exercise. Change is, therefore, seen as a mere language game in so far as the change of the language is not accompanied by changes in practice: '*there is no change at all; the language is different, the lexicon is different but everything remains unchanged*' (Teacher).

Leading Innovation by Doing Policy: A More Ecological and Inclusive View of Leadership

The idea that nothing changes, because it is just about a change in the lexicon, may be related to the perception that both principals and teachers are mere implementers or doers of endless policy initiatives that invade the school on a daily basis. However, Ball, Maguire and Braun (2012) reject the idea that policies are simply "implemented". They argue that policies are interpreted and put into practice in various ways. Arguing for the concept of "policy enactment", they state that social actors may control the process of doing policy in their schools.

Implementation is related to top-down policy, whereas enactment refers to how people interpret, accept, resist and subvert policy in context, implying teacher activism (Sachs, 2003). When conceiving schools as contexts in which policies are active and creatively produced, "micropolitical literacy" (Kelchtermans & Ballet, 2002) becomes crucial. As these authors argue, learning how to deal with the micropolitical aspects of teachers' work lives, such as power, influence and control, implies a "political" learning process.

Opposing the concepts of implementation and innovation, Frost (2010) states that the focus of implementation is: design at the centre, behavioural specifications, hierarchical accountability and training as the mode of transfer. As for innovation, it is a process marked by distributed design, proposed principles, professional accountability and practitioner-led and enquiry-based development as the mode of transfer. In this sense, a process of innovation demands "multi-level learning" (students, teachers, the school as an organisation and the educational system). However, according to Frost (2010), 'a key component in the diagram is the connection between the layers. The little sticks that link one level to the next represent "leadership"' (p. 208).

The exercise of leadership has become more complex in so far as principals and teachers have to deal with various and often contradictory demands: promoting students' learning; providing social support to children and their families, particularly in the context of the crisis and austerity; and dealing with the paradoxical discourse of school autonomy. Our study, however, shows that, in some schools, the exercise of leadership in more political, ecological and inclusive ways emerged through the promotion of decentralised and bottom-up strategies and initiatives, as well as through the capacity to build trust and collegiality and support and fostering meaningful processes and experiences to enhance pupil learning.

Issues such as teachers leading work with colleagues to improve teaching and learning were at the forefront of their accounts. For pupils, principals and teachers, leadership has to do, to a great extent, with the ways in which teachers who make a difference are seen in the school. They are able to influence colleagues, pupils and others through the development of initiatives, projects and innovation of practice, despite the constraints and difficulties they face. Expressions such as '*these teachers are respected*', '*they are key elements in the school*', '*they are able to motivate and mobilise*' and '*they take the initiative*' express this position. Another said:

> *Some teachers, even if they do not perform a formal role at school, are respected by everybody. They are the first ones to be consulted, to be asked for an opinion, to discuss an issue ... people who are respected ... this is the true leadership.* (Teacher)

Similarly, pupils spoke of the teachers who were described as '*good teachers*', '*fair*', '*they care and respect others*', '*are able to motivate pupils*' and '*are good fun but demanding*'. Younger pupils talked about their closed reality—their teacher, colleagues and friends—whereas the older ones point to the leader and leadership in a broader sense. Older pupils use the word "leader" and the younger ones talk about the "boss" and the "person who has power". For older pupils, the leader is associated with the experience and the capacity to lead teams in order to reach given goals, with comments such as: '*The leader is like a boat*', '*it is someone who has a vision for the future*', '*he knows what he is doing*', '*she knows how to sort out problems*', '*he inspires others and you have confidence in him*' and '*she is there for you*' (Pupils).

Pupils seem to share the idea that all teachers can exercise leadership regardless of the roles and responsibilities they perform. When they compare leadership of the principal and of the teachers, they highlight the proximity of the latter: '*He who makes the decisions is the principal, but who is closer to us is the teacher*' (Pupil). Also, the principals stress similar views, recognising and valuing the exercise of leadership by the teachers: '*Teachers can take initiative, the power and responsibility to make decisions and the confidence to dare ... they feel we trust them, we have confidence in them ...*' (Principal).

In a study carried out by Mullen and Jones (2008), teachers 'have shared that they want to work with principals who are willing to listen, support their decision making within reason, and trust what they say and do' (p. 337).

> Teachers are willing to take on more leadership responsibilities where they respect and admire their principals and feel supported by them. Hence, the value of building collegial relationships among teachers, and between teachers and administrators, is extremely powerful. (2008, p. 337)

One principal sees himself as exercising an 'emotional leadership' and another one stated that 'you need to respect people and give autonomy to people'. In a similar vein, when teachers talked about the principals, they identify aspects related to vision, confidence, wisdom, intuition, causes and convictions: *'the principal is a woman of causes. She never gives up'* (Teacher).

The political dimension of leadership emerges in some schools and conjunctures towards a more activist and ecological view of leadership. As one teacher stated, teachers make a difference: *'it is the people who make others believe'*, a statement convergent with Deleuze's words (2000, p. 172), *'something possible, otherwise I will suffocate'*. Frequently, an idea is only seen as impossible because we understand the real as something solid and given. However, the possible will often consist of more realities than what is now known. In the challenging circumstances faced by the schools and teachers in which our research was carried out, the dominant perspectives tended to the impossible. However, political, contextual/ecological understandings of leadership practices were also identified, deriving from believing and seeing that something is possible.

The recognition of the importance of context and the capacity to read and interpret it in its idiosyncrasy are key elements in a more ecological view of leadership. For instance, one principal spoke of the challenges he handled when he started his job as a principal. He said he saw a school *'crowded and worrying particularly in regard to pupil behaviour'*. It was necessary to *'take leadership in context'*, and he went on to say: *'the problem was not faced directly, in so far as the school tried to defend herself from the context instead of taking leadership from the context'* (Principal).

Leadership for Learning and Learning for Leading: Two Sides of the Same Coin

Principals participating in the study have a long experience as teachers and as members of management and coordination bodies and structures, and they have been serving as principals for some years in their school. In general, they state that they learn informally from the daily practice and experience.

> *I think you learn from your daily experience. It is through experience that you learn the competencies that you need. It is in practice that you learn. My professional development is informal, so to speak, and this daily professional informal way of learning is really important for me.* (Principal)

Besides experience, principals' professional development is based on In-service education and training of teachers (INSET) and specialised training, although this kind of training has often a managerialist and bureaucratic nature. It focusses mainly on administrative and legal issues, related to the policy initiatives derived from the Ministry of Education, and usually the Ministry of Education is the course provider. In terms of specialised training, at an academic level, several principals hold a Master's or PhD in areas such as school management, administration or supervision, not in areas associated with school leadership or leadership for learning.

> *I also do INSET activities and I hold a Master's in Educational Administration.* (Principal)

> *I have tried to do training. I did a specialisation in Management and School Administration and other courses run by the Ministry of Education.* (Principal)

Data from the 2013 Teaching and Learning International Survey (TALIS) report (Organisation for Economic Co-operation and Development (OECD), 2014) show that the training of school leaders in Portugal is scarce and not systematic. Data demonstrate that the situation deserves further consideration at the political, academic and professional levels. Meanwhile, the Teaching and Learning International Survey (TALIS) report 2018 is seen with great expectation. In comparison with the other Organisation for Economic Co-operation and Development (OECD) countries, Portugal has the highest proportion of school leaders who report barriers to their participation in professional development activities: the highest proportion of principals (54%) to indicate the lack of relevant opportunities available for professional development; the highest proportion (82%) of school leaders to report a lack of support from the employer for professional development; and one of the highest proportions (71%), close to Spain (79%) and Italy (73%), to state that there were no incentives for participation in professional development activities. In some countries, including Portugal, 40%

or more of the school leaders perceived that the expense of professional development was a barrier to their participation, as well as them lacking prerequisites (10% or more). Portugal has the highest proportion of principals (45%), who indicate that they have never participated in a teacher training programme or course. A substantial proportion of individuals undertake some formal preparation as teachers after they assume the principal's position (8%), or cumulatively before and after assuming that position (18%). Portugal has the highest proportion (40%) of principals who indicate no formal administrative or principal training preparation as a part of their formal education and the smallest proportions of principals reporting sufficient leadership preparation (40%). Also, it has the smallest proportion of principals who report taking part in a professional network, mentoring or research activity during the previous 12 months (11%), contrasting with high proportions (more than 80%) in other countries.

This situation reinforces the relevance of the concept of "multi-level learning" for enabling teachers to lead innovation and contribute to the development of professional knowledge (Frost, 2008, 2010). Thus, one cannot ignore that also through student leadership, it is possible to create participatory learning cultures (Frost, 2011). Turner, Christensen, Kackar-Cam, Fulmer, and Trucano (2018) state that teacher leadership flourishes within professional cultures which encourage innovation. According to these authors, professional learning communities can help change organisational and professional cultures towards innovations where school principals hold the professional capacities, beliefs and dispositions to develop their schools as learning communities in which teachers feel able to innovate, collaborate and work on their professional concerns.

In the light of this perspective, leadership for learning and learning for leading are seen as two sides of the same coin. In Portugal, policies and training institutions have not addressed these issues. Even programmes that focus on school and teachers' leadership do not take this approach to leadership for learning. It would create powerful and equitable learning opportunities for students, professionals and the system, and motivate participants to take advantage of these opportunities (Knapp, Copland, & Talbert, 2003). Leaders can accomplish this by committing themselves to establishing a focus on learning, building professional communities that value learning, engaging external environments that matter for learning, acting strategically and creating coherence (Knapp et al., 2003; Ouchi, 2003). This vision focusses on providing all learners, regardless of the difficulties they face, with the means to master challenging skills and to develop habits of mind that promote further learning, as well as independent learning (Göker, 2012).

Fairman and Mackenzie (2012) assert that teachers exercise leadership (TEL) when they extend their own and their students' learning beyond content and pedagogy: teachers reflect deeply on their beliefs in relation to their teaching; they learn how to create safe environments in which to share ideas with colleagues; they promote interpersonal skills and intrapersonal awareness and they develop skills in communicating with other stakeholders. As one participant puts it:

> *Leadership is a process that is built in context. You do a kind of pathway with others, because a leader is only a leader because he/she has got a group to lead and this group makes him/her to learn how to become a leader.* (Teacher)

Discussion

Two main tensions concerning the exercise of school leadership in Portugal emerged from the data. On one hand, principals and teachers were under pressure during the period in which the study took place. They had to deal simultaneously with the demands of increasing pupil achievement and with the need to actively invest in initiatives for social support to families and children, especially due to the increase of social vulnerability and poverty in the context of the national crisis and subsequent austerity (Flores & Ferreira, 2016). Simultaneously, they had to deal with traditional and persistent bureaucratic centralism with the new demands of managerialism, accountability and performativity.

Despite the use of the new managerialistic terms of effectiveness, efficacy, outcomes, quality and excellence, among others, a bureaucratic culture is still very much prevalent in Portuguese schools. Consequently, the image of the principals in regard to their role is that they can or should manage rather than lead. As such, leadership for learning is not embedded in their representation of their role in so far as this view entails a more closed, supportive and encouraging relationship with teachers, students and learning environments, whether in the classroom or in other contexts such as projects and activities in the community with families and other institutions.

In light of the tensions identified above, and theoretical and conceptual developments in the field, it is necessary to understand and promote new meanings for school leadership, especially those based on the perspective of leadership for learning, taking into account its potential for questioning, as a means to overcome the dominant bureaucratic culture. This is one of the reasons why Evers and Kneyber (2015) state that 'the educational system requires to be *flipped*. Replacing top-down accountability with bottom-up support for teachers' (p. 5):

> Teachers do not wait to be told what to achieve and how to achieve it; instead they show leadership in regard to the how and the what ….. To initiate this process, it is not simply a question of the government telling teachers to emancipate. It is rather a question of teachers initiating this process themselves. (pp. 6–7)

Leadership for Learning and Learning for Leading: Meaningful Challenges

In Portugal, the notion of leadership is still very much associated with the "big leader" who, through his/her singular and innate qualities, is able to mobilise his/her followers. As Frost (2011, p. 869) argues, 'The language chosen—in particular the constant use of the word "leader"—is inhibiting and reinforces the assumption that it is about special people with particular role designations and authority bestowed by officialdom'. In the Portuguese context, the use of the concept of school leadership, and even more, teacher leadership, is very recent. The concept has entered the school context through a legal framework which has ended the existence of a collegial body being replaced by the principal through the advocacy of "strong leadership". There is a scarcity of studies dealing with this topic, both theoretically and empirically, an example of which is the work by Castanheira and Costa (2007) and Silva, Amante, and Morgado

(2017). The research project conducted within the context of the Teachers Exercising Leadership (TEL) project, on which this chapter is based, was up until today the biggest study. It has attracted the national media and it has captured the picture of schools and teachers in the Portuguese context in recent years.

In teacher education programmes, issues related to leadership have not been prevalent. In some cases, it may include a curriculum unit, or even just a number of topics within a course, with the dominant issues being educational administration and management and educational policies. There are not specific courses on a regular basis for school principals either. Nor are there specific courses on school and teacher leadership. The Ministry of Education provides some courses for school principals although the focus is predominantly on educational policies, considered to be a priority. Legal and administrative issues related to new legislation are usually prevalent. In INSET, leadership is not a recurring topic either, especially for school principals who do not identify such interest.

In addition, the term instructional is no longer or seldom used in Portugal. In the democratic period, it has been subject to criticisms due to the fact that it has been associated with a narrow view of teaching as mere transmission of knowledge. Nowadays, it has been associated with the schooling or knowledge of a given person (an educated person). As such, although internationally, instructional leadership has been developing, sometimes almost as synonymous with leadership for learning, in the Portuguese context, the latter entails a great transforming potential at the level of policy, practice and research within the double perspective of leadership for learning and learning for leading.

Our research findings are in line with earlier empirical work focussing on the need to reinforce the ethical, cultural, social and political dimensions of teaching (Biesta, 2004; Tirri, 2014; Zeichner, Payne, & Brayko, 2014), for advancing social justice and democracy (Osborn, 2006; Zeichner, 2016). The moral dimension (Etzioni, 1988) and the need of "sense-making in organizations" (Weick, 1995) are the key elements for changing schools and learning. School cultures for learning need to reconnect with the question of purpose and ethical and moral project in an age of measurement and performativity (Ball, 2016; Biesta, 2009). Moral purposes include care, courage and pupils' voice (Day, 2004), which implies that children are seen as competent social actors, with voices and rights, particularly regarding issues that apply to them. The contribution of this study relates to the fact that the deconstructing and reconstructing leadership for learning lies in pupil voice. In such demanding times, it becomes more important than ever to pay attention to pupils' voices, through listening to their own views and experiences about the ways in which the school and the curriculum affect their lives, their motivation and their learning. As Mitra (2004) states, it is essential to take into account what pupils say, as well as to create dynamics that enable them to be involved in the decision-making process, school change and improvement. Pupil voice enables teachers and principals to improve their practice, enhancing the emergence of ideas and projects for the development of learning communities within a culture of leadership for learning.

Notes

1. This book had a national and international impact. Yet, one cannot ignore its limitations. In fact, it was published within the context of a specific conjuncture and it makes a generalisation which tends to reinforce the cultural traits that it aims to criticise.
2. The creation of big clusters of schools corresponded to an imposed policy from the Ministry of Education and its consequent shutting down of almost all rural schools in the country. The majority of these clusters of schools (67%) have more than 1200 students and 15% of them more than 2500 students (CNE, 2017).

References

Alexandrou, A., & Swaffield, S. (2012). Teacher leadership and professional development: Perspectives, connections and prospects. *Professional Development in Education, 38*(2), 159–167.

Ball, S. J. (2016). Neoliberal education? Confronting the slouching beast. *Policy Futures in Education, 14*(8), 1046–1059.

Ball, S., Maguire, M., & Braun, A. (2012). *How schools do policy: Policy enactments in secondary schools*. New York: Routledge.

Benavente, et al. (2014). O estado da educação num estado intervencionado. Portugal 2014. lisboa: op.edu - observatório de políticas de educação e de formação. Ces . Uc . Ceied.Ulht.

Biesta, G. (2004). Education, accountability and the ethical demand. Can the democratic potential of accountability be regained? *Educational Theory, 54*(3), 233–250.

Biesta, G. (2009). Good education in an age of measurement: On the need to reconnect with the question of purpose in education. *Educational Assessment Evaluation and Accountability, 21*(1), 33–46.

Bush, T. (2015). Editorial. Understanding instructional leadership. *Educational Management Administration & Leadership, 43*(4), 487–489.

Castanheira, P., & Costa, J. (2007). Lideranças transformacional, transaccional e "laisser-faire": Um estudo exploratório sobre os gestores escolares com base no MLQ. In J. Sousa & C. Fino (Org.), *A escola sob suspeita* (pp.140–154). Porto: Edições Asa.

Danielson, C. (2007). *Teacher leadership that strengthens professional practice*. Alexandria, VA: Association for supervision and curriculum development.

Davis, S. H., & Leon, R. J. (2009). Teaching Gil to lead. *Journal of School Leadership, 19*, 266–298.

Day, C. (2004). *A passion for teaching*. London: Routledge.

Day, C., & Gu, Q. (2018). How successful secondary school principals in England respond to policy reforms: The influence of biography. *Leadership and Policy in Schools, 17*, 332–344.

Deleuze, G. (2000). *Cinema 2. The time-image* (H. Tomlinson & R. Galeta, Trans.). London: The Athlone Press.

Dimmock, C., & Tan, C. Y. (2016). Re-conceptualizing learning-centred (instructional) leadership: An obsolete concept in need of renovation. *Leading and Managing, 22*, 1–17.

English, F. W. (2005). *The SAGE handbook of educational leadership. Advances in theory, research, and practice*. Thousand Oaks, CA: Sage.

Etzioni, A. (1988). *The moral dimension: Toward a new economics*. New York/London/Toronto, ON/Sydney, VIC/Singapore, Singapore: The Free Press.

Evers, J., & Kneyber, R. (Eds.). (2015). *Flip the system: Changing education from the ground up*. London: Routledge.

Fairman, J. C., & Mackenzie, S. V. (2012). Spheres of teacher leadership action for learning. *Professional Development in Education, 38*(2), 229–246.

Fernandes, A. S. (1992). *A Centralização Burocrática do Ensino Secundário. Evolução do sistema educativo português durante os períodos liberal e republicano (1836–1926)*. Doctoral dissertation, University of Minho, Braga, Portugal.
Flores, M. A., (Ed.). (2014). *Profissionalismo e liderança dos professores* [Teacher Professionalism and Leadership]. Santo Tirso: De Facto Editores.
Flores, M. A., & Derrington, M. L. (2017). School principals' views of teacher evaluation policy: Lessons learned from two empirical studies. *International Journal of Leadership in Education, 20*(4), 416–431.
Flores, M. A., & Ferreira, F. I. (2016). Education and child poverty in times of austerity in Portugal: Implications for teachers and teacher education. *Journal of Education for Teaching, 42*(4), 404–416.
Flores, M. A., Ferreira, F. I., & Parente, C. (2014). Conclusões e recomendações [Conclusions and Recommendations]. In M. A. Flores (Org.), *Profissionalismo e liderança dos professores* [Teacher Professionalism and Leadership] (pp. 217–236). Santo Tirso: De Facto Editores.
Formosinho, J. (1987). *Educating for passivity. A study of Portuguese education (1926–1968)*. Doctoral dissertation, Institute of Education, University of London.
Frost, D. (2008). 'Teacher leadership': Values and voice. *School Leadership and Management, 28*(4), 337–352.
Frost, D. (2010). Teacher leadership and educational innovation. *Zbornik Instituta za Pedagoška Istraživanja, 42*(2), 201–216.
Frost, D. (2011). Creating participative learning cultures through student leadership. In T. Townsend & J. MacBeath (Eds.), *International handbook of leadership for learning* (pp. 867–888). Dordrecht, The Netherlands: Springer.
Frost, D. (2012). From professional development to system change: Teacher leadership and innovation. *Professional Development in Education, 38*(2), 205–227.
Frost, D. (Ed.). (2017). *Empowering teachers as agents of change: A non-positional approach to teacher leadership*. Cambridge, MA: Leadership for Learning: The Cambridge Network.
Gil, J. (2005). *Portugal hoje – o medo de existir* (p. 2005). Lisboa, Portugal: Relógio dÁgua.
Göker, S. D. (2012). Reflective leadership in EFL. *Theory and Practice in Language Studies, 2*(7), 1355–1362.
Gordon, S. P., Jacobs, J., & Solis, R. D. (2013). *Critical issues in teacher leadership: Phase I of a national study*. Paper presented at the Annual Meeting of the American Research Association (AERA), São Francisco.

Hallinger, P. (1992). The evolving role of American principals: From managerial to instructional to transformational leaders. *Journal of Educational Administration, 30*(3), 35–48.

Henman, P. (2010). *Governing electronically: E-government and the reconfiguration of public administration, policy and power.* New York: Palgrave Macmillan.

Huang, T. (2016). Linking the private and public: Teacher leadership and teacher education in the reflexive modernity. *European Journal of Teacher Education, 39*(2), 222–237.

Kelchtermans, G., & Ballet, K. (2002). Micropolitical Literacy: Reconstructing a neglected dimension in teacher development. *International Journal of Educational Research, 37*, 755–767.

Knapp, M. S., Copland, M. A., & Talbert, J. E. (2003). *Leading for learning: Reflective tools for school and district leaders* (CTP research report). Center for the Study of Teaching and Policy, Seattle, WA; DeWitt Wallace/Readers' Digest Fund, Pleasantville, NY.

Lima, L. C. (2014). A gestão democrática das escolas: do autogoverno à ascensão de uma pós-democracia gestionária? *Education Society,* Campinas, *35*(129), 1067–1083.

Lupton, R. (2011). 'No change there then!'(?): The onward march of school markets and competition. *Journal of Educational Administration and History, 43*(4), 309–323.

MacBeath, J., & Townsend, T. (2011). Leadership and learning: Paradox, paradigms and principles. In T. Townsend & J. MacBeath (Eds.), *International handbook of leadership for learning* (pp. 1–25). Dordrecht, The Netherlands: Springer.

Meira. (2017). *A Burocracia Electrónica: Um Estudo sobre as Plataformas Electrónicas na Administração Escolar.* Tese de Doutoramento em Ciências da Educação, Especialidade em Organização e Administração Escolar, Braga, Universidade do Minho.

Miles, M., & Huberman, M. (1994). *Qualitative data analysis. An expanded sourcebook* (2nd ed.). Thousand Oaks, CA: Sage.

Mitra, D. (2004). The significance of students: Can increasing "Student Voice" in schools lead to gains in youth development? *Teachers College Record, 106*(4), 651–688.

Moos, L. (2008). School leadership for 'Democratic Bildung': Fundamentalist beliefs or critical reflection? *School Leadership & Management, 28*(3), 229–246.

Muijs, D., & Harris, A. (2006). Teacher led school improvement: Teacher leadership in the UK. *Teaching and Teacher Education, 22*(8), 961–972.

Mullen, C. A., & Jones, R. J. (2008). Teacher leadership capacity-building: Developing democratically accountable leaders in schools. *Teacher Development, 12*(4), 329–340.

Newman, J., & Clarke, J. (1997). *The managerial state: Power, politics and ideology in the remaking of social welfare.* London: Sage.

OECD. (2014). *Talis 2013 results: An international perspective on teaching and learning.* OECD Publishing. https://doi.org/10.1787/9789264196261-en.

Osborn, T. A. (2006). Teaching world languages for social justice: A sourcebook of principles and practices. *Critical Inquiry in Language Studies, 6*(1–2), 102–106.

Ouchi, W. (2003). *Making schools work: A revolutionary plan to get your children the education they need.* New York: Simon & Schuster.

Paletta, A., Alivernini, F., & Manganelli, S. (2017). Leadership for learning: The relationships between school context, principal leadership and mediating variables. *International Journal of Educational Management, 31*(2), 98–117.

Portugal, Conselho Nacional de Educação. (2017). *Organização escolar: os Agrupamentos.* Lisboa, Portugal: CNE.

Portugal, Ministério da Educação e Ciência. (2012). PERA Programa Escolar de Reforço Alimentar 2012/2013 e 2013/2014 [PERA Programme, Food Reinforcement]. Lisboa, Portugal: Ministério da Educação e Ciência.

Raelin, J. (2003). *Creating leaderful organizations: How to bring out leadership in everyone.* San Francisco: Berrett-Koehler.

Sachs, J. (2003). *The activist teaching profession.* New York: Open University Press.

Sergiovanni, T. (1992). *Moral leadership: Getting to the heart of school improvement.* San Francisco: Jossey-Bass.

Sergiovanni, T. J. (1998). Leadership as pedagogy, capital development and school effectiveness. *International Journal of Leadership in Education Theory and Practice, 1*(1), 37–46.

Silva, J. C., Amante, L., & Morgado, J. (2017). School climate, principal support and collaboration among Portuguese teachers. *European Journal of Teacher Education 40*(4), 1–16.

Stevenson. (2012). Teacher leadership as intellectual leadership. Creating spaces for alternative voices in the English system. *Professional Development in Education, 38*(2), 345–360.

Timperley, H. S. (2005). Instructional leadership challenges: The case of using student achievement information for instructional improvement. *Leadership and Policy in Schools, 4*(1), 3–22.

Tirri, K. (2014). The last 40 years in Finnish teacher education. *Journal of Education for Teaching, 40*(5), 600–609.
Torres Santomé, J. (2006). *A desmotivação dos professores*. Mangualde, Portugal: Edições Pedago.
Townsend, T., & MacBeath, J. (2011). *International handbook of leadership for learning*. Dordrecht, The Netherlands: Springer.
Turner, J. C., Christensen, A., Kackar-Cam, H. Z., Fulmer, S. M., & Trucano, M. (2018). The development of professional learning communities and their teacher leaders: An activity systems analysis. *Journal of the Learning Sciences, 27*(1), 49–88.
Weick, K. E. (1995). *Sense-making in organizations*. Thousand Oaks, CA: Sage Publications.
Wößmann, L. (2007). International evidence on school competition, autonomy, and accountability: A review. *Peabody Journal of Education, 82*(2–3), 473–497.
York-Barr, J., & Duke, K. (2004). What do we know about teacher leadership? Findings from two decades of scholarship. *Review of Educational Research, 74*(3), 255–316.
Zeichner, K. (2016). Advancing social justice and democracy in teacher education: Teacher preparation 1.0, 2.0, and 3.0. *Kappa Delta Phi Record, 52*(4), 150–155.
Zeichner, K., Payne, K., & Brayko, K. (2014). Democratizing teacher education. *Journal of Teacher Education, 66*(2), 122–135.

Part III

Responding to the Theory

7

Future-Ready Leadership Development

David Ng Foo Seong

Context and Introduction

Schools are complex and open systems with multiple sources of interdependent influences. At the macro level, global economic, cultural, political and technological influences and challenges among national institutions and economies exert tremendous pressure on schools. As schools strive to be relevant and globally connected, school reform takes on both local and international contexts. International contexts have become widely associated with comparative results from international tests, such as the Trends in International Mathematics and Science Study and the Programme for International Student Assessment, which purport to measure certain aspects of educational quality. Countries have taken it that attaining high scores on these tests is a strong indicator of being world-class. This has come to be known as world-class education reform.

D. Ng Foo Seong (✉)
Nanyang Technological University, Singapore, Singapore
e-mail: david.ng@nie.edu.sg

However, academic ability is only one of the three purposes of education. The other two purposes—preparation for vocation and citizenry development—have been conveniently overlooked. Without a doubt, academic ability counts for nothing if graduates are not able to translate their academic ability into skills and knowledge needed for jobs in the future. While there is little consensus of what world-class education means, a common fundamental question found in school reform documents worldwide is: '*How do we prepare future-ready students?*'

Being future-ready implies that learning outcomes must be dynamic and aligned to new realities that emerge over time. The future is about new realities that are context situated and context dependent. For example, if we look at Singapore's labour force by occupation in 2016, 83.5% of employment is in the services sector.[1] The services sector comprises commerce, transport and communications, finance and business, and community and social services, and accounted for more than three quarters of total employment. This new reality contrasts significantly when compared to the 1980s. In 1983, 62% of employment was in the services sector. But over the last 20 years (until 2016), a new reality has emerged.

The trends cited in the Singapore example, towards an increasing share of employment in the services sector, are consistent with developments in the other newly industrialised economies (NIEs) and more advanced economies (Fig. 7.1).

This new reality of jobs that are service oriented will challenge current assumptions of preparing students for the future beyond simply high academic grades. Specifically, school leaders must challenge current paradigms of inquiry in leadership, management, teaching and learning practices. Adopting relevant methods of inquiry (questioning, learning and knowing) will lead to new and novel solutions and practices that will meet the challenges of the new reality. Conversely, wrong methods of inquiry arising from old and outdated assumptions would only lead to ineffective practices. Fundamentally, 'future-ready' will also challenge how school leaders learn. School leadership learning and development must keep pace with a broader definition of effective schools beyond just grades and achievements. The next section will look at a new framework to define effective schools.

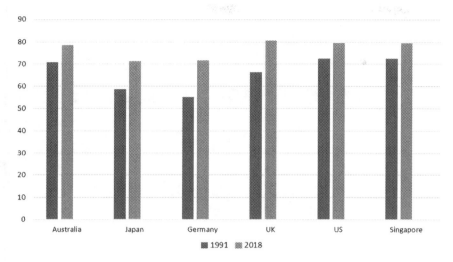

Fig. 7.1 Employment in services (% of total employment) country comparison 1991–2018

A Multi-dimensional Framework for Effective Schools

The narrow concept of effective schools looks at gains in assessment measures or standards, while the broader concept of effective schools looks at the holistic development of students. Whether it is from a narrow or broad perspective, school improvement is complex and involves multi-dimensions. This chapter proposes a new multi-dimensional framework for effective schools (Fig. 7.2). The framework provides an integrated approach to define effective schools. An effective school (successful education system) is able to develop future-ready individuals who will continue to learn beyond graduation, take on future lifework, and thrive in a changing society and environment.

Dimension 1: Purpose (Mission)

The first dimension is Purpose. The purpose or purposes of schooling provide the reasons for the existence of schools, or in other words—the

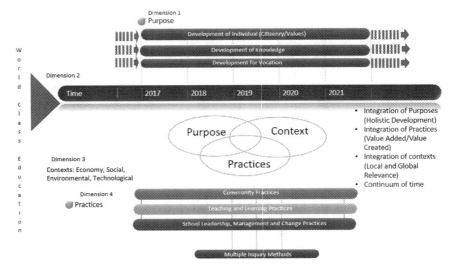

Fig. 7.2 Multi-dimensional framework for school success

mission of schools. There are three sub-dimensions in Purpose: development of values that enable individuals to live peacefully and collegially with one another in society; development of knowledge that fulfil standards of achievement and development of individuals with competencies, skill sets and habits for their chosen vocation. Effective schools must fulfil all three purposes of the school.

Dimension 2: Time (Perspective)

The second dimension is Time. Time provides perspective/focus to Dimension 1 (Purpose). The perspective of time is like the concept of vectors in Physics. A vector has direction and magnitude. Direction is past, present and future in the continuum of Time. When we relate the dimension of time to the dimension of purpose, we have an idea how much focus is required or the extent of school activities that school leaders are emphasising on fulfilling the purposes of schooling.

Magnitude is the extent or 'quantity' of school activities as per point of the continuum. Magnitude also will give us an indication of what schools value. Generally, we tend to focus on the present perspective of time and have a heavily lopsided magnitude (extent of activities) with measures that will bring immediate value to our education system. For example, high performance in assessment brings immediate high value in the form of recognition for the individual, school, system and even country. So, we have a greater magnitude of activities related to assessment. But we need to be keenly aware of the future perspective of time. The future perspective is no less important or valued. Future value is about the future-readiness of the graduates of our education system to fit into society and have the relevant qualifications and skill sets for a changing economy.

When we compare the amount of time students spend in the school system with the time in future work, it is clear that working years are about three times more than schooling years. For example, students generally finish post-secondary education at the median age of 23 but work until at least a median age of 65. The critical questions related to the dimension of time with regard to development of students for the future are as follows:

1. How do we define future value learning for students?
2. How much future value is created AS AN OUTCOME of learning? (Measures)
3. How will the value of current learning for students be translated into FUTURE VALUE for human capital? (Process)
4. What is the magnitude of school activities along the time continuum that affect a student's learning outcome—including future value? (How-to)

Effective schools, therefore, must be cognisant of the extent of learning activities and experiences—in particular, how successful the school system is in developing future-ready students. In this chapter, initial exploration to define future value is guided by Dimension 3 (Context).

Dimension 3: Context (Frames)

Context provides the frame upon which we can have specifics/details to describe Purpose (Dimension 1) and Time (Dimension 2).

There are at least five sub-dimensions of context: Political, Institutional, Cultural, Economic and Technological. In view of the limitations of this chapter, this section will only highlight pertinent ideas related to the context of economics to define future value for students.

The sub-dimension of economics looks at two aspects of vocation:

- The nature of jobs that contribute to the economy and the gross domestic product (GDP) of a country; and
- The employment of manpower across sectors.

There are typically three sectors of jobs: Manufacturing/Industrial; Services and Agriculture.

The nature of the services sector in the knowledge economy is characterised by higher skilled and higher value-added knowledge. Unlike manufacturing, which produces physical goods, services produce 'intangible' goods. These intangible goods include know-how in governance, health, education, communication, information and business. Producing services tends to require relatively less natural capital and more human capital than producing agricultural or industrial goods. With the declining natural resources, the world will have to look to developing future human capital.

The context of the economy in new, emerging and advanced economies will provide detail of what preparation for vocation (the second purpose of education) looks like. This chapter will use Singapore as a case to examine the economic changes and their implications for preparation for future vocation in the school system.

Singapore Context

The new millennium in the Asia Pacific saw the rise of large new players in the economic landscape, in the likes of China and India. These two major Asian powers bring both challenges and opportunities to Singapore. Singapore has to compete with India and China—at least in economic terms. With no natural resources and geographical constraints, Singapore's economy has been moving in the direction of a 'Knowledge and

7 Future-Ready Leadership Development

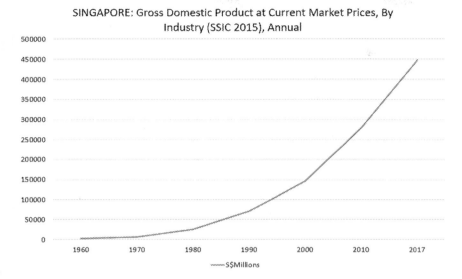

Fig. 7.3 Singapore's economy 1960–2017

Innovation Economy' from 2000 onwards (see Fig. 7.3). This move is both to compete with the Asian powers for direct foreign investment and to cement economic ties for the purpose of trade.

Characteristic of all developed nations in the world is the large component of the service sector that contributes to the growth of the economy, compared to the manufacturing sector. Singapore follows the same trend and has seen a steady rise in the service sector over the last one and a half decades. The service sector in Singapore has consistently contributed to a greater share of total economic output and employment in the economy. In 2016, the service sector accounted for about 73.4% of GDP and employed about 83.5% of the total workforce (see Fig. 7.4). Notably, if one were to step into any classroom today, eight out of ten students will be employed in the service sector upon completing their education. As inferred from the trend in developed nations, together with Singapore's geographical constraints, it is expected that Singapore will continue to have a large component of the service sector contributing to economic growth and employment even 10 years into the future.

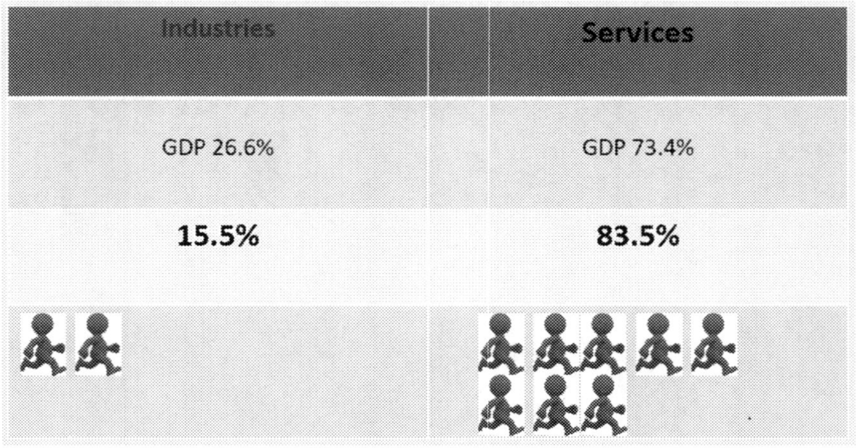

Industries	Services
GDP 26.6%	GDP 73.4%
15.5%	83.5%

Fig. 7.4 Singapore's employment by economic sectors 2016. (Source: mom.gov.sg)

What are the implications of the rise of the service sector in Singapore for the purposes of education? More specifically, how do we define future value from the sub-dimension of the economy? Consequently, how should the system develop school leaders to lead Singapore's schools to fulfil the imperatives of preparing students who are future-ready?

Defining Future Value of Students from the Sub-dimension of Economy (Singapore's Example)

Producing services tend to require relatively less natural capital and more human capital than producing agricultural or industrial goods; thus, services are well suited to Singapore's situation.

To put it in practical terms, value-added services will require employees to create innovative services and new value services. The imperative to be innovative is driven by fierce competition among countries that are producing the same type of services. Singapore can only effectively compete with other nations if the services are perceived by customers as new and value-added solutions. This poses a challenge to the purpose of preparing students for vocation. Future value for students from an economic context will require students to have an ingrained innovative mindset. Developing an innovative mindset will require consistent teaching and learning environments that will foster such a mindset. Rote and efficient learning will no longer be enough in the new economic reality. This economic context example and definition of future value are interlinked with Dimension 4 (Practices) next.

Dimension 4: Practices

The Practices dimension includes leadership and management practices, teaching and learning practices, community practices and more. Practices are based on sets of assumptions, beliefs and theories. These assumptions MUST NOT and CANNOT remain unchallenged paradigms in the discussion of future-readiness. Table 7.1 provides a contrast of the evolvement of learning assumptions in the two centuries.

What is important in terms of school success is that practices must evolve and be relevant to match the evolving realities of the purposes, time and context. Teaching and learning inquiry methods must keep up with changing realities. One example is the current dominant teaching

Table 7.1 Learning assumptions of twentieth and twenty-first centuries

Twentieth century post-war landscape	Twenty-first century landscape
General characteristics: Industrial expansion driven by surge in mechanical, technological, electronic inventions	General characteristics: Advanced industrialisation and rise of the service knowledge-based economy
Learning characteristics: Efficiency Planned Disciplined Behaviourist reinforcement Competency Knowledge acquisition Site/school-based constraints Cohort/group-based learning	Learning characteristics: Efficiency Disciplined Innovation Creativity Complexity Knowledge creation Informal, technological enhanced learning Life-wide learning Individualised learning

and learning inquiry method that is based on a set of behavioural objectives. Behavioural objectives typically are very specific proxies of change in learning. Whenever learning is defined by a set of specific behavioural objectives, it is already limiting the learning to a set of predefined and known knowledge. Objectives-driven learning will still be relevant but there is a need to include other alternative inquiry methods such as competency and complexity learning. In the latter section, the concept of complexity learning will be discussed.

Referencing the economic context example of Singapore, students must have an innovative mindset as future value that will enable them to fit into the next decade of economic development. There are three fundamental competencies that enable innovation to thrive (see Fig. 7.5). The capacity of generating and developing ideas (those that challenge current assumptions and practices) is the starting point for innovation. Without new ideas, there is no innovation. Testing the ideas and subjecting those ideas through the process of 'what, how, when, why' will allow the translation of the abstract (ideas) into reality (product). If the outcome is to turn the idea into a useful product, the final phase of entrepreneurship involves convincing users to adopt the new product. Translating these phases into the school's teaching and learning will involve creating three

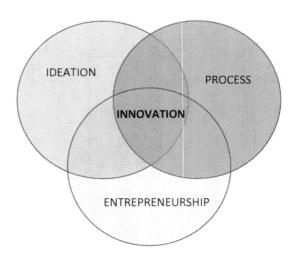

Fig. 7.5 Three learning environments in schools

learning environments that mirror the three phases. However, current practices of teaching and learning pose great challenges for these learning environments to be actualised. For example, allowing students to generate ideas and testing the ideas is often seen as a waste of time by teachers. This is because the curriculum has been planned and the outcome of learning has been predetermined. There is little room for students to generate ideas/topics/projects that are not in the planned curriculum. How should school leaders overcome the challenges?

Evolution of Leadership Learning and Developmental Programmes

Current methods of training and development of school leaders do not adequately address the challenges posed in the multi-dimensional framework of effective schools. There is a need for school leaders to generate new and novel ways to create new learning environments in schools. In recent years, the earlier conception of 'instructional leadership' has been 'reincarnated' as a global phenomenon in the form of 'leadership for learning' (Hallinger, 2009). The paradigm shift from instructional leadership to leadership for learning in schools necessitates the development of leaders in a way that parallels this shift. In instructional leadership, the focus is on instruction or teaching, and less on the process of learning. Leadership for learning places learning at the centre of focus, and together with its emphasis on creating conditions for learning, impels school leaders to bring life into the learning environment of teachers and students. (See MacBeath's chapter in this book for the five principles of leadership for learning, as well as MacBeath and Townsend [2011] and Swaffield and MacBeath [2009]. The five principles are sharing leadership, focusing on learning, sustaining a learning dialogue, creating an environment for learning and reframing accountability.) This section will trace the leadership development over the past three decades and the proposal of a new way to re-conceptualise leadership learning for the future.

In the past 50 years, educational leadership programmes have often seen incremental improvements rather than discontinuous change within a dominant design (see Fig. 7.6). In addressing this, we have conducted

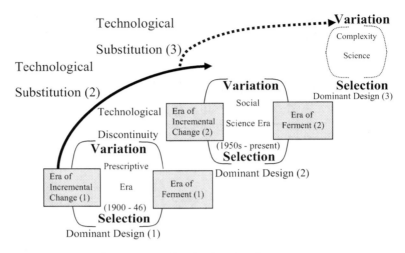

Fig. 7.6 Evolution of educational leadership development

an extensive review of literature and traced the evolution of educational leadership development to three eras: prescriptive, behavioural and the proposed complexity eras. During each era, the design and delivery of programmes have been based on the conceptual framework of the era. In each era, the discontinuation of the dominant design has come about because of a technological substitution and deep dissatisfaction with the current limitations of the design (Ng, 2014, 2015).

The following sections highlight the conceptual framework of each era and discuss how the framework determines leadership learning.

The Prescriptive Era (1900–1946)

There was little formal training in this era. Most school administrators learned their profession on the job, through trial-and-error processes. The little formal training that was provided taught courses on basic pedagogy, philosophy, school management principles and leadership characteristics. The emphasis was on the 'great man' and trait theories (Cooper & Boyd, 1987) and the application of philosophical knowledge to schools (Murphy, 1998). The 'great man' theory was based on identifying leadership traits of successful leaders (who were, almost always, men) in the political, business and battle fields. These successful leaders were deemed to have certain traits, such as being bold, being decisive and so on. Leadership development then was designed based on how best to teach these successful traits to participants (also usually men). For close to 50 years, the prescriptive approach was the dominant design for every leadership programme in the world.

In every design, the era of incremental improvement will take place where a programme will be refined within the parameters set by the dominant design. Inevitably, the law of diminishing returns sets in, where the degree of improvement becomes significantly diminished—causing dissatisfaction in the design outcome. This dissatisfaction leads to the start of an era of ferment where institutions begin to seek for alternative theoretical frameworks. The emergence of scientific research during the prescriptive era provided the platform for technological substitution, ushering in the next dominant era of design—the Behavioural Science influence.

Behavioural Science/Competency Era (1950s-Present)

In the period from the late 1940s to about 1985, theoretical and conceptual material drawn from the social sciences began to influence training programmes. This was also a period of ferment in the field of school administration. Much criticism was levelled against 'the naked empiricism, personal success stories and maxims or untested principles that constituted the knowledge base of educational administration' (Murphy, 1998). This resulted in considerable changes to the structure and content of training programmes, to mirror the perceived higher status of school administration in society. The following major changes were noted.

1. Educational administration was now viewed as 'an applied science within which theory and research are directly and linearly linked to professional practice' (Sergiovanni, 1991).
2. Social science content was the predominant yardstick used to indicate a high-quality programme (Miklos, 1992).

3. There was almost universal adoption of behavioural sciences' research techniques and instruments for research (Culbertson, 1988).
4. There was now a multidisciplinary approach to principal preparation (Culbertson, 1988). Scientific research in this era provided evidence-based decisions on learning and development.

In particular, learning could now be supported by evidence of changes in the cognitive, affective and psychomotor domains. The behavioural science era quickly supplanted the prescriptive design and became the new dominant design in leadership development. Characteristics of the behavioural science model include the following:

* a set of learning objectives;
* a specific body of knowledge (content) to be taught in order to achieve the objectives and
* adoption of the right pedagogical approach to deliver the body of knowledge.

These characteristics meant that learning could now be taught efficiently and effectively. While the behavioural science era is still relevant to a certain extent, there are inherent weaknesses in the design that again gave rise to discontent and ferment in further refining any programme. One of the inherent weaknesses of the behavioural science approach is that learning is predetermined knowledge. In addition, the increasing complexity of organisations and the influence of external factors, such as globalisation and information technology, have significant impact on emerging knowledge of how educational leaders need to lead and manage schools differently. Awareness has grown that predetermined knowledge and the body of knowledge based on known and past knowledge are no longer suitable to meet the new and current challenges. With the world changing rapidly and new knowledge being generated at a fast pace, the behavioural science era is no longer suitable as the only way to design any teaching and learning programmes.

Limitations of Behavioural/Competency Educational Leadership Learning and Developmental Programmes

The increasingly complex school system is central to the discussion of the relevance of leadership development, delivery and learning. Competency-based learning has been the dominant design in most leadership programmes for the past 50 years. The theoretical underpinning for the competency-based design is premised upon the behavioural science era where knowledge is viewed as a set of prescribed skills, roles and behaviours (Ng, 2013, 2014, 2015). Therefore, the common features in such a design will consist of specific modules or workshops designed to deliver a predetermined set of competencies, knowledge and skills. While we acknowledge the continuing importance of the behavioural sciences, there is also a recognition that such prescriptive courses are no longer sufficient to prepare leaders to lead and thrive in an increasingly complex and fast-paced changing world (Cheng & Tam, 2007; Hallinger & Snidvongs, 2005; Ng, 2015).

There is a great ongoing effort to change the delivery modes of learning and development for leadership programmes. Grogan and associates (2009) reviewed several studies and highlighted the common themes, such as the use of integrated curricular modules in place of the more traditional stand-alone college courses, the employment of intensive summer institutes, and the development of partnerships between preparation programmes and schools and school districts (Grogan et al., 2009). Hammond et al. (2007) reported similar trends in leadership preparation programmes that have moved towards non-traditional organisational arrangements, and special emphasis on the intentional integration of coursework and fieldwork.

Recent reviews of principal preparation literature suggest a common thread of the importance of integrating university course work and the students' field experiences (Lumby & English, 2009; Hammond et al., 2007; McCarthy & Forsyth, 2009). The belief is that adult learners benefit best from a 'learn-by-doing' active approach.

These new developments are a good step towards the integration of theory and practice and provide more authentic learning experiences for school leaders. However, there are still clear limitations with these approaches in learning and development. The limitations are as follows:

- Learning and development starts from a set of identified learning objectives typically written in the form of instructional objectives that measure gain in known cognitive, affective and psychomotor skills. In other words, the learning outcome is predetermined.
- Predetermined knowledge is useful for dealing with known problems and is not particularly suitable for dealing with emerging and new problems that do not fit the parameters of old problems. There is a need, then, for school leaders to constantly go back to training and developmental workshops to learn new skills to deal with new problems. By the time they learn the skills, other new problems emerge and the cycle repeats itself—each time training and development is a reactive response.
- As schools grow in complexity, there is a need for new and novel ways to solve emerging problems. The school leader is best placed in the school to deal with these new problems if they are equipped with powerful ways to generate new problem-solving knowledge. There is a need to overcome the current one-step behind, cyclical learning and developmental limitations of current programmes.

The Emerging Era of Future Leadership Development: Complexity-Based Learning for Leadership Development

The increasingly complex school system and new realities (economic, technological and cultural) will require a new paradigm in developing school leaders. Townsend, Acker-Hocevar, Ballenger, and Place (2013, p. 79) wrote:

> However, as school communities become increasingly diverse and more complex year by year, and where school leaders have to move from simple,

through complicated, to complex problems (Patton, 2008), from structured to unstructured ones (Leithwood & Steinbach, 1992, 1995), or from tame, to critical, to wicked ones (Grint, 2005), then this common-sense approach serves fewer and fewer people.

In a complex system such as a school, traditional instructional leadership, with its hierarchical approach where the principal plays the heroic individual directing others to follow his or her vision for the school, no longer applies. A complex system, which is made up of intricate relationships among various stakeholders, requires that leadership be distributed among the stakeholders. In this sense, leadership for learning might be a more fitting model here than traditional instructional learning, because of its emphasis on shared leadership rather than on leadership by one individual. Also, leadership for learning is designed to expand learning to all levels within the system (Townsend et al., 2013). Indeed, this is what complexity involves—permeation of interdependent relationships across all levels in the system. With increasing complexity, school leaders will need a set of new methods of inquiry to deal with new challenges that emerge.

As stated earlier, the dominant design for educational leadership programmes has been centred within the behavioural science era. However, in the last decade, there has been no lack of new theories—from strategic choice theory to learning organisation theory, to open systems theory, and now to chaos and complexity theory—as competing theories in teaching and learning design. This progression suggests a move to take into account the complexity of interactions, uncertainty and unpredictability, and their relationship with diversity and creativity within an organisation.

Cunningham (2000), in a conference paper submitted to the Institute of Education, University of London, proposes that complexity theory may provide a tool for tracing the emergence of simple organising principles from the complexity of social interaction and have implications for the study of schools and their communities. Morrison (2002) noted that complexity theory incorporates, indeed requires, unpredictable fluctuations and non-average behaviour in order to account for the change, development and novelty through self-organisation.

In the following section, I extrapolate from Fig. 7.6 and focus on the complexity theory era, briefly describing the concepts within this new cycle. I also discuss the approaches to learning and delivery of educational leadership programmes based on the concepts discussed.

Complexity Theory

In this section, I look briefly at key concepts of complexity theory. A relatively new perspective in the field of educational leadership, complexity theory provides an explanation in understanding the school as a complex organisation. Appearing in the twentieth century in response to criticism of the inadequacy of the reductionist analytical thinking model, it helps us to understand learning and suggests an alternative approach for knowledge in general and for the knower, the object of knowledge, method and truth.

The ability to self-organise successfully is a vital characteristic for any organisation to possess if it is to flourish in the complex world in which it exists. Leithwood and Day (2007, p. 208) add that 'Schools are dynamic organisations, and change in ways that cannot be predicted', based on their analysis of leadership studies from eight different countries.

By looking at the complexity of an organisation, leadership should consequently be viewed in a different light. A complex system is a functional whole, consisting of interdependent and variable parts. In other words, unlike a conventional system (e.g., an aircraft), the parts need not have fixed relationships, fixed behaviours or fixed quantities; thus, their individual functions may also be undefined in traditional terms. Despite the apparent tenuousness of this concept, these systems form the majority of our world, and include living organisms and social systems, along with many inorganic natural systems (e.g., rivers).

Evaluating leadership learning through the lens of complexity theory provides a different and new perspective on how individuals learn. This is so, especially for leadership development programmes that are designed with elements of complexity theory incorporated into the learning structures. The process of learning and new methods of inquiry take on a non-linear and unpredictable manner that makes setting fixed learning objectives meaningless. A complex system is a functional whole, consisting of interdependent and variable parts.

The following is a brief explanation of the key concepts of complexity theory and how they impact leadership learning.

Emergence

Emergence is a key concept in understanding how different levels in a system are linked. In the case of leadership learning, it is about how the individual, structure and system are linked. These different levels exist simultaneously and one is not necessarily more important than the other; rather, they are recognised as coexisting and linked. Each level has different patterns and can be subject to different kinds of theorisation. Patterns at 'higher' levels can emerge in ways that are hard to predict at the 'lower' levels. The challenge long-addressed in learning is how such levels are to be linked.

Non-linearity

Non-linearity in this paper refers to leadership learning and means that the causal links of the outcomes of learning are from something more complicated than a single source or single chain of events.

When there are no new patterns in conversations, there is no new idea and no novel ways to solve problems. The learning outcome is considered linear if one can add any two sources of learning or solutions derived from the teaching. Non-linearity in leadership learning would mean that the output of the learning is not proportional to the input and that the learning does not conform to the principle of additivity—that is, it may involve synergistic reactions in which the whole is not equal to the sum of its parts.

One way to understand non-linearity is to consider how small events lead to large-scale changes in systems. Within the natural sciences the example often cited (or imagined) is that of a small disturbance to the atmosphere in one location, perhaps as small as the flapping of a butterfly's wings, which tips the balance of other systems, leading ultimately to a storm on the other side of the globe (Capra, 1997).

Self-Organisation

Self-organisation happens naturally as a result of non-linear interaction among members of an organisation (Fontana & Ballati, 1999). As the word describes, there is no central authority guiding it or imposing on the interactions. Members in the organisation adapt to changing goals and situations by adopting communication patterns that are not centrally controlled by an authority. In the process of working towards a goal (e.g., solving a leadership problem), self-organising members tend to exhibit creativity and novelty as they have to adapt quickly and find ways and means to solve the problem and achieve the goal. As a result of interactions among members, the emergence of new patterns in conversation happens. This is an important aspect of self-organisation.

It must be noted that new patterns of conversation depend upon the responsiveness of members towards each other and their awareness of each other's ideas and response. As a result of the behaviour of interacting members, learning and adaptation or novel ways of solving problems emerge.

In summary, the complexity-based method of inquiry for building leadership capacity will have the following three key features:

* Learning emerged at the end—rather than predetermined at the beginning. In other words, participants generate new knowledge and new learning in solving problems at the end of the course. This knowledge is not taught or determined by faculty members.
* Learning is optimised from participating in the process of learning through multiple sources—where process itself is content. It is not the typical approach where content is packaged and delivered through courses. The phrase that can aptly describe this form of learning is: 'Process is content' and 'Courses as support'.
* Learning is largely self-organised and participant initiated rather than faculty-driven.

A Case Example of Complexity-Based Learning in the Leaders in Education Programme

True leaders often do not need to exercise hierarchical power. Instead, they persuade and influence others. The people follow their lead because the people identify with their vision. True leadership also promotes, enables, supports and creates innovations. In the Leaders in Education Programme (LEP) in Singapore, participants learn to do these. It is a 6-month full-time principalship development programme that is designed to meet the educational reforms in Singapore. The programme goal is to develop current and future 'principalship capability' in an increasingly complex world. Such principalship capability will be values-driven, purposeful, innovative and able to succeed in ill-defined conditions. The achievement of the programme's broad and deep goals demands a vibrant learning structure that is based on active and ongoing participation in a community of professional practice. What participants will learn is determined by the deep interactions and the active participation in the rich processes such as action learning, dialogue, reflection, external perspectives and so on. In other words, participants will be actively creating personal and content knowledge.

The highlight of the programme is the innovation project that each participant undergoes. In the innovation project, the participants have to get the principal and staff of the attachment school to buy their ideas by merely influencing them. The implementation of the innovation project is therefore a powerful test of their leadership capability. Not only have they to identify and plan the innovation, but also they have to paint an exciting picture of the innovation and learn to communicate the vision. In implementing the innovation, the participant plans and schedules every activity in the project. In this way, the project enhances the participants' independence and experience. Further details on the innovation project are as follows.

Knowledge Creation Through an Innovation Project

Participants are attached to a school throughout the programme and they spend regular weekly time in that school carrying out a major innovation project. They receive support and guidance from the principal of the school, the superintendent and a University faculty member. The project is expected to help the school to improve in leadership and management practices that lead to student learning and is meant to be a profound learning experience for the participant.

The school attachment provides the platform for participants to create new knowledge. In the short time that they spend in the school, they must lead others (teachers, students, parents) to do new things and/or must find different ways of doing existing things. The goal of creating new practical knowledge is to take the school to a higher level of achievement.

The process for knowledge creation through the innovation project is captured in Fig. 7.7. The innovation project is an example of how the three main vehicles, of knowledge triggers, generators and applications, work together. It is a major learning task for the LEP participants, one which illustrates how the LEP moves from a managerial model of school leadership to one that is based on an agenda of school-based innovation.

In this undertaking, the participants use the school context and readings (knowledge triggers), conceptualise an innovation project (knowledge

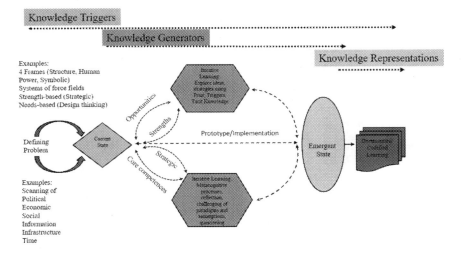

Fig. 7.7 Knowledge creation (complexity learning) through an innovation project

generator) and implement the innovation. Finally, after they have implemented the project, they represent their metacognitive learning through maxims, models, frameworks, and so on (knowledge representation). The innovation project requires each participant to design and implement an innovation in a local attachment school that can bring new value to the school and the students. The participant is to design the innovation by tapping on the strengths of the school and using an appropriate technology or know-how. Due to the time factor, the implementation of the innovation may be done as a prototype. But the participant must demonstrate the scalability and long-term sustainability of the innovation. The participants gain a basic understanding of innovation from the various courses and are encouraged to acquire more knowledge in this area through readings and discussions.

This project requires the participants to be deeply engaged in innovation so as to create a workable plan for something new. They have to scan the school's operation to understand the reality and talk to different stakeholders to gather environmental data. They have to look for strengths and opportunities, produce the blueprint of an innovation and work with the school principal and staff to implement it. The project is not a regurgitation of lecture material. Instead, the need to situate the innovation in a real school setting allows authentic learning and application of knowledge. In the syndicates, the group members discuss their innovation projects with one another. The interest is high because it is what they have to deliver. These dialogues help the participants generate new knowledge of and insights into innovation. The project allows the participants to apply the knowledge and skills of innovation in a real setting while the syndicates allow knowledge generation in a social constructivism paradigm.

Innovation is a theme that LEP participants have to grapple with when they return to school. They are keen to hear candid opinions from one another about this issue that intrigues them and matters to them. The different interpretations of the same concept, the diversity of opinions of the participants and the intellectual thrust of different people in the group greatly enrich the learning experience.

The key element in this learning project is the emergence of a workable innovative idea. This parallels complexity theory's element of emergence and autopoiesis where participants self-create knowledge (learning) during interaction with the stakeholders and components in the school system.

To date, participants have successfully completed a wide array of innovative projects and many of these projects have been sustained by the schools.

Conclusion

Future-ready leadership development needs to place an emphasis on learning, on leaders creating favourable conditions for learning, as well as sharing leadership. These are three of the five principles of leadership for learning discussed by MacBeath in another chapter in this book. Therefore, the leadership for learning model seems to be more appropriate than the traditional instructional leadership model when we discuss future-ready leadership development.

Three questions emerged in defining future-ready leadership development:

1. Knowledge development: How do school leaders continue to create new knowledge beyond courses/workshops?
2. Self-learning: How do we equip school leaders with self-learning tools that will enable them to practice lifelong learning?
3. Mixed-design leadership learning: How do training providers design leadership programmes that will address the above two questions?

In leadership development programmes, the aim is that participants will learn new and effective ways to bring about school success and reform through a well-taught programme. In programme delivery, while the international trend in education has seen a shift from teacher-centred to student-centred learning and from transmission to reflective approaches, most educational leadership programmes have remained heavily faculty centred (Barr & Tagg, 1995). In being teacher or faculty centred, the emphasis is on instructional leadership (i.e., instruction and teaching rather than learning) and this no longer serves us well. Educational programmes need to follow the paradigm shift to leadership for learning, bringing student learning to the centre of focus. The need to rethink programme delivery has gathered momentum over the years and the call for changes in programme content has been much discussed in literature even in the early 1990s (Dimmock & Walker, 1998; Hallinger & Leithwood, 1998). Universities have to shoulder an extremely difficult task in this respect, because conventional practices of course-driven programmes have been remarkably resilient over the years in the face of efforts to effect change in programme delivery and a new understanding of complexity in the world of education. School leaders have to navigate non-linear change-paths and learning how to navigate this kind of change is a critical competence for twenty-first-century change-leaders in school systems.

The complexity theoretical framework provides an alternative design for leadership development programmes that is able to meet current and future challenges that are mentioned by Cheng (2007), MacBeath (2008) and Stacey (2001). Yearly, billions of dollars are spent on training and development. It is important to ensure that the outcome of training, learning and development yields practical outcomes that are innovative and implementable.

One of the goals of this chapter is to provide a conceptual understanding of learning and design paradigms that determine eventually the outcome of learning. For more than 50 years now, the behavioural-based and competency-based designs have dominated the learning, training and development of school leaders.

Since Peter Ramus introduced the word curriculum in 1576, curriculum is usually seen as a form of planned learning. Many school leadership programmes are set and delivered in specific modules or workshops to achieve a predetermined set of competencies, knowledge and skills. In addition, these programmes are driven by faculty members and the prescribed content. The behavioural and competency concepts may still be important. However, in view of the changing reality in new emerging and advanced economies and schools, it is no longer sufficient to solely adopt behavioural- or competency-based learning for developing school leaders.

A serious implication of complexity-based design would mean shifting from 'faculty-centric' to student-centric learning. It would also mean that faculty members must be willing to step back and allow learning to emerge rather than to dictate how learning ought to proceed. Indeed, doing so involves adopting the leadership for learning model over the traditional instructional leadership model. The alternative complexity theory-based design leadership development should be considered as an alternative to generate learning that matches the challenges and complexity of the new realities in the twenty-first century. The alternate design parallels the principles of leadership for learning where the focus is on everyone learning. Future-ready and world-class education systems will need new assumptions of learning—complexity learning for school leaders.

Note

1. Retrieved from: https://data.worldbank.org/indicator/SL.SRV.EMPL.ZS?end=2015&locations=AU&start=2000&view=chart

References

Barr, R. B., & Tagg, J. (1995). From teaching to learning – A new paradigm for undergraduate education. *Change: The Magazine of Higher Learning, 27*(6), 12–26.

Capra, F. (1997). *The web of life: A new scientific understanding of living systems.* New York: Anchor.

Cheng, Y. C., & Tam, W. M. (2007). School effectiveness and improvement in Asia: Three waves, nine trends and challenges. In *International handbook of school effectiveness and improvement* (pp. 245–268). Dordrecht: Springer.

Cheng, Y. C. (2007). Future developments of educational research in the Asia-Pacific Region: Paradigm shifts, reforms, and practice. *Educational Research for Policy and Practice, 6*(2), 71–85.

Cooper, B., & Boyd, W. L. (1987). The evolution of training for school administrators. In D. Griffiths, R. Stout, & P. Forsyth (Eds.), *Leaders for America's schools* (pp. 251–272). Berkeley, CA: McCutchan.

Culbertson, J. (1988). A century's quest for a knowledge base. In N. Boyan (Ed.), *Handbook of research on educational administration* (pp. 3–26). New York: Longman.

Cunningham, R. (2000). *Chaos, complexity and the study of education communities.* A paper presented to the British Educational Research Association Annual

Conference, University of Leeds, 13–15 September 2001. Retrieved from www.ioe.ac.uk/ccs/conference2000/papers/tpm/papers/cunningham.html

Darling-Hammond, L., LaPointe, M., Meyerson, D., Orr, M. T., & Cohen, C. (2007). *Preparing school leaders for a changing world: Lessons from exemplary leadership development programs. School Leadership Study. Final Report.* Stanford, CA: Stanford Educational Leadership Institute.

Dimmock, C., & Walker, A. (1998). Comparative educational administration: Developing a cross-cultural conceptual framework. *Educational Administration Quarterly, 34*(4), 558–595.

Fontana, W., & Ballati, S. (1999). Complexity. *Complexity, 4*, 14–16.

Grogan, M., Bredeson, P., Sherman, W., Preis, S., & Beaty, D. (2009). The design and delivery of leadership preparation. In M. D. Young, G. M. Crow, J. Murphy, & R. T. Ogawa (Eds.), *The handbook of research on the education of school leaders* (pp. 395–415). New York: Routledge.

Hallinger, P. (2009). *Leadership for 21st century schools: From instructional leadership to leadership for learning.* A paper presented for the Chair Professors Public Lecture Series of The Hong Kong Institute of Education, 23 September 2009.

Hallinger, P., & Leithwood, K. (1998). Unseen forces: The impact of social culture on leadership. *Peabody Journal of Education, 73*(2), 126–151.

Hallinger, P., & Snidvongs, K. (2005). *Adding value to school leadership and management: A review of trends in the development of managers in the education and business sectors.* Nottingham, NG: National College for School Leadership.

Leithwood, K., & Day, C. (2007). What we learned: A broad view. In C. Day & K. Leithwood (Eds.), *Successful principal leadership in times of change* (pp. 189–203). Dordrecht, The Netherlands: Springer.

Lumby, J., & English, F. (2009). From simplicism to complexity in leadership identity and preparation: Exploring the lineage and dark secrets. *International Journal of Leadership in Education, 12*(2), 95–114.

MacBeath, J. (2008). Leading learning in the self-evaluating school. *School leadership and management, 28*(4), 385–399.

MacBeath, J., & Townsend, T. (2011). Leadership and learning: Paradox, paradigms and principles. In T. Townsend & J. MacBeath (Eds.), *International handbook of leadership for learning* (pp. 1–25). Dordrecht, The Netherlands: Springer.

McCarthy, M. M., & Forsyth, P. B. (2009). An historical review of research and development activities pertaining to the preparation of school leaders. In M. D. Young, G. M. Crow, J. Murphy, & R. T. Ogawa (Eds.), *The handbook* of research on the education of school leaders (pp. 86–128). New York: Routledge.

Miklos, E. (1992). Administrator preparation, educational. In M. C. Alkin (Ed.), *Encyclopedia of educational research* (6th ed., pp. 22–29). New York: Macmillan.

Morrison, K. R. B. (2002). *School leadership and complexity theory*. London: Routledge Falmer.

Murphy, J. (1998). What's ahead for tomorrow's principals. *Principal, 78*, 13–14.

Ng, F. S. D. (2013). Assessing leadership knowledge in a principalship preparation program. *International Journal of Educational Management, 27*, 425–445.

Ng, F. S. D. (2014). Complexity-based learning – An alternative learning design for the twenty-first century. *Cogent Education, 1*(1). Retrieved from www.tandfonline.com/doi/pdf/10.1080/2331186X.2014.970325

Ng, F. S. D. (2015). Leadership learning for complex organizations. *Cogent Education, 2*(1). Retrieved from www.tandfonline.com/doi/pdf/10.1080/2331186X.2015.1017312

Sergiovanni, T. J. (1991). *The Principalship: A reflective practice perspective* (2nd ed.). Boston: Allyn & Bacon.

Swaffield, S., & MacBeath, J. (2009). Leadership for learning. In J. MacBeath & N. Dempster (Eds.), *Connecting leadership and learning: Principles for practice* (pp. 32–52). Oxon, MD: Routledge.

Townsend, T., Acker-Hocevar, M., Ballenger, J., & Place, W. (2013). Voices from the field: What have we learned about instructional leadership? *Leadership and Policy in Schools, 12*(1), 12–40.

Additional Reading

Stacey, R. (2001). *Complex responsive processes in organizations: Learning and knowledge creation*. London: Routledge.

Yin, R. K. (2003). *Case study research design and methods, applied social research methods series* (Vol. 5, 3rd ed.). London: Sage.

8

Professional Autonomy and the Future of Leadership for Learning in Australia

Brian J. Caldwell

Leadership for learning is especially challenging in Australia as efforts are made to secure alignment, or at least a measure of coherence, between two levels of government, at the same time as more authority and responsibility for important decisions shifts to schools. It is a rapidly changing scene with further, possibly dramatic change, in the decade ahead.

Context

Australia has a population of 24.6 million and is a federation of six states and two territories. It was constituted from existing colonies in 1901. There are three levels of government: federal, state/territory and municipal. Municipal governments are creations of the states and territories and are not recognised in the Constitution. They provide various forms of

B. J. Caldwell (✉)
Educational Transformations, Brighton, VIC, Australia
e-mail: brian@educationaltransformations.com.au

assistance to schools in local partnership arrangements but are not considered to be a level of government in education. Federal and state/territory governments are the levels of government as far as schools are concerned.

The Constitution leaves responsibility for schools in the hands of the states, but there are factors that explain why and how an important role for the federal government has emerged. This is because Section 96 of the Constitution allows it to grant money to states/territories under whatever terms and conditions are mutually agreed. This largely arose from decisions of the High Court that upheld the exclusive right of the federal government to levy an income tax under legislation passed in 1942. This is a key factor in explaining the relatively high level of vertical fiscal inequity in Australia. The upshot is that states/territories as well as Catholic and independent schools are now dependent on the federal government for significant amounts of public funding for schools.

The federal government can create or operate within structures and processes that enable it and the governments of states/territories to work together, as illustrated in the deliberations of the Education Council (of ministers) of the Council of Australian Governments (COAG). The Australian Institute for Teaching and School Leadership (AITSL) (owned and funded exclusively by the federal government through the Minister for Education and Training) and the Australian Curriculum, Assessment and Reporting Authority (ACARA) (owned and funded jointly by the federal and state/territory governments but mandated under federal legislation) illustrate how the different levels of government have aligned their efforts in recent times.

To illustrate the foregoing, ACARA develops the Australian Curriculum that is implemented after approval by the Education Council. States/territories then adopt, adapt or incorporate it in their own curriculums, with further change by schools to meet local priorities, depending on the level of autonomy and how it is exercised. ACARA also designs and delivers a national system of tests at Years 3, 5, 7 and 9 (National Assessment Program—Literacy and Numeracy), implemented by state/territory authorities, with the online release of school-by-school results (My School). Since the federal government neither owns nor operates a school, these arrangements can only occur with the formal agreement of states/

territories. Professional standards for teachers and principals have been prepared by AITSL and approved by the Education Council. Standards related to initial teacher education have also been set but implementation is dependent on action by and agreement with universities.

Professional Autonomy and Student Achievement

The International Study on School Autonomy and Learning (ISSAL) was conducted from 2014 to 2017 and involved researchers from Australia, Canada, England, Finland, Hong Kong (China), Israel and Singapore. The study arose from a common interest in school autonomy, given that, in one way or another and under different names, it had been a priority of the government in these countries. One aspect of the study reflected an interest in the contribution of autonomy to the development of twenty-first-century skills. Reports of early progress in each of the seven countries were contained in a special issue of the *International Journal of Educational Management* (2016, Volume 30, Number 7). The study is relevant to an understanding of leadership since the extent of autonomy reflects the degrees of freedom school leaders can exercise among the various functions associated with the performance of the school.

Professional Autonomy and Leadership for Learning

The first stage of the Australian contribution to ISSAL was conducted in 2014–2016. It involved a comprehensive review of the international literature and case studies of five high-performing schools in three jurisdictions (Australian Capital Territory, Queensland, Victoria) that had at least two years of experience with relatively high levels of autonomy. Findings were reported in Caldwell (2016a) and Caldwell (2016b). Central to the findings were the following distinctions (Caldwell, 2016a, p. 4).

Autonomy For state (public, government) schools, autonomy refers to the decentralisation from the system to the school of significant authority to make decisions, especially in respect to curriculum, pedagogy, personnel and resources, within a centrally determined framework of goals, policies, curriculum, standards and accountabilities. Non-state (private, non-government) schools have traditionally had a relatively high level of autonomy.

Structural autonomy refers to policies, regulations and procedures that permit the school to exercise autonomy. Schools may take up such a remit in a variety of ways, or not at all, including ways that are ineffective if the intent is to improve outcomes for students. The granting of autonomy may make no difference to outcomes for students unless the school has the capacity to make decisions that are likely to make a difference and uses that capacity to achieve this end.

Professional autonomy refers to teachers and principals having the capacity to make decisions that are likely to make a difference to outcomes for students, and this capacity is exercised in a significant, systemic and sustained fashion. Professional autonomy calls for the exercise of judgement, with a high level of discretion in the exercise of that judgement.

The relevance of these distinctions to the future of school leadership emerged in a review commissioned by the Australian Government in July 2017 to provide advice on how to improve student achievement and school performance. The review was chaired by David Gonski who had previously chaired a review of funding for schools in Australia. The report of the second review is colloquially known as Gonski 2.0 (Department of Education and Training 2018).

Recommendation 18 in Gonski 2.0 reflected the above distinctions and cited Australia's contribution to ISSAL as its primary source (Caldwell, 2016a). The recommendation was couched in these terms: 'Ensure principals have the professional autonomy and accountability required to lead their school on the improvement journey most relevant to their starting point' (Department of Education and Training, 2018, p. 91).

The Australian Government accepted all recommendations that then formed the basis of negotiations with jurisdictions on the allocation of federal funds. Other recommendations related to the future of school leadership included 'Review and revise the Australian Professional Standard for Principals to prioritise leadership of learning and include accountability for individual student growth' (Recommendation 17) and 'Provide school leaders with high-quality professional learning' (Recommendation 20). Recommendation 17 clearly envisages principals as leaders of learning.

There are powerful implications for school leadership. It is hard to reject autonomy when the focus is on professional autonomy. Indeed, there should be an alignment of capacities for professional autonomy and those that should be addressed in programmes for professional learning. Public schools in Australia have been given significant structural autonomy for a variety of functions. Have principals and other school leaders possessed or developed the capacities to exercise professional autonomy to make decisions that lead to improvement? This takes us into the domain of professional learning. Private (non-government) schools have higher levels of structural autonomy and it is fair to ask if capacities for professional autonomy have been developed to match expectations.

Professional Autonomy and Preparation for the Principalship

The Organisation for Economic Co-operation and Development (OECD) published five volumes in its report on the Programme for International Student Assessment (PISA) 2015. Volume II (OECD, 2016a) provided an analysis of policies and practices for successful (high-performing) schools based on information gathered from students and principals. The focus was on the performance of Year 8 students in science.

Importantly as far as this chapter is concerned, the report noted that 'students score higher in science when principals exercise greater autonomy over resources, curriculum and other policies, but especially so in countries where achievement data are tracked over time or posted publicly more extensively or when principals show higher levels of educational leadership' (OECD, 2016a, pp. 230–231).

In general, there were statistically significant and positive correlations between the level of school autonomy and performance in science. There were statistically significant and negative correlations between performance and decisions made by a national education authority in the areas of resources, curriculum, disciplinary policies and assessment policies. There were no statistically significant differences between the level of school autonomy and equity in science performance (OECD, 2016a, p. 120).

Students performed better in science when principals were more autonomous, especially in countries where measures on an index of educational leadership were higher than the OECD average. 'Schools are expected to benefit more from greater autonomy when their principals are prepared for the role' (OECD, 2016a, p. 121). The positive association between principal autonomy and student performance was stronger in countries where students were assessed in standardised tests because there are 'fewer risks' if outcomes are regularly monitored.

The findings are important because they highlight the association between student achievement under conditions of professional autonomy and school leadership, especially when principals are prepared for the role. This association holds up across different national contexts.

How School Leaders Perceive Their Role in Australia

A penetrating insight into how ideas about instructional leadership and leadership for learning are played out in Australia is evident in how school leaders describe their role. OECD published an analysis of data gathered in its 2013 Teaching and Learning International Survey (TALIS) (OECD, 2016b). In 2016, there was interest in the impact of school leaders on the nurturing of professional learning communities and the environment for learning; it was not a broad-based study of school leadership or of the impact of school leaders.

The report defined certain terms that are helpful in describing what school leaders do when they adopt different styles or orientations to their work. The starting point was to describe instructional leadership and distributed leadership, each of which is considered important in creating a professional learning community and nurturing a favourable climate in support of student learning. *Instructional leadership* 'comprises leadership practices that involve the planning, evaluation, co-ordination and improvement of teaching and learning'. *Distributed leadership* is 'a reflection of leadership being shown by the principal, but also of others acting as leaders in school' (OECD, 2016b, p. 15). Four types (styles, orientations) were described:

- *Integrated leaders* are attentive to both instructional and distributed leadership in their schools and spend considerable time on curriculum- and teaching-related tasks.
- *Inclusive leaders* engage staff, students and their parents or guardians in decisions at the school, but relatively less often take up a role as instructional leaders and spend less time on curriculum- and teaching-related tasks.
- *Educational leaders* are strongly engaged in instructional leadership, but much less in involving stakeholders in decisions.
- *Administrative leaders* spend a large portion of their time on school management and administrative issues and are, as a result, less engaged in distributed and instructional leadership activities than integrated leaders. (adapted from OECD, 2016b, p. 15)

Table 8.1 contains the distribution of leadership types as reported by principals of lower secondary schools in Australia.

The responses indicate that about one quarter (26.8%) described their role in exclusively instructional leadership terms, about the same

Table 8.1 Principals' engagement in leadership activities in lower secondary education in Australia (percentage of principals reporting 'very often' or 'often' as reported in TALIS 2013)

Responses	Integrated (%)	Educational (%)	Inclusive (%)	Administrative (%)
Australia	61.5	26.8	11.3	0.5
OECD average among 35 countries	45.9	23.8	19.4	10.9

Adapted from OECD (2016b, p. 40)

proportion as did principals in the 35 countries for which data are reported in the OECD analysis (23.8%). The most striking feature of Table 8.1 is the proportion reporting an integrative style (61.5% compared to the OECD average of 45.9%), indicating a balance of instructional leadership and leadership for learning, to the extent that distributed leadership is a feature of the latter.

Table 8.2 summarises responses of principals in their reports of engagement with colleagues in aspects of leadership. Three sets of actions were identified in the OECD analysis and these may be considered indicators of leadership for learning. It is immediately apparent that the pattern of responses is about the same as the pattern in an average of responses among those reported in the OECD analysis.

The OECD report drew implications for policy and practice, especially in respect to the professional development of principals, based on the reported strength among participating countries of an integrative leadership style (Table 8.1):

> Integrated leadership, combining instructional and distributed leadership and using student outcomes to develop the school's goals, program and professional development plan, appears to be the most favourable approach to establishing such a [professional] learning community at schools. Countries and economies … can stimulate this through training programs… (OECD, 2016b, p. 17)

Table 8.2 Distribution of actions of leaders in lower secondary schools in Australia (percentage of principals as reported in TALIS 2013)

Responses	Act to support cooperation among teachers to develop new teaching practices Very often/often (%)	Act to ensure that teachers take responsibility for improving their teaching skills Very often/often (%)	Act to ensure that teachers feel responsible for their students' learning outcomes Very often/often (%)
Australia	64.0	76.1	82.5
OECD average among 36 countries	64.1	70.2	76.6

Adapted from OECD (2016b, p. 38)

Professional Learning Under Conditions of Professional Autonomy

This section summarises developments in Australia, first in respect to professional standards, and then in the findings of studies of approaches to professional learning undertaken by Jensen, Hunter, Lambert and Clark (2015) and Watterston (2015). A summary of an integrated report prepared by AITSL (2015) is also included. Then follows a summary of approaches to the preparation and professional development of principals under conditions of professional autonomy, especially in those states that have undertaken major reforms that focus on autonomy.

Standards

The Australian scene is shaped to a large extent by adoption throughout the country of two sets of professional standards, each developed by AITSL. These standards—Australian Professional Standards for Teachers and Australian Professional Standard for Principals—were approved by the Education Council of the Council of Australian Governments for adoption throughout the country. The standards serve as a touchstone for the design, delivery and assessment of professional development programmes. The following is a summary of each as they relate to the building of capacity for the exercise of professional autonomy.

The Australian Professional Standards for Teachers (AITSL, 2011a) call for capacity in three domains: professional knowledge (two standards and a total of 18 focus areas), professional practice (three standards and a total of 17 focus areas) and professional engagement (two standards and a total of 8 focus areas). The seven standards and 43 focus areas apply across each of four levels: Graduate, Proficient, Highly Accomplished and Lead. For example, the Graduate Standard for teachers who have just completed initial teacher education, calls for teachers to 'Use curriculum, assessment and reporting knowledge to design learning sequences and lesson plans' while the Lead Standard calls for a teacher to 'Lead colleagues to develop learning and teaching programs using comprehensive knowledge of curriculum, assessment and reporting requirements'.

The Standards call for increasingly higher levels of professional autonomy in the progression from Graduate to Lead. Only 9 of the 172 focus area descriptors (43 focus areas across 4 levels) explicitly refer to a system framework, although such a framework is implied in others that refer, for example, to legislated requirements. There is thus considerable scope for the exercise of professional autonomy. At issue is the extent to which legislated requirements and expectations in respect to curriculum and testing constrain that autonomy.

AITSL also developed the Australian Professional Standard for Principals (AITSL, 2011b, 2014). The Standard specifies three leadership requirements—vision and values; knowledge and understanding; and personal qualities, social and interpersonal skills, each of which is applied across five areas of professional practice: leading teaching and learning; developing self and others; leading improvement, innovation and change; leading the management of the school; and engaging and working with the community. Successful practice is intended to impact on high-quality learning, teaching and schooling, which in turn results in successful learners, confident and creative individuals and active and informed citizens. Context is recognised: school, sector and community; socio-economic and geographic; and educational systems at local, regional, national and global levels. The Standard has a robust evidence base and was the outcome of extensive consultation with stakeholders across the country.

Aspects of the Standard illustrate the role in three areas in a manner consistent with a high level of professional autonomy. Drawing from AITSL (2011a, pp. 9–11), for leading teaching and learning, principals are responsible for 'leading, designing and managing the quality of teaching and learning and for students' achievement in all aspects of their development'. For leading the management of the school, principals 'ensure that the school's resources and staff are efficiently organised and managed to provide an effective and safe learning environment as well as value for money'. For engaging and working with the community, principals 'help build a culture of high expectations that takes account of the richness and diversity of the school's wider community and the education systems and sectors'.

The Standard is silent on several matters related to autonomy. For example, a 'plan and act' element of leading the management of the school is 'Within the framework established by employing authorities/school boards manage available resources to support effective learning and teaching. Ensure budgets are integrated and aligned with learning priorities'. The 'available resources' are greater in some jurisdictions than in others; for example, in Victoria, about 90% of the state's annual recurrent budget for school education is decentralised to schools for local decision-making. The Standard is also silent on some personnel matters such as determining the mix of staff at a school and local selection of staff. Nevertheless, the processes in the Standard apply, regardless of how schools may differ on these matters.

The AITSL Studies

AITSL commissioned two reports on principal preparation and professional development. One, by Learning First (Jensen et al. 2015), provided a review of programmes, in education and other fields, national and international, and was explicitly framed by the Professional Standard for Principals. The other (Watterston, 2015) provided a systematic review of programmes in Australia. The following is a summary of findings and recommendations.

AITSL commissioned Learning First to report on the preparation of aspiring principals (Jensen et al., 2015). Programmes were described and analysed in a framework of the Australian Professional Standard for Principals. A broad perspective was adopted, with information gathered from a range of national and international sources, in education and in other fields. Practice in education included approaches in Austria, Canada, England, the United States, New Zealand and Singapore. Practice in a range of Executive MBA programmes in different countries was also summarised as well as approaches in the military. The report explicitly acknowledged the changing role of the principal, particularly under conditions of decentralisation and professional autonomy.

According to Jensen et al. (2015, pp. 3–4), the following need to be addressed in the design of preparation programmes:

1. Leadership development is an ongoing process, and a principal preparation programme is just one component.
2. Principal preparation programmes should align with an education system's strategic objectives of improving teaching and learning. Programmes should also take specific education policy objectives and context into account, as these will help shape programme content.
3. Best-practice leadership preparation includes deeper subject matter expertise, new management and leadership skills and high-order leadership capabilities.
4. Effective leadership development programmes provide a variety of learning experiences encouraging collaboration, feedback and the opportunity to practise new skills in a real-world context.
5. Programme evaluations may consider intermediate or 'proximal' outcomes … as well as longer-term student performance data.

Watterston (2015) surveyed every state jurisdiction as well as Catholic and Independent authorities in compiling her report. She identified six ingredients for programme success: (1) integration of theory and practice; (2) grounding in evidence-based research; (3) inclusion of context-related experiential activities; (4) integration of mentoring and coaching; (5) provision for shadowing, internships and school visits to help demystify the role; and (6) spaced and blended opportunities with a variety of face-to-face, online and self-directed learning opportunities.

Five weaknesses were reported: (1) inadequate funding, (2) lack of a coherent and systematic approach, (3) no clearly visible approach to the identification of potential principals, (4) lack of rigour in selection into programmes and (5) inadequate mechanisms for assessing effectiveness and impact of programmes.

Four recommendations were made for improving the 'pipeline' of applicants: (1) invest in talent identification; (2) adoption of a rigorous recruitment and selection process; (3) build partnerships between systems, universities and the profession and (4) create an evidence base to establish needs and priorities.

AITSL drew on the findings in the Learning First and Watterston reports and other studies to provide an integrated account under the title

Preparing Future Leaders (AITSL, 2015). Five recommendations were made for improving principal preparation in Australia:

1. Take a systemic, standards-based and coherent approach;
2. Identify and nurture talent;
3. Match learning to an individual's capabilities, career stage and context;
4. Use evidence-based adult learning techniques; and
5. Evaluate programmes for impact.

The report included a summary of the characteristics of 11 principal preparation programmes in several states in both government and non-government sectors. These included funding, duration, maximum number of participants, inclusion of mentoring and coaching, residential opportunities, inclusion of online experiences, project-based learning, peer learning, internship and shadowing, visits to exemplary schools, 360° profiling and university accreditation.

Professional Learning in Selected Jurisdictions

In the second phase of the Australian contribution to ISSAL in 2017 (Caldwell, 2018), interviews were conducted with leaders in professional learning in public systems in five states in response to the question: 'What approaches to the preparation and professional development of principals and teachers have proved effective in systems where higher levels of autonomy [in your state] have been extended to schools?' Brief summaries for South Australia and Tasmania are provided below. More detailed descriptions of practices in the three states with longstanding experience or recent major initiatives follow for Victoria, Western Australia and Queensland. Professional learning programmes were supported, to some extent, by the Australian Government as part of its Independent Public Schools (IPS) initiative. National Partnership Agreements (NPA) differed by state and territory to reflect priorities of jurisdictions and enable flexible implementation of the initiative. Descriptions are up-to-date at the end of 2017.

In *South Australia*, for example, funding through the NPA reflected (a) a longstanding requirement in this state that every school must have a council and (b) developments that involved a shift from a regional model for the support of the state's 528 public schools to their engagement in 60 local partnerships. Special initiatives in the NPA called for 'developing school leadership capability and capacity in managing unsatisfactory performance' and to building 'the capacity of governing councils to encourage greater parental involvement in children's learning'.

There were requirements for newly appointed principals. A mentor is assigned immediately. The principal is required to complete the Graduate Diploma in Strategic Leadership offered through the South Australian Institute for Educational Leadership by the Department of Education and Child Development Registered Training Organisation. Completion of the Graduate Diploma may gain a credit of up to 50% toward a relevant master's degree at a South Australian university. There are eight units of study in the Graduate Diploma with a key requirement that the principal successfully completes a school-based (or partnership-based) project that demonstrates the capacity to address the competencies that are specified across the units. These competencies have been mapped against elements of the Australian Professional Standard for Principals and the Leadership Framework Capabilities developed by the Department. These fall in three broad domains: (1) Self as a leader, (2) Leading change and improvement and (3) Contribute to the leadership of the organisation. Six months of executive coaching is provided for newly appointed principals to assist them during their major project.

In *Tasmania*, the focus of the NPA was entirely on the Community Empowered Schools initiative 'to increase parental engagement and involvement in school governance and decision making as part of their School Improvement Plan'. Principals may participate in related programmes. There were no formal requirements of prior professional learning for those applying for the principalship. There was a suite of modules offered by the Professional Learning Institute (PLI) from which aspirants may choose if they wish. There were no formal requirements for professional learning for serving principals although these may arise from performance and development plans as agreed with the principal's supervisor. The PLI outsources many of its modules to external providers. A pathway of professional learning for aspirants and serving leaders was under development.

The National Partnership Agreement for the Independent Public Schools initiative in *Victoria* called for the support of eight programmes for school leaders. Initially agreed in 2014, it was re-negotiated in 2016 to take account of new state priorities and initiatives. The agreement stipulated that schools would not be branded as 'independent public schools'. These eight programmes, each offered by the Bastow Institute of Educational Leadership, were building the capacity of new principals (120 each year), strategic management for principals (200 in 2014, 300 in each of the other years), leadership for business managers (80 each year), executive management for principals (100 in 2015, 200 in 2017), resourcing my principalship (200 each year), coaching for leadership (70 leadership teams in 2017), communities of practice (CoP) (120 in 2017), and technical leadership coaches (two specialist coaches available to all schools).

Bastow operates in an environment of a relatively high level of professional autonomy to meet the needs of government schools in Victoria. The current relatively high level of autonomy was established in the early 1990s but Bastow was established more than 15 years later when the need for coherence and comprehensiveness was evident, with a focus that was more on professional autonomy rather than the structural autonomy that had by then become part of the culture of schools in Victoria (although the balance of centralisation and decentralisation shifts from time to time).

Bastow is leading the design and delivery of a CoP approach. It is aimed at cultivating collaborative cultures as a lever for system-wide change that empowers highly networked principals to strengthen their capacity for leading learning which, in turn, enables a sustainable self-improving education system based on trust and mutual accountability. This approach involves the active participation of principals in collaborative professional practice networks that seek evidence, analyse data and measure the impact of strategies in the pursuit of shared goals that build the capacity for teaching and learning excellence and improved student learning outcomes.

Most of the professional learning has been delivered from the Bastow site in Melbourne. Since 2014, Bastow has significantly increased its regional delivery of courses to expand access to its professional learning suite in regional centres throughout the state. Most of the funding to support Bastow professional learning comes from the Victorian Department of Education and Training but participants are required to make a form of 'co-payment' that covers about 30% of the costs of delivery. More than 16,000 educators have participated in professional learning since 2010.

The National Partnership Agreement for the Independent Public Schools initiative in *Western Australia* contained a provision for four modules conducted over six months for principals in the IPS Leadership Program and four modules in the Empowered Governance Program for school boards. These are offered by the Institute for Professional Learning as part of its suite of programmes for IPS. There have been three reviews of IPS. One by the University of Melbourne was generally positive as was another commissioned review (Hamilton Associates, 2015). The report of a parliamentary inquiry was generally negative (Education and Health Standing Committee, 2016).

There was a measured roll-out from an initial group of 34–524 out of a total of about 800 schools. There have been changes in terminology over the years with empowerment now preferred to autonomy. The review by the University of Melbourne encouraged a shift from structural autonomy, with a preoccupation at the school level with staffing and one-line budgets, to professional autonomy, with a focus on building the capacity of principals and other school leaders before the selection of their schools into the IPS programme.

There was a high level of stability in system leadership over the life of IPS. The Director-General had served for a decade and was the longest-serving of all system leaders in Australia. The Minister for Education in the former government served for much of this period. Principals in IPS reported directly to the Director-General who met with all principals twice per year in groups of 20, with principals of remote and some regional schools participating by teleconference. Management in this unusual line management role is 'by exception' rather than ongoing with direct oversight by a regional leader. This is remarkable by national and international standards, with Western Australia (WA) geographically larger than most countries in the world and many schools in very remote locations.

Administered by the Institute for Professional Learning, the programme of preparation and professional learning for *all* principals is relatively straightforward. It contrasts with the comprehensive and coherent programme for those in or preparing for the principalship in IPS described below. This 'gateway' programme for all principals consists of principal eligibility modules that involve online learning, and which must be completed within six months of a new appointment. These are essentially compliance based, bringing appointees to an awareness level of key department policies.

In 2016–2017, the Department of Education offered five programmes in three tiers of capacity-building in the Moving from Autonomy to Empowerment initiative. The underlying rationale is that 'school autonomy in itself will not create the conditions for student success' (Hamilton, 2015) and that the following strategies are required to maximise the impact of autonomy on classrooms: principal capacity-building; intelligent accountability mechanisms; fostering an empowered mindset amongst principals and teachers; enhancing collaboration within and between schools; a focus on improving the quality of teaching and the educational experience of students; and a commitment and capacity within the central authority to deliver and support meaningful authority and not circumscribe it in such detailed ways that schools gain little benefit.

At the Entry Level, there is the IPS Development, Selection and Transition Program and the IPS Bridging Development Program. At the Consolidation Level, there is the IPS Board Development Program and the IPS Advanced Leadership Program. At the System Leadership Level, there is the IPS Principal Fellowship Program. There is no cost to participants in these programmes which are co-funded by the State and Australian Government under its Independent Public Schools initiative.

A feature is the involvement of the private sector in design and delivery. For example, Integral Development contributed to the design of the Advanced Leadership Program. The Nous Group was a contractor for the design of the IPS Board Development Program, providing training for facilitators and developing online resources.

The National Partnership Agreement on Independent Public Schools in *Queensland* is a good illustration of how Commonwealth (Australian

Government) funds can be allocated in a way that matches state priorities and work that had already been accomplished or was in progress ('scaffolding'). There are three main elements in the agreement:

- Achieve more schools with IPS status than anticipated, from 120 schools in 2015 to 250 schools in 2017 (the goal has been achieved).
- Conduct professional development programmes to build the capacity of school leaders (Leading Workforce Success) (up to 900 in first year and 10 events per year); address the needs, characteristics and contexts for delivery in schools in rural and remote areas (Capacity Building for Regional and Rural Schools) (up to 300 participants over 3 years); and strengthen school governance for principals and councils (Capable School Councils) (all members of council shall participate as they are appointed; also available to non-IPS schools with councils).
- Development of an online facility to support school-based budgeting.

As in Victoria and Western Australia, IPS schools remain part of the state school system and are required to operate in line with the same legislation, industrial instruments, directives, whole of government policy and national agreements as all other state schools. The 250 IPS schools have a direct reporting responsibility to the Director-General and, in this respect, are like the line relationship in WA. The Deputy Director-General—State Schools Performance has a broad oversight role and her prior experience as a principal has been important.

It was identified early on that IPS principals would need to set up their own professional support networks as they moved away from the close supervisor relationships with regional directors and assistant regional directors. The initial 26 schools were supported to form a collegial association of IPS schools ('Alliance') which aims to (a) facilitate professional development that furthers the goals of the IPS initiative, (b) share insights and evidence-based practice in school improvement and (c) provide advice to the Department on the implementation of the IPS initiative and influence future policy reform.

The guiding principles of the IPS Alliance are (a) students, teachers and school communities are at the centre of their work; (b) IPS schools work in collaboration with others and (c) IPS schools' work is based on strong evidence and research. While membership in the IPS Alliance is voluntary, membership has grown over the years to include nearly all 250 IPS schools. A policy framework that reflects these guiding principles was adopted by the Queensland Government in 2016.

The Alliance employs a full-time officer to support its work. Each school pays an annual fee to meet the costs of the Alliance's programmes that include three conferences each year that attract most IPS schools. Attention is given to leadership development, strengthening partnerships across the system, and innovation. A research project to draw on the experience of the initial 26 schools was underway at the time of writing.

All new IPS principals and their leadership teams receive targeted induction programmes to build their capacity and be accountable at the local level. Professional development was provided by the Department in areas such as human resources, finances and school councils, and external providers of professional development, such as the Queensland Education Leadership Institute (QELi) (see below), have also been engaged to conduct school council and leadership training. These programmes are supported by funds from the National Partnership Agreement.

Much of what has been learned with the IPS initiative has been applied in all schools and has helped contribute to a change in culture and sense of optimism in the system. Included here is the way data are being used by schools. There has been movement from an exclusively data-driven approach to an evidence-driven approach, with teachers using evidence to make informed decisions about student learning. An 'evidence hub' was formed and is now available to all schools.

The QELi was established in 2010 as a not-for-profit organisation jointly owned by the Department of Education and Training, the Queensland Catholic Education Commission and Independent Schools Queensland to help build the capacity of school leaders to drive educational reform. It is the only organisation of its kind in Australia. Participants pay a fee for their involvement in the various programmes. Offerings in 2017 included the Emerging Principals Program, the High Potential Future Teacher Leaders programme and the Middle Leadership Program and targeted events such as the Executive Leadership for School Principals Masterclass. As noted above, QELi has contributed to the IPS professional learning programme for school leaders and school councils, supported by funds that derive in part from the National Partnership Agreement.

Cross-Jurisdictional Initiatives

QELi is an example of a cross-jurisdictional initiative whereas Bastow, in Victoria, is for leaders in government schools only. Professional associations offer programmes that are cross-jurisdictional. For example, Principals Australia Institute (PAI) is a consortium of national principals' associations with membership from government and non-government sectors and membership at both primary (elementary) and secondary levels. A noteworthy initiative of PAI is the creation of a voluntary accreditation programme for those preparing for the principalship. Its creation was the outcome of international research, extensive consultation among stakeholders and trialling. It has been implemented on a voluntary basis with participants paying a fee for their engagement. A key issue is whether it will be recognised and acted upon by employing authorities.

Various professional bodies organise annual or occasional conferences that constitute another form of professional learning along with their lightly refereed journals on special themes. The most comprehensive are those of the Australian Council for Educational Leaders (ACEL). The history of this organisation illustrates the shifts in thinking about the work and study of leaders over the last half-century. Originally established as the Australian Council for Educational Administration, the initial focus was on administration, adopting the North American use of that term, and its conferences and publications reflected this. There was a high degree of separation from the fields of curriculum, pedagogy and learning. Professor William Walker, an Australian and international pioneer in the field, was its driving force. Efforts to broaden its work gathered in intensity by the turn of the century and it was renamed and restructured as ACEL. A review of its programmes and publications makes clear that its main concern is the leadership of learning, with its major conference presenters being among the leaders in the field, national and international.

Leadership in the Non-government Sector

Between one quarter and one-third of students attend a non-government (non-state, private, independent) school in Australia. This rises to more than one half at the senior secondary level in the higher Socio-Economic Status (SES) suburbs of the largest cities. These proportions are steady or in slight decline after years of growth. It is therefore of interest how these schools prepare and facilitate professional learning for their leaders.

The largest number of non-government schools are Catholic schools, with most organised into systems which organise programmes for their leaders and potential leaders. Most reflect a leadership for learning orientation with an agenda like those for government schools in the states as described in the preceding pages. Along with their non-systemic counterparts, some participate in cross-jurisdictional events. Most independent schools are supported by a professional organisation in their state or territory which organises programmes for leaders and charge a fee to participants. These programmes may be comprehensive, especially in the larger states, serving leaders at different stages of their careers. Some topics carry greater weight than those serving government schools, for example, board governance, reflecting a higher level of autonomy of non-government schools.

Summary

The Australian Standard for Principals approved by the Education Council is rigorous by international standards but some programmes for professional learning based on this standard are not as aligned with it as they might be, especially for those working under conditions of professional autonomy. The findings and recommendations of Australian studies of preparation and professional development programmes are consistent with recommendations in the international domain; indeed, researchers have contributed to international work. Details of preparation and professional development for three states were provided (Victoria, Western Australia and Queensland) and these were partly funded at the time by National Partnership Agreements for the Independent Public Schools initiative of the Australian Government. Participation is mandatory if a school is to join the IPS schemes in Western Australia and Queensland (as it was when high levels of autonomy were extended to all schools in Victoria in the mid-1990s). These and other programmes for leaders and potential leaders in government schools generally reflect a leadership for learning orientation, as do events organised by professional associations that are cross-jurisdictional, and those organised for those in non-government schools.

Discussion

There is a strong case that a profession of school leadership is emerging in Australia as a consensus settles on the practice as leadership for learning, energised by the exercise of professional autonomy. Hargreaves and Fullan (2012) distinguished between *being professional* and *being a professional*. While both are desirable, 'Ideally, of course, it's best to be professional and be a professional at the same time—to have status and autonomy and be trusted and able to make informed judgments effectively' (Hargreaves & Fullan, 2012, p. 81). They cited Etzioni's list of the characteristics of a profession:

* Specialised knowledge, expertise and professional language;
* Shared standards of practice;
* Long and rigorous processes of training and qualification;
* A monopoly over the service that is provided;
* An ethic of service, even a sense of calling, in relation to clients;
* Self-regulation of conduct, discipline, and dismissals;
* Autonomy to make informed discretionary judgments;
* Working together with other professionals to solve complex cases; and
* Commitment to continuous learning and professional upgrading. (cited by Hargreaves & Fullan, 2012, p. 80)

A high level of professional autonomy in Australia is consistent with many of these characteristics, especially those concerned with specialised knowledge, standards, making informed professional judgements and working together to solve complex cases. There is progress on processes of training and qualification and commitment to continuous learning and upgrading. A monopoly over service and self-regulation largely lies with employing authorities and their requirements for selection and appointment rather than leaders themselves, as would be achieved if current voluntary accreditation schemes such as those developed by the Principals Australia Institute become compulsory. Recognition that cases are complex is consistent with a leadership for learning orientation as is an ethic of service.

In an optimistic scenario, if high levels of professional autonomy are achieved for all leaders, especially principals, in what ways should systems of education change, especially when different levels of government are involved? Taking a systems' view, a major change cannot be made at the point of delivery—the school—without changes to other parts of the system. If an open systems' view is taken, how do all parts of the system respond, reaching new points of equilibrium? These matters were addressed in the second phase of Australia's contribution to ISSAL, the main thrust of which was to examine strategic alignment among different levels of government in 13 countries, including most of the world's top performers. A re-alignment of roles was recommended for Australia (Caldwell, 2018).

There is international interest in how higher levels of autonomy may affect the roles of different levels of government. Burns and Köster described increasing complexity in multi-level governance and the challenge of reaching an equilibrium. They singled out the trend to autonomy in response to demands from local actors who are increasingly diverse and well educated. They observed that 'Education systems are now characterised by multi-level governance where the links between multiple actors operating at different levels are to a certain extent fluid and open to negotiation' (Burns & Köster, 2016, p. 11).

A likely and preferred scenario for Australia is a deepening concern for leadership for learning among school leaders, with higher levels of professional autonomy driving the effort. A profession of school leadership is likely to emerge, with a re-alignment of roles between federal and state/territory governments and within the latter. This will call for a higher level of system adaptivity than is currently evident.

Acknowledgement The research reported in this chapter was supported by funds from the Department of Education and Training of the Australian Government.

References

AITSL (Australian Institute for Teaching and School Leadership). (2011a) *Australian professional standards for teachers.* Melbourne, Australia: AITSL. Retrieved from https://www.aitsl.edu.au/teach/standards

AITSL. (2011b). *Australian professional standard for principals.* Melbourne, Australia: AITSL. Retrieved from https://www.aitsl.edu.au/lead-develop/understand-the-principal-standard

AITSL. (2014). *Australian professional standard for principals and the leadership profiles.* Melbourne, Australia: AITSL. Retrieved from https://www.aitsl.edu.au/lead-develop/understand-the-principal-standard/leadership-profiles

AITSL. (2015). *Preparing future leaders.* Melbourne, Australia: AITSL. Retrieved from https://www.aitsl.edu.au/docs/default-source/general/preparing-future-leaders.pdf?sfvrsn=1c06e33c_2

Burns, T., & Köster, F. (Eds.). (2016). *Governing education in a complex world* (Centre for Educational Research and Innovation). Paris: OECD Publishing.

Caldwell, B. J. (2016a). *The autonomy premium.* Melbourne, Australia: ACER Press.

Caldwell, B. J. (2016b). *What the principals say.* Melbourne, Australia: Educational Transformations.

Caldwell, B. J. (2018). *The alignment premium.* Melbourne, Australia: ACER Press.

Department of Education and Training. (2018). *Through growth to achievement.* Report of the review to achieve educational excellence in Australia's Schools, Review Panel David Gonski (Chair), Terry Arcus, Ken Boston, Valerie Gould, Wendy Johnson, Lisa O'Brien, Lee-Anne Perry and Michael Roberts, (often referred to as Gonski 2.0). Canberra, Australia: Department of Education and Training. Retrieved from https://docs.education.gov.au/documents/through-growth-achievement-report-review-achieve-educational-excellence-australian-0

Education and Health Standing Committee (Western Australia). (2016). *The IPS report card.* Report of the inquiry into the Independent Public Schools Initiative, Report No. 8 of the Education and Health Standing Committee, Legislative Assembly. Perth, Australia: Parliament of Western Australia. Retrieved from http://www.parliament.wa.gov.au/parliament/commit.nsf/(Report+Lookup+by+Com+ID)/56AF902F3A6948E648258010001500F6/$file/23820473.pdf

Hamilton Associates. (2015). *School autonomy: Building the conditions for student success.* Report of research commissioned by the Department of Education, Western Australia. Retrieved from https://www.education.wa. edu.au/documents/2548175/2664299/FINAL+School+Autonomy+Buildin g+the+conditions+for+the+student+success.pdf/e6d0bc09-423b-4a1e-b569-fb1b596c462e

Hargreaves, A., & Fullan, M. (2012). *Professional capital: Transforming teaching in every school.* London/New York: Routledge.

Jensen, B., Hunter, A., Lambert, T., & Clark, A. (2015). *Aspiring principal preparation.* Melbourne, Australia: AITSL. Retrieved from https://www.aitsl.edu. au/docs/default-source/default-document-library/aspiring-principal-preparation-(print-friendly).pdf?sfvrsn=80aaec3c_0

OECD. (2016a). *PISA 2015 results (Volume II) policies and practices for successful schools.* Paris: OECD Publishing. Retrieved from http://www.keepeek.com/ Digital-Asset-Management/oecd/education/pisa-2015-results-volume-ii_9789264267510-en#.WLYFjIGGMdU#page4

OECD. (2016b). *School leadership for learning: Insights from TALIS 2013.* Paris: OECD Publishing. Retrieved from https://doi.org/10.1787/9789 264258341-en

Watterston, B. (2015). *Environmental scan principal preparation programs.* Melbourne, Australia: AITSL. Retrieved from https://www.aitsl.edu.au/docs/ default-source/school-leadership/principal-preparation/environmental-scan-principal-preparation-programs-(screen).pdf

9

Leaders of Learning: Recovering the Pedagogical Role of School Leaders and Promoting Leadership at All Levels in Scotland

Margery A. McMahon

In Scotland, in recent years, the focus on leadership for learning has intensified. This is majorly because of the *Teaching Scotland's Future* Report (TSF) (2011), which positioned school leaders as leaders of learning 'not just in relation to young people but for themselves, their staff and student teachers' (Donaldson, 2011, p. 102). This chapter provides a critical overview of how this aspiration has been realised, through a national leadership strategy to advance leadership at all levels. This imperative has also afforded the opportunity to consider how leadership is positioned and presented in initial teacher preparation as part of a more coherent professional continuum. The chapter begins by discussing the ways in which leadership at all levels has been promoted and how this articulates with government policy focused on achieving excellence and equity in education and reducing a poverty-related attainment gap. Terms such as

M. A. McMahon (✉)
University of Glasgow, Glasgow, UK
e-mail: Margery.McMahon@glasgow.ac.uk

© The Author(s) 2019
T. Townsend (ed.), *Instructional Leadership and Leadership for Learning in Schools*, Palgrave Studies on Leadership and Learning in Teacher Education, https://doi.org/10.1007/978-3-030-23736-3_9

219

leadership *for* learning and leadership *of* learning feature as a constant (the term instructional leadership is not used widely in the Scottish context) though the depth and range of application reflect the critical priorities of the government. There is a recognition that improving teacher and leader quality is central to achieving system-level change and improving educational outcomes for children and young people. The chapter concludes by considering the way in which leadership *as* learning has emerged as a third dimension, where being a lead learner and leading the learning of other practitioners, as well as pupils, is a key tenet of the teacher professionalism.

Leadership at All Levels

The promotion of leadership at all levels was an important recommendation of the *Teaching Scotland's Future* report. The subsequent articulation of this was effected through a National Implementation Board and a new leadership college. Part of this involved the development of the Framework for Educational Leadership. This mapped out a professional continuum for leadership development (Scottish Government, 2014). The framework serves as a guide for teachers and school leaders on how leadership is enacted and actions that teachers and school leaders might take to achieve and sustain it.

In spite of the inclusive and distributive approach to leadership that leadership at all levels implied, it was posited on a model of positional leadership aligned to the organisational hierarchies in schools (Mowat & McMahon, 2018). Consequently, the framework reflected a staged model linked to formal roles/positions in schools: teacher leader, middle leader, school leader and system-level leader (Mowat & McMahon, 2018). In taking forward the strategy to promote leadership at all levels, two issues emerged: (a) the implications for pre-service/initial teacher education and (b) the extent to which teacher leadership became the paradigm and vehicle to secure the wider engagement of the teaching profession in leadership. These two elements are considered in the following section.

Leadership Learning in Initial Teacher Education

Two key questions arising from the promotion of leadership at all levels consider when leadership learning should occur and whether a greater case can be made for leadership learning in pre-service or initial teacher education. In most education systems, leadership learning occurs after initial qualification, once a teacher has become established in the profession. Unsurprisingly, a search of the literature shows this to be an under-researched area of teacher education, though in some of the literature it falls under the umbrella of service-leadership.

The TSF report in Scotland set down a new marker for leadership learning in the initial phase of teacher education. A wide-scale review and consultation exercise was undertaken by the review group, led by Graham Donaldson, former Chief Inspector of Schools in Scotland. The review found that beginning teachers had limited knowledge about leadership in education and 'many early career teachers who engaged with the Review had very little awareness of leadership expectations and pathways, although local authority induction programmes often provided opportunities to learn about school and system level leadership' (Donaldson, 2011, p. 58). Donaldson proposed that the early phase of teacher education provided significant opportunities to extend understanding of the facets of leadership in education (Donaldson, 2011, p. 58) and argued for 'the importance of leadership for successful learning and the need to develop leadership qualities and skills from the outset of a career' (pp. 58, 79). When a career in teaching was seen to begin (by admission to an initial teacher preparation programme or admission to the profession post qualification) was not specified but the reform of pre- and in-service teacher education afforded opportunities to align professional programmes more closely with educational policy priorities, of which leadership was central.

Recommendations from the Donaldson report were wide-reaching, resulting in revised professional standards for teaching and in new teacher education programmes to replace the traditional Bachelor of Education programme, and the refreshment of existing programmes. Despite Donaldson's attention to leadership learning and leader development in the early phase of a teaching career, this was not fully explicated in the professional teaching standards published in 2012 (GTCS, 2012a), particularly, those pertaining to initial registration. In the preface to these standards (GTC, 2012a, p. 2), it was noted that:

> effective leadership depends on the principles of collegiality. All teachers should have opportunities to be leaders. They lead learning for, and with, all learners with whom they engage.

Within the Standards for Registration, leadership was seen as central to professionalism, listed alongside 'committing to lifelong enquiry, learning, and professional development' as core aspects of professionalism and collaborative practice (GTCS, 2012a, p. 6).

As noted above, Donaldson's recommendation for leadership at all levels was largely seen as pertaining to the post-qualification phase and a series of national initiatives and programmes were launched to take the TSF agenda forward. While initial teacher education programmes were revised significantly to advance Donaldson's recommendations for Masters-level learning, grounded in enquiry and delivered in partnership with schools, a dichotomy between pre-service and in-service education remained in relation to leadership learning in the initial phase. The extent to which this has permeated across career phases is currently being explored in a research study involving Scotland, the Republic of Ireland and Northern Ireland, funded by the Standing Committee on Teacher Education North and South. The study is investigating the extent to which leadership learning is embedded within the initial teacher education curricula in the participating systems. The project is examining models that have been successfully adopted and will then review curricula for initial teacher education to identify opportunities to further embed leadership learning. Preliminary findings from the initial phase of the study suggest three patterns: named leadership courses though the leadership element is variable; courses where leadership behaviours and practices are developed though leadership is omitted from course nomenclature and literature; and courses where leadership is deeply submerged with explicit and implicit articulations difficult to discern.

Promoting the concept of leadership learning in initial teacher education is not without controversy, and arguments are advanced about the challenges of introducing another 'subject' to an already crowded curriculum, which needs to respond to policy priorities, as well as a curriculum that increasingly comes under public scrutiny and the influence of assertive lobby groups. Moreover, there is resistance emanating from a concern that leadership learning in the initial phase will promote a 'race to the top', with new teachers accelerating through their early years to secure a leadership role, without the taking the time to consolidate their teaching practice and 'learn their craft'.

There is a concern, however, to underline that leadership learning in initial teacher education is not about creating a 'principal pipeline', though that may be a longer term consequence. Rather, it entails educating beginning teachers and equipping them with the skills to understand and contribute to the leadership they will experience as a teacher. Understanding leadership is, therefore, central to teacher professionalism, and with the focus in many schools on distributive and collaborative leadership, all teachers need opportunities to develop leadership knowledge and practices. It is, therefore, a form of socialisation into the profession. Early-career teachers are exposed to leadership in many ways and so leadership learning in initial teacher education is a means to help them understand the leadership actions and decisions that impact directly upon them and their pupils. However, it is more than this. Classrooms today are increasingly more diverse and inclusive and it is not unusual for there to be two or three other adults (or more) providing a range of pupil support. Classroom teachers are, therefore, not only leading the learning of their pupils but also are leading and managing other adults, directly in their educative role of leading learning (King & McMahon, 2017). While beginning teachers may have a slightly reduced teaching timetable and access to a school-based mentor (as in the Scottish Teacher Induction Scheme), the reality for many new teachers is that they will be working with and leading other adults from the outset. In this respect, leadership learning could be included as a 'first day competence' for new entrants to the teaching profession (Hammond, 2018).

As noted above, the literature on leadership learning in initial teacher education is limited, but from this small body, a persuasive case is made.

It is seen as a means for building leadership capacity across schools and is part of a leadership development continuum (Hamilton, Forde, & McMahon, 2018). It helps develop understandings of the school as an organisation and positions teacher leadership as a dimension expected of all teachers. It also challenges existing leadership hierarchies and where leadership is seen to reside in schools. It is a means of system-level transformation and engagement of all teachers in developing understandings and skills that support collaborative professionalism. Finally, it is part of the long-term development of a leadership pipeline (Forde, Dickson, & McMahon, 2018; Mowat & McMahon, 2018).

Pucella (2014) argues for the importance of raising student teachers' awareness of the nature of leadership to challenge their perceptions of leadership and hierarchies in schools, through which they can become more competent and confident in exercising agency and advocacy. She also sees it as central to the construction of their professional identity; through exploring power dynamics and relations in education they build a better sense of self-efficacy. It builds collaborative skills and strengthens the efficacy of student teachers in anticipation of future change agency; it enhances followership skills as well as leadership skills and fosters a sense of active participation in schools (Pucella, 2014).

Endorsing a move towards more visible leadership learning in initial teacher education is challenging. In addition to its place in a curriculum that is already seen to be overcrowded, there are questions about competing constructions of leadership, whether building secure theoretical understandings in a complex area is sufficient, and about the authenticity of experiences that may be built into programmes of study (Forde et al., 2018). There are questions about what leadership learning in the initial phase consists of. Is it, for example, seen to involve knowledge development; skills development; and values, attitudes and readiness to participate and exercise agency (Forde et al., 2018)? Questions have been raised also about whether leadership learning in the initial phase is simply a proxy for professionalism. Leadership for learning and teacher leadership are two constructs for how these questions might be addressed: for how leadership at all levels might be achieved and for how leadership learning in initial teacher education might be conceptualised and advanced. These are now considered in the following section.

Leadership for Learning and Teacher Leadership

Leadership for learning and teacher leadership are terms that are more commonly used in the Scottish context, rather than instructional leadership (which is rarely used), when discussing practices of teachers to lead learning for themselves, their pupils, and other colleagues. Both terms have gained greater currency and traction in recent years with the wider rollout of the TSF recommendations (Donaldson, 2011). In the Scottish context, leadership for learning is seen as transcending positions (i.e., remunerated roles) and is viewed as an expectation and responsibility for all teachers, from classroom teachers to headteachers (principals). Recently, however, there has been a more overt assertion of the role of the headteacher in leading learning, not to diminish the contribution of others, but to recover what is seen to be the core work of the headteacher (principal), that is, to lead learning, though this is not framed directly as 'instructional leadership'.

The promotion of leadership for learning predated TSF (2011) and in terms of the policy agenda can be traced back to the publication of the document 'Leadership for Learning: The Challenges of Leading in Times of Change' by the Scottish school inspection body—Her Majesty's Inspectorate for Education (HMIe, 2007). HMIe undertakes the inspection of schools in Scotland to provide assurance to Scottish Ministers regarding the quality of education across schools in Scotland (including schools in both the state and private sectors) (HMIe, online). A self-evaluation framework, How Good Is Our School, is available to support schools in their preparations for inspection. This framework consists of 15 quality indicators (QIs) against which schools are evaluated and self-evaluate. QI 1.2 is Leadership *of* Learning. The guidance for schools issued by HMIe relating to QI 1.2 is detailed in Table 9.1.

The 2007 *Leadership for Learning* report (HMIe, 2007) sets out a vision for the critical role of leadership in achieving the ambitions for education in Scotland. Since then there has been considerable emphasis and investment in leadership as a key driver in realising educational improvement. While the distinction between leadership *for* and *of* learning might seem insignificant, this should not be immediately dismissed as linguistic slip-

Table 9.1 Advice for schools from HMIe related to the leadership of learning

QI 1.2 Leadership of learning

This indicator relates to leadership of improvements in learning and teaching. It highlights the importance of professional commitment to improving pedagogy through a range of approaches to career-long professional learning including collegiate working. It focuses on leadership which improves outcomes for learners through enabling them to lead their own learning.

Theme 1: Professional engagement and collegiate working

Across our school, an ethos of professional engagement and collegiate working is evident. This leads to continuous improvement in learning and teaching and improved outcomes for our learners. There is evidence of strong leadership of learning by staff at all levels and in a range of contexts. We build and maintain constructive relationships, within our setting and beyond, which foster collective responsibility and mutual support. All staff undertake lead roles to motivate, support and inspire others. Our school has a collegiate learning culture demonstrated through, for example, collaborative practitioner enquiry, peer learning, constructive feedback, professional dialogue and debate. All staff work collaboratively with colleagues, learners, partners and parents to take forward improvement priorities and learn with and from each other.

Theme 2: Impact of career-long professional learning

All staff routinely engage in career-long professional learning (CLPL) and develop enquiring and coherent approaches which build and sustain our practice. The model of professional learning is understood and used by all staff. Individually and collectively, we plan and evaluate our professional learning directly on the quality of impact on learning and can evidence improvements for learners. We develop and use knowledge from literature, research and policy sources to support the process of leading and developing learning. We are proactive in extending and deepening our knowledge and understanding of curriculum areas to ensure our subject knowledge is up-to-date. We support staff to access high-quality professional learning linked to cross-cutting themes such as sustainable development education, global citizenship, outdoor learning and international education. We are improving our approaches to digital learning and teaching. We critically reflect on individual and collective professional learning. We work collaboratively to enhance teaching which leads to high-quality learning experiences for our learners. Our staff maintain effective records of their professional learning and development and create a clear professional learning action plan. We can evidence the impact our professional learning has had on our work and the progress, achievement and attainment of learners over time.

Theme 3: Children and young people leading learning

We provide a wide range of opportunities and support to ensure children and young people can take responsibility for their own learning, successes and achievements. Our learners are developing the necessary resilience and confidence to enable them to make decisions about their own learning and to lead others' learning. They demonstrate this in a range of learning contexts within the school and community. Children and young people value the professional advice and expertise of school staff and others who support their learning and decision-making. They actively engage in communication and discussions about their next steps and contribute to planning learning pathways which meet their needs and aspirations.

(continued)

Table 9.1 (continued)

QI 1.2: Features of highly effective practice	QI 1.2: Challenge questions
• Head teachers empower staff and take steps to develop leadership at all levels to improve the overall capacity of the school. • Senior leaders create the conditions for effective leadership at all levels and as a result all staff undertake leadership roles which focus on leading learning. • All staff participate in individual and collective professional learning which improves outcomes for learners. • Staff engage regularly in professional dialogue to develop collective understanding. For example, shared understanding of standards, pedagogy, assessment and strategies for raising attainment. • The school has a range of effective systems and structures to facilitate regular collegiate working to maximise opportunities for staff learning within and beyond the school. • Senior leaders facilitate a range of approaches to professional learning to enable staff to learn with and from each other. Where appropriate, this includes learning with colleagues across sectors and with partner agencies. • Senior leaders build on the skills and talents of individuals to build leadership capacity. • There is a very strong focus on improving learning among staff across the school. • There is evidence of clear and measurable impact of professional learning on outcomes for learners. • Staff work collaboratively to strengthen their understanding and implementation of key national policies including the *Scottish Attainment Challenge*, *Developing Scotland's Young Workforce* and *Learning for Sustainability*. • Staff are confident in discussing how they have improved their practice as a result of their professional learning activities. • There is evidence of a range of strategies in use to support children and young people to take responsibility for their own learning and progress. These are enabling children and young people to have greater confidence and skills in leading their own learning and that of others. • Learners regularly engage in challenging dialogue with others about their learning and progress and use this to set themselves clear targets in learning.	• How effectively do we create a learning culture within our school? • To what extent are all staff involved in leading learning across and beyond our school? • How well do we support staff to make use of the Framework for Educational Leadership and Scottish College for Educational Leadership (SCEL) to support their learning and development? • To what extent is our professional learning based on the values and actions within the GTCS professional standards? • To what extent do our quality improvement processes lead to improvements in learning and teaching? • How effective are our approaches to collegiate learning? Are we using an appropriate range of approaches which enable us to learn with and from each other? • How effective are we at building on individual skills and talents to lead improvements? • How effectively do we share our individual and collective learning across the school? • To what extent do we critically engage with research, policy sources and developments in learning and teaching? • How do we know that our professional learning is improving outcomes for learners? • How reliable is our evidence of impact on pupil learning? • To what extent do we support children and young people to take responsibility for their own learning and progress? • What strategies are we using to develop resilience and confidence in our learners to lead their own and others' learning? • How effectively are we supporting learners to initiate questions about their own learning and progress? • To what extent are our approaches improving learning for all?

Reproduced from HMIe (2014), *How Good is Our School*, 4th Edition. Livingston: Education Scotland page but rather reflects the ways in which concepts of leadership in leading school improvement have evolved and could possibly collide. Here, the emphasis is less on the leading of learning on behalf of and for others (as constructed in senior leadership roles in schools), but leading learning for all in the school community, including pupils as leaders of learners, and also other members of the school community. The tensions that have arisen as it has evolved have shown that such distinctions, conceptually and in practice, are not easily resolved, particularly, as expectations associated with more performative cultures have come to dominate.

'Leadership for Learning: The Challenges of Leading in Times of Change' (HMIe, 2007) foregrounded leadership as a critically determining factor for school improvement. It was a theme that continued to be emphasised in the subsequent *Teaching Scotland's Future* report, by the same author, former Chief Inspector of Schools, Graham Donaldson. In his TSF Report (2011), Donaldson presented his findings on a major review of teacher education in Scotland, all of which were accepted in full or in part by the Scottish Government. While 'leadership for learning' warranted only brief mention (p. 10), arguably Donaldson's recommendations on career-long professional learning and the development of leadership at all levels reflect the broader ethos and culture of leadership for learning (Donaldson, 2011, p. 10).

The rollout of the Donaldson recommendations was effected through a national implementation board and the translation from policy to practice involved key stakeholders such as, inter alia, the regulatory body for the profession, the General Teaching Council for Scotland (GTCS), the national education and inspection agency, Education Scotland and the providers of pre-service and in-service teacher education, which in Scotland resides largely with universities. The GTCS professional standards, which were revised to align with the TSF recommendations, are an important lever for effecting change in education since teacher education programmes are benchmarked against the Standards and accredited by GTCS. A professional update scheme (which requires teachers to demonstrate how they are maintaining practice against the relevant professional standard) was designed to be a further mechanism for effecting change. Leadership for learning evolves across the suite of standards, which reflects the professional continuum from early career to headship/principalship. Thus, in Scotland there are five professional teaching standards (see Table 9.2):

Table 9.2 Professional standards and career stages in Scottish education

Professional standard	Career stage
Standards for registration	
Standard for provisional teacher registration	Pre-service
Standard for full registration	Newly qualified teacher
Standard for career-long professional learning	Established/Accomplished
Standards for leadership	
Standard for middle leadership and management	Middle leader
Standard for headship	Headteacher/Principal

As noted earlier, in the Standards for Registration, mention is made of the opportunities that should be available for all teachers to be leaders and that they 'lead learning for, and with, all learners with whom they engage' (GTCS, 2012a). Though the Standards for Registration specify a focus on leadership for learning (GTCS, 2012a, p. 3), no further explication of what this means or how it is realised is provided in this entry-level standard. However, the Standard for Career-Long Professional Learning (SCLPL) sets greater expectations:

> GTC Scotland recognises that effective leadership depends on the principles of collegiality. All teachers should have opportunities to be leaders. They lead learning for, and with, all learners with whom they engage. They also work with and support the development of colleagues and other partners. The Standard for Career-Long Professional Learning includes a focus on teacher leadership and leadership for learning. (GTCS, 2012b, p. 2)

The Standard sets out the professional knowledge and understanding expected of those who are engaging with the SCLPL which involves developing deep, critically informed knowledge and understanding to enhance skills and abilities in relation to the key areas of career-long professional learning. These key areas are pedagogy, learning and subject knowledge; curriculum and assessment; enquiry and research; educational contexts and current debates in policy, education and practice; sustaining and developing professional learning; and learning for sustainability (GTCS, 2012b, pp. 8–9). Although not listed under professional knowledge and understanding, the SCLPL specifies the leadership expected from teachers working with this Standard so they are expected to develop and apply their knowledge, skills and expertise through enquiry and sustained professional learning for the following purpose:

- Deepen and develop subject, curricular and pedagogic knowledge to be able to lead learners and the learning of colleagues
- Lead curriculum development with a deep understanding of the place of subject knowledge and the wider purposes of education
- Lead and collaborate with others to plan innovative curricular programmes
- Lead and work with others to ensure effective practice in the assessment of learning, including a deep knowledge and understanding of the policies and practices of assessment as required by awarding bodies
- Lead and participate in collaborative practitioner enquiry
- Lead and contribute to the professional learning of all colleagues, including students and probationers (GTCS, 2012b, p. 8).

The Standards for Leadership and Management (which encompass the Standard for Middle Leadership and Management and the Standard for Headship) specify the leadership expectations further. As well as the opportunity for all teachers to be leaders, to lead learning for, and with, all learners with whom they engage and work, and to support the development of colleagues and other partners, the Standards for Leadership and Management include a focus on leadership for learning, teacher leadership and working collegiately to build leadership capacity in others (GTCS, 2012c, p. 2). Underpinning this is a model of the leader as 'the leading learner' who commits to their own career-long learning and encourages others to engage in career-long learning to enhance their practice (GTCS, 2012c, p. 8).

An emphasis on collegiality and working collaboratively to build capacity in self and others features as part of the professional standards. However, while standards can set out the broad expectations of teachers, their adoption and enactment require the engagement of all stakeholders. One of the ways in which this has been realised in Scotland is through the development of teacher leadership programmes which are underpinned by the principles and practices of leadership for learning. An early prototype was a new programme in teacher leadership following the publication of *Leadership for Learning* in 2007 (HMIe, 2007). This new award-bearing programme was commissioned by Scotland's largest teachers' professional association and trade union, the Educational Institute of Scotland, and was delivered jointly by two universities. Similar courses subsequently were developed by other providers.

The emergence of the Scottish College for Educational Leadership (SCEL) as a result of the TSF recommendations saw the development of a national strategy for developing leadership at all levels. An early focus of the new college was teacher leadership. Although not accredited, the structured teacher leadership programme it developed achieved a national footprint, involving teachers from across Scotland. An internal evaluative report (SCEL, 2016) provided a typology of a teacher leader as first and foremost an effective teacher, who could also work well with and influence their colleagues. They are:

> … passionate about learning and teaching. Through informed and innovative practice, close scrutiny of pupils' learning needs and high expectations they play a fundamental role in improving outcomes for children and young people. Teacher leaders are effective communicators who collaborate with colleagues, demonstrate integrity and have a positive impact on their school community. They model career-long professional learning. (Scottish College for Educational Leadership, 2016, p. 18)

Then, it could be said that within the Scottish context there has been significant progress in promoting professional cultures and creating the conditions for system-level improvement through levers such as those outlined above: professional standards for teaching; a professional update scheme for teachers; review of teacher education; enactment of a national leadership strategy through a Framework for Educational Leadership and a new leadership college; and a clear focus on leadership for and leadership of learning through the school self-evaluation and inspection process. As these have evolved there has been greater coherence, though the pace of change became an issue as the need for system uplift became a priority for the Scottish government. An Organisation for Economic Co-operation and Development (OECD) report on the implementation of Scotland's

Curriculum for Excellence also commented more generally on system-level reform (OECD, 2015, p. 3) and, while recognising what had been achieved, provided detailed recommendations for further change. The development of a coherent strategy for building teacher and leadership social capital formed one of the recommendations (OECD, 2015, p. 12).

Driven by declining performance in international league tables such as the Programme for International Student Assessment, concerns about literacy and numeracy emerging from the Scottish Survey of Literacy and Numeracy and evidence of the widening of a poverty-related attainment gap, in 2016 Scotland's First Minister boldly committed to being judged on her government's education policy. A new National Improvement Framework (NIF) and proposed Headteachers' Charter were fast-tracked as the mechanisms to bring about the required change at the scale, pace and scope seen to be necessary. These are now explored in the following section.

The National Improvement Framework and the Headteachers' Charter

In the NIF, the following four key priorities for education in Scotland were identified:

- Improvement in attainment, particularly, in literacy and numeracy
- Closing the attainment gap between the most and least disadvantaged children
- Improvement in children's and young people's health and well-being
- Improvement in employability skills and sustained positive school leaver destinations for all young people (Scottish Government, 2016, p. 7).

Six drivers for improvement would be the means of addressing these priorities consisting of school leadership; teacher professionalism; parental engagement; assessment of children's progress; school improvement; and performance information (Scottish Government, 2016, p. 9). The first iteration of the NIF, in 2016, foregrounded later versions and policy which was to set out the ambition for a school- and teacher-led self-improving system (Scottish Government, 2017). In the 2016 NIF, the emphasis was placed on the need to empower headteachers and teachers, who in turn empower others to take ownership of their own learning, and who have a strong track record of ensuring the highest quality of learning and teaching (Scottish Government, 2016, p. 10). In evaluating this, through the inspection process, the focus was to be the leadership of change, rather than the leadership of learning, which was not mentioned explicitly.

A proposed Headteachers' Charter, as part of a review of educational governance, set out 'the rights and responsibilities of the headteachers, empowering them to be the leaders of learning in their schools' (Scottish Government, 2017). The new Charter, it was proposed, would give headteachers 'freedom to lead teaching and learning in their schools, by setting out that it is for headteachers to decide how best to design their local curriculum in line with the national framework set out by the Curriculum for Excellence' (Scottish Government, 2017). While this emphasis on supporting headteachers to be leaders of learning in their schools was welcomed, wider and direct responsibilities for raising attainment and closing the poverty-related attainment gap, and for staffing and budgets, raised concerns, particularly, with the prospect that the Charter would be enshrined in legislation, as proposed. In the event, the government stepped back from legislating for a Headteachers' Charter, opting to progress it through 'consensus and collaboration' rather than legislation (Swinney, 2018).

Conclusion

This chapter has sought to show how Scotland's evolving leadership strategy has intersected with existing understandings of leadership and leadership for learning and with emerging government pressures and priorities. Many of the initiatives which have been developed can be seen to align with the principles of 'leadership for learning practice' identified by MacBeath and Dempster (2009, p. 71), which involve the following:

* Maintaining a focus on learning as an activity
* Creating conditions favourable to learning as an activity
* Creating a dialogue about leadership for learning
* The sharing of leadership
* A shared sense of accountability.

While levers for effecting change and improvement may not be intentionally benchmarked against these, they are encapsulated in the professional standards and quality indicators and are manifested in teacher leadership initiatives and programmes.

The emphasis in the Headteachers' Charter on the role of the principal as the leader of learning restores and validates a critical function, though the expansion of other areas of responsibilities through the Charter could potentially constrain this. Empowering all teachers as leaders of learning is central, therefore, for building on and strengthening distributive and collaborative approaches. While it might appear that leadership for learning waxes and wanes through the policy rhetoric, nevertheless, the focus on improving learning by improving teacher and leader quality has remained constant. Increasingly, through the NIF and research, more data and evidence are becoming available about the most effective approaches and means of improvement. Building leadership capacity and capability forms part of this and schools are responding by investing in new roles relating to curriculum and pedagogical leadership. A greater focus on collaborative professionalism (Hargreaves & O'Connor, 2017) forms part of this development, so that along with leadership for learning and leadership of learning, leadership *by* learning can also be added as a third strand. Here, leaders and teachers work collaboratively to develop and share pedagogic expertise in order to improve the quality of the pupil learning experiences and ensure achievement (Forde and McMahon (2018) in Carroll & McCulloch, 2018).

References

Carroll, M., & McCulloch, M. (2018). *Understanding teaching & learning in primary education* (2nd ed.). London: Sage.

Donaldson, G. (2011). *Teaching Scotland's Future*. Edinburgh: Scottish Government.

Forde, C., Dickson, B., & McMahon, M. (2018). *Strengthening the concept of leadership in initial teacher education*. Symposium presented at the 2018 annual conference of the Scottish Educational Research Association (SERA) 21–23 November, University of Glasgow, Scotland.

General Teaching Council Scotland. (2012a). *The standards for registration*. Edinburgh, Scotland: GTCS.

General Teaching Council Scotland. (2012b). *The standard for career-long professional learning*. Edinburgh, Scotland: GTCS.

General Teaching Council Scotland. (2012c). *Standards for leadership and management*. Edinburgh, Scotland: GTCS.

Hamilton, G., Forde, C., & McMahon, M. (2018). Developing a coherent strategy to build leadership capacity in Scottish education. *Management in Education, 32*(2), 72–78.

Hammond, J . (2018). *Training for uncertainty in veterinary education*. DHPE thesis, University of Glasgow, Scotland. Retrieved from http://theses.gla.ac.uk/9000/

Hargreaves, A., & O'Connor, M. T. (2017). *Collaborative professionalism world innovation summit for education: The wise report*. Boston: Boston College. Retrieved from https://www.wise-qatar.org/sites/default/files/rr.12.2017_boston.pdf

Her Majesty's Inspectorate of Education. (2007). *Leadership for learning: The challenges of leading in times of change*. Edinburgh, Scotland: Her Majesty's Stationery Office.

King, F., & McMahon, M. (2017, November 24). *Leadership learning in initial teacher education* (LLITE). Paper presented at the Annual Conference of the International Professional Development Association, Glamorgan, Wales.

MacBeath, J., & Dempster, N. (2009). *Connecting leadership and learning: Principles for practice*. London: Routledge.

Mowat, J. G., & McMahon, M. (2018). Interrogating the concept of 'leadership at all levels': A Scottish perspective. *Professional Development in Education*. https://doi.org/10.1080/19415257.2018.1511452

OECD. (2015). *Improving schools in Scotland: An OECD perspective*. Paris: OECD. Retrieved from https://www.oecd.org/education/school/Improving-Schools-in-Scotland-An-OECD-Perspective.pdf

Pucella, T. J. (2014). Not too young to Lead. *The Clearing House, 87*(1), 15–20. https://doi.org/10.1080/00098655.2013.818524

Scottish College for Educational Leadership. (2016). *Developing teacher leadership report*. Retrieved from www.scelscotland.org.uk/whats-happening/news/developing-teacher-leadership/

Scottish Government. (2014). *Framework for educational leadership*. Education Scotland. Retrieved from http://www.educationscotland.gov.uk/learningteachingandassessment/professionallearning/framework/index.asp

Scottish Government. (2016). *National improvement framework for Scottish education: Achieving excellence and equity*. Edinburgh, Scotland: Scottish Government. Retrieved from http://www.gov.scot/Publications/2016/01/8314

Scottish Government. (2017). *Education governance: Next steps empowering our teachers, parents and communities to deliver excellence and equity for our children.* Edinburgh, Scotland: Scottish Government. Retrieved from http://www.gov.scot/Publications/2017/06/2941

Swinney, J. (2018). *Letter to teachers and practitioners.* Retrieved from http://www.gtcs.org.uk/News/news/scottish-government-announcement.aspx

10

Instructional Leadership Development for Principals: A South African Context

Parvathy Naidoo and Raj Mestry

Introduction

Although apartheid policies and practices have been dismantled and replaced with new legislation, the South African education system has not significantly improved. Some reasons attributed to this are frequent curriculum changes, ineffective leadership of principals, poor teacher training, lack of teacher commitment, inadequate educational resources, poor school infrastructure, insufficient state funding and low levels of parent involvement. Assessment of the legacy of apartheid at the end of the era highlights major inequalities in education between white and black students. Initiatives are driven by the national and provincial departments of education to raise the educational standards of the country and to improve student performance in public education. For example, previously disadvantaged schools now receive more departmental funding, and also, school fee exemptions are granted to low-income or

P. Naidoo • R. Mestry (✉)
University of Johannesburg, Johannesburg, South Africa
e-mail: pnaidoo@uj.ac.za; rajm@uj.ac.za

unemployed parents who are unable to pay school (user) fees for their children, regardless of race. Despite these investments, there is growing concern that many educational institutions are not functioning at their optimum and that student performance is generally of a low standard. The public school system is still characterised by low pass rates, low teacher and learner morale, overcrowded classrooms, a resurgence of violence by learners, ineffective leadership and management by school managers, poor governance by school governing boards and generally declining school quality, efficiency and effectiveness, especially in schools catering for black students. Among the reasons cited above, school leadership is deemed to be one of the main reasons for the decline in educational standards.

To critically analyse school leadership in a South African context, three pertinent issues come to the fore: the professionalisation of principalship, instructional leadership and leadership for learning. The lack of stringent criteria and the absence of a qualification for the appointment of principals have resulted in many principals under-performing in their leadership and management roles (Bush, 2004). A person who holds a minimum 3-year teacher qualification and has been teaching for at least 7 years is eligible to apply for a principalship position. In South Africa, there is no overarching principal preparation or certification programme. Rather, each provincial department determines its own approach and content (mostly in-service programmes) but none has a prerequisite programme or licensure arrangement. Some provincial departments do not have the capacity to implement the in-service programmes they design (Mestry & Singh, 2007), and in many instances, in-service programmes that are provided are of an inferior quality. It should be noted that instructional leadership and leadership for learning in South African public schools have not been given the importance they deserve. Although school principals play a pivotal role in improving student learning and attaining high educational outcomes, they work under strenuous conditions and have to deal with multi-faceted transformational issues. They experience great difficulty in coping with numerous changes, partly because they are inadequately prepared for their leadership position or simply lack the necessary skills, knowledge and attitudes to lead and manage schools effectively and efficiently. In most schools, curriculum matters are delegated to deputy principals and heads of departments. We argue that principals should have the necessary knowledge, skills, values and attitudes to become effective instructional leaders. Equally important is the advancement of leadership for learning.

In this chapter, we examine the interconnectedness of instructional leadership and leadership for learning in a South African context by examining the following:

* A new leadership required for a democratic South Africa;
* Linking effective instructional leadership to student performance;
* The difference between instructional leadership and leadership for learning;
* Instructional leadership and leadership for learning in South Africa;
* School leadership preparation in South Africa;
* Challenges facing school principals in the twenty-first century and
* The type of "leadership for learning" leaders we envision for successful South African schools in the twenty-first century.

Towards a New Leadership Required for a Democratic South Africa

The advent of a democratic South Africa led to the decentralisation of schools, resulting in a significant refashioning of the education and training landscape in the country (Chisholm, 2004, p. 1). The South African government faced the enormous task of addressing the legacy of economic inequalities in education between the different race groups (Taylor, Fleisch, & Shindler, 2008, p. 6). Education control was restructured; schools, colleges, technical colleges and universities became open to all races (Chisholm, 2004, p. 1). Despite these changes, the quality of the school system has not improved as expected. Yet, there is a growing understanding in South Africa that the appointment of competent school principals is crucial to overall education quality and improvement (Heystek, 2007; Mathibe, 2007; Prew, 2007). The Department of Education thus made principal and teacher training one of their key priorities in order to address the changes in the education and training landscape in South Africa (Development Bank South Africa, 2008).

Numerous research studies emphasise the importance of principals taking on robust leadership roles in creating efficient and successful schools (Gunter, 2001). Studies in South Africa (Bush, 2013; Grobler, 2013; Naidoo & Petersen, 2015; Spaull, 2011; Spaull & Kotze, 2015) report that learner achievement and overall school performance is associated with the type of school the students attend. The more effectively the schools are run, and the more instructional leadership is provided by school principals, the more likely the students are to achieve. Tingle, Corrales, and Peters (2017) regard school principals as the curators and custodians of the school's vision, mission and values, since they provide the inspiration to achieve the school's vision and mission by directing all stakeholders towards a chosen destination. As such, principals are required to demonstrate a plethora of leadership skills, knowledge and qualities (Vick, 2004) to achieve and maintain quality schools in complex environments. The Wallace Foundation's (2006, p. 2) *Perspective, Leadership for Learning: Making the connections among State, District and School Policies and Practices* Report, and The Wallace Foundation's (2008, p. 1) *Becoming a Leader, Preparing School Principals for Today's Schools* Report, both make the point that there "are virtually no documented instances of troubled schools being turned without intervention by a powerful leader. Many other factors may contribute to such turnarounds, but leadership is the catalyst".

We now turn our attention to leadership for learning. It is asserted that principals becoming leaders for learning in schools (Kowalski, 2010) perform three interchangeable functions at school level. As **managers**, they focus on managing and controlling human, physical and financial resources. As **leaders**, they drive the vision of the institution and focus on organisational growth, development and school improvement, while as **administrators**, they deal with day-to-day operational matters, and continuously shift between leadership and management functions. These interchanging roles and responsibilities result in the principal's role being in a constant state of evolution, from navigating through instructional responsibilities (Abdullah & Kassim, 2011; DeMatthews, 2014; Du Plessis, 2017; Mestry, 2017; Naidoo & Petersen, 2015), to being a transformational leader (Balyer, 2012; Fullan, 1991, cited in Oumer, 2014; Tingle et al., 2017), with numerous other roles usually executed in a single day. Grant, Gardner, Kajee, Moodley, and Somaroo (2010) offer another perspective on how school leaders can become leaders for learning through grounded leadership roles and responsibilities. They need to focus on building a culture of accountability, mutual trust and respect among themselves and staff, adding to the already multi-faceted roles that they (school leaders) are expected to execute in their daily routines. Ultimately, the most arduous challenge for principals of the twenty-first century is not deciding whether to perform administrative duties, provide exemplary leadership or manage diverse staff, students and the school's curriculum, but rather for them to acquire the essential acuity and time to execute all the above duties and functions optimally, and often, all at the same time.

Linking Effective Instructional Leadership to Student Performance

Research confirms that high-performing schools are characterised by strong leadership that demonstrates effective instructional practices and a tangible capacity to improve teaching and learning. Harris and Muijs (2005) argue that effective instructional leadership is widely accepted as an essential to school improvement. Effective leaders exercise an indirect but powerful influence on the effectiveness of schools and also on student achievement (Leithwood & Jantzi, 1998). Internationally, the Stanford School Leadership Study Report (2007, p. 1) argues that "high-performing principals are not born, but can be made, and those who are prepared to engage in innovative, high quality leadership programmes are more likely to become effective instructional leaders, who are committed to the job and also efficacious in their work". The importance of effective principals is also highlighted by the Task Force (2000) commissioned by the Institute for Educational Leadership (IEL) to focus on developing and supporting principals as one of its five areas for improvement. The task force noted that the top challenge for principals is to become "leaders for learning". The IEL also emphasised that principals be provided with the necessary knowledge, values and skills to manage the responsibilities associated with leading and managing teaching and learning at their schools. The task force recommended that school systems must "reinvent the principalship" to meet the needs of schools in the twenty-first century (Task Force, 2000).

Hallinger and Murphy (1987) noted that principals face various challenges and a multitude of roles and responsibilities in their daily routines. These negatively impact their efficiency and effectiveness in school planning, curriculum evaluation, supervision of teachers and solving issues regarding teaching and learning. Globally, schools are the most important institutions in the socialisation of children because of schools' impact on children's cognitive development. Hallinger, Liu, and Piyaman (2017), in their comparative study of principal leadership in China and Thailand, explain that "learning-centred leadership" is a process whereby school leaders motivate, guide and support teacher learning, which ultimately leads to school improvement. Other scholars allude to principals playing a role in the various teaching and learning processes in schools, namely, methodical supervision of teachers; consistent monitoring of assessments; monitoring learners' growth and development; determining classroom management; creation of a conducive learning and teaching environment; provision of appropriate staff development initiatives and adequate training services (Hallinger et al., 2017; Keefe & Jenkins, 2002; Sim, 2011).

The consideration of leadership development in the South African context has an important historical dimension. Fleish and Christie (2004) remind us that in three core ways, apartheid undermined the authority and activity of principals by not giving principals budgetary authority or influence over the flow of resources such as textbooks; by principals having little or no influence over the hiring and firing of staff and by them having almost no decision-making powers regarding the curriculum. It can be argued that changing South Africa's education and training system is only possible if there is harmony between the vision for transformation and the day-to-day realities of those working and leading in the system.

What Is the Difference Between Instructional Leadership and Leadership for Learning?

The concept "Leadership for Learning" has a different meaning from "Instructional Leadership". One is leadership focussed on learning and the other is leadership focussed on instruction. While these concepts may have similar underlying aims, the methods used to get there are very different. One is hierarchical, where the principal makes most of the decisions and the teachers implement them, and the other is collegial and tries to build the capacity of everyone in the school, including the focus on learning for teachers as well.

Instructional Leadership

Nearly three decades ago, Evans and Mohr (1999) posed a pertinent question, which continues to have utmost relevance today: "Can principals' professional development truly improve their leadership practice?" Principals in the twenty-first century are expected to execute multifaceted roles. Their responsibilities are much more arduous and challenging than before, are at times highly complicated and are sometimes unclear, leading to principals being in danger of being seriously overloaded (Bush, 2013; Mahlangu, 2014; Mestry, 2017; Tucker & Codding, 2002). The authors allude to a principal's day usually being filled with diverse managerial activities, such as scheduling, reporting, handling relations with parents and community and dealing with unexpected multiple student and teacher crises and conflict. What coping mechanisms do principals utilise to keep them "afloat" in such complicated environments?

Kelley and Peterson (2007), The Wallace Foundation (2008) and Shipman, Queen, and Peel (2007) all offer a possible solution. Good principals create successful schools by providing teachers with relevant ongoing training and support and by providing students with continuous learning opportunities. DeMatthews (2014) claims that principals can become instructional leaders, when they take charge of teaching and learning processes by critically analysing existing curricula and the implications they have for teaching strategies and student learning. DeMatthews argues that this will be a collective activity. Furthermore, Naidoo and Petersen (2015) argue that principals only become effective instructional leaders when they engage teachers with more culturally relevant teaching strategies and practices which result in improved student outcomes. Most education scholars believe that principals are responsible for setting the tone of the school, by providing effective instructional leadership and ensuring the professional management of schools. These are, however, fundamentally different jobs requiring different leadership practices and attitudes, skills and functions (Booth, Segon, & O'Shannassy, 2010; Tingle et al., 2017).

However, in a South African context, some principals are not sufficiently ready for the principalship position, since they "are not appropriately skilled and trained for school management and leadership" (Mathibe, 2007, p. 523).

A few important questions come to the fore:

- How can twenty-first century principals be empowered to become instructional leaders?
- What types of training and development will result in principals becoming effective instructional leaders?
- What are the instructional leadership challenges facing twenty-first-century principals?

This view of instructional leadership resonates with the educational leadership and management literature both internationally and in South Africa. The authors have selected a few international scholars who offer their definitions of instructional leadership within the broader context of leadership for learning in education, and these are provided in the table below (Table 10.1):

Despite relative consensus on the views and understanding of instructional leadership, the concept "teaching and learning" is the most commonly used phrase to describe the objects of instructional leadership. However, we point out that there is not always agreement among different educational leadership and management scholars on which *leadership traits and/or practices are most likely to favour positive learner outcomes*. For example, Hargreaves and Fink (2006) and Hargreaves (2006) cite, among

Table 10.1 Definitions of instructional leadership by various scholars

Calik, Sezgin, Kavgaci, and Cagatay Kilinc (2012)	Instructional leadership seen as the behaviour displayed by principals that *directly or indirectly affects teaching and learning in their schools*.
Cuban (1984)	Instructional leaders lead from a combination of expertise and charisma, they are "hands-on" and "hip-deep" in *curriculum and instruction*, unafraid of working directly with teachers to *improve teaching and learning*.
DeMatthews (2014)	Instructional leaders have leadership functions associated with *teaching and learning*, more specifically they are the duties and responsibilities principals need to perform each day to support teachers and students to move towards educational excellence. In order to accomplish this, principals must create a safe, supportive and collaborative work environment.
Hallinger and Murphy (1985) cited in Hallinger (2009)	Conceptualises instructional leaders using a three-dimensional model for principals' leadership role: Defining the school's mission, managing the instructional programme and promoting a positive school learning climate. Each dimension is delineated into 10 IL functions, namely, framing clear school goals, communicating clear school goals, *supervising and evaluating instruction, coordinating curriculum, monitoring student progress*, protecting instructional time, promoting professional development, maintaining high visibility, providing incentives to teachers and providing incentives for learning.
Jita and Mokhele (2013), Zepeda (2007)	Instructional leaders incorporate the process of creating and sustaining an environment in which the highly complex, socially textured *tasks of effective schooling* can take place.
Mestry (2013)	Instructional leadership is the actions that principals take or delegate *to promote quality instruction, pertaining to teaching and learning in their schools*.
Horing and Loeb (2010)	Instructional leadership includes *teaching and learning being at the heart of good classroom instruction*, implying that school leaders can have a tremendous effect on student learning through the type of teachers hired, how are they assigned to classrooms and the type of opportunities created for ample learning.
Sim (2011)	Instructional leadership is conceptualised as "leadership that directly relates to *teaching and learning activities*, that creates interactions between teachers, students and the curriculum".

others, certain characteristics that promote school and organisational success and improvement:

- The creation and preservation of *sustainable learning* in schools;
- The *sustaining of the leadership* of others and
- Developing rather than depleting *human and material resources.*

Fullan (1997), on the other hand, focusses on *instruction* and claims that school leadership development must include meaningful engagement with ideas, materials and colleagues (both in and out of teaching) on intellectual, social and emotional levels to promote school and organisational success and improvement. We assess this as a collective activity as he places a great deal of emphasis on determining the context of teaching and on whether the experience of teachers is carefully accounted for.

Leadership for Learning

Hallinger (2009) cited in Bush (2013) notes that in the twenty-first century, instructional leadership has been "reincarnated" as "leadership for learning". MacBeath and Dempster (2009) argue that the term is highly problematic and that there is no firm definition. According to Hargreaves and Fink (2006) and MacBeath and Dempster (2009), there are three fundamental aspects that not only lie at the heart of effective organisational leadership but also at the centre of leadership for learning: purpose, context and human agency. In the case of school leaders, there is a clear moral purpose which should drive them; that purpose is the improvement of students and also teachers' lives through learning. Principals should see that their schools concentrate on improving students' and teachers' learning and ultimately their achievement. Leadership never takes place in a vacuum. It is always located somewhere and is influenced by its context. An important set of skills a school leader needs is the ability to "read" the context in which he or she is working (PriceWaterhouseCoopers, 2007). Third, leaders cannot work in isolation. They can only achieve the school's moral purpose through human agency. Leadership encapsulates clear movement from an individual to shared views of leadership and as a collective activity (Harris, 2009).

Mestry, Moonsammy-Koopasammy and Schmidt (2013, p. 51) argue that principals are more than capable of becoming "leaders for learning", only if they emphasise the building of an effective learning community within the school as well as creating caring education networks outside the school. This implies a strategic role for principals: as leaders for learning they need to exhibit a clear sense of direction for their schools and possess the ability to prioritise what really matters, in the school and the classroom, in terms of the learners' work. As instructional leaders, principals primarily direct teaching for learning and support teachers and students in their work towards educational excellence (DeMatthews, 2014).

MacBeath and Dempster (2009) outline five main principles that underpin leadership for learning:

1. Leadership for learning practice involves maintaining a focus on learning as an activity in which everyone (students and teachers) is a learner, and opportunities to exercise leadership enhance learning.
2. Leadership for learning practice involves creating conditions favourable to learning as an activity in which cultures nurture the learning of everyone; physical and social spaces stimulate and celebrate learning and tools and strategies are used to enhance thinking about learning and the practice of teaching.
3. Leadership for learning practice involves creating a dialogue about leadership for learning in which there is active collegial inquiry focussing on the link between learning and leadership, and coherence is achieved through the sharing of values, understandings and practices.
4. Leadership for learning practice involves the sharing of leadership in which structures support participation in developing the school as a learning community; the experience and expertise of staff, students and parents are drawn upon as resources and collaborative patterns of work and activity across boundaries of subject, role and status are valued and promoted.
5. Leadership for learning practice involves a shared sense of accountability in which a systematic approach to self-evaluation is embedded at classroom, school and community levels, and there is a continuing focus on sustainability, succession and leaving a legacy.

The first two directly address the weaknesses of instructional leadership. The first addresses shared or distributed leadership, counteracting the principal-centric approach of instructional leadership. The second is a focus on learning, in contrast to the teaching-centred dimension of instructional leadership.

Instructional Leadership and Leadership for Learning in South Africa

The terms most commonly used in a South African context are instructional leadership and managing teaching and learning. The education management and leadership landscape experienced seismic shifts in the post-apartheid period since 1994 (Hoadley, Christie, & Ward, 2009). New education policies, changes in curriculum, dismantling of apartheid practices (unequal education for different race groups and the merging of public education systems), acceptance of students from all race groups into public and private schools, use of distorted school funding models and the reclassification of public schools according to quintiles brought about massive reorganisation within the schooling system. This meant that principals were entrusted with new roles and responsibilities, making them largely accountable for student outcomes and overall school improvement (Christie, 2008; Fleisch & Christie, 2004). Most importantly, the landscape of change necessitated that the National Department of Education be given the responsibility for developing norms and standards, frameworks and national policies for the education system as a whole (Christie, 2008). Educational reform in South Africa (Heystek, 2007; Naicker, 2011) led to wide-scale devolution of power and authority to school principals and school governing bodies. Changes in the new system of governance in schools have, unfortunately, resulted in principals being unprepared for their new role. Perhaps one of the major changes in principalship has been the range of expectations placed on them and these expectations have been moved from the demands for management and control to the demand for an educational leader who can improve the academic performance of students and raise educational standards (Mestry & Singh, 2007). Instructional leadership is significant because of increasing recognition that it is one of the most important activities for principals and other school leaders (Bush, 2013). The South African Standard for School Leadership (South Africa, 2016), for example, in setting out the core purpose of principalship, focusses strongly on the need to manage teaching and learning effectively which will promote the highest possible standards of student achievement.

Education authorities and scholars seldom use the term "leadership for learning". Instead, they underscore the importance of professional development which is an aspect of leadership for learning. Drawing from studies of Leithwood, Louis, Wahlstrom, and Anderson (2004) and Leithwood and Louis (2011), we argue that leadership for learning is more significant in a South African context. There is, thus, a dire need for principals to be empowered and professionally prepared for their roles as heads of schools and to continually enhance their skills, attributes and competencies through structured continuing professional development programmes (Mestry et al., 2013). This will undoubtedly result in improved academic performance of students. Many scholars (Bush, 2008; Bush, Kiggundu, & Moorosi, 2011; Heystek, 2007; Hoadley et al., 2009; Mathibe, 2007; Mestry, 2017; Mestry & Grobler, 2003; Moorosi & Grant, 2013; Naidoo & Petersen, 2015; Van der Westhuizen & Van Vuuren, 2007) reach similar conclusions: principals leading schools in South Africa require a more specialised type of preparation together with continuous professional development to enable them to cope with the abundant roles and responsibilities that confront them.

School Leadership Preparation in South Africa

To introduce leadership for learning to practicing and aspiring principals, in 2007 the Department of Education (DoE, 2008) introduced the Advanced Certificate in Education in School Leadership and Management (ACE-SLM) as a leadership development programme for school principals (Bush, Duku, et al., 2009; DoE, 2008; Heystek, 2007; Msila, 2014; Naidoo & Petersen, 2015; Naidu, Joubert, Mestry, Mosoge, & Ngcobo, 2008). It was intended to make the ACE-SLM programme as an entry level to principalship. The implementation of the ACE-SLM programme was successful, but the educational authorities (DoE) replaced the ACE-SLM programme at a higher level, with the Advanced Diploma in Education (ADE). However, we intend discussing some pertinent matters regarding the implementation of the ACE qualification.

We argue that the ACE-SLM programme was a suitable qualification for principals to enable them to become Leaders for Learning. This was a 1-year, full-time or 2-year, part-time practice and competency-based programme aimed at developing management and leadership skills (DoE, 2008). The part-time model worked well because it enabled practicing principals and deputy principals to enrol for the programme. The assessment components were practise-based and were done in the workplace (their schools). The expectation regarding ACE-SLM was that the programme would have led to sustainable positive change in leadership practice in DoE's public schools. The rationale for the programme was to provide an entry criterion for principalship, as well as to create a vehicle for training practicing principals. In addition, the ACE-SLM served as a professional, career-related qualification and it was consistent with the job profile of school principals (DoE, 2008; Moloi, 2007; Naidu et al., 2008). According to Van der Westhuizen and Van Vuuren (2007), this was the first step towards introducing a compulsory professional qualification for principalship. To date (2019), there has not been a validation of the ACE-SLM qualification by the DoE. Although many researchers (Bush, Duku, et al., 2009; Bush, Joubert, Kiggundu, & Van Rooyen, 2009; Bush et al., 2012; Mestry & Singh, 2007; Msila, 2010) have highlighted the benefits of the ACE-SLM qualification and its importance as a professional development programme for principals, in areas of leadership and management as well as instructional and transformational leadership, the DoE was unable to make this qualification a prerequisite for any aspiring person to take on the principalship position. The Bush, Duku, et al. (2009) study, which was an extensive evaluation of the ACE-SLM programme initiated in 2007, provides a succinct account of the benefits of the programme, since there was unanimous support from service providers (Higher Institutions) and participants that the ACE-SLM programme be made an entry-level qualification for new principals; furthermore, that the ACE-SLM be revised to Advanced Diploma level, subject to four provisos (Bush, Duku, et al., 2009, p. 141), which are explained below:

1. Consideration should be given to holders of other qualifications in educational management, subject to a conversion process, involving the preparation of a portfolio for applicants to demonstrate how their management learning has been translated into effective practice in order to demonstrate the application of theory to school-based practice. This could be an interim arrangement, for approximately five years, until the supply of Advanced Diploma graduates is sufficient to meet the demand for new principals;
2. Similarly, consideration should be given to holders of the national ACE programme (the current programme). They should be regarded as eligible to become principals subject to an upgrading process to Advanced Diploma level;
3. Consideration should also be given to helping potential principals who do not obtain the support of their principals. This might require the movement of Advanced Diploma candidates to other schools where they can receive appropriate support and finally,
4. Consideration should be given to the selection process for prospective principals. Applicants should be restricted to deputy principals and heads of department, except in very small schools.

The Report recommended that suitable candidates should be funded by government, with provinces and Higher Education Institutions (HEIs) sharing responsibility for selection, following national criteria.

Challenges Facing School Principals in the Twenty-First Century

Successful schools are categorised by strong leadership instructional practices with the capacity to improve teaching and learning. That requires skilled school leaders who engage in sustained work. In the same vein, the position of school principals has shifted from a role dominated by a focus on management and administration to one focussing on instruction and systemic capacity building as explained by Grogan and Andrews (cited in Barber & Meyerson, 2007). Furthermore, twenty-first century principals are expected to become change agents who are deeply involved in the improvement of instruction and curriculum in schools. The introduction of periodic changes in curriculum programmes since 1994, namely, Outcomes-based Education (OBE), the National Curriculum Statement (NCS) and the introduction of Curriculum Assessment Policy Statements (CAPS) demanded that principals take on an instructional leadership role. Also, the abolition of corporal punishment in schools (South Africa School's Act 84 of 1996) and measures to ensure gender equity, and redress, in national policy have influenced the roles played by leadership in schools (Ngcobo & Tikly, 2008).

Studies undertaken by Mestry and Grobler (2003) and Van der Westhuizen and Van Vuuren (2007) indicate that most principals have not received adequate specialist training in leadership and the management of schools. According to Hoadley and Ward (2009), training in financial management and instructional leadership is seriously lacking for principals in South Africa. Principals are appointed based purely on their performance in the classroom, due to the absence of any prerequisite qualification for principalship. Mestry and Singh (2007) make the point that the current education environment in most South African schools requires effective and efficient school leaders and managers who possess new and improved skills, knowledge and attitudes to cope with the wide range of demands and challenges, such as (but not limited to) coping with multicultural school populations, managing change and conflict and coping with limited resources.

In addressing these demands and challenges, successful principals should embrace both innovation and transformation in their schools. In addition, the legacy of the past educational system, which was characterised by fragmentation, inequity in provisioning and the demise of a culture of teaching and learning, brings with it increasing difficulty and uncertainty in schools (Mestry & Singh, 2007; Prew, 2007).

The principal's position can now be compared to that of the managing director of a corporate company whose product is education, and whose clients are parents, students and the community (Blanchard, cited in

Loock, Campher, Du Preez, Grobler, & Shaba, 2003, p. 41). School principals are therefore required to acquire necessary skills of working with governing bodies, education authorities, parents and the general community. "Self-managing schools" in the South African context (Caldwell & Spinks, 1992, pp. 4–5) have placed more authority and responsibility on principals to make decisions within a framework of goals, policies and standards. Therefore, the recognition of the importance of specific and specialised training and development has grown as the pressures on school principals intensify and become more and more complex (Bush, 2008, p. 32). Furthermore, the expression "self-managing schools" created a determination that school leadership and management needed to be rehabilitated and given a more central role in the schooling system. This was clearly articulated by the Minister of Basic Education, South Africa, Angie Motshekga, when she stated a new vision for the role of principals in South African schools (Simeka, cited in Prew, 2007). The changes alluded to by the Minister refer to the relationship between transformational principals and effective schools, giving the relationship a systemic dimension emphasising the need to strengthen and professionalise the role of the principal, so that he/she can play a critical role as leader of the school.

What Type of "Leadership for Learning" Leaders Do We Envision for Successful South African Schools in the Twenty-First Century?

First and foremost, we require *transformational leaders* who desire to develop leadership in others by transforming them, thereby strengthening school leadership beyond themselves (Bush & Glover, 2016; Fullan, 2003). According to Mills (2005), good leadership does the following for the rest of the organisation: sets the direction, helps to visualise the end result, encourages and inspires others and jointly harnesses the efforts of others. Msila (2010) propagates a critical thinking ability in leadership while Kouzes and Posner (2001) argue that leaders should be able to mobilise others to want to act because of the credibility and trust that they display. Leaders encourage and accommodate both shared decision-making and shared leadership in their efforts to enable them to want to act and follow. Grobler, Warnich, Carrell, Elbert, and Hatfield (2002) and Nedelcu (2013) assert that transformational leaders of groups that function effectively share the following basic common characteristics:

- they provide direction and emphasise meaning to the people that they are leading and they generate trust and encourage action and favour taking risks in order to succeed;
- they display positiveness in any situation;
- they create a shared sense of purpose in the school and
- effective leaders are also regarded as purveyors of hope, and they reinforce the notion that success can and will be attained by recognising the potential in one's self as well as in others.

School principals also have a key responsibility in transforming schools: they become pace setters and pathfinders; therefore, such principals will require a different kind of training so that they will have the ability to learn and re-learn, according to Dzimbo (2007). Transformational leaders are visionary leaders with potentially historical significance who react to a crisis with great vision and great ideas and possess a willingness to foster grand experiments in solving great problems of the day. They are charismatic and imbued with passion, enthusiasm and energy. Transformational leaders also consider a problem as an opportunity to transform society and leave their legacies behind, according to Mthetha (2012).

In the last two decades, studies on instructional leadership gained momentum in South Africa: Bush (2008), Arikewuyo (2007), Du Plessis, Conley, and Du Plessis (2007), Bush (2013), Mestry (2013), and Naidoo and Petersen (2015) argue that school leaders influence student learning by seeking to achieve good outcomes by influencing motivation, commitment and capability of teachers by enhancing teaching and learning activities at schools. They further emphasise that one of the major functions and responsibilities of a school principal is to improve and facilitate efficient and effective curriculum implementation by securing adequate and appropriate financial and material resources for the school to meet learners' needs.

The Stanford School Leadership Study of 2007 explains that high-quality leadership development programmes are more likely to produce effective instructional leaders who are committed to the job and also efficacious in their work. Barber and Meyerson (2007) emphasise that high-performing schools are characterised by robust instructional practices. The schools have the capacity to improve student learning as there will be a strong presence of skilled school leaders who are able to engage in sustained work with teachers, thus improving the organisation's climate, student outcomes and school conditions. The authors further highlight that in order to maintain good schools, effective instructional leadership is required and there has to be intense collaboration of all stakeholders.

Professional collaborative leadership is fundamental to sustainable school improvement and transformation of the wider school system (Harris & Muijs, 2005). Some benefits of professional collaboration are the sharing and transferring of knowledge to improve teaching and learning (Jackson, cited in Hargreaves & Fink, 2006, p. 233). Kouzes and Posner assert that "leadership is a relationship between those who aspire to lead and those who choose to follow" (2001, p. 31). The authors emphasise that trust is at the heart of any collaborative relationship and without trust one simply cannot lead.

Forming partnerships with other local schools is beneficial since it promotes the sharing of expertise, encourages learning together and enables collective problem solving across schools. Hargreaves and Fink (2006) use the term "professional learning networks" to describe the interaction between the different stakeholders of different schools. Collaborative leadership involves influencing, giving orders, motivating and handling people, either as individuals, or in groups, managing conflict and communicating with subordinates; from a management perspective, it is the task of management to direct the activities and performance of people productively, according to Grobler et al. (2002).

The school principal is the lead learner in the school. The rapid changes in education require the school leader to embark on self-development in order to cope with the increasing demands placed on the position. The demands are, amongst others, leading and managing people, providing instructional leadership in terms of curriculum delivery, engaging collaboratively with the school community, providing exemplary leadership in staff development, and so forth. According to Barth (cited in Naidu et al., 2008), schools cannot be places where "big" people who are *learned* teach "little" people who are *learners*. Schools need to be places where both adults and young people discover the joy of learning and this is only possible if the school principal becomes the lead learner, who fosters an organisational culture that embraces continuous learning by all stakeholders. Lead principals, teachers and students envisage a notion of visionary leadership in their schools.

The fourth type of leaders required in the twenty-first-century schools, according to Mills (2005) and Fullan (2003), are visionary leaders who are prepared to take a leadership position that encompasses the following:

- leadership needs to have a vision about what can be accomplished;
- leadership should make a commitment to the mission and to the people they lead;
- leadership ought to take responsibility for the accomplishment of the mission and the welfare of those they lead;
- leadership has to assume the risk of loss and failure and lastly
- leadership needs to take recognition for success.

School principals lead the way in developing the mission, vision and values of their organisations and are therefore role models of a culture of excellence. It is an expectation that school principals provide visionary leadership to all stakeholders within their schools. Effective and efficient leadership seizes opportunities to display trustworthiness on a large scale; they also admit to mistakes and demonstrate honesty within themselves as well as their organisations. Visionary leaders become "lead learners" and are thus inspirational to the people with whom they lead and engage.

Shead (2010) and Williams-Boyd (2002) declare, visionary leaders to be forward-looking leaders: they actively communicate the level they intend taking the organisation and share their vision with their followers. Visionary leaders also demonstrate competency, take action when it is required and prove to their followers that they can display competency and declare a vision for the organisation.

Day, Harris and Hatfield (cited in Yu So, 2009), in their study of 12 schools which focussed on school heads, conclude that effective leaders communicate an informed, clear set of personal goals and educational values, which represent their moral purposes for the school. Hence, it is incumbent that school principals transfer this vision into the structures and processes of the school.

The global push is for school-based leadership and management with patterns of decision-making power and responsibility being distributed to principals, teachers and parents, who collectively take responsibility for the promotion of quality education. Democratising education also means that there is a need to recognise the indigenous cultures, while allowing room for change and development towards a type of leadership that transcends towards Ubuntu Leadership. In Africa, individual achievements frequently are much less valued than are interpersonal relations.

African societies seem to have a great capacity for tolerance and forgiveness which runs counter to Western philosophies, which espouse survival of the fittest. The Ubuntu philosophy embraces a value system that can be taught and requires a paradigm shift of thought processes, attitudes, old styles of leadership and management and human relations in the workplace, according to Msila (2014). There are few studies conducted on the Ubuntu philosophy in the African continent, more especially in South Africa, so the authors examined two studies—Brubaker's (2013) undertaken in Rwanda and Msila's (2014) conducted in South Africa. They point us to considerable emphasis being placed on the leader's ability to honour his or her obligation to values, interdependence, respect and ethnic emancipation. It is sometimes expected that the organisation will not pull together because of ethnic associations. Vision, in the Western sense, might therefore be out of place in many organisations in Africa. Followers appears not to want it, preferring a leader who is kind, considerate and understanding to one who is too demanding, too dynamic and focusses only on production. The foregoing suggests principals being authorities, rather than having authoritarian leadership; that is, leaders are seen to possess genuine authority but are expected by their subordinates to use it only sparingly and in a humane and considerate way. Msila (2014) continuously makes the point that Ubuntu leadership, based on a value system, can be taught, but it needs more than a conceptual analysis and not be seen as offensive to affirmative change. Schools must be prepared to address the climate of the institution without emphasising the differences that exist within the school's value system.

The authors scrutinised Msila's (2014) study, where a principal's journey in the introduction of "Ubuntu Leadership" was examined along with the challenges faced in the execution of leadership tasks in the school. Ubuntu is a cultural worldview, common among the Bantu tribes of Africa that emphasises the interconnectedness of self within society and the extension of humanness within shared community, according to Le Grange (2011) and Murithi (2009). Given that Ubuntu is a philosophy that extends throughout East, Southern and Central Africa, studying its implications for leader effectiveness holds tremendous potential for influencing underdeveloped leadership studies across the continent. In interrogating literature on Ubuntu leadership, the authors experienced some challenges: the only research located in South Africa is by Msila (2014) and very little research has been performed outside of South Africa.

We can make the assumption that African managers are especially concerned about the quality of their relationships, rather than individual or organisational effectiveness. We also note that internal and personal relationships dominate over those associated with the organisation's performance, its long-term strategies, its clients and its external environment. The effective manager is perceived to consult subordinates, treat them considerately, promote their self-development, support and help them and provide them with clear direction. In this view, good managers are people orientated rather than task orientated.

Msila (2014) asserts that when Ubuntu leadership is practised, the school's performance is enhanced, but this only works if there is a re-education among teachers and a concerted effort to embrace the Ubuntu philosophy by all.

Conclusion

Many of the practicing principals lack basic leadership and management training prior to, and after, their entry into principalship. According to Tsukudu and Taylor (in Bush & Oduro, 2006, p. 362) head teachers come into headship without having been prepared for their new role. Most principals in South African public schools have difficulty in finding solutions to practical problems that continuously beset them. They experience strain in balancing their managerial and administrative duties with their instructional leadership role, and this has serious implications for maintaining educational standards and improving student performance. Their work overload and the problems experienced on a daily basis with students, teachers and parents, are barriers to instructional leadership and, perhaps even more, to leadership for learning. The education authorities are rethinking the roles of principals, and if principals are relieved of their managerial and administrative responsibilities, educational standards and student performance will progressively improve by accentuating their instructional leadership role and simultaneously enhancing leadership for learning.

References

Abdullah, J. B., & Kassim, J. M. (2011). Instructional leadership and attitude towards organizational change among secondary schools' principals in Pahang, Malaysia. *Procedia-Social and Behavioral Sciences, 15*, 3303–3309.

Arikewuyo, M. O. (2007). Teachers' perceptions of principals' leadership capacities in Nigeria. *Academic Leadership: The Online Journal, 3*(5), 1–8.

Balyer, A. (2012). Transformational leadership behaviours of school principals: A qualitative research based on teachers' perceptions. *International Online Journal of Educational Sciences, 4*(3), 581–591.

Barber, M. E., & Meyerson, D. (2007). *School leadership study developing successful principals. The gendering of school leadership: "Reconstructuring the principalship"*. Paper presented at Stanford University, CA.

Booth, C., Segon, M., & O'Shannassy, T. (2010). The more things change they more they stay the same: A contemporary examination of leadership and management constructs. *Journal of Business and Policy Research, 5*(2), 119–130.

Brubaker, T. A. (2013). Servant leadership, Ubuntu, and leadership effectiveness in Rwanda. *Emerging Leadership Journeys, 6*(1), 114–147.

Bush, T. (2004, August). *Enhancing school leadership: Management development and governor training in Gauteng*. Paper presented at the Matthew Goniwe school of Leadership and Governance Conference, Johannesburg, South Africa.

Bush, T. (2008). *Leadership and management development in education*. London: Sage.

Bush, T. (2013). Instructional leadership and leadership for learning: Global and South African perspectives. *Education as Change, 1*(17), 5–20.

Bush, T., Duku, N., Glover, D., Kiggundu, E., Kola, S., Msila, V., et al. (2009). *External evaluation research report of the advanced certificate in education, school leadership and management*. Pretoria, South Africa: Department of Education.

Bush, T., Duku, N., Glover, D., Kiggundu, E., Kola, S., Msila, V., et al. (2012). *The impact of the national Advanced Certificate in Education: Programme on school and learners outcomes* (School leadership and management. Research report). Pretoria, South Africa: Department of Education.

Bush, T., & Glover, D. (2016). School leadership in West Africa: Findings from a systematic literature review. *Africa Education Review, 13*(3–4), 80–103.

Bush, T., Joubert, R., Kiggundu, E., & Van Rooyen, J. (2009). Managing teaching and learning in South African schools. *International Journal of Educational Development*. https://doi.org/10.1016/j.ijedudev.2009.04.008

Bush, T., Kiggundu, E., & Moorosi, P. (2011). Preparing new principals in South Africa: The ACE: School leadership programme. *South African Journal of Education, 31*, 31–43.

Bush, T., & Oduro, G. (2006). New principals in Africa: Preparation, induction and practice. *Journal of Educational Administration, 44*(4), 359–375.

Caldwell, B. J., & Spinks, J. (1992). *Leading the self-managed school*. London: The Falmer Press.

Calik, T., Sezgin, F., Kavgaci, H., & Cagatay Kilinc, A. (2012). Examination of relationships between instructional leadership of school principals and self-efficacy of teachers and collective teacher efficacy. *Educational Sciences: Theory and Practice, 12*(4), 2498–2504.

Chisholm, L. (2004). *Changing class in education and social change in post-apartheid South Africa*. Cape Town, South Africa: HRSC Press.

Christie, P. (2008). *Opening the doors of learning, changing schools in South Africa*. Johannesburg, South Africa: Heinemann Publishers.

Cuban, L. (1984). Transforming the frog into a prince: Effective schools research, policy, and practice at the district level. *Harvard Educational Review, 54*(2), 129–151.

DeMatthews, D. E. (2014). How to improve curriculum leadership: Integrating leadership theory and management strategies. *The Clearing House: A Journal of Educational Strategies, Issues and Ideas, 87*(5), 192–196.

Department of Education. (2008). *Advanced certificate: Education* (School management and leadership, NQF, Level 6, Course Outline, Ver.6). Pretoria, South Africa: Government Printer.

Development Bank of South Africa (DBSA). (2008). *Education roadmap, focus on schooling system*. Retrieved from www.pmg.org/za

Du Plessis, P. (2017). Challenges for rural school leaders in a developing context: A case study on leadership practices of effective principals. *KOERS — Bulletin for Christian Scholarship, 82*(3). Retrieved from https://doi.org/10.19108/KOERS.82.3.2337

Du Plessis, P., Conley, L. N., & Du Plessis, E. (2007). *Teaching and learning in South African schools*. Pretoria, South Africa: Van Schaik Publishers.

Dzimbo, P. K. (2007). *In – Service education and training of today's principals: The quest for an innovative and transformative leadership*. Presented at Mathew Goniwe School of Leadership and Governance in conjunction with the Gauteng Department of Education, Johannesburg, South Africa.

Evans, P. M., & Mohr, N. (1999). Professional development for principals: Seven core beliefs. *Phi Delta Kappan, 80*(7), 530–532.

Fleisch, B., & Christie, P. (2004). Structural change, leadership and school effectiveness/improvement: Perspectives from South Africa. *Discourse: Studies in the Cultural Politics of Education, 25*(1), 95–112.

Fullan, M. (1997). *The new meaning of educational change* (2nd ed.). London: Teacher's College Press.

Fullan, M. (2003). Leadership and sustainability. Plaintalk. *Newspaper for the Center for development and Learning, 8*(2), 1–5.

Grant, C., Gardner, K., Kajee, F., Moodley, R., & Somaroo, S. (2010). Teacher leadership: A survey analysis of KwaZulu teachers' perceptions. *South African Journal of Education, 30*, 401–419.

Grobler, B. (2013). The school principal as instructional leader: A structural equation model. *Education as Change, 1*(17), 177–199.

Grobler, P. A., Warnich, S., Carrell, M. R., Elbert, N. F., & Hatfield, R. D. (2002). *Human resource management in South Africa* (2nd ed.). London: Thomson Learning.

Gunter, H. M. (2001). *Leaders and leadership in education*. London: Paul Chapman Publishing.

Hallinger, P. (2009). *Leadership for 21st century schools: From instructional leadership to leadership for learning*. Hong Kong: The Hong Kong Institute of Education.

Hallinger, P., Liu, S., & Piyaman, P. (2017). Does principal leadership make a difference in teacher professional learning? A comparative study China and Thailand. *Compare: A Journal of Comparative and International Education.* https://doi.org/10.1080/03057925.2017.1407237

Hallinger, P., & Murphy, J. F. (1987). Principals instructional management. *Educational Leadership, 45*(1), 54–61.

Hargreaves, A. (2006). Sustainable leadership. In B. Beatty, B. Caldwell, J. Davies, T. E. Deal, A. Hargreaves, G. C. Hentschenke, D. Jantzi, L. Lambert, K. Leithwood, J. M. Novak, G. Southworh, R. Starratt, & B. Davies (Eds.), *The essentials of school leadership* (pp. 172–189). Thousand Oaks, CA: Sage Publications.

Hargreaves, A., & Fink, D. (2006). *Sustainable leadership*. San Francisco: Jossey-Bass.

Harris, A. (Ed.). (2009). *Distributed school leadership*. Dordrecht, Netherlands: Springer Press.

Harris, A., & Muijs, D. (2005). *Improving school through teacher leadership*. Berkshire, UK: Open University Press.

Heystek, J. (2007). Reflecting on principals as managers or moulded leaders in a managerialistic school system. *South African Journal of Education, 3*(27), 491–505.

Hoadley, U., Christie, P., & Ward, C. L. (2009). Managing to learn: Instructional leadership in South African secondary schools. *School Leadership and Management, 29*(4), 373–389.

Hoadley, U., & Ward, C. (2009). *Managing to learn: Instructional leadership in south African schools*. Cape Town, South Africa: HSRC Press.

Horing, E., & Loeb, S. (2010). New thinking about instructional leadership. *Kappanmagazine.org, 92*(3), 66–69.

Jita, L. C., & Mokhele, M. L. (2013). The role of lead teachers in instructional leadership: A case study of environmental learning in South Africa. *Education as Change, 1*(17), 123–135.

Keefe, J. W., & Jenkins, J. M. (2002). Personalised instruction. *Phi Delta Kappan, 83*(6), 440–456.

Kelley, C., & Peterson, K. D. (2007). *The Jossey-bass reader on educational leadership* (2nd ed.). San Francisco: Jossey-Bass.

Kouzes, J. M., & Posner, B. Z. (2001). In W. Bennis, G. M. Spreitzer, & T. G. Cummings (Eds.), *Bringing leadership lessons from the past into the future*. San Francisco: Jossey-Bass.

Kowalski, T. J. (2010). *The school principal – Visionary leadership and competent management*. New York: Taylor and Francis.

Le Grange, L. (2011). Ubuntu, ukama and the heading of nature, self and society. *Educational Philosophy and Theory*. https://doi.org/10.1111/j.1469-5812.2011.00795

Leithwood, K., & Jantzi, D. (1998, April). *Distributed leadership and student engagement in school*. Paper presented at the annual meeting of the American Educational Research Association, San Diego, CA.

Leithwood, K., & Louis, K. S. (2011). *Linking leadership to student learning*. Hoboken, NJ: Jossey-Bass.

Leithwood, K., Louis, K. S., Wahlstrom, K. L., & Anderson, S. E. (2004). *Review of research: How leadership influences student learning*. Minneapolis, MN: University of Minnesota Press.

Loock, C., Campher, P., Du Preez, P., Grobler, B., & Shaba, S. M. (2003). *Education leadership* (Module 3: Effective education management series). Sandton, South Africa: Heinemann Publishers.

MacBeath, J., & Dempster, N. (Eds.). (2009). *Connecting leadership and learning*. London: Routledge Publishers.

Mahlangu, V. P. (2014). Strategies for principal-teacher development: A South African perspective. *Mediterranean Journal of Social Sciences, 5*(20), 1738–1747. ISSN 2039-2117 (online); ISSN 2039-9340 (print).

Mathibe, I. (2007). The professional development of school principals. *South African Journal of Education, 3*(27), 523–540.

Mestry, R. (2013). The innovative role of the principal as instructional leader: A prerequisite for high student achievement. *International Proceedings of Economics Development and Research, 60*(25), 119–123. https://doi.org/10.7763/IPEDR.2013.V60.25

Mestry, R. (2017). Empowering principals to lead and manage public schools effectively in the 21st century. *South African Journal of Education, 37*(1). https://doi.org/10.15700/saje.v37n1a1334

Mestry, R., & Grobler, B. (2003). The training and development of principals in managing schools effectively. *Education as Change, 7*(2), 126–146.

Mestry, R., Moonsammy-Koopasammy, I., & Schmidt, M. (2013). The instructional leadership role of primary school principals. *Education as Change, 1*(17), 49–64.

Mestry, R., & Singh, P. (2007). Continuing professional development for principals: A South African perspective. *South African Journal of Education, 3*(27), 477–490.

Mills, D. Q. (2005). *The importance of leadership. Leadership, how to lead, how to live?* Retrieved from www.mindedgepress.com

Moloi, K. (2007). An overview of education management in South Africa. *South African Journal of Education, 3*(27), 463–476.

Moorosi, P., & Grant, C. (2013). *Preparing and developing school leaders: The African perspective. BELMAS Leadership preparation and development report*. Sheffield: BELMAS.

Msila, V. (2010). Rural school principal's quest for effectiveness: Lessons from the field. *Journal of Education, 48*, 169–189.

Msila, V. (2014). Challenges to the introduction of an alternative leadership style: A school principal's journey in the introduction of an "Ubuntu leadership model". *Mediterranean Journal of Social Sciences, 5*(20), 1738–1747.

Mthetha, R. M. (2012). Transformational leadership in the South African public sector. *African Journal of Public Affairs, 5*(3), 107–114.

Murithi, T. (2009). An African perspective on peace education: Ubuntu lessons in reconciliation. *International Review of Education, 55*(2–3), 221–233.

Naicker, I. (2011). Developing school principals in South Africa. In T. Townsend & J. Macbeath (Eds.), *International handbook of leadership for learning* (Vol. 25, pp. 431–443). Dordrecht, Netherlands: Springer International Handbooks of Education.

Naidoo, P., & Petersen, N. (2015). Towards a leadership programme for primary school principals as instructional leaders. *South African Journal of Childhood Education, 5*(3), 371–379.

Naidu, N., Joubert, R., Mestry, R., Mosoge, J., & Ngcobo, T. (2008). *Education management and leadership: A South African perspective*. Cape Town, South Africa: Oxford University Press.

Nedelcu, A. (2013). Transformational approach to school leadership: Contribution to continued improvement of education. *Change and Leadership, 17*, 237–244.

Ngcobo, T., & Tikly, L. (2008, September). *Key dimensions of effective leadership for change: A focus on township and rural schools in South Africa*. Paper presented to the CCEAM Conference, Durban, South Africa.

Oumer, W. (2014). *Principal instructional leadership performances and influencing factors in secondary schools of Addis Ababa*. MA thesis unpublished, Addis Ababa University, Ethiopia.

Prew, M. (2007). Successful principals: Why some schools succeed and others struggle when faced with innovation and transformation. *South African Journal of Education, 3*(27), 447–462.

PriceWaterhouseCoopers. (2007). *Independent study into school leadership*. London: Department for Education and Skills.

Shead, M. (2010). *Five most important leadership traits*. Retrieved from http://www.leadership501.com/five-most-important-leadership-traits/27/

Shipman, N. J., Queen, A., & Peel, H. A. (2007). *School leadership with ISLLC and ELCC*. New York: Eye on Education.

Sim, Q. C. (2011). Instructional leadership among principals of secondary schools' in Malaysia. *Educational Research, 2*(12), 1784–1800.

South Africa. (2016). *Policy on the South African standard for principals*. Pretoria, South Africa: Government Printers.

Spaull, N. A. (2011). *Preliminary analysis of SACMEQ 111, South Africa* (Working papers 11/11). Stellenbosch, South Africa.

Spaull, N. A., & Kotze, J. (2015). Starting behind and staying behind in South Africa. The case of insurmountable deficits in learning mathematics. *International Journal of Educational Development, 41*, 13–24.

Stanford School Leadership Study Report. (2007). *School principal training and development programme.* The Wallace Foundation.

Task Force. (2000, October). *Institute for educational leadership. Leadership for student learning, reinventing the principalship* (Report), Washington, DC.

Taylor, N., Fleisch, B., & Shindler, J. (2008, February). Changes in education since 1994. Paper commissioned by the presidency. Pretoria, South Africa. Retrieved from https://www.jet.org.za/resources/Taylor%20Fleisch%20Shindler%20Changes%20in%20Education%2015%20year%20review.pdf

The Wallace Foundation. (2006). *Perspective, leadership for learning: Making the connections among state, district and school policies and practices* (Task report). New York.

The Wallace Foundation. (2008). *Becoming a leader, preparing school principals for today's schools* (Task report). New York.

Tingle, E., Corrales, A., & Peters, M. L. (2017). Leadership development programs: Investing in school programmes. *Educational Studies.* https://doi.org/10.1080/03055698.2017.1382332

Tucker, M. S., & Codding, J. B. (2002). *The principal challenge.* San Francisco: Jossey-Bass.

Van Der Westhuizen, P., & Van Vuuren, H. (2007). Professionalising principalship in South Africa. *South African Journal of Education, 3*(27), 431–445.

Vick, R. C. (2004). *The use of SREB leadership development framework in preservice preparation programs: A qualitative study.* Department of Educational Leadership and Policy Analysis, East Tennessee State University. Retrieved from http://etd-submit.etsu.edu/etd/theses/available/etd-0809104-151312/unrestricted/VickR081904f.pdf

Williams-Boyd, P. (2002). *Educational leadership – A reference handbook.* Oxford, CA: ABC-CLIO Inc.

Yu So, V. (2009). Principal leadership for private school's improvement: The Singapore perspective. *Journal of International Social Research, 8*(1), 714–749.

Zepeda, S. J. (2007). *Instructional supervision: Applying tools and concepts* (2nd ed.). Larchmont, NY: Eye On Education.

Part IV

Practising School Leadership: Putting the Theories into Practice

11

Principals as Literacy Leaders (PALL): Leading Learning by Improving Instructional Practices in Australia

Anne Bayetto and Tony Townsend

Background

Since 2009, when it was funded as part of a Commonwealth "Closing the Gap" initiative, the *Principals as Literacy Leaders* (PALL) programme has been undertaken by more than 1500 school leaders from around Australia. Of the 43 grants that were provided to improve literacy and numeracy in Australian schools under that programme, this was the only one that was not focussed on classrooms or teachers. The premise behind the development of the PALL programme was that effective leadership could be used as a means for improving students' reading and that this could be better achieved if principals understood the significance of their being a leader

---

A. Bayetto (✉)
Flinders University, Adelaide, SA, Australia
e-mail: anne.bayetto@flinders.edu.au

T. Townsend
Griffith Institute for Educational Research, Griffith University, Mt Gravatt, QLD, Australia
e-mail: t.townsend@griffith.edu.au

of learning; that is, if they could talk from an informed stance, they would be better placed to promote and embed effective instructional practices in reading in classrooms.

While the original plan in 2010 was just for principals to attend the PALL programme, it was soon realised that PALL's reach needed to be expanded to include other leaders in their schools (e.g., assistant/deputy principals, Advanced Skills Teachers, heads of sections, and literacy coaches). This was in response to recognising that *one* principal attending from a single school was unlikely to be enough for them to effect long-term change and improvement because:

- It placed too much responsibility on the principal to "do it all";
- If a principal stepped away from their school, it was possible that any previously established impetus could be diminished; and
- A principal needed a critical mass of colleagues in their school who were talking the same language and with whom s/he could collaboratively work in order to keep a focus on reading improvement.

Although the PALL programme was originally designed for primary school principals, it has since been modified to provide targeted programmes for leaders in secondary and Indigenous schools, and leaders wanting to learn more about improving transition from primary to secondary school and about the ways for increasing family and community engagement and involvement in reading.

PALL Programme Structure

The PALL programme has been composed of five spaced professional learning (PL) sessions across a school year, along with an associated research. Module 1 focussed on the processes for sharing leadership where there was a consideration of eight dimensions in the leadership for learning (LfL) blueprint (Fig. 11.1).

The PALL programme has iterated that school leaders needed to focus on the moral purpose of ensuring that all students became independent and successful readers and that this could be guided through reference to

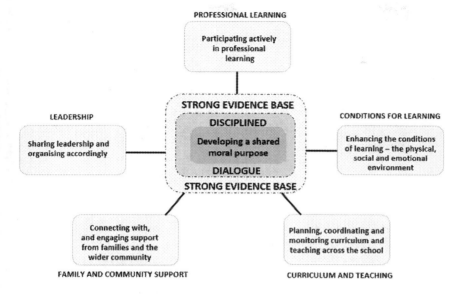

Fig. 11.1 The leadership for learning blueprint

evidence-based teaching and learning practices and by using a disciplined dialogue approach to drill down to the achievements and needs of individual students in any analysis of worthwhile diagnostic data. The five dimensions evolving from the three core dimensions were identified as being essential for reading improvement.

It has been maintained that:

- *Leadership* in a school should be shared and that everyone, at different times, may be a leader, a teacher, and a learner. It has also been highlighted that with a collective focus on reading improvement, it would be more likely to create its own energy, be generative, and sustainable;
- *Professional learning* focussed on reading improvement should be undertaken by teachers, learning support staff, *and* leaders, so they could all develop core knowledge and understandings and be able to "speak the same language" when discussing programming, planning, and instruction;

- *Conditions for learning* made a difference, for example, ensuring that the school environment and resource allocations were focussed on making reading a priority and that the emotional and supportive tone would influence students' willingness and desire to read in classrooms, to read with learning support staff outside of classrooms, and to read beyond the school day;
- *Curriculum and teaching* decisions, when well planned, coordinated, and monitored, had a significant impact on school culture, self-esteem, self-efficacy, and teaching and learning approaches; and
- *Family and community support* strengthened schools' endeavours towards reading improvement.

While the PALL programme has acknowledged that even just one of these dimensions was suggestive of a considerable amount of work, it has highlighted that when the LfL blueprint is focussed on in its entirety, it increased the likelihood of achieving longer term traction. This also supported the PALL approach of ensuring that more than one person in a school should be involved in any reading improvement focus. As Bernhardt and Hebert (2017, p. 103) maintained, "Incremental change is simply not enough to meet the needs of *every* student".

Based on recommendations from international reports about reading development (National Reading Panel, 2000; Rose, 2006; Rowe, 2005), Module 2 has outlined what school leaders needed to know in terms of content knowledge (Shulman, 1986; Stein & Nelson, 2003) by focussing on the BIG 6 of reading: oral language; vocabulary; phonological awareness; letter-sound knowledge (phonics); comprehension; and fluency, with particular emphasis being placed on the significance of oral language and vocabulary as foundational for the development of the other reading skills (Beck, McKeown, & Kucan, 2013; Murphy et al., 2018).

Module 3 has considered processes for collection, analysis, and use of reading achievement data. There has been a particular focus on the selection of valid and reliable assessment processes and for the necessity to triangulate data so that decision-making could be well supported. Building on this premise, there has been emphasis placed on using this information for teachers' programme planning. As Venables (2014, p. 1) stated, "… *not* to review … data is to put our students at certain, even measurable, disadvantage".

Module 4 has cast the lens over ways of designing and implementing effective reading instruction in the everyday class programme and through the use of other intervention processes if students had been identified as needing more intensive instruction. Particular attention has been given to the processes involved in the Response to Intervention (RtI) model that recommended the use of tiers or waves of intervention (Deshler, 2015).

Module 5 has looked at ways of evaluating approaches to intervention and has reflected on how to keep focussed on continuous improvement with reference to Simmons (2015, p. 50), who recommended that approaches should be based on the same principles used by structural engineers: "… fortified foundations, aligned instruction, bridged transitions, and flexible interventions".

In between each of the modules, leaders were asked to work with their teachers and school communities to identify and develop strategies to address identified growth points for reading improvement and, by the end of the year, they were expected to have developed an intervention plan to be implemented the following year.

Since PALL's inception in 2010, and arising from school leaders' involvement, there have been seven pieces of research reviewing the effectiveness of the PALL programme with data collected through pre- and post-PALL programme surveys and by working in case study schools, where researchers looked to document and develop finer grained understandings about which leadership practices facilitated effective instructional reading practices.

Using the eight dimensions in the LfL blueprint, what follows is a discussion of some key points that have been learned so far from the participants' involvement in the PALL programme and from the case study research.

The Research

Although each of the specific research projects on PALL had their own set of objectives, the overall aim of the PALL research was to identify how PALL impacted on, and what school leaders actually did to improve, reading outcomes within their school. Some specific research questions that are responded to in the current chapter are:

1. What effect does PALL have on the participants' perceived ability to lead reading improvements in their schools?
2. What effect does PALL have on leadership practices?
3. What specific activities do school leaders undertake to improve the reading performance in their schools?
4. What effect do these activities have on changing teacher practices?
5. What effect do these activities have on changing student engagement and changing student achievement?

Over the course of the seven studies, a variety of data were collected. Both quantitative and qualitative data-collection methods were undertaken. The data reported on in this chapter include:
Quantitative data:

- *Personal Leadership Profile* and a *School Improvement instrument* completed by the participants in the PALL programme;

Qualitative data:

- Visits to *case study schools*, where qualitative data were collected:
  - *Interviews with principals/leadership teams;*
  - *Focus group discussions with selected teachers and selected parents of students involved in the everyday class reading programme and/or the reading interventions;*
  - *Student work samples; and*
  - *Student learning experience survey.*

In many of the research reports and again below, the responses collected could be referred back to the various elements of the LfL blueprint.

Developing a Shared Moral Purpose

Fullan (2001, p. 1) made the point that, "Moral purpose is about both ends and means. In education, an important end is to make a difference in the lives of students. But the means of getting to that end are also crucial" and with this in mind, the LfL blueprint has been used by leaders in the case study schools as the focal point for planning, initiating, implementing, and sustaining reading improvement for all students. The PALL programme has maintained that all students can learn to read, including those who attended schools located in disadvantaged areas, but upon speaking with leaders, some admitted that when previous initiatives had not developed the traction that they wanted, they had used students' disadvantaged backgrounds as an explanation for their lack of success. However, having been involved in PALL, where they gained contemporary knowledge about possible ways of working, they had become more focussed on *how* they could tenaciously focus on reading improvement as they now more clearly saw it as an equity imperative plus they better understood that, for all students, being able to read was a passport for life opportunities and choices.

> *I think the belief that every child can achieve and it's up to us to make the difference. And really my heart says that that's our job. That's what we're here for and it's not easy. And every school has got different cohorts of parents and teachers and children. So, it's up to us to find the key that's going to work within the school.*
>
> *… we planned literally a whole day on getting people to understand that every kid could learn, given enough time. And then even with our interventions, we'll put up stuff to show that if time is the variable, then learning will be the constant. So, there is an understanding of that, that everyone will get there by people doing interventions – they've started to see the ones they didn't think are going to, are going to. We just weren't doing it the right way.*

This need for a shared moral purpose had clearly impacted on one of the case study schools, where researchers noted that all of the interviewed leaders and teachers could explain their understandings about the school's common goals for reading improvement, while another leader cited that over 90% of the school staff was clearly committed to this shared moral purpose and that with this their moral compass had a clear direction. The challenge for this leader, though, was to consider how to engage with the other 10% who, at that point, were not as convinced about the students' rights to be taught to read. Overall, the majority of leaders and teachers, who were interviewed, could convey their school's shared goals for improvement and this commitment, both at the individual class and whole school levels, was expressed on many occasions. What was distinctive in some schools was when families could also articulate the shared moral purpose and their role in supporting their child's reading development.

Not unexpectedly, a shared moral purpose varied according to each school's context but, generally, there was an understanding that every student, whatever their background, warranted the instruction they needed for them to become independent and successful readers.

Strong Evidence Base

Many PALL participants shared that their prior knowledge about the selection of reading assessments, and endorsement of appropriate instructional practices, had not been made with reference to current evidence-based research and they had, on occasions, referred back to what they learned as undergraduates or to what they had picked up from a range of sources, while working in-service.

As part of each module, participants were given access to a range of evidence-based research articles and asked to read one or more that caught their attention. In the subsequent module, there was a time set aside for participants to discuss what they had read and the implications for work in their schools. This collegial process was particularly valued by leaders because they had the opportunity to share responses with PALL colleagues, and often with their colleagues back in schools, as the articles were often used to initiate conversations in staff meetings or professional learning sessions. Notable, though, were the challenges for some leaders who had teachers reluctant to read evidence-based research because they were more focussed on reading about everyday instructional strategies. In response to this feedback, the first author was asked by the Australian Primary Principals' Association (APPA) to write a series of research-to-practice papers for all of the components of the BIG 6 and these were made freely available on the APPA website: *https://www.appa.asn.au/publications/principals-as-literacy-leaders/*. These articles have been particularly well received by teachers, and leaders reported that they often used them to open up discussions about the current and potential ways of working.

By the end of Module 5, leaders were very clear about the merits and logic of reading and reflecting about evidence-based research as it had been stressed that the research "covered their backs", when they were engaged in professional conversations, particularly in conversations where they may encounter reluctance to engage, or push-back, from some colleagues who were not presently open to considering changes in the ways they worked. It was noted in both written and verbal feedback that leaders appreciated the research-informed structure of the PALL programme and that they valued the LfL blueprint that was used as the reference point.

Disciplined Dialogue

Many leaders acknowledged that prior to involvement in PALL, their reading data (formative and summative) had often been collected in idiosyncratic ways and that not all of the BIG 6 components had been assessed. They also conceded that there had not been surety that any collected data had been thoughtfully scrutinised or acted upon in relation to programme planning. Swaffield and Dempster (2009) maintained that when data were viewed in a disciplined way, it would lead to more considered and aligned programming and planning decisions. In the PALL programme, this staged process has been referred to as using a *disciplined dialogue* approach where leaders and teachers engaged in professional conversations about data. There are three steps/questions for using a disciplined dialogue approach:

1. *What do we see in these data?*
2. *Why are we seeing what we are seeing?*
3. *What, if anything, should we be doing about it?*

This methodical approach was well received by PALL participants and it was clear in the case study schools that by working through the three questions, they became more focussed on data than had previously been the case.

> [W]e have always collected data however how effectively we were taking on board the results of the data were probably a concern, so we needed to make sure we had a whole school approach to the data that was coming back externally and also our internal data.
>
> [I]t's breaking it down. It's not like, "Oh, well, this child is not reading so well." It's about, "Why not? And what part is lacking? What's the component there that's stopping this child from progressing?" So, they're a lot more analytical with what they're doing, really drilling down into the data a lot more, and then planning for that.
>
> [I]f you went back to 2011 they may have spent some of that time organising the excursion and the next camp and having a chat about whatever it might be, whereas the focus is only on what do we want the kids to learn, how are we going to know when they learn it and the assessments what are we going to do if they do know it and what are we going to do if they don't know it.

This shift to using disciplined dialogue showed improved effectiveness in the analysis and use of data in many schools. Both leaders and teachers not only knew which assessment processes focussed on the BIG 6 were diagnostically most helpful, but also how they might use the data for programme planning. When they also ensured triangulation of their data, they felt more secure in having discussions about the patterns in students' learning and also in looking for trends in classes, across year levels, and across "like" schools.

[U]sing sometimes more than one assessment to clearly identify levels of performance. In many schools it was claimed that "no child escapes assessment" and this was used to establish a detailed understanding of each individual's literacy capabilities.

An outcome of this more collegial focus on data was the enhanced conversations regarding students at all levels of learning such that each student was monitored, not just the underperforming students.

Leaders made it clear that they were a work-in-progress regarding their knowledge base about data collection and analysis but, when speaking with researchers, many indicated they were continuing to find ways to strengthen their understandings about how to analyse data so that it could be meaningfully used to inform teachers, students, and their families about what was already known and what needed to be learned next.

We are now continually collecting and analysing data with a shared understanding of how this informs future teaching practice.

With the PALL schools there's a sharper focus than with principals in other schools because we've been involved in a common journey. With the PALL schools we've used a disciplined dialogue framework, and in looking at NAPLAN results recently we immediately went to unpack the data, not try to go into any reasons at that stage. And I have taken that approach on board with the non-PALL principals too.

The data recorded during the discussion showed that several principals spoke of their increased focus on the use of evidence coupled with disciplined dialogue leading to better understandings of the here and now and where to go next.

When speaking with leaders and teachers in the case study schools, it became apparent that they were becoming more proficient at using data as a basis for their decision-making, but that they still had some way to go for their practices to be robust. Overall though, they were now feeling more capable and confident about making informed decisions. PALL participants also reported that they felt better when they were able to identify a *range of ways* of assessing students' progress and, in some case study schools, they had started their own inquiry projects focussed on assessing students' progress.

Leaders shared that they aspired for all educators in their schools to be capable of interrogating data and making informed decisions based on what had been noted. Arising from that was the recognition that school staff members needed to keep data collection, analysis, and translation into practice on the radar so they could continually finesse their knowledge, understandings, and skills, as well as be able to meaningfully discuss and report progress with families and students. This suggested the need, in some case study schools, for further targeted professional learning.

Shared Leadership

The PALL programme has held a strong stance about the importance of developing *shared leadership* rather than leadership being seen as that of position. Principals in the case study schools reported that their involvement in the PALL programme had supported them in developing and sharpening their capacities to more effectively guide teachers when making decisions about assessment practices, programming, lesson planning, and monitoring instructional practices but that the decision to "share/distribute the load" made sense as it strengthened the likelihood that initiatives would be better embedded in classrooms. One of the terms often iterated in the PALL programme has been that "everyone in a school was a leader, a teacher, and a learner" and this clearly struck a chord with many participants as it was often restated when speaking with leaders in the case study schools. They had come to recognise that, depending on the focus, educators with secure background knowledge and skills could often take the lead, while, on other occasions, those same educators would learn from others. The logic of not placing full responsibility for reading improvement on the principal became more apparent to PALL participants as they delved further into thinking about the ways of working. However, that was not to say that principals did not have an active part to play in showing deep interest in teacher and student learning. The difference, though, was that leaders were more positively vested in the merits of the BIG 6 components being part of reading programmes. In some schools, there was a move to shared decision-making between leaders and teachers regarding priorities (e.g., which of the BIG 6 to focus on first) and this created its own across school energy: teachers were more prepared to problem-solve and to try something new because they understood that the principal had their backs. Both leaders and teachers began asking questions and, with the materials shared in the modules, leaders could often share ideas about the ways of working.

This mutual sense of everyone working towards the same goal became generative and how it was achieved looked different across the case study schools. A number of case study schools already had professional learning communities/teams (PLCs/PLTs) so these were a natural platform for focussing on the BIG 6: some teams were solely comprised of teachers at the same year level, others were at the cohort level (e.g., early years, primary years, middle years), while others were vertically grouped. Whatever the configuration, the teams in many of the case study schools were active and intentional, with teachers often taking the lead and decision-making responsibility about the priorities and ways of working being shared.

I would say that there's been a shift in terms of team leaders wanting to take it on.
… you're going to commit to the school for a number of years. It's not like the next big thing. This is the big thing.

One of the biggest challenges in many case study schools was that of having long-term leaders and teachers. Schools that had the same staff in place for a number of years understandably had gained better traction than those where there had been a high turnover: just when shared understandings and practices were put into place, newcomers needed to be inducted into how the school addressed reading improvement. This turnover had immediate ramifications for professional learning and moderation of expectations. It was noted that a particular case study school that had a notable churn in leadership was the one with the least long-term effect on reading improvement.

Each case study school saw leaders differently approach use of the LfL blueprint and implementation of the BIG 6. In some schools, leaders were heavily involved in all the activities; in others there was evidence of shared work between the leadership team, and in others an abrogation to others with little leader involvement (and in some instances, not all that successfully). Perhaps unsurprisingly, researchers found that the more active the leadership team, the more there was momentum at all levels in the school. What the more successful case study schools found was that all educators benefited from making leadership opportunities available. One principal noted that prior to having been involved in PALL "… *if I was successful, it was more good luck than good management*" and for another principal, "*PALL and the Blueprint have helped her, in a school that was floundering, with finding her way and having staff come on board and gain a sense of cohesion*".

Further, some principals restructured the way they worked:

One of the principals (at Module 5) has rejigged their admin role and given duties to others so they can be in the classrooms for 2 hours every morning, and it's a shock to see what it's actually like, potentially every day, and it's made them more human, or humane, about expectations.

and:

The school has taken a slow but firm approach with the expectation that everybody would be involved.… The principal has a good understanding of literacy but her leadership style has been very effective, not in-your-face, but let's look at the data, what's best for students, and let's agree about how we're going to achieve that. She would often refer to the Blueprint in conversation with her assistant [and say] well what are the links?

It has been evident that "buy-in" of the leader and leadership team has been essential to keep focussed on the LfL blueprint and the BIG 6 and as such, it was clear that those working in the case study schools had learned a great deal about both leadership and the teaching and learning of reading.

Professional Learning

Having been a part of the PALL programme, participants felt they could better make more informed decisions about the "why", "what", and "how" of professional learning and that this had led to them becoming more strategic. They found that by using the LfL blueprint, and considering the BIG 6 components, it helped to centre the discussion about priorities at both the individual teacher and whole school levels. It was indicated by leaders that through teachers accessing professional learning about one or more of the BIG 6, it had led to more comprehensive and enthusiastic uptake because teachers understood the logic of why these components were so essential to systematically and explicitly teach and how it might be done. Further, some leaders recognised that they already had teachers with considerable expertise in their schools and that they needed to creatively establish ways for those educators to be released to work with their colleagues or to take the lead in professional learning sessions.

For some leaders, it was the Literacy Practices Guide (LPG) booklets that had a big impact. These were the documents that listed some points for consideration when observing classroom layouts, programmes, lesson plans, and the instructional practices that teachers used. For some leaders, this in-between-module "homework" provided an entry point into some previously inaccessible classrooms. The LPGs were used in other ways too, for example, in some case study schools, they were used for class observations by a team that included a leader and a class teacher from the year below and the year above the teacher being observed. This was found to be an excellent conversation starter regarding seamlessness of instruction in the school. Leaders commented that through using this process they were better able to acknowledge and commend teachers' formative attempts to teach components of the BIG 6 and it was a way of opening conversations about professional learning needs, "… *for others it was a light bulb moment*", and for experienced and capable teachers "… *it was just an endorsement of what they're doing*".

For some of the case study schools, it was identified that they would benefit most if they had a regular timetable of peer observation in order to develop an ethos of continuous and supported feedback to ensure that "… *every classroom is an intentional, literacy rich classroom*".

Another major factor arose when some leaders recognised that for the BIG 6 to be embedded in their schools' instructional programmes, they too should attend key professional learning sessions so they could hear the same presentation and later talk with their colleagues about it. *PALL and the BIG 6 were part of the language used by principals and teachers.*

Significant too was the realisation for some leaders that learning support teachers and teacher aides should also hear the same information as teachers so that programme planning and intervention approaches could be better aligned. In particular, questions were asked, in the PALL programme, about the expectations and work of teacher aides. Stewart (2018, p. 5) commented that they "… have a direct impact on a student's ability to make progress both academically and socially" and as such deserved to be very well informed about efficacious instructional practices.

What the research showed was that professional learning sessions (whether in or out of the school) were still the main processes used for the dissemination of information about reading improvement. However, involvement in PALL saw schools become more discerning in their selection of commercial providers of professional learning and often more interested in using their own on-site staff for developing effective instructional practices by their teachers. Whatever the direction chosen, once a need had been identified:

> PL [was] *provided … to identify and support students to become independent readers.*

This process had, in turn, strengthened the PALL premise that everyone in a school can be a leader and that leadership skills in reading could also be used in other subject areas. From research so far in the case study schools, it has been apparent that leaders accepted the need to provide continuous, goal-oriented, and evidence-based professional learning in order to maintain the focus on the teaching of reading.

> *And that's the best professional learning, when you're sitting with your colleagues, someone's delivering it, you're observing that, and then you know you're going to have to, you know, deliver it as well based on the recommendations of the group. It's really powerful, powerful learning.*

Perhaps unsurprisingly, one of the key outcomes of more targeted and prioritised professional learning in the case study schools was increased teacher confidence. This was of particular note in schools where it had been identified that some everyday Tier/Wave 1 programmes were not yet meeting all students' learning needs and that they needed to be revised.

> *The model of professional learning through sharing practice, examining specific data, planning for teaching and reviewing outcomes is becoming a powerful tool to create consistency across our primary campus.*

Overwhelmingly, the case study research confirmed the significance of the role of principals as they led their school while also developing the leadership qualities of middle managers and teachers. One way of "walking the walk" was for principals to show that they were still learners as well.

Curriculum and Teaching

It was suggested to PALL leaders that the planning, coordinating, and monitoring of curriculum and teaching should be shared by all educators in their school because everyone was collectively responsible for the progress of all students. While individual teachers still had their class lists, it was imperative that they aligned their instructional practices to support seamless curriculum delivery as students moved through the school.

As previously highlighted, a number of case study schools had already well-established professional learning communities/teams (PLCs/PLTs) and part of their remit had been to probe data in relation to instructional practices with the intention of further strengthening the quality and consistency of instruction in their schools. As Venables (2018, p. 82) stated, "Looking at student and teacher work is the most difficult and sensitive task teams can undertake, and arguably the most important".

This use of teams across the school had enabled the development of common purposes, ways to share effective instructional practices, and opportunities for teachers to take the lead.

> *We have introduced a collaborative working pattern to the staff, and they have accepted and embraced a collective responsibility for all students' learning.*

How this was done was understandably different according to each school's context, but one common practice often noted was teachers collaboratively mapping their scope and sequence, and collaboratively developing units of study. A number of principals had reworked their timetables to ensure that teachers at the same year level were simultaneously released at least fortnightly, if not weekly. However, this was not seen as a priority in some schools and it was apparent that there were still some instructional practices not aligned with other teachers' work.

> *So we get together in grade groups, and have a focus student or focus group of students who are probably struggling with the same issue, or problem, and then we come out together as a group with a bit of a focus … we all have a think about what ideas we've done similar that we could help her with.*
>
> *Our staff now engage in collegial dialogue re literacy practices across the K-10 continuum, when a few years ago there was a clear obstacle based on ignorance, self-doubt and lack of shared responsibility for literacy.*

It was reported from some of the case study schools that after analysing data, some teachers' organisational processes were altered to better focus on the range of students' reading abilities in their classes, for example, with use of fluid, needs-based groups rather than groups that had been formed based on a single reading age test score from earlier in the year.

> *This shift demonstrated commitment to action around what students needed to be learn next.*

When schools were asked to identify the focus for their reading intervention, it was noteworthy that a number had come to the realisation that the Tier/Wave 1 everyday class programme of all their teachers was not necessarily meeting students' learning needs. Nelson, Oliver, Hebert, and Bohaty (2015, p. 15) made the point that "Achieving fidelity of universal programs requires that a majority if not all individuals in the school implement them with fidelity". Feedback from some leaders indicated they had to get this right first before they could logically focus on Tier/Wave 2 or 3 intervention approaches. For some other case study schools that were further along in their focus on reading improvement, they found that what was shared in PALL reinforced what they had already been doing but they now had the evidence-based research that supported their decisions and interventions.

The challenge of teacher transfer in and out of schools was a concern but one principal made the observation that:

> [W]e've got sets of teachers here who have been with us since the start, who have come on board sort of halfway through the journey, and then we've got some that are new. So it's just keeping them all together, supporting each other, making sure that they're aware of what the literacy intervention plan is—what is it that we need to do to implement the BIG 6 in my room? What are the needs of my students?

One of the biggest impacts reported was from schools where all educators used a shared language, for example, when teaching the core reading comprehension strategies.

> Students being able to go from class to class and be faced with the same language when discussing reading and reading comprehension has made significant differences to the time needed to introduce topics; all students are beginning to show common understandings when using the 7 [comprehension] strategies.
>
> [T]hey would all know those key words. They know in their reading time if they were doing something about fluency. They would know that—what they were doing with prosody [the rhythm and sound in language], they would know what fluency was and what they were trying to improve. They would know they were doing comprehension. They have full understanding of what comprehension was and what area of comprehension they were covering.

Another strength noted was in the schools where the same language was also used when speaking with families and in school reports, so that everyone in the school was "on the same page" when it came to knowing what students were learning.

> [Teacher capacity is] growing. Good and growing. They are very collegial and collaborative; some of the essentials that are needed for a team to work together are there.

Some leaders asked that all of the BIG 6 components be evident in teachers' term and weekly planning documents and one principal commented that PALL had created a "unified approach" with teachers "focusing on all students".

Some schools chose to include information about the BIG 6 in their weekly staff bulletins, while others built in allocated time during staff meetings for teachers or teams to report back about their achievements in teaching the BIG 6. When some teachers were hesitant to teach new content or to use different instructional practices, leaders reported that they had achieved a more relaxed uptake when they told teachers to at least have a go and even if it was not as successful as anticipated then they could discuss alternative ways forward.

> *I think until we felt comfortable with the BIG 6, we didn't want to talk to it. But once everyone in that team got their head around exactly what all the changes meant they were using it. Now [the BIG 6 and its language is] in all of our planning and that will be the next step I think, to start using it properly.*

However, it was acknowledged that there was still much to be done regarding meeting all students' learning needs and that leaders and teachers were a work-in-progress:

> *Some teachers need more assistance to move forward than do others and in this case classroom observations and conversations about teaching practice are useful. In some cases, teachers provide these observations and in other cases, the leaders do so.*
>
> *We still need to differentiate better in our classrooms, with explicit teaching that targets individual needs, interests and abilities. We need to be better at collecting and interpreting data, for intentional and explicit purposes. We need to ensure that no students slip through the gaps. We need to make more time for collaborative planning and evaluation; timetabled, intentional, weekly case-management meetings. We will introduce the "BIG 6" to all classrooms and ensure that every classroom is an intentional, literacy rich classroom. We need to continue to build a "feedback culture" within our school, for teachers and students. We also need to share the journey, and involve our parents in a more intentional way. We need to ensure that all teachers implement the scope and*

sequence documents in their teaching practice, explicitly delivering literacy every day, in every learning task to every child.

Conditions for Learning

While teaching the BIG 6 components is essential, these reading skills are in the service of students becoming independent and successful readers and a contributing factor for this to happen has to be that students feel physically, socially, and emotionally supported as they learn to read. Dempster et al. (2017) asserted that students must not only feel at ease with teachers and peers but also be interested in what was being taught and what they were choosing to read or being asked to read.

> *Although the leaders of the PALL professional learning workshops have focussed on literacy interventions with and for students, and the impact these have on student achievement, our leadership team decided that it was beneficial for [our school] to focus on changing the culture at [our school] to raise aspirations and expectations among staff, students and parents.*

This raised the question of programming and time allocation whereby PALL participants were invited to respond to recent evidence-based research and commentary about the use of literacy/English blocks.

> *Principals indicated that literacy blocks in the school would be continued or developed following the intervention, noting the need for them to be defined (embed non-negotiables for daily 90-minute literacy block) and uninterrupted (e.g., through ongoing monitoring of events and organisation.)*

Another way of ensuring students' generalisation of their developing BIG 6 skills was developed in one case study school when they recognised that students' phonological awareness skills would be more successfully developed if teachers used cross-curricular perspectives, so they sought guidance from their speech pathologist about the ways of infusing practice of phonological awareness skills into other subject areas.

It also became evident to a number of leaders that they needed to audit their current collection of reading resources for both teachers and students. Some schools recognised that they must dramatically increase the amount of texts in classroom libraries, especially by increasing the number of non-fiction titles. Other schools made a concerted effort to involve students in meaningful text selection for their school libraries because student feedback had highlighted that the types of texts that they wanted to read were not currently available. With this bulking up of class and school libraries, some leaders reported that teachers had increased the amount of allocated time for independent reading and that there had been an immediate and heightened interest to read on the part of many students. Other schools focussed on freshening and updating core reading materials (e.g., guided reading texts) and when reviewing commercial products, referred back to their assessment data to guide their purchases. Added to this was the need for some schools to improve the quality of home reading texts so that students would want to read beyond the school gate.

However, new and different resources are not necessarily going to lead to reading improvement and it was recognised in some case study schools that, again, they needed to cast a lens over their instructional practices.

Family and Community Support

Teale (2018, unpaginated) recently made the point that "The research is clear, consistent, and convincing: When schools succeed in working cooperatively with families, children experience academic and social benefits". However, all case study schools reported that meaningfully connecting with families had been, and continued to be, their biggest challenge. The case study schools were in a difficult situation as they had communities that were experiencing financial and social challenges; a further complexity in some schools was the low literacy skills of some of the parents. This presented a conundrum when the researchers undertook parent interviews because it was probable that those who agreed to be interviewed were parents who were already motivated in supporting their children and whose children perhaps least needed reading support. The difficulty for the case study schools (though anecdotally it had been reported as a major issue in many schools) was how to reach out to the families who most needed the information but who seemed reluctant to be involved perhaps for a range of reasons: they did not appear to be interested in supporting their children, they lacked knowledge about reading development, they did not have the prerequisite literacy skills for supporting their children, and they may not have been able to understand some of the information made available to them.

Schools reported that they wanted to do more to engage and involve families and communities with their focus on reading improvement but that they needed to re-think how they did it as the current approaches were not often well aligned and not drawing in the number of families they had anticipated. Yet the interest was there in some schools as it had been made clear from survey feedback that "… parents were asking for schools to communicate with them more about their children's learning". Case study schools had moved to make use of more targeted communication processes such as social media to share photos with families of their children reading, speaking, and writing and this had been well received. A number of schools had already stopped using printed newsletters as the primary source of information and had moved to the use of digital versions.

First and foremost, it was recognised by the case study schools that they could not assume that families knew how to help their children and that "We also need to share the journey, and involve our parents in a more intentional way". To avoid falling into using "edu-speak", some schools became more focussed on using clear and concise language about the BIG 6 as well as sending home fresher reading texts with more contemporary titles and themes, while some schools developed their own "Home Literacy Practices" guides for families.

> [T]he need to be more explicit with parents, about the importance of what they do with their child, but also to provide them with advice on how to do this best.
> I think they underestimate the power they have too, that they don't understand that even just talking to their child and asking them about things makes such a huge difference. They think—oh, well, that doesn't make any difference but it actually does and they don't understand that that can be important.

Most of the case study schools had provided information sessions about reading development and the ways that families could assist but reported that, on many occasions, the numbers were low and it was the same families who attended any and every event; often they were the very families the school did not necessarily need to be involved as their children were already reading very well. It was the families who had not yet met their child's class teacher/attended acquaintance nights/come to parent-teacher interviews and so on that they wanted to meet. Another issue in all of the case study schools was that family involvement tended to fall away as their children entered the middle primary years and it was all but non-existent by the secondary years. All of the schools felt they had quite some way to go when working with families and while some approaches were encouraging, they still had much to do but there were plans afoot.

> *Yeah, it is a bit of a challenge when you're a parent and you're given a lot of information, a lot of, you know, things coming backwards and forwards that ... I think for me that the school does communicate the things that are found, to me the best things are the summaries, like you get the goals, the student goals, the personal student goals, and for me that really helps. [For instance] in comprehension, fluency, so you know what you should be working on this term, and the school sends a copy with the kids home, letting you know what you're meant to be working on this time, and you do know what to expect and what you should be working on in that.*

Some schools made deliberate efforts to connect with local childcare providers and preschools/kindergartens so that relationships were developed prior to school entry. For some children, this involved a lengthy transition programme that started well before they turned five, while other schools hosted playgroups, social events, and workshops. Some leaders and teachers paid a great deal of attention to developing family trust and raising awareness.

> *School X also reaches out to the community to involve the people who will work with children before they enter the school. School X now has an active coalition with local kindergartens and child care facilities, and people from these*

> *organisations are invited to participate in the school's BIG 6 programs to encourage the common language of PALL and the BIG 6 to move outside the school.*
>
> *It became bigger than just staff too because [name] had a big involvement with the kinders, the local kinders. And so, we recognise that oral language didn't just start with us ... so it was about getting those conversations out to the community ... and I think we all work with people like the parents.*

Beyond a focus on families, some case study schools had come to recognise that they needed to connect with other "like" schools, or ones in close proximity that may not have been schools formally in their nominated zone. Some leaders who attended PALL found that they could better stay focussed on their schools' reading improvement intentions when they knew that other leaders were also focussed on the BIG 6, as this common focus enabled conversations between schools at a range of levels. This collegial approach often saw arrangements made for a group of schools to share professional learning sessions. Interestingly, current PALL programme participants were active in encouraging non-PALL leaders to attend these shared professional learning days and this saw a number of these leaders choose to undertake the next PALL programme.

Impact on Student Learning

Some students in the case study schools were asked to complete a survey to establish how they felt about various aspects of reading. Data indicated that most of them liked to read though some felt insecure about their actual reading abilities. When asked about their teachers' reading instruction, it was evident they had appreciated some changed instructional practices: they stated that they were now more engaged and involved in their reading lessons and high numbers of students shared that their teacher talked to them about how to improve their reading and that they taught them in interesting ways.

> *[T]eachers do have a conversation now with children about what is interesting, what do you find stimulating and why? ... Get their opinion, get their thinking.*

> Because you might look at the group of kids and think they're engaged because they're nice kids and they're well behaving kids, but really, are they engaged? You know, what is "being engaged"? What does that mean to them?

A number of case study schools had moved to using the language of "learning intentions" and "success criteria", whereby teachers shared with students what reading skills they were about to teach them and what the success criteria would look and feel like for students. These very clear descriptions resulted not only in students having common understandings about why they were learning to develop the selected skills but it also enhanced their abilities to talk about their own learning and to explain what reading strategies they had used (or decided not to use) to understand the author's message.

However, the data also showed that students were not often reading in their free time at school or after the school day and neither were family members involved in their reading development at home. This admission seemed to support schools' frustrations about the lack of family engagement and that more needed to be done. In response to this feedback, some of the schools started with their school library: they updated their texts to reflect students' current interests, they increased the number of books that each student could borrow at any one time, and a few schools actively worked with their local council libraries on initiatives.

> [W]hat we did on that this year in this sense is we tried to sort of buy, with home reading, books that were non-fiction. And it was interesting because when I did a little survey one day when they were doing free reading and I said well who's reading a non-fiction book, and there were only three. And those three continually read non-fiction as opposed to the ones that were reading fiction. So I thought that was interesting, and then we had, yeah, discussions about that in terms of trying to broaden our genres as well.

It was very clear in most schools that there was much work for them to do to encourage increased family involvement with their children.

Conclusions

While the researchers had not wished PALL case study participation to be viewed as another "job to do" for leaders and teachers, it was noted that, for some case study schools, they seemed to generate a subtle level of professional tension regarding their imminent visits and responses to their verbal and written observations and recommendations.

When asked what had been learned about taking on the challenge for reading improvement, there were commonalities across the case study schools. While enthusiastic and committed about what needed to be done, the leaders understood that they had to take their teachers with them without teachers feeling overwhelmed and potentially pushing back. Leaders knew they had to be focussed on developing processes that became embedded and they did so by prioritising one or two key goals and staying focussed on them until they were *"just what we do in this school"*.

Some of the case study leaders offered a cautionary warning about not taking on an approach/commercial product that was being used at another site as they had come to realise that their plans for reading improvement needed to be based on "THEIR" students' data and "THEIR" teachers' current skill sets. They also commented on the need to achieve quick wins with teachers, asking questions about instructional practices rather than immediately judging, and staying focussed on increasing the quality of some teachers' instructional practices.

It was evident to the researchers that there was a heightened awareness and confidence shown by school leaders about leading literacy improvements in their schools.

> *[I]t's now a consistent approach, where before I think we had some whole school strategies in place, but they weren't as consistent as they are now that we have PALL.*

But it was not just about the changes in the ways of working for leaders. The researchers saw evidence of common understandings among staff, collaboration amongst class teachers and learning support staff, more consistent practices *across* a school, and raised aspirations among staff, students, and families.

> *The model of professional learning through sharing practice, examining specific data, planning for teaching and reviewing outcomes is becoming a powerful tool to create consistency across our primary campus.*
>
> *So for some people who are beginning teachers it was just wonderful. Some of the checklists, some of the how to set your classroom up, and then to have the six important elements of PALL, the BIG 6, that was just brilliant.*

All leaders maintained that it was essential for them to hold their nerve when initiating, sustaining, and maintaining change, and it was a case study principal who commented that *"PALL has made all the difference to this school. When I did it, it was like a light came on"* that has affirmed that they can be leaders of learning about reading improvement.

References

Beck, I. L., McKeown, M. G., & Kucan, L. (2013). *Bringing words to life* (2nd ed.). New York: The Guilford Press.

Bernhardt, V. L., & Hebert, C. L. (2017). *Response to intervention: RtI and CSI. Continuous school improvement* (2nd ed.). New York: Routledge.

Dempster, N., Townsend, T., Johnson, G., Bayetto, A., Lovett, S., & Stevens, E. (2017). *Leadership and literacy. Principals, partnerships and pathways to improvement*. Cham, Switzerland: Springer.

Deshler, D. D. (2015). Moving in the right direction but at what speed and how smoothly? *Remedial and Special Education, 36*(2), 72–76.

Fullan, M. (2001). Moral purpose. *National College for School Leadership*. Retrieved from https://www.nationalcollege.org.uk/cm-mc-ssl-resource-moral-purpose.pdf

Murphy, P. K., Greene, J. A., Firetto, C. M., Hendrick, B. D., Li, M., Montalbano, C., et al. (2018). Quality talk: Developing students' discourse to promote high-level comprehension. *American Education Research Journal*. Retrieved from https://doi-org.ezproxy.flinders.edu.au/10.3102/0002831218771303

National Reading Panel. (2000). *Teaching children to read: An evidence-based assessment of the scientific research literature on reading and its implications for reading instruction*. Retrieved from http://www.nichd.nih.gov/publications/nrp/upload/smallbook_pdf.pdf

Nelson, J. R., Oliver, R. M., Hebert, M. A., & Bohaty, J. (2015). Use of self-monitoring to maintain program fidelity of multi-tiered interventions. *Remedial and Special Education, 36*(1), 14–19.

Rose, J. (2006). *Independent review of the teaching of early reading: Final report*. Retrieved from http://www.standards.dfes.gov.uk/rosereview

Rowe, K. (2005). *Teaching reading: Report and recommendations of the National Inquiry into the Teaching of Literacy*. Canberra, Australia: Department of Education, Science and Technology.

Shulman, L. S. (1986). Those who understand: Knowledge growth in teaching. *Educational Researcher, 15*, 4–14. https://doi.org/10.3102/0013189X015002004

Simmons, D. (2015). Instructional engineering principles to frame the future of reading intervention research and practice. *Remedial and Special Education, 36*(1), 45–51.

Stein, M. K., & Nelson, B. S. (2003). Leadership content knowledge. *Educational Evaluation and Policy Analysis, 25*(4), 423–448. https://doi.org/10.3102/01623737025004423

Stewart, E. M. (2018). Reducing ambiguity: Tools to define and communicate paraprofessional roles and responsibilities. *Intervention in School and Clinic*. Retrieved from http://journals.sagepub.com/toc/iscc/0/0

Swaffield, S., & Dempster, N. (2009). A learning dialogue (principle 3). In J. MacBeath & N. Dempster (Eds.), *Connecting leadership and learning: Principles for practice* (pp. 106–120). London: Routledge.

Teale, W. H. (2018). *Reading education internationally*. Retrieved from https://www.literacyworldwide.org/blog/literacy-daily/2018/08/23/reading-education-internationally?utm_source=TW09042018&utm_medium=email&utm_campaign=ThisWeek&utm_content=Story-3

Venables, D. R. (2014). *How teachers can turn data into action*. Alexandria, VA: ASCD.

Venables, D. R. (2018). *Facilitating teacher teams and authentic PLCs. The human side of leading people, protocols, and practices*. Alexandria, VA: ASCD.

12

Promoting Teacher Collaborative Learning in Lesson Study: Exploring and Interpreting Leadership to Create Professional Learning Community

Toshiya Chichibu, Tetsuro Uchizaki, and Yumiko Ono

Introduction

Lesson study is known as a professional development activity in which teachers collaboratively plan, teach, observe, analyse and revise actual class lessons (Fernandez & Yoshida, 2004; Lewis & Tsuchida, 1998; Stigler & Hiebert, 1999; Watanabe, 2002). Japan's practice of lesson study has been the focus of attention in many overseas countries, which led to the establishment of the World Association of Lesson Studies (WALS) in 2007. Every year, over 800 participants from 30 countries get

---

T. Chichibu
National Institute for Educational Policy Research of Japan, Tokyo, Japan
e-mail: chichibu@nier.go.jp

T. Uchizaki
Himeji University, Himeji, Japan
e-mail: tetsu-515@docomo.ne.jp

Y. Ono (✉)
Waseda University, Tokyo, Japan
e-mail: y.ono6@kurenai.waseda.jp

© The Author(s) 2019
T. Townsend (ed.), *Instructional Leadership and Leadership for Learning in Schools*, Palgrave Studies on Leadership and Learning in Teacher Education, https://doi.org/10.1007/978-3-030-23736-3_12

together. Japan's practice of lesson study has over a century of tradition and it is implemented in nearly all schools. According to the survey results of the 2017 National Assessment of Academic Ability by the Ministry of Education, Culture, Sports, Science, and Technology (MEXT) in Japan, 0.1% of elementary schools and 0.4% of middle schools do not implement lesson study at all. In other words, at least 99.5% of elementary and middle schools implement lesson study at least once a year; 71.2% of elementary schools and 49.6% of middle schools implement lesson study at least seven times a year; and although the rate of implementation at middle schools is lower than at elementary schools, it can be seen that more than half of schools implement lesson study at least seven times a year.

Although Japan's practice of lesson study has gained worldwide attention and has a high rate of implementation, there are also many studies that cast doubt on its substance and effectiveness. Such doubts include the following:

- Lack of motivation due to an excessive examination of lesson plans (Hargreaves & O'Connor, 2018);
- Lack of depth in discussion in pre- and post-lesson meetings stemming from contrived collegiality (Hargreaves, 1994);
- Some schools continue implementing ineffective lesson study meetings around three times a year without substantial effects (Sato, 2012);
- The conflict between different opinions among teachers (Sato, 2012); and
- Resistance to change habituated practices (Sako, Kakiuchi, Matsuoka, & Kubota, 2015; Blake & Mouton, 1976).

The harmful effects of habituated practices are particularly significant. The frequency of lesson study and the methods for the examination of lesson plans become routine in each school. For example, each school has established its own policy and procedure for conducting lesson study: the number of annual demonstration research lessons, the organisational system for examination of the lesson plans to be implemented in research lessons, the duration of post-lesson discussion meetings and the external resource persons to invite to the research lessons and post-lesson discussion meetings. These are some elements that have become customary at each school and are difficult to change. If it is proposed to increase the frequency of lesson study, there is an opposition that it will be difficult to secure class time and time for school events. If it is proposed to reduce the frequency, there is an opposition that the quality of lessons will fall. The survey conducted by Japan's National Institute for Educational Policy Research (NIER) in 2014 identified a prefecture where there are more schools whose perception of the effectiveness of lesson study is low despite holding frequent lesson study meetings. Some of the causes behind this result are thought to lie in the absence of a careful and critical examination of lesson plans or post-lesson reflective sessions (Chichibu, 2017). Chichibu visited the same middle school located in this prefecture for three years as a lesson study advisor and proposed increasing the opportunities for examining lesson plans. However, the school did not attempt to change the way they had conducted a lesson study (Chichibu, 2017).

Leadership by school principals is essential for changing the problem areas outlined above. Prior research to date on leadership in organisational change suggests the following styles as effective:

- transformational leadership (Bass, 1985; Bass & Avolio, 1990; Leithwood & Jantzi, 1997);
- instructional leadership (Hallinger & Murphy, 1985; Townsend, Acker-Hocevar, Ballenger, & Place, 2013);
- cultural leadership (Deal & Peterson, 1990, 1994; Schein, 1985); and
- supportive leadership (Rinehart, Short, Short, & Eckley, 1998; Wall & Rinehart, 1998).

All previous research observes that leadership is crucial for changing organisational culture and that encouragement is needed until the members of an organisation reach a consensus to achieve change in the organisational culture. With regard to transformational leadership and instructional leadership, there are many situations in which school principals propose concrete ideas for improvement, while a school principal often encourages ideas for improvement to come up from the teachers through cultural leadership and supportive leadership. However, even with transformational leadership and instructional leadership, school principals do not neglect how teachers perceive the ideas for improvement, and they provide encouragement in order to increase the motivation of teachers. Conversely, a vision of organisational change is not lacking with cultural leadership and supportive leadership. The leadership of one school principal is a mixture of multiple elements, and an effective principal is capable of applying different leadership styles, according to the needs and contexts of the school. Effective change should be judged from the perspective of which kind of leadership predominates at different occasions and contexts in the change process.

Principal in Focus

Currently, there is no school administrator licence in Japan. All educational staff at a school, including the nurse teacher, must hold a teacher licence issued by the prefectural board of education (an equivalent of state or provincial board of education). A licence is valid for 10 years and it must be renewed every 10 years. Deployment of compulsory school teachers (elementary and middle schools) is under the responsibility of each prefecture. More competent and effective teachers are recruited as subject advisors (*Shido Shuji*) of local boards of education who visit schools to give instructional support as well as school management advice and often serve as external experts at lesson study meetings. In general, a school principal must pass the examination to be a qualified candidate for a post. About 10% of principals have experience working as subject supervisors, and they are promoted as principals at a faster rate. Teachers and principals are relocated within an administrative boundary after a certain number of years. Typically, a principal serves about 3 years in one school before being transferred to another school.

Tetsuro Uchizaki, the co-author of this paper, served as a principal for 8 years from 2004 to 2008 and from 2009 to 2011 at two elementary schools. At both schools, he worked on reforming lesson study with a focus on curriculum management to be successful in improving student attendance and average achievement assessment scores. The number of teachers at Japanese elementary schools is around 20, but the two schools where Uchizaki served as principal were both classified as large schools, with more than 50 teachers. Uchizaki succeeded with reforms at two large schools one after the other. His leadership is interpreted as an instructional leadership, and he focused on lesson study reform centred on curriculum management. This paper will look at how Uchizaki identified the problems of the schools and how he developed and implemented school improvement strategies.

The Strategy of Principal Uchizaki

Japan's practice of lesson study is spreading around the world as an effective model of a school-based continuous professional development program for enhancing teacher competency, and many achievements have been observed. However, there are many schools that face the problems mentioned above. The schools, called 'research schools', hold open demonstration lessons almost every year and conduct high standard lesson studies which attract many visitors. They are few in number at around 1% of all schools. At research schools, lesson study meetings are held more often: five to six times a year at a regular school, but at least ten times a year at a research school. It is not uncommon for the meetings to examine lesson plans to last until late at night. Since research schools are regarded as municipal or prefectural training schools to prepare lesson study advisors, the teachers assigned to research schools are highly motivated and voluntarily engage in challenging lesson study. On the other hand, in ordinary schools, teachers try to practice lesson study during working hours. External lesson study advisors who have their On-the-Job Training (OJT) in research schools tend to apply research schools' way of doing things without much consideration or contextualisation, and it often results in ineffective lesson study.

In addition to being a large school, Kamijima Elementary School, where Uchizaki was first assigned as principal, was designated in 2005 as the hub school for professional development for lesson study leaders of the school research section. The teachers in charge of the research section from 100 public elementary schools in the city gathered at Kamijima Elementary School three times a year with the aim of building their capacity to lead research by observing lesson study at their school. In other words, Kamijima Elementary School was expected to become the research school for Hamamatsu City. However, the lesson studies that Kamijima Elementary School used to practice differed considerably from what was expected from research schools. Teachers in the school prepared a simplified lesson plan for open demonstration lessons when an external lesson study advisor visited the school.

Uchizaki felt the need to make a fundamental review of how to conduct a lesson study in order to reform its practice at Kamijima Elementary School. The conclusion he arrived at, after a great deal of consideration, was that lesson study should be based on a unit curriculum. The practice of lesson study based on the unit curriculum that Uchizaki started at Kamijima Elementary School was also implemented and established at Kami Elementary School, the second school where he served as principal.

Reform of Lesson Study Based on Unit Curriculum

The unit curriculum was uniquely developed by Kamijima Elementary School. Shizuoka Prefectural Board of Education provided a model curriculum specifying the knowledge, skills and attitudes to be learned in each subject. Using this model as a reference, Kamijima Elementary School specified the knowledge, skills and attitudes required to develop in each unit of a subject. The completed unit curriculum plan composed of around 10 hours of lessons, which looked completely different from the usual lesson plan. Research schools prepare thick and detailed descriptions of the objectives and an analysis of teaching and learning materials, the conditions of children, the lesson procedures, the board writing plan and other processes for a 1-hour lesson on around ten pages. Lesson plans prepared by regular schools were varied. Some of them were as thick as that of research schools while others described the lesson flow in only one page. The unit curriculum plan created at Kamijima Elementary School summarised the progress of about ten lessons of a unit on two pages. For teachers at Kamijima Elementary School who became accustomed to writing a one-page simplified lesson plan, the volume of description increased. However, it was perceived to be too brief as a lesson plan prepared by a designated school for the training of teacher leaders for research, which Kamijima Elementary School was expected to be.

The items in the unit curriculum plan consisted of unit objectives, assessment standards and the unit teaching plan. Describing the unit objectives required a deep understanding of the subject objectives, the content of the descriptions of the curriculum standards set out by the national government and the content of textbooks. Discussions on the unit curriculum plan promoted deep understanding of unit objectives among the teachers. A 1-hour lesson in the unit curriculum plan specified, in one sentence, the competency children were to develop in a given time and the learning activities to achieve it. It was agreed to use a common unit curriculum plan collaboratively created by the teachers of the same grade. When one teacher of a certain grade had an open demonstration lesson, s/he used the unit curriculum plan only and stopped using lesson plans prepared by individuals (see Fig. 12.1).

Though the unit curriculum plan is slim when compared with the regular research school lesson plan, it is difficult to prepare it for all subjects and all units at once. Uchizaki decided to limit the subjects and units covered each year and to increase a stock of the unit curriculum plans gradually over years. In conventional lesson studies, a detailed lesson plan was prepared only for the lesson demonstrated and the other

Unit title		
Unit objectives		
Unit assessment standards	(Knowledge)	
	(Thinking skills)	
	(Attitudes)	

Number of periods	Knowledge/Skills/Attitudes to be taught in lessons	Main learning activities
1		
2		
.		
.		
.		
10		

Fig. 12.1 Unit curriculum plan form

lessons not covered by a lesson study were conducted following a much-simplified annual curriculum plan. By developing the unit curriculum plan, which is something between an annual curriculum plan and a detailed lesson plan for lesson demonstration in lesson study, Uchizaki aimed to create a stock of practical curricula plans useful in daily lessons over a number of years.

It was the first time for either the Board of Education or the teachers to see such an innovative curriculum plan form, and it must have been confusing and difficult to accept. Uchizaki first visited the Board of Education and gained agreement from the manager in charge: Firstly, the school was to use the new unit curriculum plan in lesson studies instead of a lesson plan, and secondly, the lesson studies based on the unit curriculum plan would be shared with teacher leaders as professional development opportunities for future lesson study advisors. Two factors are considered to work in favour of approval of Uchizaki's proposal. Firstly, his proposal and the curriculum model formulated by Shizuoka Prefecture shared the basic principles. Because Uchizaki worked as a subject advisor before being appointed as a principal, the board of education staff including the manager in charge knew him well and trusted his professional decisions.

Having obtained the agreement of the manager at the Board of Education, Uchizaki next explained the new unit curriculum plan form to the teachers at Kamijima Elementary School. The proposed form was totally new to the teachers, but it was accepted by them. For the teachers accustomed to writing a one-page lesson plan, a two-page-long form looked easier than a ten-plus-page lesson plan prepared by research schools.

Kami Elementary School, where Uchizaki transferred as principal after Kamijima Elementary School, implemented lesson studies more vigorously than Kamijima. However, the lesson study practice at the school faced some issues:

* Attempting to standardise lesson plan format leaves little room for creativity;
* Unnecessary criticism of lesson plans in lesson plan review meetings while claiming it was for the benefit of teachers;

- Teachers copied the opinions shared in the lesson plan review meetings without critical examination and reflection, so the lesson plans were products of compromise without a clear focus; and
- In a post-lesson discussion, there was either superficial praise or severe criticism of the lesson.

As a result, teachers became reluctant to present research lessons.

Although Kami Elementary School was implementing lesson study actively, it was not effective enough to support teachers to develop professional knowledge or skills. Considering these challenges, Uchizaki changed the practice of lesson study into the one based on unit curriculum plans as he did at Kamijima Elementary School. The teachers at Kami Elementary School showed some initial resistance to the new approach, but it was established within 6 months.

Implementation System for Unit Curriculum

Uchizaki made efforts to create an enabling environment to develop the unit curriculum plan. Firstly, he grouped teachers by the grade they taught as a base unit for both lesson study and developing the unit curriculum plans. Whole-school lesson study involving all teachers of different grades is commonly practised in Japan. However, as both Kamijima Elementary School and Kami Elementary School were large schools with five classes in one grade, Uchizaki reduced the occasions for meetings of all the teachers but tried to hold weekly grade group meetings. The grade group leader served concurrently as the lesson study leader and led the construction of the unit curriculum in meetings held every week. A standard class schedule in Japanese schools is four lessons in the morning and two lessons in the afternoon. As a matter of fact, many schools schedule one afternoon lesson period weekly to secure time for a staff meeting or lesson study meeting. Kamijima Elementary School designated the sixth period of every Wednesday as the time for meetings on lesson study.

The teachers did not organise research lessons separately for the sake of lesson study. Instead, they observed each other for regular classroom teaching and sat down in every Wednesday grade teacher meeting to discuss issues on teaching and learning and unit curriculum planning. In addition, they agreed to work intensively on creating the unit curriculum plans during the long school holidays in summer and winter.

Secondly, Uchizaki assigned a competent teacher as lesson study leader and released him from teaching to focus on the management of lesson study. In Japanese schools, many mid-career teacher leaders are appointed by the principal to the posts such as the curriculum organisation leader, the lesson study leader, the grade group leader, and the student guidance leader, among others. It is common to all schools to appoint a more capable teacher as the curriculum organisation leader, but the policy on appointing other leaders differs depending on the school. Many schools appoint competent teachers as grade leaders rather than lesson study leaders, but Uchizaki appointed a talented teacher next to the curriculum organiser as the lesson study leader. In response to Uchizaki's intentions, the lesson study leader observed day-to-day lessons and gave teachers advice on their lessons. In addition, the lesson study leader took photographs of lessons and uploaded them onto the intranet to promote individual as well as collective reflection on their teaching practices. The lesson study leader also took part in grade-level meetings and attempted to provide coordination between grades (Fig. 12.2).

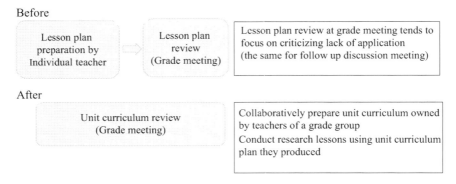

Fig. 12.2 Lesson study reform based on unit curriculum

Strategies Other Than Unit Curriculum

Although Uchizaki entrusted the improvement of lessons to grade meetings, where teachers were expected to collaborate in preparing the unit curriculum, commitments varied from teacher to teacher and from grade to grade. As he had reduced the occasions for whole-school meetings, Uchizaki decided to communicate his values and beliefs with all teachers by means of the Principal's Newsletter.

The topics covered in the Principal's Newsletter were the basic principles for classroom management and lesson management. Not only did it communicate the basic principles, but it also contained his feedback on what he had noticed from daily rounds of schools and casual observation of lessons. Starting with five issues of the Principal's Newsletter in April at the beginning of the school year, he sent two to three newsletters a month to teachers in the following months. The first issue in April touched on the objectives of school education, teachers' attire and greetings to students, and it encouraged frequent contact and consultation with the principal. The second issue presented some hints for effective classroom management and his definition of good and poor lessons, as identified below.

Practical hints for effective classroom management:

- Always take a firm attitude on not doing the wrong thing.
- Do not leave students to do what they like on the pretext of student autonomy.
- Do not overlook minor changes in the children.
- Neither regard parents with hostility nor pander to them.
- Be sure to use greetings such as Good morning and Goodbye.
- Bring everyone's attention to greetings at the beginning and the end of lessons and be polite.
- Call attention if there are children who look away or do not listen during lessons.
- Always keep lockers and helmet storage areas tidy and organised.

Definition of a good lesson:

* The lesson is conducted with a firm objective of the unit and the particular period.
* It is easy for any child to understand the learning tasks.
* The questions have been carefully selected and formulated so that they require no supplementary explanation after being asked.
* The teacher continuously monitors and assesses the children's efforts and progress.

Examples of poor lessons:

* The teachers sit and give instructions.
* The teachers do not move from the blackboard.
* The teachers do all the talk and students listen.
* The teachers teach the textbook.
* The children are not aware of the objectives of the activities they are engaged in.

In the third issue, he once again briefly communicated to the teachers the hints of classroom management. The fourth issue focused on classroom management at a time when 2 weeks had passed since the start of a new academic year. Uchizaki urged the teachers to review how they were managing their classrooms and to discuss the issues in a grade group meeting. The newsletter provided practical guidance on how good lessons and classroom management that he believed in looked like by using positive expressions: 'Touring around the classrooms, I can see all kinds of things each of you has done. A classroom where the desks are arranged orderly. A classroom without any litter. A classroom where the children and the teacher are working together enthusiastically. A classroom where the children are happily engaged in learning.'

The fifth and the last issue in April expected teachers to reflect on how the demeanour of children had been. It emphasised the rules on how to interact with children. 'Please reflect on your way of instruction and the attitude of children this month.' 'We have come to see different sides of children but aren't we trapped by fixed ideas about our children?' and

'Even if you intend to treat all the children fairly, some children may feel that treatment is unfair. It is important for us teachers to be aware of this when interacting with the children'.

Achievements of Reform Efforts

Uchizaki's school management as described above brought about positive changes in lessons, teachers and children. The main reason for focusing on Uchizaki's school management was that both experienced and younger teachers in the same grade showed common characteristics in the lesson organisation when all their lessons were demonstrated openly, using the aforementioned unit curriculum plan. Furthermore, the children expressed their ideas actively, and the teachers' instruction proceeded flexibly while accepting students' comments as much as possible. There are many research school lessons prepared that have a very detailed lesson plan, minutely describing questions to ask and what to write on the board. Despite those efforts, we have observed often that a teacher was not able to handle the responses from children flexibly. In this case, however, it was heartening to see that five classes in one grade achieved practically the same level using a simplified unit curriculum plan.

The lessons Uchizaki aimed at and promoted were those where all learners were encouraged to speak their own thoughts freely and listen to others. As such practices became established, the children's self-esteem increased and non-attendance decreased. Although there had been a number of children who were school-phobic at Kamijima Elementary School before Uchizaki was appointed, the number continued to fall over the 5 years he served as principal and eventually dropped to zero. The school's results in the National Assessments of Academic Ability held in the fourth and fifth years of Uchizaki's service at Kamijima were significantly better than the city average, and the percentage of correct responses for questions requiring higher order thinking skills was particularly high. In Kami Elementary School, after he transferred from Kamijima Elementary School, the number of long-term absentees decreased and the percentage of correct answers for questions requiring higher order thinking skills increased. Uchizaki's leadership made a difference for both teachers and children.

Characteristics of Uchizaki's Leadership

In this section, we try to underscore the factors that contributed to his school reform from the instructional leadership point of view.

Uchizaki had a clear vision of organisational reform and introduced various proposals to achieve it. Of course he made some revisions of his plans and policies by considering the views of the assistant principal and lesson study leaders, but as the principal he made a decision in most cases in a top-down manner: the analysis of school problems, the reform of teaching/learning approaches, organisational change for effective lesson study, the change from the conventional lesson plan form to the unit curriculum form, and guidance of teaching methods and classroom management through the Principal's Newsletter. In particular, the development of the unit curriculum was innovative and represents Uchizaki's strong motivation for reform.

Uchizaki aimed to transform the mindset of teachers. Five issues of the Principal's Newsletter in April were evidence that he was aware of the necessity to repeatedly communicate his ideas to the teachers about classroom management, school management, and how teaching/learning should be. The same messages appeared again in the newsletters toward the end of a school year. The objective seemed to be a warning to the teachers. When he found some signs of disorder, or a problem in classroom management or in teaching, during his regular casual classroom visits, he sent a message to the teachers to remember the rules and hints on classroom management shared at the beginning of the year and to re-establish them firmly. Research lessons using the unit curriculum plan was another strategy of freeing teachers from the obsession with an excessive review of lesson plans. He sought to create a system of practising lesson studies accepted and supported by both experienced and less experienced teachers.

It is often pointed out that a mere demonstration of instructional leadership has not necessarily resulted in teacher change. As Schein (1999) argues, when a leader serves as an expert who provides a solution (expert model) or an authority who diagnoses and prescribe solutions (doctor-patient model), transformation of the organisational culture was hard. Schein puts forward the clinical process consultation model that facilitates clients to bring out their own ways of thinking or solutions. Uchizaki's leadership style shares the common awareness of the problem with Schein. He supported transforming teachers' perspectives toward teaching and learning through the process of developing the unit curriculum model and reforming their approach to lesson study.

There were some teachers who resisted Uchizaki's lesson study reform initiative at both schools. There were also a couple of teachers who insisted on preparing the conventional detailed lesson plans and who did not agree with the significance of the unit curriculum. Even these teachers admitted that the children who were taught by the teachers supporting and implementing the unit curriculum model took the initiative in their own learning. The teachers who were not sympathetic to Uchizaki's lesson study reform did follow the principle of active learning and the basic rules to maintain effective classroom management. It is thought that this was made possible because Uchizaki repeatedly advocated for the vision of good lessons and effective classroom management that he was aiming for through the Principal's Newsletters and other communication channels. The case may have something in common with the concept of leadership through storytelling by Denning (2007).

Summary

The case of Uchizaki can be regarded as the successful implementation of lesson study and teaching/learning reform through instructional leadership. But what lessons should we learn from this case to reform school organisation into a professional learning community?

In organisational development theory, workshop approaches such as 'open space technology' and 'future search' have been used recently to bring out teacher's initiatives and commitment. Sako and Takezaki (2011) demonstrated that setting common objectives to work on through teacher workshops is effective for organisational reform. Besides, servant leadership (Greenleaf, 1977/2002) and supportive leadership (Rinehart et al., 1998), which are similar to Schein's consultation model, have also become popular as a model for leaders.

The case of Uchizaki clearly differs from these leadership approaches seeking motivating participation by organisational members and bottom-up decision-making. Rather, it is close to a picture of a leader with a clear vision, advocated by Drucker (2002). As Mintzberg (2009) asserts, any kind of leadership may function effectively, but Uchizaki's case can be evaluated as instructional leadership, illustrating the significance of presenting a vision at the same time as creating strategies that are acceptable to the teachers. However, as Boyce and Bowers (2018) argue, the high degree of overlap is observed between the theories of instructional leadership and leadership for learning. If we agree that effective human resource management is within leadership for learning, Uchizaki's leadership can be regarded as leadership for learning. It is clear that his staff support did contribute to teacher satisfaction and more teacher commitment: for example, concern for teachers' feeling for burden, providing practical and concrete hints for effective classroom management and creating work environment for professional learning.

Lesson study practice with an emphasis on the examination of lesson plans, which Uchizaki felt to be a problem, is Japan's traditional approach to lesson study practice. Researchers specialised in subject pedagogy continue to advocate the significance of lesson study that emphasises rigorous examination of lesson plans. It is a fact that many teachers continue to practise it despite being aware of some adverse effects described in Uchizaki's case. How could we change school organisation to minimise the feeling of a burden of lesson study and maximize students' learning at the same time? The case of Uchizaki presented one possible solution that worked in a specific context. Further research is needed to explore the relationship among leadership, teacher collaborative learning and students' learning.

References

Bass, B. M. (1985). *Leadership and performance beyond expectations*. London: Collier Macmillan.

Bass, B. M., & Avolio, B. J. (1990). *Transformational leadership development: Manual for the multifactor leadership questionnaire*. Palo Alto, CA: Consulting Psychologists Press.

Blake, R. R., & Mouton, J. S. (1976). *Consultation*. Reading, MA: Addison-Wesley.

Boyce, J., & Bowers, A. J. (2018). Toward an evolving conceptualization of instructional leadership as leadership for learning: Meta-narrative review of 109 quantitative studies across 25 years. *Journal of Educational Administration, 56*(2), 161–182.

Chichibu, T. (2017). The relationship between the coaching by supervisors of boards of education and the school culture. *Japan Bulletin of Educators for Human Development, 20*(2), 37–46 (in Japanese).

Deal, T. E., & Peterson, K. D. (1990). *The Principal's role in shaping school culture*. Washington, DC: U.S. Department of Education.

Deal, T. E., & Peterson, K. D. (1994). *The leadership paradox: Balancing logic and artistry in schools*. San Francisco: Jossey-Bass.

Denning, S. (2007). *The secret language of leadership. How leaders inspire action through narrative*. San Francisco: Jossey-Bass.

Drucker, P. (2002). *Managing in the next society*. New York: St. Martin's Press.

Fernandez, C., & Yoshida, M. (2004). *Lesson study: A Japanese approach to improving mathematics teaching and learning*. New York: Routledge.

Greenleaf, R. (1977/2002). *Servant leadership: A journey into the nature of legitimate power and greatness*. New York: Paulist Press.

Hallinger, P., & Murphy, J. (1985). Assessing the instructional management behavior of principals. *The Elementary School Journal, 86*(2), 217–247.

Hargreaves, A. (1994). *Changing teachers, changing times: Teachers' work and culture in the postmodern age*. New York: Teachers College Press.

Hargreaves, A., & O'Connor, M. T. (2018). *Collaborative professionalism: When teaching together means learning for all*. Thousand Oaks, CA: Corwin Press.

Leithwood, K., & Jantzi, D. (1997). Explaining variation in teachers' perceptions of principals' leadership: A replication. *Journal of Educational Administration, 35*(4), 312–331.

Lewis, C. C., & Tsuchida, I. (1998). A lesson is like a swiftly flowing river: How research lessons improve Japanese education. *American Educator, 22*(4), 12–17. 50–52.

Mintzberg, H. (2009). *Managing*. San Francisco: Berrett-Koehler Publishers.

Rinehart, J. S., Short, P. M., Short, R. J., & Eckley, M. (1998). Teacher empowerment and principal leadership: Understanding the influence process. *Educational Administration Quarterly, 34*(1_suppl), 630–649.

Sako, H., Kakiuchi, M., Matsuoka, S., & Kubota, M. (2015). Practice and outcomes of team consultation about School Organizational Management (1):

Action research by Consultation Team made by Kochi Prefecture School Board and Naruto University of Education. *Research bulletin of Naruto University of Education*, 30: 147–167 (in Japanese).

Sako, H., & Takezaki, Y. (2011). A case study on construction and availability of methodology for step-wise organizational development of school. *Journal of Japan Association of Educational Administration, 53*, 75–90.

Sato, M. (2012). *Reforming schools*. Tokyo: Iwanami Shoten (in Japanese).

Schein, E. H. (1985). *Organizational culture and leadership*. San Francisco: Jossey-Bass.

Schein, E. H. (1999). *Process consultation revisited: Building the helping relationship*. Reading, MA: Addison-Wesley.

Stigler, J. W., & Hiebert, J. (1999). *The teaching gap: Best ideas from the world's teachers for improving education in the classroom*. New York: Free Press.

Townsend, T., Acker-Hocevar, M., Ballenger, J., & Place, A. W. (2013). Voices from the field: What have we learned about instructional leadership? *Leadership and Policy in Schools, 12*(1), 12–40.

Wall, R., & Rinehart, J. S. (1998). School-based decision making and the empowerment of secondary school teachers. *Journal of School Leadership, 8*(1), 49–64.

Watanabe, T. (2002). Learning from Japanese lesson study. *Educational Leadership, 59*(6), 36–39.

13

Creating and Leading Powerful Learning Relationships Through a Whole School Community Approach

George Otero

Instructional leadership now focusses on the interplay of achievement, well-being and life chances, when student performance is considered. Instructional leadership also now demands a focus on each learner, his or her context, needs, talents and motivation.

This personalization therefore requires that curriculum, instruction and assessment becomes a *social process* characterized by (a) continual consultation between teachers, students, families and communities about who they are, what's worth learning and how to learn together; (b) focussing on the student as the subject of at least five basic learning relationships—student to self; student to subject; student to peers; student to teacher; and student to family and the wider community and (c) creating a culture of trust, discovery and dialogue that allows the social, personal and environmental factors in a child's life to be integrated into the educational experiences offered in the classroom and the school (Otero & West-Burnham, 2009).

G. Otero (✉)
Center for RelationaLearning, Santa Fe, NM, USA
e-mail: sunmoon@newmexico.com

Leading learning relationally will require school leaders to become outward facing in their orientation, moving beyond delivery and management perspectives, towards community and relationship perspectives. Recently, Paul Reville, the Director of the Educational Redesign Lab at Harvard University, stated, "Schools alone, as currently conceived, are insufficient to do the job of educating all students for success." The Redesign Lab is initiating a project to help school and community leaders to work together to address both in-school and out-of-school factors that affect student learning, including personalizing learning, integrating services, providing enrichment activities outside of school and school governance (*Education Week*, February 24, 2016, p. 9).

The call for schools to be more outward facing is not new. Jack Minzey and Clyde LeTarte in their landmark book, *Reforming Public Schools Through Community Education* (1994), set out the implications of decades of exploration of the impact of out-of-school factors on achievement and life chances. They argued for a change in the paradigm of what we call schools. They saw community education as both the vehicle for the change and the result of the change: moving from a focus on schooling to a focus on education, everyone in the community could be a learner and a teacher at different times.

Instructional leadership and leadership for learning are both practices of school leadership that encourage school leaders to maintain a steady resolve on improving learning. Yet, many school leaders realize that managing internal school processes, procedures, and personnel within school are necessary but insufficient when student learning is understood as the effect of multiple ongoing relationships and factors beyond the control, and often the influence, of the school.

School improvement in recent years has identified two types of school leadership (among others): instructional leadership and leadership for learning. School leadership was centred on improving what happened in classrooms and to learners in the confines of the school building, curriculum and school day. Instructional leadership focusses on achievement, wellbeing and life chances where student performance is concerned, but also on each learner, his or her context, needs, talents and motivation (Elmore, 2000). Leadership for learning now understands learning to be multifaceted and multidimensional, the result of the relationships between family, school and community and between student and subject, student and peers, student and teacher and student and the wider community, all of which need nurturing and support (Hattie, 2009; Otero, 2016; Townsend, 1994). Both theories now require school leaders to consider, and attend to first and foremost, the social relationships that surround learning.

Few school leaders would deny that student learning is nested in multiple social contexts. Bronfenbrenner's (1979) ecological framework for human development describes the relationships beyond the school that influence student learning. His theory describes the social systems in which children and youth develop and learn, strongly suggesting that student learning is influenced significantly by relationships that are occurring simultaneously in several contexts. Bronfenbrenner's ecological framework for human development is concerned with systems in society and suggests that for young people, the family is the primary unit to which children belong, who in turn are part of school and community, with each student belonging to a broader network of groups and systems, all of which impact their experience and learning in school. In their recent research on school belonging, Allen, Vella-Brodrick, and Waters (2016) propose that even school belonging is a socio-ecological phenomenon, and they examine Bronfenbrenner's framework, and multiple research studies since, to consider school belonging, in order to explore the various systems of relationships that affect a student's sense of school belonging that occurs beyond the school gate.

As the principles and practices of both instructional leadership and leadership for learning have developed over the years, both approaches to school leadership must adapt to the emerging broader view of the purpose and role of a school in the education of the young, and the leadership required to support these new understandings. Leading learning will require school leaders to become outward facing in their orientation, moving beyond delivery and management perspectives to engage with community and relationship perspectives.

Given the need for schools and their leaders to be more outward facing, this chapter presents a rationale and framework for school leaders, one that integrates instructional leadership and leadership for learning for the purpose of creating powerful learning relationships throughout the entire educational community, and that directs school leadership. It will describe a practical model for leading learning relationally, one that posits the school as a hub for the development of social capital and positive relationships between youth, family, staff and community. School life, practices and procedures are focussed on (a) connecting parents to their children's learning, (b) linking the community to the school and vice versa, (c) developing community-based extended learning opportunities for all stakeholders and (d) personalizing the learning for each and every student. First, the chapter provides a brief description of each of these domains.

The Four Relational Domains

Parent Connectedness: "Schools partnering with families to support their child's learning"

Parents are their child's first and most constant teachers and that makes them pivotal in learning. In essence, we, as educators, have the privilege of partnering with parents to raise their children, and by deeply connecting parents to the school, we enhance the parent, teacher and student relationships. Parents must be valued and encouraged to interact with the school, as we know that this has clear benefits for student learning. Connecting parents to school is one of the five key components driving success in Chicago schools (Consortium on Chicago School Research [CCSR], 2006)

> The evidence is consistent, positive and convincing: families have a major influence on their child's achievement. When schools, families and community groups work together to support learning, children tend to do better in school, stay in school longer and like school more. (Henderson & Mapp, 2002, p. 7)

Partnering with teachers, volunteering, being part of committees and making sure that students are ready to learn when they arrive at school, all enable high-quality learning to take place. These actions firmly solidify a sense of community and can all be undertaken by parents. Schools have the space, opportunity and expertise to engage parents in supporting learning on many levels. Parents' capacity to partner will vary and has the potential to be enhanced as the partnership grows. This will be mutually beneficial.

Community Links: "Engaging in mutually beneficial activities to make us all partners in raising local children"

The result of connecting the school to the community and the community to the school will be a greater number of community members working directly with children. Opportunities for the community to work with the school to enhance learning and make it more relevant should be a priority for every school leader.

Having community members and their organizations volunteer, provide expertise and share their talent leads to true partnering. The idea that the community must partner with the school to improve achievement, wellbeing and life chances for young people gives the community a purpose and direction that is to the betterment of all. The school looks to the community for the investment of time and energy as much as, if not more than, it does for their financial support.

In every community, there is a range of organizations with a breadth of experience, expertise and resources that can be harnessed to support the extension of student learning beyond the environment of the school. The short- and long-term benefits of partnering between the community and school can transform the lives of children and families and strengthen the community itself. The opportunity for this partnering to be mutually beneficial to everyone involved should not be underestimated.

Community-Based Learning: "Exploring alternative pathways"

Using community-based learning, leaders of learning endeavour to:

- engage students in authentic learning to enhance future learning experiences;
- cultivate the rich knowledge and willingness of a range of community members to support the learning of young people; and
- build meaningful relationships for young people with their peers and other community members.

Working in this domain, leaders look beyond the regular school offerings and further engage students in their learning. This enhances instructional leadership. To achieve this, we have to let learners take control of their learning in an environment that is different from the classroom. It requires having adult and young-adult mentors teaching, coaching and playing with the students. Mentoring is the core teaching and learning methodology for this domain.

The reality is that we have students who require different opportunities to demonstrate their skills and talents, and fare better learning in a community context. Community-based learning focusses on enhancing the learning of students by allowing them to personalize it through stimulating programmes and experiences that are child-centred, developmentally appropriate and structured in a different way from their classroom. At the heart of this domain, students are working on self-determined learning goals and are being involved in engaging workshops and ongoing projects. The opportunity to further engage the community, universities and other local schools in enhancing learning is available. In fact, the involvement of parents, local organizations and businesses is integral to the success of community-based learning. When community members give their time to teach something they know and love to young people, everyone benefits.

The idea of community-based learning is to provide a revision, or extension, to the school day. It should not be seen as more of the same, nor as more time at school, but as an opportunity to pursue student-generated learning goals and to engage in stimulating activities—all the while broadening the students' experiential base and developing new skills. These experiences must be relevant to the student, and not just organized to meet the artificial construct of a curriculum to be surmounted or powered through.

Community-based learning at its best provides students with an opportunity to work on collaboratively determined learning goals. The students come up with what they want to get better at and work with people who can actively help them get better at that skill or talent. Community-based learning is about further learning and that applies to children and adults alike. In the long term, future programmes could be running both within and after regular school hours. With community members successfully sharing their skills and recognizing that they can make a significant contribution to student learning, the school will be more accepting of them mentoring within school hours in the future and community members will feel more comfortable sharing that expertise during the school day. This furthers the notion of schools becoming genuine community-learning organizations.

Personalizing the Curriculum: "Connecting students to their learning"

As practitioners, we find it challenging to cater for the range of abilities in a classroom. Yet as the famous educator, John Dewey, stated, "If we teach today's students as we taught yesterday's, we rob them of tomorrow." Today, educators are more aware than ever that all learning is social. Vygotsky (1978) was key in establishing this awareness and helped change the way educators think about children's relationships with others. His work shows that social and cognitive development work together, build on each other and are unique to each learner.

Systems and schools recognize that students have different needs and learning dispositions, and in recent times, the push to ensure that educators cater for a range of abilities has had a renewed emphasis. This is due in part to the data-rich world in which we live and the advent of new technologies and new teaching methodologies. Personalizing the curriculum is about ensuring that learning for all students is relevant, supportive of those who require additional assistance to make progress, and challenging, satisfying and playful for all.

Personalizing the curriculum means much more than adapting the presentation of a curriculum to the learning dispositions and different range of abilities of students. To truly personalize the curriculum, the school leader must build a strategy for learning and teaching that makes each individual student a partner in the teaching and learning process. We partner with the student, parent and community to make the learning richer, to access all the available learning environments, resources and contexts and to make more meaning from their learning experience.

Our goal must be to teach every child at their point of need and then take them further with their learning. This must include opportunities for children to make choices in their learning and co-construct learning goals. Instruction must be personalized to allow students to continually develop their skills, talents and unique identity. The learning must be child-centred and can only occur successfully when we have built strong, interdependent and personal relationships with our students that allow us to understand them as whole people. Working together, the student and teacher can utilize a range of assessment to allow the child to access the curriculum at their point of need. The role of the teacher is critical; we must allow them to be risk-takers and teach in ways they haven't taught before.

Rationale for the Four Domains

Good leadership is always cognizant of the purpose being served. School leaders serve learning. Leaders of learning therefore focus time and attention on the relationships that impact student learning. Instructional leadership focusses more on how instruction happens in ways that support critical learning relationships. Learning happens in a community. Schools are part of the community. Dedicated to serving learning, future-oriented school leaders define and expand their role by enhancing, supporting and developing learning relationships, both within school and across the community. In addition, if schools seek to increase learning for all children and youth, leaders must operate in ways that address all the interdependent factors that contribute to learning in schools. So, teaching children to read, write, add and subtract becomes a set of strategies to be understood and practised in school, in the family and in the wider community.

School leaders have a better idea of what to do when they are clear about what success looks like. Townsend, Clark and Ainscow, in their 1999 chapter, "Third Millennium Schools: prospects and problems for school effectiveness and school improvement", analyse why schools of the third millennium might have to be totally different from those we have today. As society changes, schools will change not only their structure and procedures but also their conception of purpose. Further, Leadbeater and Wong in "Learning from the Extremes" (2010) outline four ways that learning in the twenty-first century may unfold. They prefer innovation over improvement when looking at how schools address learning needs in future and suggest that the purpose of a school is to respond to the specific learning needs and learning contexts of the communities being served.

Australian sociologist Edgar (2001), in *Patchwork Nation*, explored all the factors that create and are creating Australian society and suggested this specific purpose for a school in Australia today. "The purpose of a school is to help a family educate a child." If one asks school leaders, teachers, parents and community members how much they agree with this purpose, as I have hundreds of times, you will hear strong support and general agreement. Recently, groups have suggested that in today's society, school, family and community might see themselves as necessary allies in the education of the nation's children, more of a three-way learning partnership instead of placing too heavy an emphasis on what the school must do.

With reference to the "moral" purpose of school, Fullan (2003) and others such as Feinberg (1990) ask school leaders to continually ponder the deeper purpose of a school in order to understand how to lead successfully. This following quote (Otero, Csoti, & Rothstadt, 2018) states the moral purpose behind the framework described below.

> Sometimes we wonder if our schools are really helping people to be better human beings, and so as leaders we need to reflect on whether we are actually doing the right thing to achieve this. The three of us got into education because we wanted to make a difference, yet we have all wrestled with understanding how we can achieve this as educational leaders. This book is about what we know is important for every child to succeed, and describes

a framework for leading a school that focusses on the factors that deliver the best learning outcomes. The school leader can use this handbook to create opportunities for learning and teaching that connect and mobilise all stakeholders. We, as leaders, have found that this framework has helped us lead by a moral imperative rather than by personal preferences.

The Leadership Challenge: Working Better Together

How can a school respond to the challenge of working better together in partnership with students, families and communities to increase learning for everyone? First, by having leaders, teachers and support staff, parents and community members understanding the factors that determine a child's achievement, wellbeing and life chances. Second, by seeing school leadership as primarily about building and sustaining positive relationships between and among students, staff, parents, families and the larger community. Third, by focussing school leadership efforts on building positive relationships in the four domains (referred to above) that impact learning as described in the whole school-community approach.

Framework for Leading Learning

The whole school-community framework described here has emerged over several years and is grounded in theory and practice. It is based on the power of positive relationships to connect school, family and community in ways that increase or enhance student learning, wellbeing and life chances (Otero, 2016).

For example, educators can safely say we now have enough data to suggest what factors impact a child's achievement, wellbeing and life chances (West-Burnham, Farrar, & Otero, 2007). The data have been coming into discussions of schooling for years. The most significant early research was conducted over 50 years ago. The Coleman Report, "Equality of Educational Opportunity", is considered to be the foundational research that altered the lens through which analysts, policymakers and the public at large view and assess schools (Hanushek, 2016). The report summary challenges all schools to look at their success by looking beyond the school walls (Coleman et al., 1966, p. 325):

> Taking all these results together, one implication stands out above all: That schools bring little influence to bear on a child's achievement that is independent of his background and general social context; and that this very lack of an independent effect means that the inequalities imposed on children by their home, neighborhood, and peer environment are carried along to become the inequalities with which they confront adult life at the end of school.

Since then, literally hundreds of research efforts have documented the community, social and personal factors that influence not only student achievement but also wellbeing and life chances. Most school leaders would also agree that achievement, wellbeing and life chances are basic aspects of being a whole person and should not be addressed in isolation from each other. This is reflected in the Association for Supervision and Curriculum Development's Whole Child Approach (www.ascd.org/whole-child.aspx) and in England's Every Child Matters Policy, begun under the Labor government in September 2003, but sadly abandoned in 2010 by a new government bent on focussing solely on student academic achievement, which led to more siloed approaches.

For the sake of argument then, let us assume that the purpose of education can be summarized by the simple proposition that schools are part of a process that is designed to maximize the achievement, wellbeing and life chances of every child and young person. If this is true then the role of schools, educators and school leaders might be seen as managing all the contexts, relationships and variables that influence student success to ensure the most propitious learning circumstances possible.

The framework embedded in the whole school-community approach attempts to activate key factors that are known to influence student learning, wellbeing and life chances (West-Burnham et al., 2007). Figure 13.1 shows the potential variables operating on any individual in terms of their personal life chances, wellbeing and learning. Wellbeing can be best understood as the overall effectiveness of a person's life—where the key

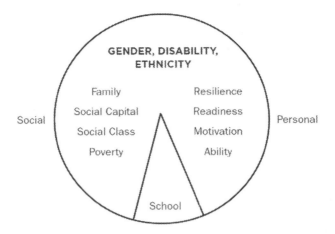

Fig. 13.1 The variables influencing a child's life chances and wellbeing. (West-Burnham et al., 2007)

variables are largely positive, for example, physical and mental health, the quality of family life and friendships, living in a safe community, economic security and an overall sense of personal fulfilment and a positive view of personal futures and potential.

The four factors at the top of the diagram, which are italicized, were in a different category to the rest when this was graphic was developed; they were seen as being essentially inherited, and in the normal course of events, there is nothing that can be done to change them. We now know, more than a decade later, that gender and disability, in particular, may not be as immutable as we thought previously. What is still clear is that in certain circumstances, gender, ethnicity, disability and family history can have significant positive or negative implications in terms of life chances, especially in terms of achievement in school. In some circumstances, they can have highly beneficial implications—it seems to depend on context. They are not neutral influences on learning.

The other three variables, social, personal and school, are not set in the same way as the first four factors; that is, they can be influenced, changed and mitigated in ways that the more personal physical and family characteristics cannot. Yet, there are clear patterns in the nature of these variables and their impact on children. The social variables are essentially contextual; they describe the social situation of every child and young person. The personal variables, our views and attitudes about ourselves, are the factors that explain the distinctive identity of every person—the attitudes to life that help to make us who we are. The school as a variable is significant in that it is probably the one common factor in almost every person's life, and in some respects, is the most controllable of all. Regardless of the community one finds oneself a part of, there is always a school, even if it under a tree or at home. Of course, we need to recognize that there are still millions of children, mostly girls, who don't get to go to school at all, and this in itself is a factor that impacts their lives.

There will obviously be a complex interplay between the most significant variables identified in Fig. 13.1, and there is an almost infinite number of permutations possible for the interactions between the social and personal variables. However, certain implications are very clear in each significant category. If school is the one common factors in all of our lives, then instructional leadership and Leadership for Learning are approaches that need to be exercised in the context of understanding and appreciating the social, personal and community factors that lead to achievement, wellbeing and positive life chances. Below are some of the factors in the figure that strongly influenced the development of the framework.

Family

The quality of family life is fundamental to life chances and educational success. There are obvious cultural, social and moral issues directly related to childhood experiences of family life. There are also very real issues in terms of cognitive and neurological development, which have profound implications in terms of personal academic potential. Two pivotal factors in the family are play, as the key to socialization, and language, as the basis for all learning. Both of these require active parent involvement in their children's lives.

In a review of research from across the world, Desforges (2003, p. 4) draws very explicit and highly confident conclusions:

> [P]arental involvement in the form of 'at-home good parenting' has a significant positive effect on children's achievement and adjustment even after all other factors shaping attainment have been taken out of the equation. In the primary age range the impact caused by different levels of parental involvement is much bigger than the differences associated with variations in the quality of schools. The scale of the impact is evident across all social classes and all ethnic groups.

He identifies a range of other factors at work:

* The higher the level of a child's attainment the greater the parental involvement;
* Maternal education, social class, material deprivation and maternal psychosocial health influence the extent of involvement; and
* Engagement diminishes with the child getting older and the level of engagement is mediated by the child.

In essence, the impact of a child being born into an effective family has a greater impact on wellbeing and life chances than the quality or nature of schooling:

> [A] great deal of the variation in students' achievement is outside of the schools' influence. Family social class, for example, accounts for about one third of such variance. Second, parental involvement in the form of home discussion has, nonetheless, a major impact on achievement. Other forms of involvement have insignificant effects. (Desforges, 2003, p. 21)

In effective families, there are high levels of social and emotional engagement and ongoing rich and complex dialogues around stories, ideas and the daily life of the family. The absence of such engagement and dialogue just makes school that much harder. There is a long-understood correlation between social class, family life and language. Children raised in higher social classes may have richer social and linguistic family lives, and by doing so, they increase their educational potential. All of these possibilities are reinforced one way or another by the community in which a family resides.

Social Capital

Quite apart from any intrinsic merit there might be in living in an effective community, it is clear that where an individual resides is a very significant element in determining their educational, social and personal success, measured by a wide range of criteria. For Putnam (2000, p. 296), the link between community and educational success is an absolute one:

> [C]hild development is powerfully shaped by social capital ... trust, networks, and norms of reciprocity within a child's family, school, peer group, and larger community have wide-ranging effects on the child's opportunities and choices and, hence, on behavior and development.

Putnam goes on to establish a precise correlation between the quality of community life and educational outcomes and the level of social capital in a community:

> [S]tates with high social capital have measurably better educational outcomes than do less civic states. The Social Capital Index is highly correlated with student scores on standardized tests taken in elementary school, junior high and high school, as well as the rate at which students stay in school. (p. 299)

Putnam's overview of the whole country is reinforced by the detailed study of the impact of the neighbourhood on school improvement by CCSR in 2006. The positive aspect of community is very clear:

> We found that schools with strong essential supports were more likely to exist in school communities with strong social capital—active religious participation, collective efficacy, and extensive connections to outside neighborhoods. (CCSR, 2006, p. 3)

The negative corollary was equally explicit:

> Communities with weak social capital—low levels of religious participation, collective efficacy, and few social connections beyond the neighborhood—were likely to have weak essential supports in their schools. Weak

> supports also were more typical in communities with high crime rates and relatively higher percentages of abused or neglected children. Taken together, these results suggest that positive school community conditions facilitate the development of the supports, while the presence of crime and a high density of students living under extraordinary circumstances inhibit them. (CCSR, 2006, p. 3)

Quite simply, where communities are linked to the life of the school and when the community becomes a base for learning, positive social capital is reinforced and built. The framework within the whole school-community approach enables the school to bring out the best in a community. The school assists the community in developing strong social capital to support the education of the children. This was recognized by the Audit Commission in the UK—the agency charged with reporting on value for money in public expenditure:

> School improvement and renewal are inseparable issues from neighborhood improvement and renewal, particularly in the most disadvantaged areas. While schools are profoundly affected by their neighborhoods, they equally have a key role in promoting cohesion and building social capital. (Audit Commission, 2006, p. 6)

Social Class

There is a clear and direct correlation between social class, well-being and life chances. Examination of school impact on learning and achievement indicates that social class trumps school and classroom practice. Confronting the myth in America that private schools do a better job than public schools, in a recent interview (Strauss, 2018), Dean of the Curry School of Education in Virginia, Robert Pianta, argued:

> You only need to control for family income, and there's no advantage. So, when you first look, without controlling for anything, the kids who go to private schools are far and away outperforming the public-school kids. And as soon as you control for family income and parents' education level (social class indicators), that difference is eliminated completely. (*Santa Fe New Mexican*, Monday, July 30, 2018, p. A-6)

And yet, those who attend private schools in the United States have better life chances, from income opportunities to health and life expectancy. This success has less to do with school performance and a great deal to do with the social class of the child and family. In most respects, the higher the social class, the better the life chances and wellbeing of the students in that community.

Movement between social classes is even more difficult today and education contributes negatively to closing the gaps (Putnam, 2015). In most countries, social class is a major influence on wellbeing and life chances and the separation and lack of mobility between classes is growing. Schools ignore these trends at their peril.

In working with school leaders over the last 15 years, I have found it essential to take time to understand these factors before moving on to discussions of strategies or programmes. Instructional leadership and leading learning are approaches that need to be exercised in the context of understanding and appreciating the social, personal and community factors that determine achievement, wellbeing and life chances.

Based on years of analysis and exploration of the personal, social and situational factors influencing wellbeing, life chances and success, especially in school, I and colleagues have proposed that school leaders can enable success in school and life for all learners by focussing their leadership on building relationships that acknowledge, support and develop the impact on learning that are seeded in the four domains, connecting parents to children's learning, linking school and community, extended learning opportunities and personalizing learning. It might be argued that school leadership is primarily about building and sustaining positive relationships between and among students, staff, parents, families and the larger community.

Learning Relationships That Matter: A Whole School-Community Approach

In this part of the chapter, I look in more detail at the Framework for Creating and Leading Powerful Learning Relationships through a whole school-community approach, focussing school leadership efforts on building positive relationships in the four domains that impact learning.

Current efforts to improve schools mostly miss the point. First, they fail to understand what John Goodlad and his researchers documented years ago in *A Place Called School* (2004): "A school is not a school is not a school". Every school is a dynamic and integral part of the local community. Goodlad promoted a context-based assessment to individualize reform efforts where the critical context for every school *is* the local community. Therefore, we contend that a school is best seen as a local community organization.

Second, as discussed earlier, the school alone does not adequately control the factors that make a difference to what a school can achieve. Only when schools, students, families and communities collaborate in specific ways do schools "perform" well. When schools—whether they are public, private, charter schools, community schools, core social centres or full-service schools, to name just a few—address the relevant social and personal factors that influence student achievement in their locale, achievement, wellbeing and life chances tend to rise.

West-Burnham et al. (2007) propose the rationale, practice and policy for schools that see their primary purpose as connecting school, family and community to increase learning in ways that focus on the primacy of relationships in learning, are accessible to all and are socially just.

Following on from the imperatives of the book, and action research conducted in New Mexico, school leaders in Melbourne, Australia, collaborated with the author to create a framework for school leaders that assists them in addressing the relationships that research indicates will have the highest impacts on learning. The framework describes a practical model for leading learning relationally, in ways that posit the school as a hub of social capital and positive relationships between youth, family, staff and community. School life, practices and procedures are focussed on the four domains referred to above.

The whole school-community approach is based on a core realization: schools cannot prepare all children with twenty-first-century skills unless the school becomes a place where parents, carers and local community members can partner with educational staff to provide learning experiences that uniquely address each and every child. Figure 13.2 shows the framework for building dynamic, relational, school cultures.

This framework builds on the evidence. High-level parent involvement leads to: better student achievement (Henderson & Mapp, 2002); strong in-depth relationships with students critical to their success in school (Hattie, 2009); a curriculum that needs to engage every student; and partnerships and support from the community that are positive influences on school success (Barnes & Schmitz, 2016). The framework creates an integrated picture, or map, of how to develop learning and

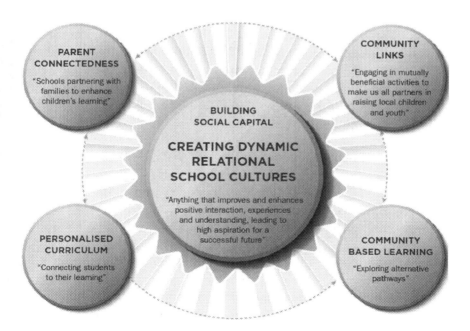

Fig. 13.2 A framework for leading learning relationally

teaching relationships that bring these four domains to the forefront of school activity. When school leaders and school staff direct their professional energy and action to address these four critical relationships, good things happen for kids.

Dozens of examples of the relational leadership needed to connect school, family and community using the framework and mindsets above can be found in the book, *Leading and Creating Powerful Learning Relationships, A Whole-School Community Approach* (Hawker Brownlow, 2018).

The Leadership Challenge: Building and Sustaining Positive Relationships

The Need for Relational Leadership

Relationships are not a factor in learning; they are the context for all learning. Positive relationships connect school, family and community in ways that increase learning (Otero, 2016). Therefore, the quality of the relationship will always determine the quality of the learning. Knowing what relationships matter in learning and having the skill and ability to influence those relationships is one key to better outcomes for children and youth.

The importance of making relationships the focus of school leadership was stated in no uncertain terms by Michael Fullan: "Any school reform effort that improves relationships has a chance for success, any that doesn't is doomed to fail" (Fullan, 2003). He argues that school leaders must pay attention to the context that informs any interaction with others and to pay attention to the little things they do and say that impact their relationship with stakeholders. He encourages school leaders to help people see new possibilities and situations knowing that people rarely change through a rational process only.

David Giles, from Flinders University, goes further and insists that all leadership is relational, so we have only to focus on how we live within this reality. His research prompts him to propose the following:

- We are always already 'in' relationships;
- Relationships are always mattering whether we are aware of this or not;
- Relational leadership is **not another style of leadership** rather a "*way of being*" in leadership;
- The term "Relational Leadership" is a **reminder** of what is critical to our practice as leaders; and
- *Leadership is always relational, and relationships are the essence of leadership.* (Giles, 2018, p. 46)

Nicholas and West-Burnham (2016, p. 188) emphasize that school leaders today must lead through relationships and they suggest several leadership behaviours that characterize relational leadership. Of those, several are especially useful when leading the whole school-community approach.

- Being comfortable and confident in seeing leadership as essentially relational;
- Understanding the relational climate of the school;
- Maintaining an appropriate balance of love and power;
- Balancing fast and slow thinking;
- Developing an empathic foundation to effective leadership;
- Nurturing your intuitive responses to leadership issues; and
- Reviewing the quality of relationships across the school and intervening as appropriate.

Leading a Whole School-Community Approach: Implications

It will be difficult to implement a whole school-community approach as described here using the conceptual frameworks, mindsets and approaches to school leadership that currently dominate discourse around schooling. In the whole school-community framework, we suggest it is not only that we emphasize relationships but also emphasize those relational domains where trusting and authentic relationships are to be built and supported. These relational domains have been clearly researched and demarcated over the past several decades. They are a new way to conceptualize schooling. Too often, aspects of these domains have been added on, or into, traditional conceptions of the structure of schoolwork. As I have found working with school leaders over the past two decades, taking a whole school-community approach to leadership as described will require school leaders to reconceive many aspects of their role and work.

The relational domains described here cannot be managed or even supported in the ways school leaders have grown accustomed. One cannot direct or manipulate the interdependent dynamic social, personal and community factors that influence learning by managing the interactions of staff, families and community members, or by presiding over the delivery of services boxed into programmes, standards, outcomes, procedures, curriculums, instructional models and pedagogies, that currently make up school discourse. The shift from management leadership to relational leadership will require a wholesale change in our understanding of the why, what and how of education. This framework and approach are freeing school leaders to change the way they change.

Guidance on understanding the relational leadership needed to lead learning in a whole school-community approach is becoming more available as school leaders take on the challenge of being part of the educational efforts of the community and not just the school. Again, Giles (2018) has identified through his research what he terms 'ways of being', the sensibilities, rather than the standards, that school leaders will exhibit in making a whole school-community approach a reality. As a relational way of 'being in' leadership, Relational Leaders were found to:

- **live "towards"** a deep moral and ethical commitment to critical, humane and connected interrelationships;
- **live "out"** a way that authentically models and embodies "care-full" relationships (individually and organizationally);
- **"attune" to** the subtleties of the immediate, dynamic and relational context through refined relational sensibilities; and
- **"enact" a** phronesis (practical wisdom, tacit knowing) which is context-specific and involves relational sensibilities (such as attunement, tact, nous, resoluteness, improvization and moral judgment amongst other sensibilities). Giles (2018, p. 12)

Even research from the business world identifies the kind of leadership best suited to a whole school-community approach. George (2003) proposed a new kind of leader, one whose character was the ingredient that mattered most—more than other characteristics or style. He challenged older models of leadership, including the "great man theory" and competency-based leadership models. Previous generations of business people spent more time trying to "market" themselves as leaders, rather than undertaking the transformative work that leadership development requires. Authentic leadership, now the gold standard in business leadership is, at its heart, relational leadership practice. According to George (2016),

> Authentic leaders monitor their words and behaviors carefully to be attuned to their audiences and to enroll their colleagues and teammates. They do so because they are sensitive to the impact their words and actions have on others, not because they are "messaging" the right talking points.

As with Giles' relational sensibilities, authentic leaders are developing their leadership in relationship to those they work with and depend upon. Therefore, research on authentic leading explores specific character behaviours such as how and when to be vulnerable, cognitive distortions, making meaning of who we are by integrating the constructed self with the true self—or True North—and going from purpose to impact (Working Knowledge, HBR, 2016).

Relational leadership in the context of a whole school-community approach also applies to instructional leadership. The whole school-community approach asks teachers to personalize learning and teaching by focussing on five critical relationships: student to self, student to content, student to peers, student to teacher and student to the wider community (Otero & Chambers-Otero, 2000). Ross Bevege, a seasoned principal from Melbourne, Australia, has exercised instructional leadership by supporting the school staff to focus on these five relationships in all their teaching efforts. After success in personalizing learning this way in two secondary schools, he has turned his attention to coaching school leaders in relational learning. He is suggesting school leaders use the five learning relationships to guide the formation and practice of their own leadership. He is exploring what I would call a capability framework for leaders to assess and monitor their relational ability and skill. For example, in relating to self, leaders would possess a strong and positive relationship with self as well as a firm self-belief as a leader and learner. In their relationship with staff they would possess a positive relationship with the staff they lead/work with and understand the impact their leadership has on others, and in relating to students, parents and the wider community they would possess and seek to build supportive and constructive relationships between the home, the school and the local community (Bevege, personal email, April 20, 2016).

In the whole school-community approach, leading learning and instructional leadership must support building key relationships. For this approach, a new form of instructional leadership is required, one that will focus on five relationships referred to in this chapter. Leading for Learning will focus on connecting family, school and community, building positive relationships around learning and developing a school culture that activates and embraces the power and resources everyone brings to the education of communities' children and youth. Leading learning with a whole school-community approach means knowing what makes a good school culture and understanding social capital, then leading the development of a good school culture and constantly helping the school community build social capital that supports achievement, wellbeing and success.

Beliefs and Mindsets

Leading for Learning in the context of a whole school-community approach as outlined depends on behaviours and actions that support honest, open, equitable and trustworthy dialogue and conversation. The messages below give school leaders' signposts that they are indeed connecting school, family and community and working together and identify new ways of thinking. School leaders need to:

- See the purpose of the twenty-first-century school as helping a family and community educate a child, rather than the multitude of purposes that dominated twentieth-century schooling;
- Understand that many important resources needed to educate children and youth are located outside the school and are not within it;
- Recognize that if you don't know your students, you cannot hope to personalize their learning. Knowing the whole child becomes the baseline for determining teaching and learning strategies;
- Understand that a personalized curriculum is the best way to achieve the holistic development of the child;
- Understand that the "invitation" to parents to engage in all aspects of school life must be visible and authentic;
- Move beyond the regular school offerings to engage all students in meaningful learning;
- Provide students with different learning opportunities that will lead to high levels of engagement;
- Understand that the more adults involved in the learning/mentoring of students, the richer the experience will be;
- Be conscious of the importance of the "village" and the assets within, that will enable them to see opportunities and act upon them;
- Seek out people within the broader community who possess expertise and skills in a range of areas that can complement the school's work; and
- Invite the community to be part of the school as well as bringing the school to the community.

A whole school-community approach to education is gaining ground in schools and school systems across the globe. The San Francisco Public Schools *Comprehensive Community Schools Framework and tool kit* (2017) addresses the four relational domains, but in distinctive ways. All schools in San Francisco Unified School District (SFUSD) address four foundational elements: (1) Strong Instructional Core, (2) Student-Centred Learning in a safe and supportive Culture and Climate, (3) Strong Family-School-Community Partnerships and (4) Authentic and Inclusive School-based Governance. For example, under Student-Centred Learning, school leaders should support and ensure that teaching and learning takes place in a safe and supportive environment, one that emphasizes positive relationships and a sense of community. Under Authentic and Inclusive School-based Governance, schools are asked to actively support and encourage families to be advocates for each and every student, to ensure they are treated fairly and have equitable access to learning opportunities.

Leading schools with this focus on the relationships between and among students, teachers, parents, families and the wider community, requires specific behaviour from school leaders. Below are a few examples of the actions that leaders should keep in mind when connecting school, family and community for better outcomes for students (SFUSD tool kit, 2017).

- Every interaction with a student's family is an *opportunity to build trust*—or to erode it.
- Supporting equitable participation in school leadership and governance relies on *fundamental approaches to family engagement in general*, such as active outreach, two-way communication and effective facilitation.
- *Use multiple ways for outreach and communication*, including newsletters, school websites, email/texting—as well as personal invitations and encouragement.
- *Make connections* among the school's formal and informal decision-making groups, and *include all families in conversations about the school.*

Another example of system transformation towards a whole school-community approach is the Sandhurst Catholic Schools in regional Victoria. Instead of seeing parent and community involvement as a strategy for school improvement, they see family and community engagement as a vital pathway for working together as full partners in creating school and learning environments where everyone can contribute to and benefit from learning together. The work is housed in the Wellbeing Team, where school leaders are supported to let the voice of students, families and community co-create the vision, priorities, programmes and practices that allow everyone in the school community to contribute positively to student learning. This approach requires more listening than telling, an emphasis on who we are, as well as what we say or do and a commitment to positive solutions as opposed to a welfare approach to life, health and learning. Utilizing a number of conversational and discussion formats, schools, families and the wider community constantly seek to answer the three basic questions mentioned above. Who are we? What's worth learning? How do we learn that together?

The results are impressive after two years of implementation. School leaders no longer see their primary role as a manager but as a mentor and an activist working with students, families and the wider community, to create a whole school-community approach to learning together.

Another example is the Indigenous Support Unit serving State Schools in Far North Queensland. Here the indigenous support leaders took advantage of the regional office's attempt to make connecting families to children's learning an equal priority for school leaders, right beside improving teaching, refining and embedding data-based decision-making and refining and embedding planning and accountability structures. The service commitment of the region recognized that connecting parents and caregivers with their children's learning was equally important. These leaders, charged with serving the specific needs of Aboriginal and Torres Strait Islander families and communities, emphasized a strength-based approach to supporting the families and local communities to build connections and engagement with their local schools. They used community-based engagement strategies that would connect families to student learning, as well as link the community to the school and the school to the community, highlighting three of the four domains of the whole school-community framework. All efforts required the school to operate from a culture of respect and embrace the history, language, passions and hopes of the local families and communities. This version of the whole school-community approach is the essence of whole-school activity, from visioning, governing, teaching and learning, and family and community engagement, in Tagai State College. This independent school is a school with about 20 island locations where education is of, by and for, the families and communities (Tagai State College Web Site).

Conclusion

In order to survive and succeed in a rapidly changing world, all schools will need to become more outward facing and to adopt a version of a whole school-community approach (England School definition). Leading learning and improving instruction will rely on the ability and skill of school leaders to connect everyone in the school community to learning. The actions, behaviours and beliefs of leaders described above indicate that instructional leadership and leadership for learning are seen as companion aspects of the kind of relational leadership necessary to ensure the achievement, wellbeing and success of every child and young person in the community.

References

Allen, K.-A., Vella-Brodrick, D., & Waters, L. (2016). Fostering school belonging in secondary schools using a socio-ecological framework. *The Australian Educational and Developmental Psychologist, 33*, 1–25. https://doi.org/10.1017/edp.2016.5

Audit Commission. (2006). *More than the sum*. London: Audit Commission.

Barnes, M., & Schmitz, P. (2016). Community engagement matters (Now more than ever). *Stanford Social Innovation Review*, Spring.

Bronfenbrenner, U. (1979). *The ecology of human development, experiments by nature and design*. Cambridge, MA: Harvard University Press.

Coleman, J. S., Campbell, E. Q., Hobson, C. J., McPartland, J., Mood, A. M., Weinfeld, F. D., et al. (1966). *Equality of educational opportunity*. Washington, DC: U.S. Government Printing Office.

Consortium on Chicago School Research (CCSR). (2006). *The essential supports for school improvement*. Chicago: University of Chicago.

Desforges, C. (2003). *The impact of parental involvement, parental support and family education on pupil achievements and adjustment: A literature review* (Research Report RR433). London: Department for Education and Skills.

Edgar, D. (2001). *The patchwork nation: Rebuilding community, rethinking government*. Sydney, Australia: HarperCollins.

Elmore, R. (2000). *Building a new structure for school leadership*. Washington, DC: The Albert Shanker Institute.

Feinberg, W. (1990). The moral responsibility of public schools. Contained in J. I. Goodlad, R. Soder, & K. A. Sirotnik (Eds.), *The moral dimensions of teaching* (pp. 155–187). New York: Jossey Bass.

Fullan, M. (2003). *The moral imperative of school leadership*. Thousand Oaks, CA: Corwin Press.

George, W. (2003). *Authentic leadership: Rediscovering the secrets to creating lasting value*. San Francisco: Jossey-Bass.

George, B. (2016). The truth about authentic leaders. *Working Knowledge*, Harvard Business School. Retrieved from https://hbswk.hbs.edu/item/the-truth-about-authentic-leaders

Giles, D. (2018). *Relational leadership in education: A phenomenon of inquiry and practice*. London: Routledge.

Goodlad, J. (2004). *A place called school: Twentieth anniversary edition*. New York: McGraw Hill Professional.

Hanushek, E. A. (2016). What matters for student achievement. *Education Next, 16*(2), 18–26.

Hattie, J. (2009). *Visible learning: A synthesis of over 800 meta-analyses relating to achievement*. London: Routledge.

Henderson, A. T., & Mapp, K. L. (2002). *A new wave of evidence: The impact of school, family and community connections on student achievement. Annual synthesis 2002* [online]. Austin, TX: National Center for Family and Community Connections with Schools, SEDL. Retrieved from https://www.sedl.org/connections/resources/evidence.pdf

Leadbeater, C., & Wong, A. (2010). *Learning from the extremes*. San Jose, CA: CISCO Systems, Inc.

Minzey, J. D., & LeTarte, C. E. (1994). *Reforming public schools through community education*. Dubuque, IA: Kendall/Hunt Publishing.

Nicholas, L., & West-Burnham, J. (2016). *Understanding leadership: Challenges and reflections*. Bancyfelin, UK: Crown House.

Otero, G. (2016, July). *Connecting school, family, and community: The Power of positive relationships* (Seminar series 256). Melbourne, Australia: Center for Strategic Education.

Otero, G., & Chambers-Otero, S. (2000, November). *RelationaLearning, Towards a human ecology in 21st century schools* (Occasional paper, IARTV, No. 67).

Otero, G., Csoti, R., & Rothstadt, D. (2018). *Leading & creating powerful learning relationships* (2nd ed.). Melbourne, Australia: Hawker Brownlow Education.

Otero, G., & West-Burnham, J. (2009, February). *Leadership for personalizing learning: Critical shifts in understanding* (Seminar series #181). Melbourne, Australia: Centre for Strategic Education.
Putnam, R. (2000). *Bowling alone*. New York: Simon and Schuster.
Putnam, R. (2015). *Our kids, the American dream in crises*. New York: Simon and Schuster.
San Francisco Public Schools Tool Kit. (2017). Retrieved from www.sfusd.edu/toolkit
Strauss, V. (2018, July 30). *Study: Private schools aren't better than public schools. Santa Fe New Mexican*.
Townsend, T. (1994). *Effective schooling for the community*. London/New York: Routledge.
Townsend, T., Clark, P., & Ainscow, M. (1999). Third Millennium Schools: Prospects and problems for school effectiveness and school improvement. In T. Townsend, P. Clark, & M. Ainscow (Eds.), *Third Millennium Schools: A world of difference in effectiveness and improvement* (308p.). Lisse, the Netherlands: Swets & Zeitlinger.
Vygotsky, L. S. (1978). *Mind in Society: the Development of Higher Psychological Processes*. Cambridge, MA: Harvard University Press.
West-Burnham, J., Farrar, M., & Otero, G. (2007). *Schools and communities working together to transform children's lives*. Stafford, UK: Continuum.

14

The Power of Collective Leadership for Learning

Suzanne Cridge

Introduction

In 2013, Social Ventures Australia (SVA) launched The Bright Spots Schools Connection (The Connection), a collaborative, connected network designed to engage school leaders in collective learning within, and across, their school communities. In 2019, The Connection is a thriving network of leaders that represent 50 schools from across Australia, all serving the education needs of challenged communities with low socio-economic indicators.

The power and influence of effective school leadership is an underestimated leverage point of system transformation and change to build quality learning and school improvement. This chapter will explore the opportunity provided by collaborative networked learning, the power of what can be achieved and the impact that emerges when the principles of leading for learning are enacted in a network model where the expertise

S. Cridge (✉)
Social Ventures Australia, Sydney, NSW, Australia
e-mail: scridge@socialventures.com.au

of the individual becomes the expertise of the collective. This model of leadership support and collaboration is catalytic in building education impact and improvement, as everyone is a learner, everyone has a role to play and value to add. Drawing on the experience and insights of participating school leaders and their teams, this narrative will propose refined ways of building the ecosystem necessary to support powerful school leadership. These ideas will be discussed in more detail.

Education and School Leadership: The Opportunity and the Challenge

Knowledge today is more pervasively available than ever before. It can be readily accessed by most with advances in technology and is no longer the domain of some or just a few. Both knowledge and information are exchanged in ways and at rates which were almost unimaginable even a decade ago. The accessibility of knowledge, however, does not guarantee that it gets to where it can be used or mobilised for action to create systems' impact. Education knowledge, although readily available, also needs mobilising within and across systems. It relies on translation into the nuanced actions necessary to deliver the learning improvements within communities where it matters most, and where education systems need it to be, to achieve the maximum desired impact.

Knowledge is also empowering. As knowledge and the mobilisation of knowledge increases, traditional system hierarchies of knowledge management, where knowledge has been less mobile, become less relevant and potentially less effective.

Knowledge is now being shared and exchanged in more accessible and dynamic ways. This phenomenon has the potential to inform and empower education practitioners and leaders, both more efficiently and effectively, to move to action. The challenge, and the opportunity, is to get this growing knowledge resource to the practitioners and leaders, where it can be put into action efficiently across systems. There are also risks in ensuring the consistency of the standards of quality of that knowledge, so increasing the accessibility of quality knowledge needs to be intentionally managed, creating the best-leveraged opportunities, in ways where it cannot be ignored. We need to design with intention mechanisms in systems to make this happen and not leave it to chance.

The good news is that quality educational leadership knowledge, expertise and practice exists as a largely untapped resource in education systems. Highly effective school leaders are building new knowledge and understanding of what works within this complex ecosystem in everyday practice. However, this knowledge often lies randomly located within, and stubbornly stuck and stranded in, pockets of expertise across traditional systems. How can education systems find, connect and enable this invaluable and largely untapped resource, one that might raise quality levels across the system?

The role of educational leadership as a mobilising mechanism for building capacity is a fundamental and important consideration in resolving complex education challenges. Growing complexity in education ecosystems requires a strategic move to a devolved, action-based approach to leadership, supported with explicit and shared responsibilities and accountabilities. There is an opportunity to evolve, enable and empower education leadership knowledge and practices at the school level by mobilising people and technology. The intentional design of a coordinated system-wide response to persistent challenges and wickedly entrenched issues is an important action for creating a more accessible and equitable Australian education system.

Complex problems cannot be solved with silver bullet solutions. The obstacles and stumbling blocks encountered in the evolving journey of education systems are rarely simply addressed. As mentioned, there is, however, an enormous amount of leadership expertise, knowledge and insight that sits within the education ecosystem, across multiple contexts, waiting to be connected and mobilised to create aligned responsive actions. This new and growing opportunity can develop mechanisms and structures to unleash, empower and align this asset of systems' leadership capacity and then direct it to create the targeted actions needed to deliver new learning momentum and improvements. This essentially is profession-led education action, aligned and directed at the school level where the real work is delivered to create the conditions for learning. It could be argued that this is systems-based leadership for learning.

It is a time-sensitive challenge to explore what different paradigms of school leadership might bring to the conversation and what actions might exist for creating new value in a complex system. What is more fundamental to these bigger questions confronting education systems globally, is to consider the subsidiary questions, namely what leadership approaches and styles are still relevant, and what needs to change to respond to these changing and evolving conditions. For many in education practice at the school level, it sometimes feels that they are building the plane and flying it at the same time, and so arises the issue of what is most important. Where should school leaders start? Some would certainly suggest that instructional leadership is critical, and for others, it is leading for learning that is more important. But perhaps, is it something completely different, such as hybrid blends of a number of approaches?

This chapter will focus on the enabling conditions for school leadership practices that are relevant to emerging shifts in education systems. Perhaps it is how we build collaborative insights, informed by evidence of what works, to connect the expertise and knowledge that matters most. Networked collaborative leadership support creates these conditions and is a powerful emerging mechanism to create collective efficacy for the catalytic actions necessary for systems' impact. Progress in education is no longer about exclusively adopting only one type of leadership approach, but the opportunity to create conditions for the marriage of specific actions and shared learning to create the perfect storm for learning impact.

In any given school or system context, we need to create the best learning opportunities for young people to progress successfully through learning at school. Of critical importance then, is how educational leaders are best supported to build those contextually aligned and nuanced conditions to achieve success within the schools situated in the complex communities they lead. Put simply, how can education systems best support school leaders to connect their knowledge and expertise to deliver greater impact for learning? How can the actions of growing knowledge and expertise be best shared across systems to inform and support all leaders in ways that will build systems leadership capacity effectively and provide the momentum for new systems action?

Networked Leadership for Learning

Education is a complex human interaction. Education and school leadership on every level are both very human responsibilities. As our community evolves, more sophisticated human interactions and ways of knowing, sharing and learning together, and the degree of complexity for the needs within the education ecosystem, also increase. The importance and necessity of great leadership in this changing context is, broadly speaking, an uncontested premise.

Leadership can be an isolating responsibility in schools when there are limited mechanisms to connect with like-minded professionals grappling with similar challenges and decisions to be made. Education systems, traditionally, have been set up in transactional hierarchies where accountabilities and responsibilities to deliver are clear, but in reality, the nature of the journey to deliver varies and is context specific. Professional leadership in this climate does not come with an instructional handbook. School leaders are essentially the directors of their leadership and learning journey. It is not possible that one leader or even a small group of leaders in a school could have all the knowledge and experience they need to respond to rapidly changing learning contexts, challenges and opportunities. System support for leaders needs to become more efficient to be more effective.

The complexities of leading learning in school communities are challenging, but knowledge and expertise are pervasive across systems. The opportunity provided by the convening of collaborative networking for school leaders is that it connects them to the necessary knowledge, at their point of need, in both highly effective and efficient ways. It also has the potential to embed the practice in effective sustainable ways. Collaborative leadership networks provide a catalytic professional connection where the resources of expertise, knowledge and learning are collected and exchanged for the improvement of the collective. Access to additional and new knowledge is empowering; it can also be very affirming. The value of the collective wisdom of leaders working across contexts builds whole systems' capacity and efficacy.

Louise Stoll (2015) declared that collaboration is the name of the game, proposing that it is a smart and logical move for schools to pool their expertise to develop actions that best respond to need. In England, for example, schools at least are expected to work together to create what Stoll refers to as a 'self-improving system'. School-to-school support and peer-to-peer learning are identified as important actions to raise standards and improve the quality of teaching and learning. Stoll also refers to the 2013 Organisation for Economic Co-operation and Development's (OECD) Teaching and Learning International Study (TALIS) (OECD, 2018a) that highlights the importance of professional collaborations, suggesting that the most successful countries and jurisdictions that have continued to improve consistently include opportunities for peers to work together.

In Australia, the Report of the Review to Achieve Educational Excellence in Australian Schools: Through Growth to Achievement, produced by a panel chaired by David Gonski on behalf of the Australian Government (Commonwealth of Australia, 2018), provides the view that school leadership support is a priority action. Review recommendation 20 specifically refers to the importance of supporting school leaders and enabling them to share their expertise with one another. Sharing expertise and knowledge productively does not, however, happen without process, intention and purpose.

Networked inquiry developed by Judy Halbert and Linda Kaser is another example of how the expertise of a collaborative network can be captured and directed with rigour and intention. Halbert and Kaser (2016) see collaboration as a fundamental systems-transformation practice. Originating in British Columbia, Canada, their model, based on inquiry, develops collaborative practices with intention, by connecting the moral purpose of the work and the strong inquiry mindsets of school leaders with a powerful equity and quality agenda. This Spirals of Inquiry (Halbert & Kaser, 2016) methodology is a powerful tool that has been embraced by many of the Social Ventures Australia Connection schools to guide and provide structure to their learning in shared collaborative practices across the network.

The purposes of networked collaboration for schools are to produce better learning outcomes, to become more effective and efficient in their work and to build the conditions for success collectively. The shift to a collaborative professional team practice in schools and classrooms has not emerged by accident but is driven by need and has a clear purpose. Humans work better together. Living in communities is an evolutionary fact that has provided a long history of benefits to the human race for thousands of years; collective efficacy is not a new phenomenon.

Collaborative professionalism is a notion described by both Hargreaves, et al. and Fullan in their separate publications on Leading from the Middle (Fullan, 2015; Hargreaves, Shirley, Wangia, Bacon, & D'Angelo, 2018). They describe the value of solving growing education complexities through collaborative professional relationships, such as those being exemplified in the high-performing Canadian education jurisdiction of Ontario. According to both Fullan and Hargreaves, the notion of 'collaborative professionalism' in education practice typically features effective feedback, and rigorous professional dialogue guided by processes and protocols.

The premise of collaborative professionalism described by Hargreaves et al. (2018) moves professional dialogue towards developing learning for meaning and purpose, in contrast to focusing on primarily narrow achievement goals. It also builds an embedded culture where educators are the professional experts and recognised as such. Professional judgements, however, are built through collaborative inquiry. Leaders share collective responsibilities for both delivery and the outcomes that create the impact gains for the school in which they operate. This shift is not a 'hands-off' approach from the government but a guiding and empowerment role for systems to play.

Middle leaders generating action together is identified as a core element of the Ontario education strategy in the Leading from the Middle initiative (Fullan, 2015; Hargreaves et al., 2018). Education system change occurs when school practices are impacted. In Ontario, Hargreaves and Fullan describe the opportunity for responsive new policy and leadership in education as a devolved leadership model where hierarchy has less relevance and a self-improving system becomes the priority focus.

Accomplished and successful school leaders are resourceful, creative and strategic. It takes a rare leadership talent, however, to deal with the complexities of the contemporary leadership responsibilities in schools in isolation. Connecting the collective leadership talents across schools to build systems' efficacy provides improvement leverage points for education systems in multiple dimensions of practice.

The value of collaborative action within systems cannot be underestimated. If we think of ecosystems being the sum of community actions, and the community actions as the sum of all actions collectively, then systems change is quite a random process. On the other hand, if we can activate collaborative leadership action within an ecosystem, the opportunity to cut through the complex multi-layers of community actions to support the spread of high-impact action more efficiently becomes possible. It cuts through the system's 'noise' to reduce distractions. This concept can be represented simply in Fig. 14.1.

Moving collaboratively in delivering action provides the opportunity to create intentional climates of shared motivation with a clear moral purpose to drive action. Collaborative action promotes a notion of shared appetite for collective efficacy and impact that can cut through complexity to transform and improve systems.

Convening the 'right people' to build trust and culture cannot be underestimated as a necessary precondition for success where sharing and pooling knowledge and expertise is a necessary feature (Erlichman, Sawyer, & Spencer, 2018). Investment in due diligence to identify the right contributors is astute and critical.

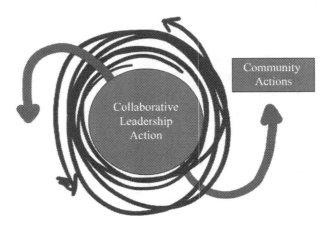

Fig. 14.1 Collaborative action cuts through complexity

14 The Power of Collective Leadership for Learning

Creating the conditions for successful collaboration also requires significant cultural shifts in systems. In the not-for-profit social sector, collaborative networking has been emerging over the last decade as an opportunity to drive stronger outcomes. Jane Wei-Skillern and Nora Silver suggest that there are mindset shifts that are counterintuitive principles for success in collaborative network design (Wei-Skillern & Silver, 2013). These shifts are outlined as moving:

From	To
Focus on growth	Focus on mission
Focus on control	Focus on trust
Focus on yourself	Focus on others
Focus on garnering resources	Focus on sharing resources
Focus on the particular—bright stars	Focus on the whole—building constellations

Wei-Skillern and Silver (2013)

As complexity in education grows, it provides the rationale for thinking differently and creatively. Participation rates and retention in both formal and informal Australian education systems continue to grow yet equity and achievement gaps remain stubbornly entrenched (OECD, 2018b). Both the opportunities and the challenges continue to coexist despite significant financial and resource investment into Australian education systems. There are clearly both big opportunities for improvement and competing challenges to be overcome.

The notion of increasing complexity provides a good place from where to develop to this important conversation, as it is fundamental to the challenges of delivering learning improvement and greater impact within systems of education. Core to the conversation are the following questions:

* What are the leadership actions that will develop new thinking and create deeper understanding?
* Where are the best opportunities for evolving school leadership practices?
* What is the potential for the new design of structural mechanisms to support and grow improved education and school leadership for greater impact?

- Is it enough to think about developing school leaders' capacity as individuals within schools or should we be moving towards building the capacity of Leading for Learning into systems' leadership frames?
- And if so, what does that look like in practical terms for school leaders?
- Can systems be organised more effectively to support and develop great school leadership?

The logical place to start is where action for impact happens, at the school level, posing the question: what can we learn from successful school leaders? This question leads to the work of Social Ventures Australia and their attempts to build a network that will enable school leaders to do their job effectively and efficiently to deliver great learning.

Social Ventures Australia

In 2013, Social Ventures Australia launched a consultative process to better understand the education equity context in Australian schools. The process uncovered interesting practical insights with data collected from practising school leaders. A shared concern expressed by the school leaders was that school leadership practices in Australia were generally disconnected. There were new initiatives being shared with school leaders but they were not always perceived as aligned to a real need. Practitioner school leaders reported feelings of professional isolation and were even constrained in their professional learning opportunities to learn from and with each other.

The schools consulted in 2013 rarely worked collaboratively and demonstrated few consistently maintained and ongoing professional relationships with other schools, other than those consistently described as superficially meeting the requirements of systems, such as local area meetings. Some professional learning and support were reported as being self-managed and identified, but it was often ad hoc and much of it was directed and dominated with high-level, broad system priorities. Much was identified as imposed or 'top-down' and therefore not always deeply contextually aligned to local needs. There appeared to be little filtering or even consistency of knowledge and expertise sharing applied, particularly within and across disadvantaged school contexts. Checking in with colleagues across schools with the explicit intention and for the purpose of sharing learning and expertise exchange was randomly organised. There was no evidence reported of practitioner ongoing collaboration across Australian states.

There was also little differentiation of professional learning strategies identified by schools, given the range of contexts and the different and similar challenges identified. Many school leaders reported feelings of isolation, stress, challenge, frustration and concern which was exacerbated with the added complexities of those schools located in disadvantaged and challenged communities. The perception was that they worked in isolation despite being part of a bigger system of practice.

High-impact education practices, expertise and knowledge did exist but sat within these isolated pockets within education systems. Quality school leadership was identified as a driver for both developing and delivering the impact observed in the schools that were identified as doing well. The problem seemed to be that this important leadership knowledge and expertise was only shared with other schools and across systems by chance and not necessarily by design. Understanding this dynamic provided both a new opportunity and a new challenge to consider.

The commitment from SVA was to create the actions and mechanisms needed to connect and unleash the expertise and knowledge of powerful educational leadership for growing learning impact so that it could become pervasive practice. School leadership was identified as an untapped leverage point for improving learning, particularly in challenged school communities. School leaders can either enable great teaching and learning, or disable it, through decisions made on the basis of their knowledge and expertise in any given context. This is a huge responsibility. If high-quality teaching and learning is the non-negotiable of a high-performing system, then building school leadership capacity is a critical opportunity to explore opportunities for greater system-level impact.

Successful school leaders hold considerable expertise and knowledge about how to create the conditions to impact student learning and improve outcomes. The schools led by successful leaders are the hotspots of leadership knowledge and expertise and are significant assets to education systems. New questions emerged:

- Could this expertise be connected and mobilised to build greater capacity?
- What are the mechanisms that are necessary for school leaders to collaboratively share their experiences efficiently and effectively, to both build and bolster school leadership capacity within and across systems collectively?

Through these questions, a new premise also emerged, that of collective expertise generated by a collaborative network design for school leaders, which has the potential to become a catalytic influence as a model for systems change. Collaborative leadership network designs have the potential to embed and sustain actions for increased systems capacity development, through building the high-impact practices across more schools within the system.

Building a Collaborative Leadership Design Network in Practice: The Bright Spots Schools Connection

What Is a Collaborative Network?

For purposes of this discussion, a collaborative leadership network is a community alliance defined by the following design attributes:

- A shared common moral purpose;
- An aligned commitment to action;
- Voluntary inclusive participation with a flat hierarchy of shared leadership;
- A willingness to share and exchange expertise;
- Collective and mutual responsibility and accountability for shared success and impact; and
- Respectful relationships in a culture of trust and goodwill.

It is not a Community of Practice or a Professional Learning Community in the traditional sense, but these complementary structures may flourish within a Collaborative Leadership Design Network (in future called a CLDN), by creating the targeted response to a particular focus area as may be identified within the collaborative network.

The Bright Spots Schools Connection (in future called The Connection) is a model of a 'for purpose and convened, collaborative network community'. The Connection is an initiative created by Social Ventures Australia (SVA) that supports exceptional school leaders in disadvantaged schools to connect and improve the learning outcomes of students collectively.

The Connection is a tiered collaborative leadership network of 50 Australian selected schools representing three Australian states and approximately 2900 educators in a community of 30,000 student learners in 2018 and approximately 50,000 student learners across 5 years (Social Ventures Australia, 2018). Each school serves a community with a socio-demographic rating either on, or below, the average Australian Index of Community Socio-Educational Advantage (ICSEA) scale of 1000 (Australian Assessment and Curriculum Reporting Authority, 2011). There are four key objectives of the CLDN of The Connection. They are as follows:

* Identify successful practices in schools serving disadvantaged communities;
* Build the capacity and mobilise the knowledge and expertise of school leaders through modelling, coaching and exchanges of knowledge and understanding;
* Spread evidence-informed practices through exposure to new thinking and developments in new practices to improve student learning; and
* Influence the education landscape, building the system capacity to deliver impact for disadvantaged communities where it might be needed most.

The overarching goal of The Connection is to improve the student learning outcomes of participating schools. It aims to do this by bringing the schools together and sharing new educational ideas and evidence, so that the schools will apply new effective practices, build effective partnerships and increase their capacity to implement school improvement, thereby improving the school's teaching and learning environment.

The Connection initiative is built around a Programme Logic framework (see Fig. 14.2). It is a strengths-based design and starts with identifying a combination of both successful mature and emerging schools demonstrating actions placing them on the improvement journey continuum. It then connects the leaders of these schools through convening and tiered networking activities which are designed to build and connect the knowledge and expertise of each group of school leaders. The model promotes a distributed leadership approach by engaging a minimum of three or more school leaders from each school in these tiered interaction opportunities. The goal of the activities and interactions is to create an exchange and inform an evidence base of what practices and action contribute to achieving maximum impacts for education success.

The next two figures demonstrate the models for action, with Fig. 14.3 providing an overview of how collaboration is leveraged to support action.

Figure 14.4 identifies the core features of the Collaborative Leadership Network Design.

The school leadership teams are invited to participate in the network voluntarily after a rigorous screening and a due diligence process that informs the selection of participants. School leadership teams make an investment to participate based on the role that they play in the group. The investment cost is offset by contributions from both the sponsoring state education systems and philanthropy. The state-based systems share responsibility for the selection of the school leadership teams that are invited to participate. State systems leverage the opportunity to develop the capacity of targeted school leaders in schools as systems influencers. The actions of the supported school leaders also build the momentum for developing learning improvement from within the system itself, essentially embedding actions to grow 'self-improving' systems.

In addition to the convened interactions, each school develops a Project Action Plan (PAP) which identifies a strategic improvement

14 The Power of Collective Leadership for Learning

Issue

Systems
Systems have not explicitly identified the best practices, the mechanisms and enabling conditions that promote, support and share high performance practices to develop education success in disadvantaged communities.

School leaders
Systems have not leveraged the experience and expertise that exists in successful schools to effectively share and diffuse the strategies that enable schools in low SES communities to consistently provide excellent education opportunities.

Activities

Build evidence base

Talent Scout
Identify school leaders and schools that are Bright Spots in the system, to understand the priorities, practices and approaches capable of achieving successful outcomes in schools in Low SES communities. Build and strengthen that practice with action research support, and develop skill and capacity to be modelled to others.

Researcher
Investigate these schools to identify the active ingredients that lead to excellent outcomes; and capture, articulate and harness this evidence and expertise.

Support diffusion

Convenor
Convene systems leaders, school leaders and others to showcase Bright Spot schools, and build the mechanisms for diffusion and scaling of excellent practices.

Broker
Strategically connect the schools to each other and to others who can support their improvement and outcomes with human, social, financial or thought capital.

Capacity-builder
Build and strengthen the skills and knowledge of the systems and school leaders, with the insights and expertise to drive evidence informed decision making aligned to low SES schools and related needs

Influencer
Model and advocate for policies and practices that sustainably enable schools to share, improve and accelerate their performance using evidence and experience from The Connection.

Outcomes

Systems
Systems have improved capacity demonstrated by;
1. Connected schools that share and develop effective practice together.
2. A stronger evidence base of what works in schools within low SES communities.
3. Developed mechanisms for guiding school leaders to make evidence-informed decisions

School leaders
School leaders have;
1. Better knowledge of evidence base for effectives practice
2. Access to peer to peer sharing and expert professional support
3. Increased capacity and strong implementation skills

Impact

School leaders and systems know what it takes to improve student outcomes within schools in low SES communities and they effectively leverage the available resources within systems to provide high quality teaching and learning.

This leads to improved and equitable education provision across systems which provides all students access to excellent education opportunities.

Fig. 14.2 Programme Logic Frame Bright Spots Schools Connection, Social Ventures Australia

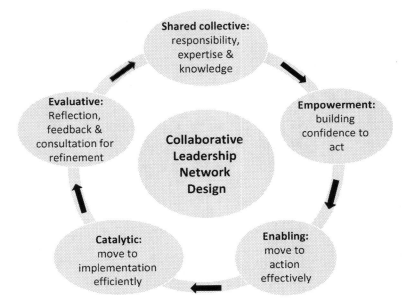

Fig. 14.3 Leveraging the cycle of collaboration for action

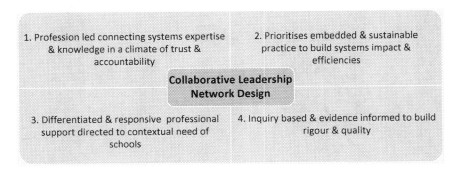

Fig. 14.4 Core features of CLDN

action of focus and priority for their engagement in the Connection network. The PAP is designed for a 3–5-year interaction and is in every case an embedded part of the school's strategic plan. The Connection school PAPs are context specific to each school, although there are shared identified themes across the cohort. Each plan is rigorously built around a

Programme Logic frame with monitoring and evaluation of progress with actions, outcomes and identified success measures. The shared processes of developing and implementing PAPs provide an important language and focus for the network interactions and underpin the many cultural elements of the networked collaborations which build the important underpinning relationships. The PAPs also provide both a mechanism and a purpose for the currencies of professional knowledge and expertise to be traded and shared around and within the collaborative network.

Table 14.1 Summary of SVA connection activities

SVA connection collaborative network convened activities & interactions
Thought Leadership Gatherings   Two-day national gatherings of the network cohort of leaders (up to three leaders from each school) held four times a year for all Connection schools. They are designed to challenge and to enable reflection and exploration of both existing and new practices.   *Hub days*   Collaboratively designed professional learning and exchange sessions held four times a year for each state group cohort of school leaders (up to three leaders from each school) as well as a target STEM specialist group of schools. The hub days are smaller state-based groups and are tailored to local and group priorities.   *School visits*   Coordinated, full-day school visits hosted by a Connection school leadership team. These take place on the day after Thought Leadership Gatherings four times a year. School visits are designed to observe schools in practice and provide feedback and opportunity for shared learning for leadership teams.   *Direct support from SVA Convenor*   Visits to schools by the SVA Convenor to provide tailored professional support on request for Project Action Plans. Engagement support visits are provided at a minimum of two to four times a year for each network school or cluster. These visits are conducted to provide tailored support to the school leadership team in the implementation of Project Action Plans.   *Connection international explorations*   International investigations of education practices in other countries conducted annually since 2017. International experiences are provided for school leaders to build insights, expertise and expand networks of influence.   *Additional activities by design and request*   These are activities that are delivered and aligned to emerging opportunities or new activities supported upon request. They might include hosting a visiting education expert, supporting a Teach Meet professional convening or developing a twilight professional learning opportunity.

The activities provided to engage the school leaders in professional interactions are presented within a tiered approach starting at the school level graduating up to the national aligned focus areas (see Table 14.1). They are mostly co-designed and aligned to identify the needs of the collaborative network. All activities delivered are evaluated against engagement levels and feedback is collected from participants to then inform the design of new activities and to gauge the quality of the experiences and interactions. Every convened activity provided is optional and invitational which honours the professional expertise and judgements that each school leader brings to the collaboration relationship. It also provides differentiation of the experience which is necessary to ensure the engagement in activities efficiently respond more appropriately to the many diverse contextual nuanced needs across the collaborative networked group. The collaborative school leadership network is a hotspot of creative and rigorous professional practice.

The activities are delivered across three states (Victoria, South Australia and New South Wales) in both school-based and alternative capital city locations within Australia. The Connection collaborative leadership network has engaged a growing number of 'experts' from within and outside education circles who have contributed to the learning of the participating school leaders. Many have remained critical friends of the collaborative networked group, providing access to additional support and social capital for the school leaders. The school leaders indicate that the networked relationships have offered significant value to their engagement with The Connection community and with each other. The group of critical friends include academic experts, industry experts, philanthropic partners and education system leaders at all levels, creating access to a broader resource of expertise for the school leaders to draw from to inform their leadership actions and decisions.

Measuring The Connection Impact

The emerging impact of The Connection design to date is described in two parts but is not fully complete or exhaustive. The evaluation of this work is current and ongoing.

The first section describes, in summary, the impact of eight Powerhouse schools after 4 years' participation in The Connection collaborative network design. The second section describes, in summary, the impact of the participation of The Connection Hub schools in two groups after 1 year in The Connection collaborative network design. The two evaluations referred to include (a) the 2016 Pilot Evaluation of 18 schools participating for 1 year from three Australian states, Victoria, South Australia and New South Wales; and (b) the first year Progress Report 2017 of a 3-year evaluation for an expanded Hub group representing 24 schools from the school cohort including representation from all three states, and also including the Science, Technology, Engineering and Mathematics (STEM)-focused group of Hub schools added in 2017. These evaluations were completed by Social Ventures Australia Consulting, a group independent of the Social Ventures Australia Education team.

Powerhouse Schools Impact Study

Background

In 2014, SVA commenced The Connection with the selection of eight Powerhouse schools. These Powerhouse schools were identified from a referred list of 84 schools as being schools that had demonstrated significant impact in the development of student learning outcomes. This Powerhouse school cohort of leaders initiated the work of the CLDN of The Connection. The following summary has been adapted from the final evaluation report produced by the Australian Council Education Research (ACER) (2018).

> *The focus of the evaluation was to test The Connection's Theory of Change with an emphasis on understanding what competencies and capabilities are required of Powerhouse school leaders to be successful. The three areas of interest were as follows:*
>
> * *To identify what might be some of the 'unique' or 'special' competencies and capabilities of effective school leaders;*
> * *To see if, through participating in The Connection collaborative design, such school leaders would further develop their leadership competencies and capabilities; and*

- To see whether these competencies and capabilities are capable of being imparted to other school leaders.

Methodologies used to collect data points informing the evaluation included three online surveys, three face-to-face interviews with school leaders at each school site, including leaders at all school levels, classroom teachers and two representative case study narratives.

What was the impact after 4 years of collaborative networked leadership support?

The ACER evaluation was able to confirm that each of the eight Powerhouse school principal leaders demonstrated the following eight competencies and capabilities:

- *An unwavering belief that all students deserve the right to quality educational outcomes, and that all students can, and will, succeed;*
- *A deep, and continually developing, knowledge and understanding of the curriculum (including research, developments in pedagogy, assessment and student wellbeing);*
- *Personal qualities, social and interpersonal skills to lead and mediate change (including evidence of optimism; enthusiasm; confidence; perseverance; resilience; open-mindedness; willingness to learn; personal reflection);*
- *An ability to take responsibility for developing a culture of effective teaching and learning;*
- *An ability to build trust and collegiality with teachers and community;*
- *An ability to work with others to produce and implement evidence-informed improvement plans;*
- *An ability to develop their own professional learning and skills and to encourage their staff to develop their professional learning and skills; and*
- *An ability to engage and work with the wider community to build partnerships.*

The evaluation also found that participation in The Connection collaborative network design allowed the eight Powerhouse school principal leaders to develop and refine their leadership competencies and capabilities as outlined.

The Powerhouse school leaders demonstrated agility, creativity and integrity in their leadership. The learning journeys were shared in case study formats and provided a small snapshot of the experience of leading in complex educational contexts. The narratives suggest no one clear strategy for action but a blended approach designed with an intentional purpose in response to the identified needs. The specific case study details of the activities of Powerhouse schools and their impact on student learning can be found in the report (ACER, 2018).

The Impact of the Connection Collaborative Network for Powerhouse Schools

The impact of The Connection on Powerhouse schools was assessed as 'significant', 'positive', 'major', 'pivotal' (Australian Council of Education Research, 2018). Powerhouse school principals believe that the impact of The Connection on their schools' work is considerable, transforming and long-term. The schools involved in The Connection expressed that they were privileged to be part of an important initiative. School leaders agreed that The Connection provided the impetus—'the catalyst'—for changes their schools needed. The Connection affects, in a positive way, the overall teaching and learning environment in their schools. Principals reported changes they observed in staff who participate in the school's Bright Spots project. They witnessed 'increased teachers' capacity and understanding'. Participation in The Connection led principals, school leaders and teachers to change their thinking and behaviour; this is perhaps the strongest indication that the impact of The Connection was indeed significant and that The Connection on Powerhouse schools was likely to be long-term.

The Connection's model of supporting schools to design and undertake a project of significance in their school provides a valuable model to promote long-term systemic change. The Bright Spots Schools Connection Powerhouse schools project was assessed as being an important initiative.

The Connection was given a strong endorsement by the Powerhouse school leaders stating that they would encourage other schools to participate in similar initiatives in the future. The Powerhouse school principal leaders value the networks that they have made with other schools, and do not underestimate what they have learned, and continue to learn, from the collaborative networked experience. One Powerhouse school leader stated, '*The Connection is having a huge impact. We would not be where we are now without it*' (ACER, 2018).

Connection Hub Schools Evaluation

Pilot Evaluation 2016 of the Star Hubs Initiative: Connection Collaborative Network Model.

In 2015 and 2016, The Connection collaborative network was expanded with an additional 18 schools to test the design and gauge the outcomes of hub-based professional collaboration within the network. Each of the additional schools was selected based on an analysis of National Assessment of Progress in Literacy and Numeracy (NAPLAN) trend data (Australian Curriculum Reporting Authority, 2016), the socio-economic demographic rating of the school—ICSEA (Australian Assessment and Curriculum Reporting Authority, 2011), and responses and performance characteristics compared to the National School Improvement Tool (Masters, 2012). These schools all demonstrated promise to become emerging Powerhouse influencers in their respective state systems.

The group of 18 schools included 13 primary schools and 5 secondary schools from three Australian states: Victoria, South Australia and New South Wales. The evaluation was conducted (Social Ventures Consulting, 2016) to investigate the potential to scale up the work of the Connection to increase impact and value. The methodology included a mix of aligned surveys and interviews with school leaders and teachers, asking them to reflect on the changes at their school that occurred as a result of their participation over the 12 months.

Table 14.2 summarises the outcome responses reported by schools in the pilot evaluation report. Case studies of the actions taken by specific schools, and the impact of those actions, can be found in the report (Social Ventures Consulting, 2016).

For the respondents surveyed, 76% of schools agreed or strongly agreed that Star Hubs played a catalytic role in driving changes at the school and 71% reported that it has already impacted the overall teaching and learning environment across the school in the first year of participation.

Table 14.2 Summary of pilot Hub school participation 2015–2016, after 1 year of participation

Outcome	Changes reported by schools
Overall value of the hub as reported by participating schools	76% agreed Star Hubs has played a catalytic role in driving change in my school
	71% agreed Star Hubs has impacted the overall teaching and learning environment across my school
	94% agreed in order to sustain the changes supported through Star Hubs my school needs to stay engaged in the initiative
Increased knowledge and connections	96% agreed I have acquired new knowledge that is relevant to my role in the school
	93% agreed I have increased connections with like-minded leaders
	85% agreed my thinking and underlying beliefs have been positively challenged and changed
Collaboration between schools	100% agreed my school feels like a part of a collegiate network with other Star Hub participants
	100% agreed my school is willing and able to work in partnership with others
	100% agreed my school has identified opportunities for mutually beneficial working relationships with other schools
Schools reporting new practices	94% agreed we have developed a plan for change (in one or multiple areas) informed by evidence of great practice
	94% agreed we have implemented new practices
Improvements in the learning environment reported by schools	82% agreed as a result of the new practices my school has experienced positive changes in the teaching and learning environment
	65% agreed as a result of the new practices students in my school have experienced improved learning outcomes
Schools opinion of likely outcomes without participation	35% agreed without participating in Star Hubs, my school would still have developed partnerships with other schools
	88% agreed without participating in Star Hubs my school would still have implemented new practices
	24% agreed without participating in Star Hubs my school would have experienced comparable improvements in learning outcomes

Connection Hub Schools Progress Report 2017

Building on the favourable indications from the pilot evaluation, The Connection hub school design was expanded further in 2017. An additional 15 schools were added to create a specialist STEM Learning Hub with support from a corporate philanthropic partner, Samsung Australia. The Star Hub group of schools was also expanded from 18 to 27 schools located across Victoria, New South Wales and South Australia. The Hub schools represented, in total 42 schools, each entering into a 3-year commitment supported by respective state education systems, commencing in the school year 2017. This brought the total group of participating schools to 50, inclusive of the eight original Powerhouse schools.

The first year of progress was evaluated by Social Ventures Australia Consulting (Social Ventures Australia Consulting, 2017). An overview of participating schools' feedback regarding the changes that occurred at their school in their first year, in line with target outcomes, as a result of participating in The Connection hub is included in this summary snapshot. The methodology included collecting survey responses to an end-of-year survey of school leaders and teachers, school self-assessments against the Project Action Plans implemented in their schools and interviews with selected school leaders. The target outcomes, both short-term and longer-term, are outlined in Fig. 14.5.

Schools' feedback throughout the year was analysed, together with the end-of-year survey and interviews. There were a number of common themes that participating schools reported:

- The Connection provides schools with *a unique and valued opportunity to be part of a national network and with other schools on a similar journey*. Schools valued highly the opportunity to discuss educational ideas and thinking with other school leaders. The Connection also provided a valued opportunity to engage in broader networks with people outside of education, thus providing new perspectives.
- Participation in The Connection helped *accelerate* the work that schools were doing to pursue partnerships and introduce new practices. Schools acknowledged that they take part in a number of net-

14 The Power of Collective Leadership for Learning 371

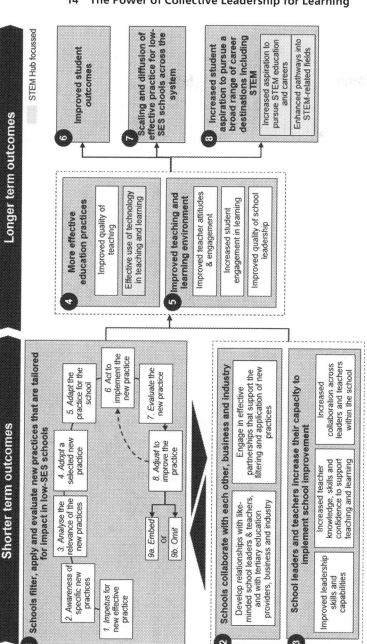

Fig. 14.5 Connection Hub school target outcomes for evaluation of progress in 2017

working and professional development opportunities outside of The Connection, and that it is difficult to credit school improvements specifically to Star Hubs. However, school comments affirm that participation in The Connection played a key role in driving those changes.
- Several schools commented that The Connection provided a *'one-touch' point* for planning and tracking school goals and change. It helped schools to articulate the focus of their work and *'set the path'* towards school improvement.
- In terms of the most evident school improvement changes, schools highlighted that being part of The Connection has strengthened *leadership capacity* across the school and promoted *growth and confidence* across teachers.

The data related to the short-term outcomes identified in Fig. 14.5 is summarised in Table 14.3.

The Impact of the Opportunity to Collaborate in Education

The SVA Connection initiative has been an opportunity to walk alongside both accomplished and aspiring school leaders as they deliver critical work in schools. The 5-year journey since 2014 has provided many valuable insights into real-world practice of school leaders who are making a difference in challenging contexts. It is clear from the interactions with The Connection schools that every education context that sits within a school community is nuanced with, and directed by, its own set of challenges. At the same time, there are overarching themes for the challenges identified across the cohort of schools. While evidence is still emerging through ongoing evaluations, it appears that there is a clear trend that collaboration across schools brings value to the school leadership role both within individual schools, but also system-wide.

In the instance of the 50 Connection schools, the challenges that the school leaders have identified are not definitively the same, but they are aligned. The opportunities to become connected with the other leaders

14 The Power of Collective Leadership for Learning

Table 14.3 Outcomes analysis after 1 year of a 3-year planned engagement

Outcome	Changes reported by schools
Schools filter, apply and evaluate new practices	92% of schools have developed a plan for change informed by evidence on great practice
	88% have implemented new practice(s)
Schools collaborate with each other	88% of leaders and teachers have increased connections with like-minded leaders
	75% of schools have identified opportunities for mutually beneficial working relationships with other schools
School leaders and teachers increase their capacity to implement school improvement	91% of schools met/exceeded their expectations of progress in improved school leadership (as set in their Project Action Plans)
	83% of schools met/exceeded their expectations in increasing teacher skills or capacity (as set in their Project Action Plans)
	61% of leaders and teachers have changed how they use colleagues within their own school
More effective school practices	71% of STEM schools said that technology has been an enabler of STEM practice
Improved teaching and learning environment	81% of schools have experienced positive changes in the teaching and learning environment
	83% of schools met/exceeded their expectations in increasing student engagement (as set in their Project Action Plans)
Improved student outcomes	54% of schools report that students have experienced improved learning outcomes in the first year
Increased student aspiration in STEM	71% of STEM schools have observed change in their students' interest and inspiration to pursue STEM
Scaling and diffusion of effective practice for low-SES schools across the system	86% of STEM schools share practices adopted through the STEM Learning Hub with schools in our broader networks

who are committed to the similar core goals creates the shared insights to solve for challenges together and is therefore highly valued. School leaders in The Connection have reported consistently that they value being connected. The schools they are leading are learning together with others outside of their own context and they are implementing new and refined practices that they believe are having an impact on student learning. The overall benefit of the collaboration has been the catalytic impact on driving new action both in schools and across systems. A significant majority of the participating schools, across all cohorts, report that participation has developed new actions that are progressing their work collectively much faster than they ever anticipated.

The value of collaborative networks, however, extends beyond just developing and sharing new practices. Mechanisms for strategic networking for collaboration in learning also promote sharing of expertise and critical thinking and problem solving which are enabling; efficiently connecting and creating leverage for assets and knowledge across systems.

The interactions in a trusted collegiate network can also be affirming and are a confidence booster to the leadership team of a school, identifying if they are on the right track towards building the conditions for learning impact. The network is a place to rely on to check perceptions, refine assumptions and seek feedback on strategy actions with like-minded colleagues who share an investment in the value of the success of the collective. There is no room for egos in the culture of professional trust that has developed, as every participant has value to add, an insight to share or a question to explore. There is no power dynamic or hierarchy as the network is an inclusive culture with shared values across the group.

The CLDN has emerged as a supportive, creative and rigorous learning culture where participants keep each other accountable yet are also comfortable enough to expose vulnerabilities in the shared quest to improve together. The silos created by school competition are broken down by the intention to become successful together. Within the CLDN, similar principles to those of the Ontario context described above by Hargreaves and Fullan have been applied to Australian school leaders. School leaders are powerful influencers as they translate policy priorities into teaching and learning practices. School leaders (also the middle players) are a critical leverage point for enacting responsive professional action. When school leaders demonstrate shared responsibility, trust, humility, intention and professional initiative together, they are also more confident to act. When they are collaboratively engaged in the decision-making processes to developing the intention to act, they have an opportunity to be evidence-informed and to benefit from a bigger pool of collegiate expertise. When these school leadership teams are then placed in a position of influence within systems, their action and the learning contribute to important systems leadership modelling responsibilities. In systems design, the school leaders become the nodes of knowledge and expertise to be leveraged so that great practice has then the opportunity to become pervasive practice. Leading for learning becomes collaborative, inclusive and influential to create systems change.

Conclusion

Where does this leave the concepts of leadership discussed in this book? instructional leadership and leading for learning are both dimensions of this evolving culture of practice but cannot be solutions in isolation. The Connection schools have demonstrated that evolving school leadership practice is dynamic, multi-dimensional, responsive, creative and certainly professional. The most successful leaders create actions that are fit for context, responsive to need and driven by a quest for excellence with shared priority support of the collective. Successful school leaders are the emerging system leaders for learning improvement: Australian education excellence is a shared priority.

The CLDN is built around the shared insight that the complexity of the challenge requires creative expertise that is pooled, curated, rigorously challenged and informed by evidence of what works and how. It is a leadership that can be both instructional and is clearly focused on learning, but at the same time, it is learning for all participants.

Collaborative networking design builds an open inclusive exchange and enrichment of learning and sharing of leadership expertise. The act of collaborating creates collective responsibility so that new learning and shared efficacy work catalytically to translate practice into learning impact in real schools located in real communities. It is a practice-based response which has a purpose and real intent to make a difference. The Connection schools' preliminary data suggest that school leaders, when connected with a shared purpose, analyse, adopt, adapt and enact new practice as they learn both with and from each other. The evaluation data collected also suggest that the participating Connection schools value the collegiate trust and the opportunity to build and explore evidence-informed practices together because it meets their professional needs to grow, which also supports them to lead more effectively.

Expressed within the experiences of the Australian Bright Spots Schools Connection, linking 50 schools in a CLDN over 5 years, the messages from school leaders are clear:

- Collective and shared practice is catalytic;
- Consultative practices are empowering, affirming and challenging;
- Empowerment is enabling;
- Collaborative practice shares the responsibility and accountabilities to grow impact; and
- Collaborative Network Leadership design taps into a diversity of ideas, knowledge and expertise, assets within systems to build better learning outcomes for all participants.

It is the opportunity of positioning and aligning quality-driven leadership expertise to the nuanced challenges of learning communities that will deliver renewed momentum in education practice.

Knowledge is pervasive in all learning communities. Cultivated expertise in collaborative learning networks can unleash its potential and direct it more broadly so that it can make a difference where it will be of most value. Successful school leaders can then move beyond adopting just one approach to deliver leadership actions, to practices that are about adapting and blending to create hybrid leadership practices and actions that are tailored and responsive to need more efficiently and effectively. Leaders' expertise can both grow and be cultivated to build highly effective learning communities across systems.

School leaders do have reason to take a seat at the table for system leaders and there is an important purpose for why they should be there. After all, individually we can make a difference but together we can and will have much more impact.

References

Australian Assessment and Curriculum Reporting Authority. (2011). *Guide to understanding ICSEA*. Retrieved from ACARA: http://docs.acara.edu.au/resources/Guide_to_understanding_ICSEA.pdf

Australian Council of Education Research. (2018). *Evaluation of the bright spots schools connection final report*. Melbourne, Australia: ACER.

Australian Curriculum Reporting Authority. (2016). *National assessment program*. Retrieved from ACARA My School: https://nap.edu.au/naplan

Commonwealth of Australia. (2018). *Through growth to achievement report of the review to achieve educational excellence in Australian schools*. Canberra, Australia: Commonwealth Department of Education and Training.

Erlichman, D., Sawyer, D., & Spencer, N. (2018, March). Cutting through the complexity: A road map for effective collaboration. *Stanford Social Innovation Review*.

Fullan, M. (2015, December). Leadership from the middle, a system strategy. *Education Canada, 55*, 22–26.

Halbert, J., & Kaser, L. (2016). *System transformation for equity and quality: Purpose, passion and persistence* (Seminar series 260). Melbourne, Australia: Centre for Strategic Education.

Hargreaves, A., Shirley, D., Wangia, S., Bacon, C., & D'Angelo, M. (2018). *Leading from the Middle: Spreading Learning, Well-being, and Identity Across Ontario*. Toronto, Canada: Council for Directors of Education (CODE).

Masters, G. N. (2012). *National school improvement tool*. Retrieved from Australian Council Education Research: https://research.acer.edu.au/tll_misc/18

OECD. (2018a). *The OECD Teaching and Learning International Survey (TALIS) – 2013 results*. Retrieved from OECD Better Policies for Better Lives: http://www.oecd.org/education/school/talis-2013-results.htm

OECD. (2018b). *Equity in education: Breaking down barriers to social mobility*. Paris: OECD Publishing.

Social Ventures Australia. (2013). *Social ventures Australia education: Business & project plan, bright spots schools connection*. Melbourne, Australia: Social Ventures Australia.

Social Ventures Australia. (2018). *Bright spots schools connection*. Retrieved from Social Ventures Australia: https://www.socialventures.com.au/education/the-sva-bright-spots-schools-connection/

Social Ventures Australia Consulting. (2017). *The Connection Hub 2017 progress report*. Melbourne, Australia: Social Ventures Australia.

Social Ventures Consulting. (2016). *Star Hubs initiative 12 month evaluation*. Melbourne, Australia: Social Ventures Australia.

Stoll, L. (2015). *Enhancing teaching and learning through enquiry-based collaborative R&D* (Occasional paper 140). Melbourne, Australia: Centre Strategic Education.

Wei-Skillern, J., & Silver, N. (2013). Four network principles for collaboration success. *The Foundation Review, 5*(1), 121–129.

15

Leading Place-Based Interventions to Improve Outcomes in Low Socio-economic Settings

Christopher Chapman, Alison Drever, Maureen McBride, Craig Orr, and Sarah Weakley

Introduction

In their book *The Spirit Level*, Wilkinson and Pickett (2010) argue that more equal societies are more successful societies. However, despite this analysis and a significant body of supporting evidence combined with high levels of investment in tackling poverty and inequalities, the relationship between poverty, inequalities and poor educational, economic and health outcomes remain as steadfast as ever.

Poverty in Scotland is highest amongst families with children. One in four of Scotland's children are officially recognised as living in poverty

---

C. Chapman (✉) • C. Orr • S. Weakley
University of Glasgow, Glasgow, Scotland
e-mail: chris.chapman@glasgow.ac.uk; criag.orr@glasgow.ac.uk; Sarah.Weakley@glasgow.ac.uk

A. Drever • M. McBride
Children's Neighbourhoods Scotland, Glasgow, Scotland
e-mail: alison.drever@glasgow.ac.uk; Maureen.McBride@glasgow.ac.uk

(Scottish Government, 2018), with the Institute for Fiscal Studies forecasting an increase of more than 50% in the proportion of children living in poverty in the UK by 2020/2021 (Browne & Hood, 2016). There is also widespread recognition among researchers and practitioners that children from low-income households do significantly worse at school than their more affluent peers (Joseph Rowntree Foundation, 2014). These sets of interrelated and compounding issues result in individual services that struggle to adequately tackle the range of issues around inequality and disadvantage that negatively impacts children and young people. By taking an ecosystem perspective (Grossman, Lombard, & Fisher, 2014), working collaboratively with other services, some organisations hope to develop an adaptive shared system of service delivery more suited to tackling such complex issues. The Scottish Government is committed to developing collaborative leadership to realise integrated collaborative working across services to serve community, city and national level requirements (Christie Commission, 2011). However, despite this laudable aspiration, the realities of achieving this in practice remain challenging.

Place-based approaches are one response to the situation set out above. Over the last two decades (and the last decade in particular in the UK), these approaches to educational change have gained in both prominence and popularity. Increasingly, governments across the Western world appear to be recognising the multiple factors within and beyond the school system that impact children and young people and the complex problems that face children in an unequal society call for collaborative solutions (Whitehurst & Croft, 2015). Our approach draws on some ideas, concepts and lessons from other place-based models such as the Harlem Children's Zone (2018), Strive Partnership (2016) and explicit models based on capabilities in Northern Ireland (Greater Shankill Children and Young People Zone, 2018; Hall, 1995) and Wales (Welsh Government, 2017) to develop an approach that will achieve its aims and ambitions in a complex Scottish context.

As with place-based approaches in general, and in particular, those which follow a collective impact approach, the impacts on the 'big' aims are realised in the long term, and therefore, results on some of these initiatives, particularly in the UK, are only just emerging. However, existing research on more established initiatives continues to assert that the problems of poverty and disadvantage, and the problems associated with poverty and disadvantage, have the potential to be addressed by establishing collaborative, holistic and ambitious initiatives within the places where children and young people grow up. This requires long-term commitment and investment of resources rather than short-term, politically driven funding cycles.

In an attempt to move beyond the challenges outlined above, we have developed Children's Neighbourhoods Scotland (CNS). The CNS model uses the principles of collective impact to add value and synergy to the application of services at the neighbourhood level (Hanleybrown, Kania, & Kramer, 2012; Kania & Kramer, 2011). CNS is a place-based approach (cf. Bynner, 2016) underpinned by capabilities theory (cf. Brunner & Watson, 2015; Sen, 2009) to improve outcomes for children and young people in neighbourhoods with high levels of poverty. CNS uses design-based research to create interactive cycles of developmental and research activity to create a context-specific, evidence-based activity to improve conditions, and outcomes within the neighbourhood.

In this chapter, we offer a practical example of leadership for learning as an extended practice beyond a school setting. We provide an overview of the context and background of CNS and highlight some of the issues associated with initiating, and leading, a collective impact approach. Finally, in conclusion, we reflect on some of the early lessons pertaining to leadership in this complex high-octane setting and offer the public service reticulist as a potential form of leadership for learning within the context of place-based approaches.

Context and Background

The University of Glasgow and the Glasgow Centre for Population Health (GCPH) have drawn on the learning from place-based approaches in the UK (cf. Batty et al., 2018; Dyson, Kerr, Raffo, & Wigelsworth, 2012; Greater Shankill Children and Young People Zone, 2018; Welsh Government, 2017) and beyond (cf. United States Department of

Education, 2018) to establish Children's Neighbourhoods Scotland (CNS). Currently, this programme works with partners and local people in Bridgeton and Dalmarnock in the East End of Glasgow to improve services, resources, opportunities and chances for the children and young people who live there. CNS aims to build on the good work and investment already happening locally and to place a greater focus on making sure efforts across a range of services and support systems are collaborative, coordinated and better delivered for children and families in the communities in which they live. To achieve this aim, CNS, serving as the backbone organisation, chose to follow the model of collective impact within this large neighbourhood project (Kania & Kramer, 2011).

Bridgeton and Dalmarnock, two adjacent neighbourhoods in the East End of Glasgow, historically have some of the highest levels of socio-economic disadvantage in the city; where 50% of children live in poverty, over half of the households with dependent children are single-parent households, there is a higher proportion of community members claiming means-tested unemployment and/or disability benefits, and the life expectancy for both women and men is lower than the city average (Glasgow Indicators Project, 2012).

The last decade has brought significant changes to the neighbourhood's landscape, primarily due to developments related to Glasgow as the host city of the 2014 Commonwealth Games as well as additional local government resources committed to the area in two separate initiatives. The 2014 Commonwealth Games Athletes' Village was reconfigured after the event as a combination of social and private housing serving 700 families and growing the population, particularly in the primary school. The neighbourhood is also the site of local government regeneration activities, which focus on both economic regeneration and children and young people's services, with a community hub based in the primary school. In the coming years, the neighbourhood anticipates more growth, with more housing planned as well as a primary and nursery school. Importantly, the neighbourhood is an area with established local services, third sector organisations and schools. As well as local partners, there are many other statutory partners in the area such as health visiting, social work, community safety and private sector organisations (Clunie & Leman, 2017). Together, these organisations as well as national partners serve as the network of partners that CNS works with in a collective impact approach to educational and community improvement.

The concept of CNS was developed during 2016–2017, with the first phase of the project (initiation phase) occurring in 2017. An inaugural meeting of local and national stakeholders and potential partners took place in December 2016 and began planning for a long lead in to working with this complex and over-intervened community, who have experienced decades of investment and project overload. This has included a number of 'false dawns', unfulfilled promises and a churn of outsiders offering another silver bullet. We were very clear that CNS was not another intervention, but rather, a new way of thinking about how to tackle issues by building on existing assets within the area. The key role of CNS is brokering and facilitating collaboration that could lead to new ways of thinking and working arrangements within the neighbourhood. The following year focused on building relationships with key stakeholders and securing resources to appoint key personnel.

By August 2017, support from the Local Education Authority had been secured to backfill the headteacher position of a local primary school as a local coordinator, funding was secured through an Economic and Social Research Council Impact Acceleration Account for a knowledge exchange and impact fellow (KEIF), and funding from business and philanthropy supported the appointment of two research and evaluation associates (1.5 FTE). The University and GCPH also provided senior academic support and operational leadership on a pro bono basis to pump-prime developments.

The project was formally launched in February 2018 (implementation phase). Initial activity included the preparation of evidence reviews on capabilities and place-based approaches and a detailed analysis of the context of the neighbourhood to identify priorities for action. The five priorities identified were social life, family life, career and education, transitions and mental health. The local team has worked with the community and young people on a number of projects focused in these areas including within the themes of play, developing student researcher teams to explore pressing issues within the neighbourhood and, more recently, investigations into pathways into and out of NEET (which considers

16–19-year-olds that are not in any of education, employment and training).

Soon after the formal launch of CNS, the Scottish Government committed to embedding and extending this approach into a number of new sites containing high concentrations of children living in poverty in other urban, town and rural areas of Scotland. It might be surprising that this investment occurred so quickly; however, given the long lead in time for the project's initiation, perhaps it is understandable, especially as there is proof of concept both within CNS and other sites in similar settings elsewhere.

As we have noted, a key feature of CNS is to bring together professionals and services to break down boundaries and silos to promote collective impact. We now move on to outline our approach to collective impact.

Leading a Collective Impact Approach

The collective impact approach for both place-based and national networks of cross-sectoral educational improvement initiatives has gained in prominence since its introduction by Kania and Kramer in 2011. The approach is defined as 'the commitment of a group of important actors from different sectors to a common agenda for solving a specific social problem' (2011, p. 3). This approach is primarily associated with initiatives in the US and has been utilised in health, community development and educational change projects (DuBrow, Hug, Serafini, & Litzler, 2018). What ties collective impact initiatives together is their aim to solve complex and multifaceted problems; the same type of problems that face the neighbourhoods of Bridgeton and Dalmarnock and the type of problems that CNS aims to solve. While existing examples of successful, smaller scale collaborative projects are common in neighbourhood initiatives to tackle poverty and increase educational attainment, including in CNS sites, a collective impact initiative differs by its focus on a structured process to create a shared agenda; coordinate action, communication, and measurement; and broker and facilitate relationships by a backbone organisation at its centre (Hanleybrown et al., 2012; Henig, Riehl, Houston, Rebell, & Wolff, 2016). This is a developing methodol-

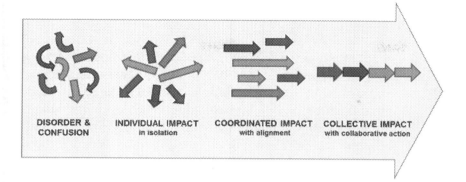

Fig. 15.1 Harnessing models of collaboration for collective impact. (Henig et al., 2015)

ogy in the field of educational improvement: in 2015, Henig and colleagues first outlined the collective impact approach for education, and in 2016 published a review of collective impact approaches across the US. In all of the projects they reviewed, the goal of collective impact is to move from disorder, isolated impact and coordinated impact to collective impact among partners in each initiative (Fig. 15.1).

Kania and Kramer (2011) detailed the five conditions of collective impact that differentiate these projects from other types of collaborations, and work in the first phases of the CNS project has been active in each of these five conditions: backbone support, common agenda, mutually reinforcing activities, continuous communication, and shared measurement. As full implementation (and now expansion) of CNS is an ongoing process, some aspects of these conditions are more advanced than others. However, using these conditions as a guide we can begin to understand the value of a systematic way of working in a complex, multifaceted change project such as CNS.

Creation of a Backbone Organisation

A defining feature of the collective impact approach is the backbone organisation, a separate organisational entity with a dedicated staff who can 'plan, manage, and support the initiative' through ongoing leadership and facilitation, data collection, evaluation, and logistical support to make sure the initiative runs smoothly (Hanleybrown et al., 2012; Kania & Kramer, 2011). Recent work on the role of backbone organisations has emphasised their role as more than simply administrators and the 'glue' that holds the partners together. Instead, backbone organisations should serve as 'incubators for change' by facilitating, coaching and serving as the nexus of respectful accountability among all partners (DuBrow et al., 2018). They are the central impartial body to support the neighbourhood approach and the collaborations that are to be established to achieve this and serve to guide and support partners to fulfil the other four conditions of collective impact (Clunie & Leman, 2017). Notably, during initiation, the backbone organisation carried no funding on its own; rather, the team worked in collaboration with partners within existing funding streams and contributed to joint funding bids. To date, the CNS backbone role has been fulfilled by a Planning Group led by a collaboration between university partners and local government, and works alongside a Research and Evaluation Group and an Advisory Group.

The Planning Group and its members as the backbone organisation spent 2017 building a local presence in the neighbourhood, with a local coordinator serving as a key factor in the organisation. This member was a well-established community leader who worked within an existing hub of activity; in this case as a leader in the primary school with a reputation for having strong relationships with the community and third sector partners. Like the Harlem Children's Zone (2018), the team recognised that a key site for intervention and collaboration among many partners was at the school, and indeed existing local government initiatives were already connected there. With this site recognised as a hub of activity, community-based interventions could sit alongside school-based interventions in the implementation phase. During the planning and early implementation phase of CNS, the backbone organisation gathered data and evidence, built the network of partners, linked the work to existing policy areas and engaged with community members to understand the capabilities and needs of the variety of stakeholders involved in this project. After the establishment of the backbone organisation and its roles in the project, action in the other four collective impact areas could commence.

The latter half of 2018 saw a number of changes in staffing. The KEIF moved on to a promoted post in a third sector organisation, and the local coordinator returned to lead the school and the establishment of a new school in the area. On the one hand, this was challenging, particularly in relation to a temporary loss of capacity on the ground by individuals who had invested significant resources in building relationships and also putting additional stress on pro bono support at a time when the system was having its expectations raised about CNS. On the other hand, it provided an important opportunity to bring an experienced third sector practitioner with a strong reputation within the community and one, for the first time, who came from the community. These interim arrangements also enabled CNS to increase the time commitment of one of the research and evaluation team to take on some of the KEIF roles.

The learning from these early phases of development of the backbone organisation has led us to conclude that while it is helpful to have a KEIF for the initiation of a backbone organisation, for the longer term a local coordinator, with leadership experience across a range of services and sectors and the community and, where possible, who is from within the community, is a preferable model. As CNS moves into the next phase of development with 3-year funding in place for a backbone organisation, this is the model that will be adopted and the job descriptions have been collapsed accordingly.

CNS is also in a position where the pro bono support cannot be sustained. The appointment of a National Director, dedicated administrator, communications officer and lead research and evaluation officer in early 2019 ensures the backbone organisation has both the capability and leadership capacity to develop the programme over the next 3 years.

Setting the Common Agenda

The first phases of the CNS project were characterised by mapping the current neighbourhood landscape of services and working with local community partners and children and their parents to set a common agenda built on the holistic approach to improvement. The priority action areas and outcomes—long-term, intermediate and short-term—

were developed from engagement activities into a Theory of Change for the project. Although the collective impact approach does not generally use Theory of Change models (as their focus is on models that involve greater co-production) (Hanleybrown et al., 2012), the CNS planning team felt it was valuable to have this framework to guide discussions of the overall approach, given the lack of familiarity of other partners working in a collaboration of this type. The Planning Group worked with existing evidence about the neighbourhood to map the current neighbourhood context and activities to create the key contextual evidence for the Theory of Change. This included gathering statistical and demographic data, local private investment initiatives, third sector reports and evidence from the other public sector initiatives into a Context Report for all partners (Clunie & Leman, 2017). A major aspect of this work was to then meet with local partners individually to understand their assets, capabilities and experiences—network- and capacity-building actions that are fundamental to the creation of a common agenda. Further follow-up questions were sent to all identified partners, and only then was a draft Theory of Change created (see Fig. 15.2). Questions of this type may be valuable to consider when working with a variety of partners in other improvement projects in complex systems.

Creating a common agenda: questionnaire sent to partners in the planning phase of CNS

1. What are the most important needs of children and young people in Bridgeton and Dalmarnock?
2. What are the current challenges/ barriers to your work having a bigger impact in the neighbourhood? (Please think specifically about the aspects of your work that affect children, young people and families.)
3. Can you describe any examples you've noted or experienced of successful partnership working?
4. What in your experience have been the barriers and facilitators to successful partnership working?
5. How can we get successful partnerships established in Bridgeton and Dalmarnock?
6. What action does this require?

Fig. 15.2 Creating a common agenda: questionnaire sent to partners in the planning phase of CNS

The Theory of Change is a living document that serves as an open approach that can adapt as the project progresses and our learning about key processes deepens. Local stakeholders in CNS were also invited to comment on the draft Theory of Change in an all-day workshop, and this type of facilitation and engagement activity is a foundational activity of a backbone organisation. The iterative process of consultation with community partners is what allows a shared set of aims and objectives to form, and in turn develops into identifying activities by which partners will provide the greatest impact.

The development of the analysis of context and Theory of Change have been important processes in developing a shared understanding with local and national stakeholders on the advisory group and other partners and interest groups. The process and associated documents have acted as stimuli to surface difficult issues, expose misconceptions and challenge norms and assumptions of behaviours and practice.

Mutually Reinforcing Activities

A collective impact model aims to harness the existing resources of neighbourhood or project area to achieve the aims of the common agenda. This is led by a backbone organisation acting to understand the capabilities of partners (and individuals) in the area it works, and 'coordinat[ing] their differentiated activities through a mutually reinforcing plan of action' (Kania & Kramer, 2011, p. 7). In the initiation phase of CNS, extensive work was undertaken to identify and engage existing partners who are already working within the priority areas for children and young people identified by partners and community members: in 'transitions' (e.g., nursery to primary school, primary to secondary school and school to career), career and education, mental health, family life and social life.

Engaging with partners focused on these community-identified priority areas can determine what existing resources can be leveraged for collective impact and through these conversations may also be able to identify more actors in the community that are working in the area but may not be currently connected to the CNS programme.

The CNS team is working to bring a range of front-line practitioners together on a range of issues. A more recent development has involved the generation of vignettes of 'families in crisis' to document how services have missed opportunities and failed to support individuals and their families in extreme need. The vignettes highlight the critical incidents, systems failure and fault lines that have prevented positive action. These artefacts provide an important resource for professional learning purposes to explore how these situations might be avoided in the future.

In addition to some of the developments outlined earlier in the chapter, CNS is developing working groups of partners in each of the priority areas, which will then create subnetworks for coordinated action. With the establishment of the new backbone organisation it is anticipated that the pace of this work will be accelerated through multi-agency and interdisciplinary partnerships and professional learning activities that draw on a number of resources, including the reviews of evidence, analysis of context, place-based tools, case studies and other resources to build stronger inter-professional relationships within the neighbourhood and with the community itself.

Continuous Communication

Relationship building among the wide variety of partners and actors is a fundamental aspect of any collaborative enterprise, and in a collective impact project it is crucial to success. It allows for all those involved in the project to build trust, assure mutual objectives and create common motivation (Hanleybrown et al., 2012; Kania & Kramer, 2013). This relationship building occurs among partners, between partners and community members, and between all of these groups and the backbone organisation.

The CNS team has therefore invested considerable effort in cultivating channels of communication and then formalising feedback mechanisms among partners by holding neighbourhood-wide events. These lines of communication must also be cultivated with the children and young people who stand to benefit from the CNS interventions. The coproduction activities of the capabilities-focused approaches in Northern Ireland and Wales were reflected in the engagement of children and young people in the first and second CNS phases, particularly in the activities with children and young people to develop the five priority areas of action.

CNS has sought to ensure that both vertical and horizontal lines of communication have been developed. Continuous communication has an important role to play in stimulating the cultural change required to achieve collective impact. This is particularly important in relation to building flatter networked collaborative leadership that cuts across organisational and professional boundaries and breaks down silos. Working in this way means that professionals have to detach their leadership from position and authority, instead focusing on solving the issues in hand and identifying where the knowledge, expertise and problem-solving power is located within the neighbourhood irrespective of the position held by the practitioner.

Shared Measurement

This final condition of a collective impact initiative is less developed at present for CNS, but it is no less important. The profiles generated by GCPH (see below) are helpful and cover an area in the East End of Glasgow but do not cover the exact geographical CNS. It is an ongoing task for the neighbourhood team to collate more precise data specifically for CNS. The data contained in this profile combined with the detailed analysis of context are fundamental to the CNS approach. This diverse range of information is used to provide a holistic picture of the neighbourhood we are working with and to inform our decision-making. The programme leadership is constantly revisiting and refining this analysis to identify changes in the context and to draw out the learning and lessons offered by the analysis (Table 15.1).

There are also issues regarding data sharing agreements across areas, services and organisations that the team continues to navigate. Indeed, 'agreement on a common agenda is illusory without agreement on the ways success will be measured and reported' (Kania & Kramer, 2011, p. 6). Fulfilling this condition requires that a group of shared metrics for improvement are agreed upon by all partners, and more importantly

Table 15.1 Neighbourhood profile for Parkhead and Dalmarnock

Domain	Indicator	Count	Rate	Difference from Glasgow	Period
Demography	Population aged 0 to 4	820	9%	+53%	2015
	Population aged 5 to 11	762	8%	+24%	2015
	Population aged 12 to 17	574	6%	+13%	2015
	Population aged 18 to 24	791	9%	-27%	2015
	Birth rate (per 1,000 pop'n)	108	15.5	+27%	2013
	Under 25s from a minority ethnic group	223	9%	-46%	2011
Infant Health	Infants who sleep in the supine position	126	85%	-9%	2015
	Babies exposed to passive smoking	N/A	26%	+72%	2014/15
	Babies with birth weight below 2500g	9	3%	+3%	2013 - 2015
Culture and Environment	Children who walk to primary school	N/A	65%	+22%	2008 - 2015
	Under 16s living within 400m of green space	907	61%	-23%	2014
	P1 children who are obese or severely obese	N/A	8%	+26%	2012/13 - 2014/15
	Hospitalisations for dental treatment (per 1,000 pop'n under 16)	26	17.5	+32%	2014
Crime and Safety	Referrals to Scottish Children's Reporter Administration	63	4%	+136%	2015/16
	Offenders (per 1,000 pop'n aged 8 to 18)	41	38.5	+29%	2015/16
	Victims of crime (per 1,000 pop'n aged 8 to 18)	42	39.4	+87%	2015/16
	Emergency hospitalisations due to assault (per 1,000 pop'n under 25)	N/A	2.6	+97%	2010/11 - 2014/15
	Emergency hospitalisations for unintentional injuries (per 1,000 pop'n under 15)	N/A	11.4	+13%	2010/11 - 2014/15
Socio-Economic	Children in poverty	770	46%	+58%	2013
	Lone parent households	563	61%	+52%	2011
	Overcrowded households with children	319	22%	+24%	2011
Learning and Education	Children with communication delay at 27 to 30 months	45	22%	-6%	2014
	S4 pupils achieving 5 or more qualifications at SCQF Level 5	9	18%	-48%	2012 - 2013
	Secondary school attendance	N/A	88%	-4%	2013/14
	School leavers with a positive destination	52	85%	-5%	2013
	16 to 19 year olds not in employment, education or training	217	65%	+134%	2012
Health and Wellbeing	Pre-school children with likely development difficulties	N/A	12%	+66%	2012 - 2014
	Referrals to Children and Adolescent Mental Health Services	69	4%	+12%	2015/16
	Male healthy life expectancy (years)	N/A	47.3	-16%	2011
	Female healthy life expectancy (years)	N/A	49.7	-15%	2011
	Under 25s whose day-to-day activities are limited by disability	200	8%	+38%	2011

Glasgow Indicators Project (2012)

the process for reporting those metrics to the backbone organisation needs to be put into place as the project evolves. Developing this system of shared measurement occurs in tandem with establishing the common agenda (or Theory of Change in the case of CNS), and the processes for reporting are dependent upon the capabilities and partners involved in carrying out the agenda. For CNS this is a primary area of action in the first year after the official launch of the project, as the project team works with partners to establish, manage and adapt as necessary a system of measurement and accountability across all of the key indicators in the Theory of Change. As noted by Kania and Kramer (2013), the wide variety of partners working in the neighbourhood combined with the complexity of the problem will likely result in emergent solutions arising during the project, which may call for what is being measured to change; however, the commitment to shared measurement remains consistent.

In the final section of this chapter we move on to reflect on the leadership lessons that have emerged during the initiation and implementation of CNS over the past 2 years.

Some Initial Reflections on CNS Leadership: Learning, Challenges and Potential

The initiation and implementation of CNS highlight a number of leadership challenges that must be overcome to successfully operate in a challenging, highly fluid and volatile context that involves working across a set of complex organisational, professional and political domains. The leadership challenges include the following:

- *Pace and momentum*: The first leadership challenge relates to ensuring that CNS maintains an appropriate pace so that the momentum is not lost, whilst also ensuring authentic buy-in from professional and community stakeholders so that they are empowered to co-produce the solutions needed to progress the project. This is particularly challenging when significant time has been invested in building the interpersonal relationships necessary to empower stakeholders which can be easily lost when CNS staff leave. In order to mitigate this challenge, CNS ensured a structured handover with an overlap and induction period. Relationships are documented and archived to ensure institutional memory is maintained.
- *Managing expectations and maintaining focus*: A second key leadership challenge involves managing multiple expectations from the community and other key stakeholders, services including those imposed by the local and national government. In managing these often-conflicting expectations, it is important for the leadership to maintain focus on the key activities related to delivering impact rather than being diverted to serve others' agendas that fall out with the aims and objectives of CNS. In order to achieve this, the CNS team has drawn on a range of

expertise from within the team to ensure that the CNS leadership plays to their strengths and where possible can draw on social capital from pre-existing relationships.

- *Balancing research and development activity*: One strength of CNS is the extent to which evidence and research guide developmental activity: the extent to which CNS is a 'Learning Programme'. This can also create a leadership challenge about where to focus resources and energy at any given time. Leaders need to be clear about the quality and robustness of the research and evaluation evidence generated in order to make research-informed decisions whilst at the same time maintaining developmental action. This is linked to the first leadership challenge of maintaining pace and momentum. To ensure an appropriate balance between research and development is maintained, that they inform one another, and that 'research' and 'development' silos are avoided, the membership of the planning and research and evaluation groups are mixed and the senior leaders of the project have an oversight of all research and development activities.
- *Building and sustaining authentic relationships*: This leadership challenge is particularly important when operating in challenging, highly fluid and volatile contexts. Leaders require high-level influencing, facilitation, brokerage and negotiating skills. CNS leaders cannot rely on their professional position, power and authority which are likely to have little credibility when working in an unusual, different or multi-disciplinary professional setting to their own. In order to build these relationships, CNS leaders have deliberately operated at different levels within hierarchical structures to build authentic networks and communities of practice across a range of organisational, professional and political domains.
- *Managing competition and fostering collaboration*: Fluid and volatile contexts often have a competitive edge. This may be between different services or third sector organisations that are providing services in return for resources. This can be further complicated by local histories and the alliances that have developed over time. This presents a complex leadership challenge when attempting to build a collaborative culture underpinned by a common agenda with mutually reinforcing

activities and shared measurement systems. CNS leaders have sought to achieve this through constant communication and professionalism and by being transparent in their actions and decisions at all times.
- *Politics and vested interests*: The previous five leadership challenges all form part of the requirement to manage politics and vested interests at all levels. This requires leaders to understand the micropolitics of local communities and to understand, and be able to influence, politicians and leaders in local government and other organisations that serve the communities. CNS leaders also need to understand, and be able to respond to and influence, national policymakers and politicians. The team has achieved this by ensuring there is a mixed skillset across the leadership profile and through careful selection of a National Director with a diverse range of experience and expertise, rarely found in any one individual.

These leadership challenges and the emerging messages about the nature of leadership practices required to mitigate them offer a potential way forward that resonates with the types of leadership necessary to support educational and wider public service reform agenda in Scotland (cf. Christie Commission, 2011).

These reforms are attempting to improve the performance of public services and outcomes for citizens by shifting from a dominant hierarchical culture with its associated bureaucratic, managed organisations underpinned by leadership based on position and power to a much flatter, non-hierarchical culture. This culture has the potential to support high levels of social cohesion underpinned by collaborative leadership, partnership and co-production between service providers (and the communities they serve).

As already noted, this is particularly important for CNS where, for example, the team might be facilitating a meeting or planning a development with a number of leaders from a range of public, third and private sector organisations, which may also involve senior university academics and senior practitioners in the field. It is CNS's experience, and there is increasing evidence from our own empirical research on public service leadership, in Scotland (Chapman, 2018) and the wider literature (cf. Sullivan & Skelcher, 2002), that in these complex settings, traditional patterns of leadership fall way short of building the trust or relationships necessary to deliver the intended outcomes. Rather, a more nuanced collaborative form of leadership has the potential to build a sense of community and shared endeavour across a range of boundaries.

The leaders who seem capable of providing successful leadership in these complex settings are those who exhibit the characteristics of 'public service reticulists' (Chapman, Watson, & van Amersfoort, 2017), that is, they are sophisticated learners and are adaptive and effective in a range of complex settings. These public service reticulists are the following:

- *Skilled communicators*: Public service reticulists use adaptive language to empathise with others through negotiation and see challenging and complex situations from a range of perspectives. They can demonstrate empathy with other perspectives whilst influencing individual and group positions.
- *Excellent networkers*: Public service reticulists use their expertise and social and emotional intelligences to gain access to a diverse range of settings, both locally and nationally. They seek out and connect with those who have similar interests to build coalitions and alliances that can lever the outcomes that they desire in different parts or levels within the system.
- Strategic in orientation: Public service reticulists see the 'big picture' and understand the contributions that partners can make. These leaders have the ability to get the appropriate expertise and experience around the table and can make the case for collaboration, so individuals can see the value added in working together strategically to generate long-term productive relationships.
- *Contextually astute*: Public service reticulists understand the relationship between organisational conditions, individuals' behaviours and outcomes. These leaders understand the power of context and are astute in developing solutions that optimise the capability and capacity residing in specific settings.
- *Problem solvers*: Public service reticulists think laterally and creatively to seek solutions. These leaders are not linear thinkers. They make con-

- *Self-managing*: Public service reticulists are adept at risk-taking within a framework that understands organisational capacity. These leaders dare to challenge the status quo and take risks without being reckless. When something is not working, or looks problematic, they fail fast and adapt their approach to achieve success.

The early experiences from CNS suggest leadership challenges associated with developing successful place-based interventions are complex and often not straightforward. However, there are three messages from this chapter that we should reflect on. First, traditional forms of leadership that find solace in their own professional identity and working within rather than across professional boundaries are outmoded and undermine holistic place-based approaches such as CNS. Second, we need leaders who are comfortable working at different levels within the system, rather than being pigeonholed in a hierarchy, and can work across a range of different boundaries. Therefore, CNS will need to build a team of public service reticulists who are confident boundary spanners over the next phase of development and finally, that this situation presents a significant professional learning challenge for the system. As of yet, there is no systematic professional development in place to support growing this type of leadership. Perhaps this is an opportunity for CNS to begin to grow a new cadre of public service reticulists from the ground up?

Commentary

In summary, and to draw us back to the main themes of this volume, we argue that the insights presented in this chapter provide us with an example of leadership for learning that goes beyond notions of leadership for learning in schools. We suggest that the emergence of public service reticulists is an indication that we need a rethinking of leadership, one that goes beyond current conceptions of the principles which suggest that leadership for learning is a predominantly school-based concept. We require a more holistic approach that involves focusing on leaders' own learning and the learning of others by creating the conditions for learning across professional and geographical boundaries, promoting communication and dialogue in complex settings, sharing their leadership and developing systems of joint accountability and responsibility to improve outcomes for children living in the most disadvantaged communities. If we are to achieve this then we may optimise the potential of leadership for learning.

References

Batty, E., Pearson, S., Wilson, I., Coldwell, M., Steill, B., & Willis, B. (2018). *Children's community evaluation report 2017*. Sheffield Hallam University. Retrieved from: https://www4.shu.ac.uk/research/cresr/sites/shu.ac.uk/files/childrens-community-eval-2017-report.pdf

Browne, J., & Hood, A. (2016). *Living standards, poverty and inequality in the UK: 2015–16 to 2020–21*. London: Institute for Fiscal Studies. Retrieved from: https://www.ifs.org.uk/uploads/publications/comms/R114.pdf

Brunner, R., & Watson, N. (2015). *What can the capabilities approach add to policy analysis in high-income countries?* (What Works Scotland working paper). Retrieved from: http://whatworksscotland.ac.uk/wp-content/uploads/2015/03/workingpaper-capabilities-approach.pdf

Bynner, C. (2016). *Rationales for place-based approached in Scotland* (What Works Scotland working paper). Retrieved from: http://whatworksscotland.ac.uk/wp-content/uploads/2017/03/RationalesforPlacebasedApproachesinScotland.pdf

Chapman, C. (2018). *Public service leadership: What works?* (What Works Scotland working paper). Retrieved from: http://whatworksscotland.ac.uk/wp-content/uploads/2018/12/WWSPublicServiceLeadershipWhatWorks.pdf

Chapman, C., Watson, N., & van Amersfoort, D. (2017). *What works in public service leadership: Exploring the potential* (What Works Scotland working paper). Retrieved from: http://whatworksscotland.ac.uk/wp-content/uploads/2017/07/WWSPublicServiceLeadershipExploringThePotential.pdf

Christie Commission. (2011). *Report on the future delivery of public services by the Commission chaired by Dr Campbell Christie*. Retrieved from: http://www.gov.scot/Publications/2011/06/27154527/0

Clunie, N., & Leman, L. (2017). *Children's neighbourhoods context report.* Retrieved from: https://childrensneighbourhoodsscotland.com/our-neighbourhoods/bridgeton-and-dalmarnock/

DuBrow, W., Hug, S., Serafini, B., & Litzler, E. (2018). Expanding our understanding of backbone organizations in collective impact initiatives. *Community Development, 49*(3), 256–273.

Dyson, A., Kerr, K., Raffo, C., & Wigelsworth, M. (2012). *Developing children's zones for England.* London: Save the Children.

Glasgow Indicators Project. (2012). *Neighbourhood profiles: Parkhead and Dalmarnock.* Retrieved from: https://www.understandingglasgow.com/profiles/neighbourhood_profiles/1_ne_sector/21_parkhead_and_dalmarnock

Greater Shankill Children and Young People Zone. (2018). *Generation Shankill Zone.* Retrieved from: http://shankillzone.org/

Grossman, A. S., Lombard, A., & Fisher, N. (2014). *Strive together: Reinventing the local education ecosystem.* Boston: Harvard Business School. Retrieved from: http://web.lemoyne.edu/courseinformation/Ridzi/341%20HS%20Case%20Mgnt/Strive%20Together%20Case%20Study.pdf

Hall, M. (Ed.). (1995). *A new beginning: Shankill think tank.* Newtownabbey, UK: Island Publications.

Hanleybrown, F., Kania, J., & Kramer, M. (2012). Channeling change: Making collaborative impact work. *Stanford Social Innovation Review.* Retrieved from: https://ssir.org/articles/entry/social_progress_through_collective_impact

Harlem Children's Zone. (2018). *Our results.* Retrieved from: https://hcz.org/results/

Henig, J., Riehl, C., Houston, D, Rebell, M., & Wolff, J. (2015). *Putting collective impact in context: A review of the literature on local cross-sector collaboration to improve education.* New York: Teachers College, Columbia University. Retrieved from: https://www.wallacefoundation.org/knowledge-center/Documents/Putting-Collective-Impact-Into-Context.pdf

Henig, J., Riehl, C., Houston, D., Rebell, M., & Wolff, J. (2016). *Collective impact and the new generation of cross-sector collaborations for education.* New York: Teachers College, Columbia University. Retrieved from: https://www.wallacefoundation.org/knowledge-center/pages/collective-impact-and-the-new-generation-of-cross-sector-collaboration-for-education.aspx

Joseph Rowntree Foundation (JRF). (2014). *Closing the attainment gap in Scottish education.* Retrieved from: https://www.jrf.org.uk/sites/default/files/jrf/migrated/files/education-attainment-scotland-summary.pdf

Kania, J., & Kramer, M. (2011). Collective impact. *Stanford Social Innovation Review.* Retrieved from: https://ssir.org/articles/entry/collective_impact

Kania, J., & Kramer, M. (2013). Embracing emergence: How collective impact addresses complexity. *Stanford Social Innovation Review*. Retrieved from: https://ssir.org/articles/entry/social_progress_through_collective_impact

Scottish Government. (2018). *Poverty and income inequality in Scotland: 2015/16*. Retrieved from: http://www.gov.scot/Resource/0051/00515392.pdf

Sen, A. K. (2009). *The idea of justice*. London: Penguin.

Strive Partnership. (2016). *2015–16 Partnership report: Every child, every step of the way, cradle to career*. Retrieved from: http://www.strivepartnership.org/education-results-resource/partnership-report

Sullivan, H., & Skelcher, C. (2002). *Collaborating across boundaries*. London: Palgrave.

United States Department of Education. (2018). *Programs: promise neighborhoods*. Retrieved from: https://www2.ed.gov/programs/promiseneighborhoods/index.html

Welsh Government. (2017). *Written statement – Children first*. Retrieved from: http://gov.wales/about/cabinet/cabinetstatements/2017/childrenfirs/?lang=en

Whitehurst, R., & Croft, M. (2015). *The Harlem children's zone, promise neighborhoods, and the broader, bolder approach to education*. Washington, DC: Brown Center on Education Policy, Brookings Institute. Retrieved from: https://www.brookings.edu/research/the-harlem-childrens-zone-promise-neighborhoods-and-the-broader-bolder-approach-to-education/

Wilkinson, R., & Pickett, K. (2010). *The spirit level: Why equality is better for everyone*. London: Penguin.

Part V

Summary and Conclusions: What Do We Now Know About School Leadership?

16

Leadership for Learning: Embracing Purpose, People, Pedagogy and Place

Neil Dempster

In the first chapter of this book, Tony Townsend posed its central question, a summary of which provides the stimulus for the final chapter:

> Are *instructional leadership* and *leadership for learning* two sides of the same coin or are they two very different approaches to leading school improvement?

The short answer I offer is that *leadership for learning (LfL) is* very different from the more widely known and more frequently cited concept, *instructional leadership*. I back the position I am taking with a series of themes exposed through my reading of the chapters in this volume as well as in other research and scholarly writing published over the last three decades. That said, there are discernible elements of *instructional leadership* resident in *leadership for learning*. These will become apparent as I explain my views. As a starter, I offer a quick scan across broad shifts

---

N. Dempster (✉)
Griffith University, Brisbane, QLD, Australia
e-mail: n.dempster@griffith.edu.au

in the literature over the period from the 1980s to the present in order to highlight some of the background to my argument.

The Evolution of Approaches to School Leadership

There is no doubt that the concept *instructional leadership* found its way into the school leadership literature in the 1980s. It was individualist in perspective with power vested in the principal, reinforcing leadership as supervision. Slowly over the next 30 years, hierarchical dominance has shifted towards explanations of leadership as a collective activity focused on agreed purposes, thus downplaying the hierarchical position and the "power of one". This evolution is evident in changes in the language resulting from research findings published over this period: for example, from *instructional leadership* (Hallinger & Murphy, 1985), to *shared instructional leadership* (Marks & Printy, 2003), to *transformational leadership* (Bass & Avolio, 1994; Leithwood, 1994), to *integrated leadership* (Robinson, Lloyd, & Rowe, 2008), to *distributed and networked leadership* (Harris & Spillane, 2008; Johnson, Dempster, & Wheeley, 2016; Spillane, 2006). Ultimately, important findings from decades of work have been dissected and coalesced into what is now increasingly frequently being called *leadership for learning* (Hallinger, 2011, 2018; MacBeath, 2006; MacBeath, Dempster, Frost, Johnson, & Swaffield, 2018; Townsend & MacBeath, 2011). Getting to this point, however, has required the analysis of many studies of school leadership in different cultural settings across the globe, as the chapters in this book have shown.

As a consequence of these changes over time, what can be said about the difference between *instructional leadership* and *leadership for learning* at a deeper philosophical level is that explanations are moving, though by no means universally, from a determinist view of human nature to a voluntarist view. This is not to say that hierarchical power in schools is "dead" or "dying". Far from it: positional authority and structural hierarchy are "facts of life" in educational organisations. Nonetheless, it is clear that if improved student learning and school performance are the primary purposes of education, then much of the accumulating body of contemporary research is pointing to a broad conception of leadership—one rooted in understandings of human agency and autonomy. In other words, it points to power *with* rather than power *over*.

Having given a brief overview of some of the visible movements in conceptions of leadership, I now identify and examine seven themes which, to the eyes of authors in this volume, are essential contributors to the present-day prominence of *leadership for learning*. These themes are the result of the additive nature of international school leadership research, which has now reached a point where particularly significant leadership practices influencing effective professional pedagogy have been isolated, described and evaluated in the studies conducted by, for example, Leithwood, Seashore, Anderson, and Wahlstrom (2004), Dinham (2005), Hallinger (2005), Robinson, Hohepa, and Lloyd (2009), Louis et al. (2010), Sammons, Gu, Day, and Ko (2011), Leithwood (2012), Day, Gu, and Sammons (2016), Hitt and Tucker (2016) and MacBeath et al. (2018). Taken together, these themes show that school leadership is undeniably a multidimensional construct subject to application variations in different social, economic and cultural circumstances. Nevertheless, at its heart and in its ideal form, *leadership for learning* demands a commitment to the practices which assist principals, teachers and families to focus on the moral purpose of education.

Embracing Moral Purpose

In the face of challenges impacting on teaching and learning brought about by globalisation and its ubiquitous policy influence, principals and teachers have been confronted with the effects of an international test-driven agenda. This has tended to narrow the school curriculum, defining what is an effective school and a good education often through test results. The moral purpose of education appears infrequently in the intensity of this competitive test-driven environment. However, a number of authors in this book have reminded us, as did Gerald Grace (1995), that: "For school leaders and the profession as a whole, the moral purpose is to enhance the lives and life chances of children and young people"

(p. 5). Doing so is not possible, Michael Fullan (2001) has argued, without strong system alignment placing trust and confidence in school personnel to meet this moral obligation. Moreover, it is the responsibility of professional educators to make it clear whose interests they serve because the hallmark of the professional is to work in the client's interests; in the case of educators, those "clients" are children and young people. Added to this, however, is the integrity issue of being able to put aside their own interests as they respond to the circumstances and situations children face in the communities and schools they attend. Being able to see the "bigger picture" for each child on entry to school and to use the school's resources and its pedagogical capabilities to respond to the child's interests, needs, talents and capacities, rather than to reduce schooling to "scores" as a proxy for a quality education, is what defines a true professional educator. What seems to me to distinguish *instructional leadership* in this regard is the tendency for "instruction" to be something linked to a predetermined narrow suite of outcomes overvalued by politicians and policymakers at the expense of outcomes valued by teachers, parents or caregivers and students themselves. *Leadership for learning* starts with a clear focus on learning as liberating—learning that will be valuable to children and young people as they grow and develop, readying themselves for an autonomous adult life well-prepared to make useful contributions as citizens in the societies in which they will live. Unashamedly, the moral purpose of education in democratic economies is about this end.

Listening to Student Voice

Inclusivity is immediately apparent in the explanation of the *leadership for learning* principles enunciated by John MacBeath in Chap. 3. Leadership is observable in activities, which include principals, other position holders, teachers, students, parents and community members, all engaged in improving learning for young people. Students themselves, therefore, have a particularly significant role to play in the leadership of their own learning, and so their voices must be heard. Indeed, student voice should be integral to the learning process.

How might principals, teachers and parents bring student voice into the foreground? Some useful ideas can be gleaned by turning to research studies aimed at gaining accurate understandings of young people's views on a range of matters, not the least of which is opinions about their own learning needs, as Dempster, Lizzio and colleagues have written (2010, p. 4):

> Some studies employ visual stimuli as the preferred method to elicit young people's experiences and perceptions. For example, O'Grady (2008) employed a process of 'photovoice' which involved young people taking photographs of aspects of their daily lives which were then used as stimuli for interviews and small group discussions. Similarly, Marquez-Zenkov, Harmon, van Lier, and Marquez-Zenkov (2007) in their 'Through Students' Eyes' project utilised photographs taken by students (as well as the students' written descriptions of the photographs) to seek their ideas about 'quality' teachers. Leitch and Mitchell (2007) also found that image-based methods (in this case impromptu drawings) were effective for revealing students' experiences of their school's culture that might not otherwise be so easily articulated, while Leitch, Gardner et al. (2007) successfully employed a variety of methods including image-based pupil activities (student drawings and co-interpreting video-taped classroom observations) in their efforts to consult students on their experiences of learning and assessment. A second approach has employed the narrative method to more directly sample students' experiences. Thus, Albert and Valda (2009) had students construct stories about themselves and other individuals or groups of students as a means of developing an authentic leadership voice. Finally, some researchers have employed interview methods to engage students in the recall and reflection of relevant 'critical incidents' in their daily lives (Carter, Bennetts & Carter, 2003).

Whatever method is chosen to seek out student views, I suggest that there are at least four sets of questions students should address with their teachers, when they are engaged as genuine co-leaders in their learning.

1. What do we need to understand about our learning? What is the topic about which we need to be heard?

2. How should we go about enabling students to give their views freely? What inquiry method will be most useful?
3. How will we process the information to make sense of what we hear? Who will we involve in this?
4. What processes should we employ to translate information into helpful practices to improve learning? How can we lead this together?

Questions such as these rest on several assumptions: (a) that students should experience an authentic measure of control over the leadership of their own learning; (b) that no topic important to students, but seemingly trivial to adults, is "off limits"; (c) that understanding should be focused on the direct experience of students in their particular circumstances; and (d) that there is a deep respect for the views of all learners which builds trust and rapport with teachers in a "culture of listening" (Leitch & Mitchell, 2007).

I turn to a report by MacBeath, Sugimine and others (2003) to illustrate the nature of adolescent student views provided by them about their learning whilst engaged in cross-cultural visitation well away from their native Scotland. They spoke of how their own values and assumptions had been challenged in unfamiliar cultural contexts; how they had learnt to see things from different perspectives; how important team work had been; how flexibility and compromise accompanied activity in new settings; how important the completion of tasks to reach milestone points is; the usefulness of holding judgement back, lest personal bias interfere with open verbal or written communication; how to face, rather than avoid, difficult decisions in potential conflict situations; finding the understanding necessary to lead initiatives; and all the time increasing self-knowledge and the capacity to lead personal learning. When student voice provides such a rich tapestry of views, it is contingent on teachers and others contributing to the learning environment to take them seriously as they work to maximise the shared social nature of learning.

Promoting Learning and Pedagogy

There is little doubt that *instructional leadership*, particularly as critiqued in the chapters by David Ng, then by David Imig, South Holden and Dale Placek, has concentrated in the United States of America on scripted learning according to the diktats of national, international, district and local test regimes. When this is the case, what is considered worth learning is what is prescribed and evaluated. And what can be reliably evaluated in the school curriculum has been limited most often to basic skills. Hence, it is a restricted inventory of evaluation results against which principals and teachers are held accountable. At worst, what occurs is that the dominant pedagogical focus becomes what is measured and for which the school is held publicly accountable in league tables or in other direct forms of comparison describing, for example, "successful", "failing" or "turnaround" schools. Pedagogical quality becomes linked to a series of performance numbers rather than to the breadth of experiences to which teachers may introduce their students. Concomitantly, high-stakes testing reduces the influence students have on the curriculum, their teachers and the learning experiences they are likely to encounter. Pedagogy in these circumstances is much less about children and young people's voices, drives and motivations than it is about the economies of nation states and their international status.

As I read it, *leadership for learning* begins with the child, *not* the state. From her or his earliest days, as Charles Fadel argues from the Harvard University Centre for Curriculum Redesign, the child should experience "a deeply versatile curriculum" (Fadel in Earp, 2017, p. 1), one which moves from the dominance of content knowledge reproduction to the higher order skills of creative problem solving, as well as collaborative personal qualities such as resilience, cognitive agility, respect and compassion. Classroom learning, if it is responsive to the learner, needs to balance prescription with spontaneity, structure with serendipity, stress with fun, compliance with choice and accountability with responsibility. If this balance is to be achieved, then traditional subjects such as Mathematics, Languages, Science, Music and the Arts, Health and Physical Activity, Geography, Social Studies and History need to become charged with lived experiences rather than being reduced to multiple-choice test items. Teachers know that real-life experience is where lasting learning power resides, and given the opportunity, are rarely loath to lead learning with their students in this direction. There is also no doubt that if students are to experience a "deeply versatile curriculum", parents and family members are automatically implicated in *leadership for learning*. More is said about this when I discuss Networked Leadership for Collective Impact.

Leadership for learning, as noted in MacBeath's chapter, is also about a focus on learning for all, not on student learning alone. Therefore, teachers' learning is an important subsidiary component in achieving the moral purpose of education. Developing a personal commitment to learning in an increasingly pervasive technological world requires teacher development initiatives responsive to the information overflow of the digital age. Knowledge and understanding of globalisation and technological change are imperatives for today's and tomorrow's teachers. Knowledge that once had to be memorised can now be obtained in an instant. The new skills for teachers relate to how to access, manage, synthesise, evaluate and critically assess information as they co-construct new personalised knowledge with their students—students who are often more digitally savvy and socially networked than their teachers. This more positive and futurist perspective is and should continue to be prominent in pedagogy for youth in the modern era.

Engaging People

Leadership is not about individual position holders, as I have already said: it is about people coming together in the pursuit of common ends and, in doing so, turning leadership away from unremitting recourse to positional power and towards the acceptance of shared power through collective human agency. This philosophical and practical shift is evident, as I indicated at the outset to this chapter, in the steady accumulation of research findings published over the last three decades. This has resulted in a synthesis of *leadership for learning* domains and practices in which

16 Leadership for Learning: Embracing Purpose, People...

Table 16.1 Domains and dimensions of a Unified Leadership Framework

Leadership domains and dimensions
1. Establishing and conveying the vision
Creating, articulating and stewarding shared mission and vision
Implementing vision and setting goals and performance expectations
Modelling aspirational and ethical practices
Communicating broadly the state of the vision
Promoting use of data for continual improvement
Tending to external accountability
2. Facilitating a high-quality learning experience for students
Maintaining safety and orderliness
Personalising the environment to reflect students' backgrounds
Developing and monitoring curricular programme
Developing and monitoring instructional programme
Developing and monitoring assessment programme
3. Building professional capacity
Selecting for the right fit
Providing individualised consideration
Building trusting relationships
Providing opportunities to learn for whole faculty including leaders
Supporting, buffering and recognising staff
Engendering responsibility for promoting learning
Creating communities of practice
4. Creating supportive organisations for learning
Acquiring and allocating resources strategically for mission and vision
Considering context to maximise organisational functioning
Building collaborative processes for decision making
Sharing and distributing leadership
Tending to and building on diversity
Maintaining ambitious and high expectations and standards
Strengthening and optimising school culture
5. Connecting with external partners
Building productive relationships with families and external partners in the community
Engaging families and community in collaborative processes to strengthen student learning
Anchoring schools in the community

Hitt and Tucker (2016)

principals, teachers, students and other stakeholders committed to improved learning and achievement may have great confidence.

Hitt and Tucker (2016) have analysed three well-known, research-informed North American leadership frameworks to produce a *Unified*

Table 16.2 *Carpe Vitam* Leadership for Learning principles and practices

Carpe Vitam LfL principles	Leadership for learning practices
1. Focusing on learning as an activity	A focus on professional learning
	A focus on organisational learning
	Teaching with a focus on learning
2. Creating a learning dialogue	Tools for disciplined dialogue
	Dialogue purpose and scope
	Scaffolding disciplined dialogue
3. Fostering an environment for learning	Everyone has opportunities to reflect on the nature, skills and processes of learning
	School culture nurtures the learning of everyone
	Physical and social spaces stimulate and celebrate learning
	Tools and strategies are used to enhance thinking about learning and the practice of teaching
4. Sharing accountability	Embedding a systematic approach to self-evaluation at classroom, school and community levels
	Developing a shared approach to internal accountability as a precondition of accountability to external agencies
	Reframing policy and practice when they conflict with core values
	Maintaining a continuing focus on sustainability, succession and leaving a legacy
	Taking account of political realities and exercising informed choice as to how the school tells its own story
	Maintaining a focus on evidence and its congruence with the core values of the school
5. Sharing leadership	Collaborative patterns of work and activity across boundaries of subject, role and status are valued and promoted
	The experience and expertise of staff, students and parents are drawn upon as resources
	Structures support participation in developing the school as a learning community
	Shared leadership is symbolised in the day-to-day flow of activities of the school
	Everyone is encouraged to take the lead as appropriate to task and context

MacBeath and Dempster (2009)

Leadership Framework comprised of five domains elaborated with 28 practices. The five domains are: establishing and conveying the vision; facilitating a high-quality learning experience for students; building professional capacity; creating supportive organisations for learning; and connecting with external partners. These domains are listed in Table 16.1 together with their accompanying practices or dimensions as Hitt and Tucker call them.

To illustrate the similarities and some of the subtle differences observable in different versions of leadership frameworks, I provide an earlier example produced as a set of five principles and practices developed as an outcome from the Cambridge University-led *Carpe Vitam* Leadership for Learning Project (MacBeath & Dempster, 2009). These principles and practices are reproduced in Table 16.2. When Tables 16.1 and 16.2 are compared, it is clear that there is an underlying assumption that leadership is about people working together on practices which they acknowledge are intrinsic to improved learning. Indeed, the centrality of shared leadership underpins both frameworks and is self-evident in the activities from Hitt and Tucker's (2016) framework such as "building trusting relationships", "building collaborative processes for decision making" and "engaging families and community in collaborative processes to strengthen student learning". MacBeath and Dempster's framework depicts similar sentiments but in statements such as: "Collaborative patterns of work and activity across boundaries of subject, role and status are valued and promoted"; "Structures support participation in developing the school as a learning community" and "Everyone is encouraged to take the lead as appropriate to task and context".

When taken as a whole, both frameworks reinforce the view that leadership is now being conceived by researchers as a set of activities or practices which are explicitly described. Implicit throughout is the understanding that shared leadership is a necessary condition if research promise is to be realised in improved student learning and achievement.

Downplaying Hierarchy

An examination of the two frameworks included above suggests that while positional power always lies behind what occurs in schools, its prominence is being downplayed so that leadership responsibilities may be opened up to any of the parties with student learning interests at heart. Inside the school, this opening up is not automatic, as Murphy, Smylie, Mayrowetz, and Louis (2009, p. 185) have argued in their research into distributive leadership. They describe the strong grip that hierarchical structural arrangements have in schools and the long-standing political sanctioning that lies behind them. They also found, even when changed leadership opportunities are initiated, that there is a reluctance to take on the teacher leadership challenge, leaving eyes constantly turned towards positional leaders for approval. Murphy et al. concluded that the encouragement of distributive leadership faces barriers, not the least of which are historical organisational inertia, and the fact that teachers do not see teacher leadership as "instinctive". Notwithstanding these difficulties, those adopting a *leadership for learning* stance understand that collective human agency is the most powerful ingredient in achieving the moral purpose of education and that headlining "purpose" and "agency" as opposed to "position" and "authority" creates the circumstances for transformative action on learning. MacBeath et al. (2018), in the conclusion to their discussion of leadership based on Simpson's (2016) three perspectives: (a) the "leader-practitioner" or position holder, (b) leadership as a set of distributed practices and (c) leadership in the flow of practice, argue that:

> All three perspectives on leadership ... find a home in school settings. The leader-practitioner looms large, almost as a fixed "object" in education systems, intractably hierarchical with layers of positional leadership dominating organisational structures. These are unlikely to be discarded while one person in each school is designated as the accountable officer for what takes place there. The shifts being made in recent years to conceptualise and implement leadership as a set of (distributed) practices retain and often enhance the influential role of the school principal. His or her business it is to "gird the loins" of followers in order to undertake tasks which contribute to the leader's vision, albeit with others who share in its pursuit. While the

positional leader may want to define himself or herself as "first among equals", this appears to us to be rather more rhetorical than real in the light of a decade of research into distributed, collaborative, or shared leadership. As we have shown, however, such a "norm" may, in fact, materialise.

Movement towards the idea of leadership emerging in the flow of practice, when and where activity occurs, invests a collective power in those who want to put pedagogical practice under scrutiny. This contributes to enhanced understanding, influencing future practice, adding meaning to one's own agency, and the concept of leadership itself in the process. Put succinctly, our thinking about the three perspectives, when applied to LfL in schools, suggests that we would all be better off with less of the first perspective and more of the second and third. (pp. 105–106)

Networking Leadership for Collective Impact

The statement above, that "collective human agency is the most powerful ingredient in achieving the moral purpose of education", leads quite justifiably to the view that the wider and more active the collective (provided its focus is on students' learning and well-being), the more potent its impact will be. Outside the school, just as there has been inside it with teachers, there has been an oft-cited reluctance for parents, families and other community members to take up leadership opportunities. Such a view disregards decades of research findings which underscore the all-embracing influence parents, caregivers and the child's community circumstances have on learning and achievement (Coleman et al., 1966; Gamoran & Long, 2006; Jacobson, 2011; Jacobson, Brooks, Giles, Johnson, & Ylimaki, 2007). *Leadership for learning* brings so-called outsiders right into the leadership mix, eschewing any perceived parent and family reluctance or disinterest, replacing it with a commitment to local leadership partnerships. This practice is well articulated in Table 16.1 in the words: "Anchoring the school in the community".

More than this, however, is evident in contemporary research as it continues to engage scholars in examining how the effects of leadership activities may be maximised. The term *networked leadership for collective impact* is a shorthand description for the combinations of insiders and outsiders, individuals and agencies, working in coalitions to improve the lives and life chances of the young, as Chapman et al., Otero and Cridge have argued in their contributions to this book. The companion term, "leadership both ways", puts into shorthand a call for schools to reach out into their communities as they accept, simultaneously, the potential benefits of parent, family and community leadership reaching into the school.

What is being added this decade to *leadership for learning* practices is a concern to create and transform the functioning of partnerships between community agencies and schools, especially in disadvantaged communities, to improve the well-being and life trajectories of children and young people (Branch, Homel, & Freiberg, 2012; Homel, Freiberg, & Branch, 2015). Doing so enables schools and community agencies to transcend the limitations caused by the system silos of government initiatives, countering with the collaborative actions that foster respectful relationships and deliver goal-directed, quantitatively evaluated, evidence-based assistance using differentiated resources and processes that promote child social-emotional well-being, school engagement and academic success (Wandersman et al., 2008). These are lofty aims, but it is clear in the 50 years, since the Coleman Report, that the school alone will not win the battle for long-term, sustainable improvement without networked allies teamed in interventions which bring outside and inside school conditions together in the interests of disadvantaged children and young people.

Understanding Context

In his review of 40 years of leadership research, Hallinger (2011) remarked on the need for much more attention to be directed to understanding the context in which school leadership actions are implemented. This is because a sense of "place" is a necessary precursor to the connections school leaders and teachers need to make with the communities in which they serve. This sense of place is both cognitive and emotional. Having deep empathy for their students, founded on an understanding of the economic, social and cultural conditions surrounding them, informs how leadership actions are implemented. An understanding of place also informs and shapes how family and community members may be drawn into leadership roles and partnerships with the interests of their children firmly in mind. It provides a concrete knowledge base for decisions on the use of school and community resources.

Where wide cultural diversity occurs, as it does in many schools, the task of "reading" the context is much more difficult than it is in monocultural environments. Likewise, principals and teachers drawn from a cultural orientation dominant in particular country contexts have an obligation to open their minds to learning led by cultural knowledge holders. This is where the concept of "leadership both ways" comes to the fore (Ober & Bat, 2007; Priest, King, Nagala, Nungurrayi Brown, & Nangala, 2008) and where Fraser's (2007) notion of "parity of participation" must take hold. Context knowledge should be a process of mutual exchange amongst peers with equal voices. Joint ownership of the leadership actions designed to benefit students is the promised result.

To sum up, as I have indicated earlier, research into the context in which school learning occurs has been shown to matter markedly. Thinking about conditions outside the school gate is imperative, because privileging learning the school's way, more often than not, reinforces a failed status quo. *Leadership for learning* "both ways" is less familiar, but certainly it is the direction in which well-connected schools and communities are headed when they undertake together, place-based interventions for a collective impact.

Conclusion

Undoubtedly, we have come a long way from the three dimensions and ten functions Hallinger arrived at in a review of *instructional leadership* in 2005. While (a) *defining the school's mission,* (b) *managing the instructional programme* and (c) *promoting a positive school learning climate* are observable in *leadership for learning* practice today, they are there, not as an unmodified mantra for principals, but as elements embedded in a much more comprehensive view of what it takes to lead learning for student and school improvement. As the two frameworks reproduced in this chapter, in Tables 16.1 and 16.2, show, over the last three decades, researchers have defined a much more fine-grained analysis of what it takes to lead learning. The themes emanating from the work of authors in this book highlight the need for networked leadership by people tightly connected in their commitment to the purpose of education, people who know and understand children and the needs, hopes and aspirations they and their communities have. *Leadership for learning,* seen in this light, is much more than *instructional leadership.* It relies less on positional power and more on principals, teachers, students and community agents exercising autonomy in collective actions committed to making a difference in the life journey of learners. In a nutshell, it is about embracing the moral purpose of education, listening to those whose interests should be served, searching out and developing helpful pedagogy, engaging with people in shared leadership initiatives that over-ride hierarchy, networking with agents external to the school to enhance the impact of leadership actions, and in doing so, being responsive to and liberating for students, no matter their circumstances or place of learning.

References

Bass, B. M., & Avolio, B. J. (Eds.). (1994). *Improving organisational effectiveness through transformational leadership.* Thousand Oaks, CA: Sage Publications.

Branch, S., Homel, R., & Freiberg, K. (2012). Making the developmental system work better for children: Lessons learned from the Circles of Care Programme. *Child and Family Social Work, 18,* 294–304.

Coleman, J., Campbell, E., Hobson, C., McPartland, J., Mood, A., Weinfeld, F., et al. (1966). *Equality of educational opportunity.* Washington, DC: US Government Printing Office.

Day, C., Gu, Q., & Sammons, P. (2016). The impact of leadership on student outcomes: How successful school leaders use transformational and instructional strategies to make a difference. *Educational Administration Quarterly, 52*(2), 221–258.

Dempster, N., Lizzio, A., Keeffe, M., Skinner, J., & Andrews, D. (2010). The contributions of research design and process facilitation in accessing adolescent views of leadership. *Leading and Managing, 16*(2), 77–89.

Dinham, S. (2005). Principal leadership for outstanding educational outcomes. *Journal of Educational Administration, 43*(4), 338–356.

Earp, J. (2017). Global education: 21st century skills. *Teacher Magazine*. Retrieved from www.teachermagazine.com.au/article/global-education-21st-century-skills

Fraser, N. (2007). *Abnormal justice*. Retrieved from http://www.fehe.org/uploads/media/Fraser_Abnormal_Justice_essay.pdf

Fullan, M. (2001). *Leading in a culture of change*. San Francisco: Jossey-Bass.

Gamoran, A., & Long, D.A. (2006). *Equality of educational opportunity: A 40-year retrospective* (Working paper no. 2006–9). Madison, WI: Wisconsin Center for Education Research.

Grace, G. (1995). *Beyond education management*. London: Taylor and Francis.

Hallinger, P. (2005). Instructional leadership and the school principal: A passing fancy that refuses to fade away. *Leadership and Policy in Schools, 4*, 221–239.

Hallinger, P. (2011). Leadership for learning: Lessons from 40 years of empirical research. *Journal of Educational Administration, 49*(2), 125–142.

Hallinger, P. (2018). Bringing context out of the shadows of leadership. *Educational Management Administration & Leadership, 46*(1), 5–24.

Hallinger, P., & Murphy, J. (1985). Assessing the instructional management behaviour of principals. *The Elementary School Journal, 86*(2), 217–247.

Harris, A., & Spillane, J. (2008). Distributed leadership through the looking glass. *Management in Education, 22*(1), 31–34.

Hitt, D. H., & Tucker, P. D. (2016). Systematic review of key leadership practices found to influence student achievement: A unified framework. *Review of Educational Research, 86*(2), 31–69.

Homel, R., Freiberg, K., & Branch, S. (2015). CREATE-ing capacity to take developmental crime prevention to scale: A community-based approach within a national framework. *Australian and New Zealand Journal of Criminology, 48*(3), 367–385.

Jacobson, S. (2011). Leadership effects on student achievement and sustained school success. *International Journal of Educational Management, 25*(1), 33–44.

Jacobson, S. L., Brooks, S., Giles, C., Johnson, L., & Ylimaki, R. (2007). Successful leadership in three high-poverty urban elementary schools. *Leadership and Policy in Schools, 6*(4), 291–317.

Johnson, G., Dempster, N., & Wheeley, E. (2016). Distributed leadership: Theory and practice dimensions in systems, schools and communities. In G. Johnson & N. Dempster (Eds.), *Leadership in diverse learning contexts* (pp. 3–31). Cham, Switzerland: Springer.

Leitch, R., & Mitchell, S. (2007). Caged birds and cloning machines: How student imagery 'speaks' to us about cultures of schooling and student participation. *Improving Schools, 10*(1), 53–71.

Leithwood, K. (1994). Leadership for school restructuring. *Educational Administration Quarterly, 30*, 498–518.
Leithwood, K. (2012). *Ontario leadership framework with a discussion of the leadership foundations.* Ottawa, Canada: Institute for Education Leadership, OISE Ottawa.
Leithwood, K., Seashore, K., Anderson, S., & Wahlstrom, K. (2004). *Review of research: How leadership influences student learning.* Minneapolis, MN/Toronto, Canada/New York: Centre for Applied Research and Educational Improvement, University of Minnesota/Ontario Institute for Studies in Education at the University of Toronto/The Wallace Foundation.
Louis, K. S., Leithwood, K., Wahlstrom, K. L., Anderson, S. E., Michlin, M., & Mascall, B. (2010). *Learning from leadership: Investigating the links to improved student learning.* Minneapolis, MN/Toronto, Canada/New York: Centre for Applied Research and Educational Improvement, University of Minnesota/Ontario Institute for Studies in Education, University of Toronto/The Wallace Foundation.
MacBeath, J. (2006). A story of change: Growing leadership for learning. *Journal of Educational Change, 7*(1–2), 33–46.
MacBeath, J., & Dempster, N. (Eds.). (2009). *Connecting leadership and learning: Principles for practice.* London: Routledge.
MacBeath, J., Dempster, N., Frost, D., Johnson, G., & Swaffield, S. (2018). *Strengthening the connections between leadership and learning.* London: Routledge.
MacBeath, J., Sugimine, H., & with Sutherland, G., Nishimura, M., & The students of the Learning School. (2003). *Self-evaluation in the global classroom.* London: Routledge.
Marks, H. M., & Printy, S. M. (2003). Principal leadership and school performance: An integration of transformational and instructional leadership. *Educational Administration Quarterly, 39*, 370–397.
Murphy, J., Smylie, M., Mayrowetz, D., & Louis, K. S. (2009). The role of the principal in fostering the development of distributed leadership. *School Leadership & Management, 29*(2), 181–214.
Ober, R., & Bat, M. (2007). Paper 1: Both ways: The philosophy. *Ngoonjook: A Journal of Australian Indigenous Issues, 31*, 64–86.
Priest, K., King, S., Nagala, I., Nungurrayi Brown, W., & Nangala, M. (2008). Warrki Jarrinjaku 'working together everyone and listening': Growing together as leaders for aboriginal children in remote Central Australia. *European Early Childhood Education Research Journal, 16*(1), 117–130.

Robinson, V., Hohepa, M., & Lloyd, C. (2009). *School leadership and student outcomes: Identifying what works and why. Best evidence synthesis iteration.* Wellington, New Zealand: Ministry of Education.

Robinson, V., Lloyd, C., & Rowe, K. (2008). The impact of leadership on student outcomes: An analysis of the differential effects of leadership types. *Educational Administration Quarterly, 44,* 635–674.

Sammons, P., Gu, Q., Day, C., & Ko, J. (2011). Exploring the impact of school leadership on pupil outcomes. *International Journal of Educational Management, 25*(1), 83–101.

Spillane, J. P. (2006). *Distributed leadership.* San Francisco: Jossey-Bass.

Townsend, T., & MacBeath, J. (Eds.). (2011). *International handbook on leadership for learning.* Dordrecht, Netherlands: Springer.

Wandersman, A., Duffy, J., Flaspohler, P., Noonan, R., Lubell, K., Stillman, L., et al. (2008). Bridging the gap between prevention research and practice: The interactive systems framework for dissemination and implementation. *American Journal of Community Psychology, 41,* 171–181.

Index

A

Accomplished Principal Standards, 122
Accountability, 20, 21, 33–34, 50, 52, 53, 57–60, 71, 82, 95, 107, 109, 111, 113, 118, 120, 121, 127, 134, 137–138, 141, 146–149, 154, 155, 175, 196, 197, 207, 209, 233, 241, 247, 343, 349, 351, 358, 376, 386, 392, 398, 409
Administrators, 3, 7, 21, 33, 107, 109, 117, 119, 125, 150, 176, 240, 302, 386, 387
Alignment (coherence), 193
  among levels of government, 193
Assessment data, 117, 290
Assessment practices, 280
Assessment standards, 305
Australia
  Australian Council for Educational Leaders (ACEL), 94, 212
  Australian Curriculum, Assessment and Reporting Authority (ACARA), 194
  Australian educational leadership research, 94, 97
  Australian Effective Schools Project, 86
  Australian Institute for Teaching and School Leadership (AITSL), 96, 97, 194, 195, 201–205
  Australian model of successful principal leadership, 91
  Australian Primary Principals Association (APPA), 92, 277

Australian Professional Standard for Principals, 197, 201–203, 206
Australian Professional Standards for Teachers, 201
Constitution, 193, 194
Council of Australian Governments (COAG), 194, 201
Education Council, 194, 195, 201, 213
future of leadership for learning, 193–215
Gonski Report (2018), 196, 352
principals' perceptions of role, 95
programs for professional learning of principals, 206, 209
role of federal government, 194
role of state and territory governments, 194, 215
studies of principal preparation, 203, 205
The Australian School Principal: A National Study, 83
Authority, 60, 62, 67, 68, 106, 108, 127, 145, 155, 184, 193, 194, 198, 203, 204, 209, 212, 214, 221, 242, 248–250, 253, 257, 259, 312, 391, 394, 404
Autonomy
  autonomy and student achievement, 195
  professional autonomy, 9, 95, 193–215
  structural autonomy, 9, 196, 197, 207, 208

B
Backbone organisation, 382, 384–387, 389, 390, 392
BIG 6, 93, 272, 277, 278, 280–284, 287–289, 291, 293, 296
Bright Spots Schools Connection, 347, 358–364, 376
Building capacity, 349
Bureaucracy, 58, 140, 146, 147

C
Capabilities theory, 381
Centralisation, 138, 207
Challenged communities, 347, 357
Children's Neighbourhoods Scotland (CNS), 10, 381–397
Coleman Report, 78, 326, 327, 416
Collaboration, 23, 24, 26, 28, 32, 51, 52, 80, 86, 88, 92, 98, 107, 125, 134, 204, 209, 210, 233, 255, 295, 348, 352, 355, 357, 360, 362–364, 368, 372, 374, 383, 385, 386, 388, 394, 396
Collaborative action, 354, 416
Collaborative leadership action, 354
Collaborative Leadership Design Network (CLDN), 358–365, 374–376
Collaborative leadership network, 351, 358, 359, 364
Collaborative learning, 24, 112, 115–117, 299–314, 376
Collaborative professionalism, 224, 234, 353
Collective efficacy, 331, 350, 353, 354

Index

Collective impact, 380–393, 415–417
Collective responsibility, 23, 59, 118, 121, 127, 285, 353, 375
Communication, 27, 28, 83, 166, 170, 184, 291, 313, 342, 384, 385, 387, 390–391, 395, 398, 408
Community, viii, 6, 16, 33, 57, 81, 134, 166, 228, 243, 270, 299–314, 317–344, 347, 380, 406
Community-based learning, 321–323
Community education, 318
Community links, 321
Complexity theory, 181–184, 187, 189
Compliance, 51, 62, 65, 108, 136, 209, 409
Comprehensive Assessment of Leadership for Learning (CALL), 125
Conditions for learning, 8, 93, 175, 188, 272, 289–290, 349, 374, 398
The Connection, 347, 359, 360, 362, 364–368, 370, 372, 373, 375
Connection Hub, 365, 368, 370–373
Connection impact, 364–373
Construction, 93, 224, 307
Contexts, 7, 9, 17, 18, 22, 24–26, 33–34, 37, 55, 66, 68, 78, 82, 85, 86, 91, 92, 94, 96, 97, 120, 135–140, 143–145, 148, 149, 151, 154–156, 165–166, 169–174, 186, 193–195, 198, 202, 204, 205, 210, 220, 225, 229, 231, 237–259, 276, 286, 302, 314, 317–319, 322, 324, 325, 327–329, 333, 334, 336, 338–340, 349–351, 356, 357, 362, 367, 372–375, 380–384, 388–391, 393, 394, 396, 408, 413, 416–417
Continuing professional development programmes, 249
Continuous learning opportunities, 243
Control, 21, 26–28, 58, 79, 136, 141, 146–149, 239, 248, 318, 322, 332, 334, 408
Coordinating curriculum, 79
Council of Chief State School Officers (CCSSO), 120, 121
Cultural leadership, 301, 302
Culture, ix, 17, 23, 37, 55, 56, 59, 60, 62, 65, 81, 84, 86–89, 91, 96, 119, 138, 144, 153–157, 202, 207, 211, 228, 231, 241, 247, 252, 256, 257, 272, 289, 301, 312, 317, 340, 341, 343, 353, 354, 358, 366, 374, 375, 394, 395, 407
Curriculum and instruction, 70, 107
Curriculum and teaching, 21, 93, 199, 272, 285–289
Curriculum management, 302, 303

D

Data, 31, 32, 35, 36, 64, 93, 113–115, 117–119, 124, 127, 136, 140, 141, 148, 152, 154, 187, 197, 198, 200, 204, 207,

211, 234, 271–274, 277–280, 282, 285, 286, 288, 293–296, 326, 356, 366, 368, 372, 375, 376, 386, 388, 391
Deliverology, 50
Democratic management, 137–138
Department of Education (United States), 106, 126
Disciplined dialogue, 56, 271, 277–280
Discourse, 18, 19, 34, 50, 52, 65, 66, 135, 137–139, 144, 149, 337, 338
Distributed leadership, 7, 19, 22–24, 26, 29, 37, 54, 94, 134, 199, 200, 248, 360
Donaldson report, 221

E

Ecological leadership, 141, 148–151
Educational resources, 237
Effective classroom management, 309, 313, 314
Effective leadership, 61, 71, 139, 204, 222, 229, 269, 337
Effective schools, 15, 17, 70, 78, 79, 83, 86, 108, 166–172, 175, 253, 347, 349, 365, 405
Efficiency, 4, 52, 139, 238, 242
Elementary and Secondary Education Act (ESEA), 105, 109–111
Emergence, 35, 36, 80, 81, 138–139, 157, 177, 181, 183, 184, 187, 231, 397
Emotion, 70, 71

Empowerment, 208, 209, 353, 376
Equity, 121, 198, 219, 252, 275, 352, 355, 356
Every Student Succeeds Act (ESSA), 105–120, 124–128
An Exceptional Schooling Outcomes Project (ÆSOP), 87–89, 95

F

Family, 3, 94, 121, 124, 149, 154, 155, 270, 276, 279, 280, 287, 290–294, 296, 317, 319–321, 324–326, 328–334, 336, 338, 340–343, 379, 382, 383, 389, 390, 405, 410, 413, 415, 416
Family and community support, 272, 290–293
Formal leadership, 54
Future-ready, 165–190

G

General Teaching Council for Scotland (GTCS), 222, 228–230
Gonski, David, 196, 352
Good lesson, 310, 313
Grade group meeting, 307, 310

H

Harlem Children's Zone, 380, 386
Headteachers' Charter, 232–234
Heroism, 113–115

Hierarchy, 50, 52, 54, 55, 58–63, 71, 134, 135, 220, 224, 348, 351, 353, 358, 374, 397, 404, 414–415, 418
Holistic, 167, 341, 381, 387, 391, 397

Improvement, 3, 8, 17, 23, 54, 59, 84, 93, 97, 105, 113, 118, 119, 121, 135, 144, 157, 175, 177, 196, 197, 199, 202, 206, 231, 232, 234, 239, 241, 246, 252, 270, 273, 276, 295, 301, 309, 325, 332, 348, 349, 351, 354, 355, 360, 366, 375, 383–385, 387, 388, 391, 416
Inclusive leadership, 93, 141, 148–151
Inequalities, 237, 239, 327, 379, 380
Inert ideas, 49, 71
Informal leadership, 125, 134
Innovation, 23, 26, 28, 36, 83, 88, 97, 135, 137, 141, 148–151, 153, 174, 185–188, 202, 211, 252, 325
Innovative Designs for Enhancing Achievements in Schools (IDEAS), 88, 89, 94, 95
In-service programmes, 238
Instructional leader(s), 8, 9, 19–21, 23, 70, 106–108, 113, 119, 134, 199, 239, 241, 243, 244, 247, 255
Instructional leadership (IL), viii, 7, 15–39, 49, 105, 134, 175, 220, 237–259, 301, 317, 350, 403, 404, 418

International School Leadership Development Network (ISLDN), 90, 97
International Study on School Autonomy and Learning (ISSAL), 195, 196, 205, 215
International Successful School Principalship Project (ISSPP), 90, 92, 95, 97
Interstate School Leaders Licensure Consortium (ISLLC), 120, 121, 123

Knowledge building, 39

Language, ix, 49–52, 57, 62, 63, 65, 71, 93, 119, 123, 124, 148, 155, 214, 270, 272, 284, 287, 288, 291, 293, 294, 329, 330, 343, 363, 396, 404, 409
Leader responsibility, 22, 24, 95, 123, 150, 241, 351, 353, 414
Leadership and management roles, 238
Leadership as learning, 220
Leadership development, viii, 8, 9, 165–190, 204, 211, 220, 224, 237–259, 339
Leadership for learning (LfL), viii, 8, 49–71, 105–128, 134, 175, 193–215, 219, 238, 270, 314, 318, 329, 347–376, 381, 403–418
Leadership for learning blueprint, 271

Leadership for learning (LfL) project, 81, 85, 92, 413
Leadership for Organisational Learning and Student Outcomes (LOLSO), 87, 88, 95
Leadership impact, 87, 92
Leadership learning, 82, 85, 166, 175–180, 182, 183, 188, 221–224, 393–397
Leadership learning in initial teacher education (LLITE), 221–224
Leadership preparation programmes, 179
Leading Australia's Schools, 84
Leading learning, 50, 62, 106, 108, 111, 121, 122, 127, 128, 133–157, 207, 223, 225, 228, 269–296, 319, 326–333, 340, 344, 351
Leading learning relationally, 318, 320, 334
Leading learning relationally framework, 335
Learning Forward, 112, 118, 119
Learning relationships, 317–344
Lesson plan, 201, 280, 283, 300, 301, 303–307, 311–314
Lesson study, 10, 299–314
 advisor, 301, 303, 304, 306
 leader, 307, 308, 312
Leverage, 107, 347, 354, 357, 360, 374
Life chances, 317, 318, 321, 326–330, 332–334, 405, 416
Life history, 84
Literacy Practices Guides (LPG), 283, 291

Los Angeles Unified School District (LAUSD), 123, 124
Low socio-economic settings, 379–398

M

Managerialism, 139, 154
Managers, 19, 27, 82, 113–115, 133, 134, 207, 238, 240, 252, 258, 285, 306, 343
Market, 4, 84, 339
Mentoring, 28, 120, 153, 204, 205, 322, 323, 341
Middle leaders, 87, 89, 92, 220, 230, 353
Ministry of Education, Culture, Sports, Science and Technology (MEXT), 300
Misconception, 50, 389
Monitoring student progress, 17, 79, 80, 108
Moral purpose, 7, 10, 82, 84, 93, 156, 246, 257, 270, 275–276, 325, 352, 354, 358, 405–406, 410, 414, 415, 418
Multi-faceted transformational issues, 238

N

National Assessment of Academic Ability, 300
National Association of Elementary School Principals (NAESP), 110
National Improvement Framework (NIF), 232–234

National Institute for Educational Policy Research (NIER), 301
National Policy Board for Educational Administration (NPBEA), 107, 120–122
A Nation at Risk (1983), 4, 120
Neighbourhood, 56, 331, 381–384, 386–392
Network, 10, 33, 36–37, 58, 153, 319, 347, 352, 355, 356, 358–360, 362–368, 370, 374, 376, 383, 386
Networked leadership for learning, 351–356
Network model, 347
New York City Public Schools, 124
No Child Left Behind Act (NCLB), 107, 109–111, 125
Non-linearity, 183–184

Obama administration, 106, 109, 125–126
Organisational culture, 86, 256, 301, 312
Organisation for Economic Co-operation and Development (OECD), 19, 54, 70, 152, 197–200, 231, 232, 352, 355
Outcomes, vii, 4, 8, 17, 20, 31, 32, 34, 35, 52, 55, 81, 86–91, 94, 95, 105, 113–115, 142, 154, 166, 169, 174, 175, 177, 180, 183, 189, 190, 196, 198, 200, 202, 204, 212, 220, 231, 238, 244, 248, 254, 255, 274, 279, 284, 285, 296, 326, 331, 336, 338, 342, 352, 353, 355, 357, 359, 363, 366, 368, 370–373, 376, 379, 381, 387, 395, 396, 398, 406, 413

PALL programme structure, 270–273, 277
Parallel leadership, 89, 90
Parental engagement/parental involvement, 206, 232, 330
Parent connectedness, 320–321
Partnership, vii, 64, 120, 179, 194, 204, 206, 211, 222, 255, 321, 325, 326, 335, 360, 366
Pedagogy, 10, 27, 61, 65, 68, 88–90, 94, 95, 154, 176, 196, 212, 229, 314, 338, 366, 403–418
Personalising the curriculum, 323–324
Personalization, 128, 317
Place-based approach, 380, 381, 383, 397
Policy drivers, 51
Poor lesson, 309, 310
Poverty, 139, 140, 154, 219, 232, 233, 379–382, 384
Power distance, 52
Principal, 3, 16, 50, 79, 105, 134, 178, 195, 225, 237, 269, 301, 339, 366, 404
Principal evaluation (in the United States), 123–125
Principal leadership, 20–24, 61, 83, 84, 88, 95, 106, 109, 121, 135, 242

Index

Principals as Literacy Leaders (PALL), 92–94, 97, 98, 269–296
Principalship, 185, 197–198, 206, 207, 209, 212, 228, 238, 242, 244, 248–250, 252, 258
Principal's newsletter, 309, 312, 313
Process, ix, 3, 8, 22, 23, 26, 32, 33, 50, 56, 57, 60, 65, 81, 83, 85, 87, 89, 114, 119, 124, 127, 135, 137, 138, 142, 148, 149, 154, 155, 157, 169, 174, 176, 184, 185, 194, 203, 204, 214, 233, 242, 243, 251, 257, 270, 272, 273, 276–278, 283, 284, 286, 291, 295, 302, 304, 312, 313, 318, 324, 327, 336, 352–354, 356, 360, 363, 374, 384, 385, 389, 392, 406–408, 413, 415–417
Process of learning, 114, 115, 175, 182, 184
Profession
  characteristics of, 214
  principalship as a, 250
Professional development, 19, 22, 27, 56, 79, 80, 86, 93, 95, 111, 114, 118, 124, 125, 135, 152, 153, 200, 201, 203, 205, 210, 211, 213, 222, 243, 249, 250, 299, 303, 306, 372, 397
Professionalisation of principals, 238
Professional learning, ix, 10, 86, 88, 89, 92, 111, 112, 114–118, 120, 197, 201–213, 229–231, 270, 271, 277, 280–285, 289, 293, 296, 314, 356, 357, 366, 390, 397

Professional learning communities/teams, 281, 285
Professional learning community (PLC), 7, 88, 89, 107, 115, 117, 127, 153, 198–200, 281, 285, 299–314, 359
Professional Standards for Education Leaders (PSELs), 121–123, 127
Professional standards for teaching, 221, 231
Programme Logic frame, 363
Project Action Plan (PAP), 360, 362, 370
Promotion of quality instruction, 80
Public schools, 5, 6, 123, 126, 197, 206, 238, 248, 250, 258, 332, 341

R

Reading improvement, 270–276, 280, 281, 284, 286, 290, 291, 293, 295, 296
Reading interventions, 274, 286
Recentralisation, 137, 138
Reinvent principalship, 242
Relational domains, 320–324, 337, 338, 341
Relationships, 3–5, 10, 23, 28, 31–33, 35, 36, 54, 59, 63, 67, 68, 83, 97, 109, 117, 124, 125, 135, 150, 155, 181, 182, 210, 253, 255, 258, 292, 314, 317–344, 353, 356, 358, 363, 364, 379, 383, 384, 386, 387, 390, 393, 394, 396, 416

Index

Research school, 303–306, 311
Reticulist, 381, 396, 397
Risk, 53, 63, 70, 71, 254, 256, 348, 397

S

School administration, 137, 146, 177
School-based continuous professional development, 65, 249, 303
School capacity, 91
School effectiveness, 3, 70, 79, 80, 86, 325
School funding, 123, 248
School governing board, 238
School improvement, 8, 9, 20, 38, 84, 88, 90, 92, 93, 106, 107, 113, 119, 124, 167, 210, 228, 232, 240–242, 248, 255, 274, 303, 318, 325, 331, 332, 342, 347, 360, 372, 403, 417
School leadership, viii, 1–10, 20, 70, 77, 106, 135, 166, 196, 232, 318, 348, 404–417
School management, 3, 137, 152, 176, 199, 244, 302, 311, 312
School self-management, 5
School's vision, mission and values, 240
Self-organising, 184
Shared accountability, 8, 119
Shared leadership, 7, 8, 19, 52, 93, 112, 116, 117, 124, 143, 181, 254, 280–282, 358, 413, 415, 418
Singapore, 9, 22, 25–28, 50, 68, 166, 170–174, 185, 195, 203

Skills, attributes and competencies, 249
Social capital, 232, 320, 331–332, 334, 340, 364, 394
Social class, 330, 332–333
Socialisation, 223, 242
Social Ventures Australia (SVA), 347, 356–359, 361, 363, 365, 372
Standards for Registration, 222, 229
Standing Committee on Teacher Education North and South, 222
State ESSA Plans, 111–113, 124
Student learning, 9, 10, 20, 27, 34, 59, 77, 78, 84, 86, 89, 91, 93, 96, 98, 106, 108, 114, 186, 189, 199, 211, 238, 243, 254, 255, 274, 280, 318–321, 323, 324, 326, 327, 342, 343, 357, 359, 367, 374, 404, 410, 413, 414
Student learning impact, 78, 81, 83, 92, 293–294
Student learning outcomes, 26, 78, 94, 207, 360, 365
Student performance, 117, 118, 124, 198, 204, 237–239, 241–242, 259, 317, 318
Subject advisor, 302, 306
Successful school leadership, 25, 77, 82, 89
Supervising and evaluating instruction, 17, 79
Supportive leadership, 301, 302, 313
Sustainability, 89, 90, 95, 187, 247
SVA, *see* Social Ventures Australia

T

Teacher and School Leader Incentive Grants, 111
Teacher coaching, 95
Teacher leadership, ix, 7, 9, 19, 22, 23, 29, 54, 60, 61, 63, 87, 89, 93, 107, 112, 115–117, 127, 134–136, 145, 153, 155, 156, 220, 224–232, 234, 414
Teacher practices, 34, 274
Teaching and learning, vii, viii, 15, 21–24, 27, 59, 65, 66, 81, 85, 87, 89, 90, 96, 97, 144, 149, 166, 173–175, 178, 181, 199, 202, 204, 207, 233, 241–244, 248, 249, 251, 252, 254, 255, 271, 272, 282, 304, 308, 313, 322, 324, 341, 343, 352, 357, 360, 366–368, 374, 405
Teaching and Learning International Study (TALIS), 152, 198–200, 352
Teaching Scotland's Future (TSF), 219–222, 225, 228, 231
Terminology, 7, 49, 50, 57, 69–70, 112, 208
Theory of Change, 388, 389, 392
Title II (of ESSA), 110, 111, 126
Transformational leadership, 7, 19, 20, 81, 87, 91, 94, 250, 301, 404
Trump administration, 111, 126
Trust, 54–56, 58, 60, 88, 89, 149, 150, 207, 241, 253–255, 292, 317, 331, 342, 354, 358, 366, 374, 376, 390, 396, 406, 408

U

Underperforming schools, 90
Unit curriculum, 304–313
Unit curriculum plan form, 305, 306
Unit objectives, 305
Unit teaching plan, 305
United States (US), 1–5, 7, 9, 10, 15, 52, 70, 81, 105–128, 203, 333, 384, 385, 409

V

Vouchers, 5
Vulnerability, 60–62, 70, 71, 154, 374

W

Waves of intervention, 273
Wellbeing, 10, 318, 321, 326–330, 333, 334, 340, 342, 344, 366, 415, 416
Whole school-community framework, 326, 337, 343
World Association of Lesson Studies (WALS), 299

Printed in the United States
By Bookmasters